D1095667

MAPS AND CHARTS PUBLISHED IN AMERICA BEFORE 1800
A BIBLIOGRAPHY

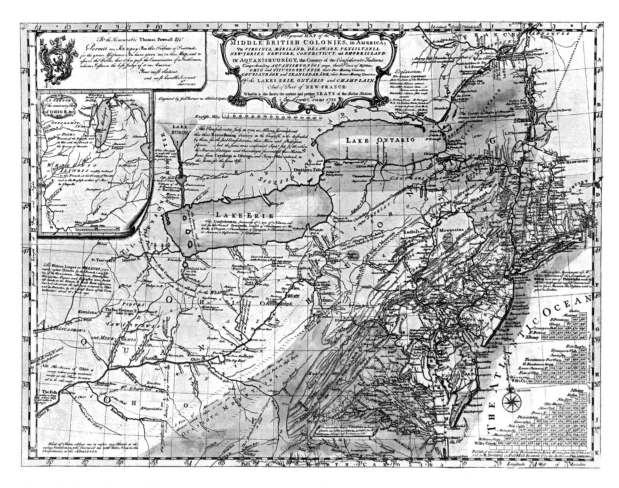

Evans, A General Map of the Middle British Colonies, 1755 (No. 298)

MAPS AND CHARTS PUBLISHED

IN AMERICA BEFORE 1800

A BIBLIOGRAPHY

by

JAMES CLEMENTS WHEAT

and

CHRISTIAN F. BRUN

New Haven and London: Yale University Press

1969

Published with assistance from the Acorn Foundation, Inc.

Library of Congress catalog card number: 69–15464

Designed by John O. C. McCrillis,
set in Baskerville type,
and printed in the United States of America by
Connecticut Printers, Inc., Hartford, Conn.
Distributed in Great Britain, Europe, Asia, and
Africa by Yale University Press Ltd., London; in
Canada by McGill University Press, Montreal; and
in Latin America by Centro Interamericano de Libros
Académicos, Mexico City.

Preface

While there have been a number of lists and bibliographies of maps and charts published within the borders of the United States, this is the first which attempts to describe the entire known cartographical contribution of the American press prior to 1800. Included are not only the maps and charts published separately but also those used as illustrations in books and pamphlets and from all other sources such as atlases, gazetteers, almanacs, and magazines.

The present effort grew from the late James Clements Wheat's original intention of preparing a descriptive list of American printed maps and charts in the William L. Clements Library of American History. Soon realizing the value of a bibliography of all such maps and charts which could be located in the major map collections in the United States and Great Britain, he expanded his objectives to this new goal. In gathering the information presented here, as many as possible of these collections were visited in person, although the resources of the William L. Clements Library were of great advantage. The various photoduplicate materials assembled during this period have been retained in the Map Division of that library and are available there for future research.

The published maps, plans, and charts which are described on the following pages reflect very definitely the gradual advances of the American press during the period before 1800. Some of these maps are American engravers' copies of European efforts (some American maps were also copied or adapted by European engravers), but most are the published results of the work of American surveyors and cartographers. In some cases the engraver himself was the author as he tried to incorporate the best features of several source maps into what became his own creation. As the demand for better maps and charts grew, native American map makers and engravers strove to provide them. The marked improvement of the maps of the last decade of the eighteenth century are a testimony to their skill.

As can be seen by a review of the geographical headings in the Contents, not all the maps are of the immediate American scene, many being of the world and of Europe, Asia, and Africa. One hundred and fourteen are of Europe. The third known map published in America was an engraved map by Captain Cyprian Southack in 1717 showing North America. The first known atlas published in the United

States, the "War Atlas" published by Mathew Carey in 1794, contained seven maps, one of American interest (showing the West Indies), the balance being of the nations of Europe.

A number of the maps described are relatively famous milestones in the history of American cartography. The first known map published in the United States was John Foster's "A Map of New-England, Being the first that was ever here cut . . ." it appeared in William Hubbard's *A Narrative of the Troubles with the Indians in New-England* (Boston, 1677). In 1722 John Bonner issued his map of Boston, the first American town plan, reissued in at least nine separate states or editions, the last in 1769. The James Lyne survey of New York City was published by William Bradford in 1735. Probably the most famous map published before the American Revolution was Lewis Evans' "A General Map of the Middle British Colonies, in America . . ." 1755, which, like a number of other of the better American maps, was immediately reproduced in Europe and continued to be reissued over a period of years.

The first map of the original United States as it existed after the Revolution was engraved and published by Abel Buell in March 1784, and the second by William McMurray in December of the same year. The first pilot book was the work of Matthew Clark, whose individual charts were issued in atlas form in 1789, followed in 1791 and the years after by the many issues of pilots published by John and William Norman. The various known states or editions of these charts are identified and listed, some for the first time. Some few further contributions have also been provided here concerning the famous Joshua Fisher large chart of Delaware Bay (1756) and its later states. Among other well-known maps are the following: The John Filson "Map of Kentucke" [1784] (nine states of this plan have so far been identified, with perhaps even more indicated); the large map of the United States by Abraham Bradley, first published in 1796, detailing the roads of the new nation, which became in its successive states the official map of the Post Office Department. Perhaps the best-known map of the United States is in Christopher Colles, *A Survey of the United States* (New York, 1789), with 83 maps known to be issued.

There are still others which deserve even more recognition than they have thus far received in their contribution to American cartography: the Bernard Romans chart of Florida, published in 1774, one of whose engravers was Paul Revere; the Manasseh Cutler "A Map of the Federal Territory from the Western Boundary of Pennsylvania to the Scioto River . . . ," printed in Boston circa 1787 and known in only six copies today; the Nicholas Scull and George Heap map of Philadelphia printed there in 1752, which gives the first known reproduction of the building we know today as Independence Hall; the A. P. Folie detailed "Plan of the Town of Baltimore . . ." printed in Philadelphia in 1792; and the Thomas Hutchins "A

Topographical Plan of that part of the Indian-Country . . ." printed in Philadelphia in 1765, which showed the route of Colonel Henry Bouquet in his successful effort to awe the Indians in the Ohio Country.

A number of the maps in this bibliography have never before been recorded or have been noted only in very specialized sources difficult to obtain. The inclusion here of a number of maps of which no copy is known to exist today is based upon some valid proof of their issuances. An example is the second map known to be printed in America, the Captain Cyprian Southack chart of the lower St. Lawrence River, printed in Boston in 1711. Fifty copies of this chart were printed and distributed to captains of a British naval expedition against the French, yet no copy is known today. Another map of this category is the Phillip Cockrem map of North America, which, as evidenced by two newspaper advertisements appearing in New York City in 1730, was available for sale for "Twenty Shillings, each New York Money." In the instance of Captain Abner Parker's "Chart of Saybrook Bar," only one copy of the second state survives in the Connecticut Historical Society; no copy of the first state is known.

Guide to Editorial Principles

The individual map descriptions are arranged by geographical and political area beginning with the maps of the world. A list of these areas is given in the table of contents. The maps and any resulting states or editions are given chronologically within these divisions. "See" references are given at the appropriate dates of maps showing two major areas such as a map incorporating two adjoining states. A brief description of the map is given, a summary appearing below. Subsequent states of the map through 1799 and sometimes 1800 and later are noted at the respective dates of their issuance together with the changes occurring on the plate at that time.

The form of individual entries is as follows: The individual unit number is followed by the year of publication of the map. If the date does not appear upon the map it is enclosed in brackets; if the date is uncertain, it is bracketed and followed by a question mark or designated "c." followed by the date. If the map has more than one state this will be noted by Roman numeral designation; following this number will be a parenthetical cross reference to all states of the same map both those preceding and following in the chronological sequence of the map. States printed after 1799 are noted in the *Description*. The *Description* includes all descriptive material not specifically designated for another section. This includes imprint information, author identification, comments upon the map's history, errors on the map which may serve to identify other earlier or later states, interesting features of the map and its publications, and so forth. Following the *Description* is the *Size* of the maps given in inches, vertical and then horizontal measurements. The *Scale* of the map is then provided using the term of measurement given on the map itself. If no unit of measurement is given on the map this is stated in this way: *Scale* None. If a scale has been determined by the authors this is given in parentheses, i.e. (1″ = 300 yards). *Size* and *Scale* are given only in the first state entry for a map. If no copy of the first state was found, this information will be given in the *State* II. Any change in scale designation on a later state of a map will be noted in the *Description* of that particular entry. In the case of a map of which no copy was found but some reasonable evidence of its issuance exists, *Size* and *Scale* are both listed as Unknown. *Insets* are described next. If several are noted they are listed thus: [a], [b], [c]. The contents of each *Inset* description are given as follows: Title (if any), short descriptive notes as needed, then size and scale using the same criteria as above. Next the map's publication is noted, whether the map is *Published* separately or "in" a larger work, or in conjunction with it, followed by the page reference or map number. If the map has been published both separately and in one or more briefly listed sources this is noted as far as is known. Selected Reproductions are listed following the publication notice. *References* used in conjunction with the map are listed in this section. This is not a compilation listing of all known sources but cites only those references used in conjunction with work done here. Known copies of each map are given at the end of each section. It is important to note, however, that no attempt was made to compile a complete census of all copies. *Locations* are noted of maps examined by the authors, discovered through their correspondence, or gained from listings in catalogs or other reference works. The abbreviations used are taken from the Library of Congress *Abbreviations used,* and are listed on pp. xvii–xix.

Beginning on page 187 is a complete list of *References* indexing all works cited in the individual map entries. Included are all of the books, pamphlets, and periodicals published in America before 1800 and cited under *Published.* Books and periodicals cited under *Description* and *Reference* are also listed here. The works are listed alphabetically by author, or if anonymous, by the first significant word of the title. The briefly listed entries are followed by location symbols of known copies though no attempt was made to make a census of all extant copies. The respective map item numbers are given after each listing. To be used in conjunction with this section is the following *Index of Names.* Authors of publications cited in the *Description, Published,* and *Reference* sections of the individual map entries will have their own entries in the *References* section. In the *Index of Names* are listed all the other names mentioned in the *Description* sections—cartographers, engravers, recipients of dedication, printers, editors, publishers, translators, and so forth.

The maps described here represent a considerable portion of the maps actually published within the United States before 1800. It is hoped that this bibliography will provide a reliable reference to future carto-bibliographical research and will be an aid to further discoveries of previously unknown examples of early American cartography and other states of maps listed here. The references throughout the text give testimony to the value to us of the excellent studies made by other individuals. I indicate below our appreciation to the many who have aided us in answering our manifold questions. The responsibility for the final results is, of course, our own. Any new or supplementary information concerning these maps or any newly discovered issues or states will be very much appreciated.

The original author of this bibliography, James Clements Wheat, has contributed to it not only with his fundamental thorough scholarship but also with his enthusiastic spirit of research. Mr. Wheat, an engineer by profession, was the nephew of William L. Clements, the donor of the Library which bears his name. During the academic year 1933–34, Mr. Wheat served as the first Curator of Maps in this library, and it was then that he began this project. After that year he returned to the engineering field, working whenever possible on the bibliography. He died in December 1958 at the age of seventy. I had the privilege of assisting Mr. Wheat for several years before his death and since then have continued to complete the final research for the volume.

The results which are given here have been made possible through the fine spirit of cooperation shown by many individuals who have aided us in the compilation of this study. We wish to give special recognition to the William L. Clements Library for its original and continuing support. We have had the valued cooperation of the various members of its staff over the years, especially the counsel and advice of the late Randolph G. Adams, its first director, and Howard H. Peckham, the present director. We have been fortunate also in the valuable assistance given us by the Library of Congress and especially its Map Division; by the late Col. Lawrence C. Martin, and by Arch C. Gerlach, former chiefs of the division; and by Walter W. Ristow, the present chief, Mrs. Clara Egli LeGear, and other members and former members of the division.

Our appreciation is extended to Lawrence C. Wroth, Librarian Emeritus of the John Carter Brown Library, whose expert knowledge of early American cartography and printing has been a constant and welcome aid; to Thomas R. Adams, the present librarian; and to Miss Jeannette D. Black. We wish also to express to Alexander O. Vietor, Curator of Maps at Yale University, our appreciation for his assistance.

We wish to acknowledge our gratitude to the Acorn Foundation for its generous support toward the publication of this volume.

We are indebted to many other individuals and institutions for their aid and for the information they have provided, especially the following: Gerard D. Alexander, Chief of the Map Division, New York Public Library; Burton Collection of Detroit Public Library; Carey S. Bliss and Ed Carpenter, Henry E. Huntington Library and

PREFACE

Art Gallery; Clarence S. Brigham, retired Director, American Antiquarian Society; Library, University of California, Santa Barbara; the late Lloyd A. Brown, former Librarian, The Peabody Institute; Mrs. Kirk Bryan, former Assistant, Winsor Map Room, Harvard University; Boston Athenaeum; the late Arthur B. Carlson, former Curator of Maps, New-York Historical Society; the late Barney Chesnick, former Assistant Librarian, Library Company of Philadelphia; Connecticut Historical Society; the late bibliographer Charles Evans; the late Allyn B. Forbes; the late James M. Foster, former Director, Maryland Historical Society; Massachusetts Historical Society; Mrs. Hazel S. Garrison of Harrisburg, Pennsylvania; Zoltan Haraszti, former Keeper of Rare Books, Boston Public Library; British Museum; James J. Heslin, Director, New-York Historical Society; Gertrude D. Hess, Assistant Librarian, American Philosophical Society; Gerald D. McDonald, Chief, American History and Genealogy Division, New York Public Library; North Carolina State Department of Archives and History; the late Mrs. Ella M. Price; Pennsylvania State Library; Stephen T. Riley, Director, American Antiquarian Society; Mrs. Lori Ritchie; R. A. Skelton, former Superintendent of the Map Room, British Museum; Colton Storm, former Curator, The Ayer Collection of the Newberry Library; the late Thomas W. Streeter, collector, Morristown, New Jersey; the late Robert W. G. Vail, former Director, New-York Historical Society; Nicholas B. Wainwright, Librarian, Historical Society of Pennsylvania; Mrs. Helen White, former Head, Map Division, Free Library of Philadelphia; Edwin Wolf II, Librarian, Library Company of Philadelphia; Yale University Library. My special thanks to Eleanor Olds Batchelder, Katherine H. Robinson, David Horne, and John Gudmundsen for their editorial guidance. And to my wife for many hours of unfailing assistance.

University of California, Santa Barbara   CHRISTIAN F. BRUN
Santa Barbara, California

Contents

Illustrations

Norman, J., A New General Chart of the West Indies [1790]. This copy from his *American Pilot*, Boston, 1794. Courtesy of John Carter Brown Library, Brown University.

Plan of the Blockade of Cadiz [1797]. Courtesy of William L. Clements Library.

Carey, A Map of the Countries situate about the North Pole [1796]. Courtesy of William L. Clements Library.

Abbreviations

AMERN.	American
ATTESTR	Witness
B.	Bay
Bart.	Baron
Br	Bridge
BR	Branch (of a river), brook
c.	Circa
CAP	Cape
CH	Courthouse
CI	City
Co	Company, county
Col, Coll	Colonel, College, collection
Cr	Creek
DAB	Dictionary of American Biography
Dart Col	Dartmouth
Dedicd	Dedicated
DEG	Degree
Del, Delin, Delinvt, Delineavt, Delt	Delineator, cartographer, author
Diam	Diameter
ED	Edition, editor
ENGD	Engraved
ESQ, ESQR	Esquire
F	Fort, feet
FC	Fecit
Fig	Figure
FLL	Falls
Foll	Following
Front	Frontispiece
Ft	Fort, feet

ABBREVIATIONS

GEN, GENL	General
GENTM	Gentlemen
GR	Grand
HAR, HARB, HARBR	Harbour or Harbor
HAVERL	Haverhill
HBLE	Humble
HONE, HONLE	Honorable
HR	Here
I, ID	Island
INCIDIT	Author
INV, INVT	Author
JR, JUNR	Junior
L	Lane
Lat.	Latitude
Long.	Longitude
MAG.	Magazine
MESS.	Messeurs
MH	Meeting House
MSS	Manuscript
MTS	Mountains
N	New, North
N.B.	Note
ND	North
NE	New England
No	Number
N.W.	North West, Northwest
Obet	Obedient
Opp.	Opposite page
P or p.	Page
PD	Pond
PENNA	Pennsylvania
Pl	Plate
Prop.	Proprietor
PT	Point

R.	River
REVD	Reverend
S	Street
S, Sc, Scp, Sct, Scu, Sculp., Sculpt, Script.	Sculptor or engraver
SD	Sound
SEBR	September
Ser.	Series
Servt.	Servant
SEVL	Several
SN	San
SR	Sir
St	Street
T	Town, township
T.p.	Title page
Twn	Town
UD States	United States
V	Versus
W	West
YAL COLL	Yale College
YOR	Your
&C	and so forth

Library Symbols

BM	British Museum
CaNSHD	Dalhousie University, Halifax, Nova Scotia
CSmH	Henry E. Huntington Library, San Marino, California
Ct	Connecticut State Library
CtHi	Connecticut Historical Society
CtHT	Trinity College, Hartford, Connecticut
CtHT-W	Trinity College, Watkinson Library
Cty	Yale University
DGU	Georgetown University Library
DI-GS	U.S. Department of the Interior Library, Geological Survey Library
DLC	Library of Congress
DN	U.S. Department of the Navy Library
IC	Chicago Public Library
ICHi	Chicago Historical Society
ICN	Newberry Library, Chicago
ICU	University of Chicago
KyLoF	Filson Club, Louisville
M	Massachusetts State Library
MB	Boston Public Library
MBAt	Boston Athenaeum
MdBE	Enoch Pratt Library, Baltimore
MdBP	Peabody Institute, Baltimore
MdHi	Maryland Historical Society
MeHi	Maine Historical Society
MH	Harvard University
MHi	Massachusetts Historical Society
MiD-B	Detroit Public Library, Burton Historical Collection
MiU	University of Michigan
MiU-C	University of Michigan, William L. Clements Library
MSaE	Essex Institute, Salem, Massachusetts
MWA	American Antiquarian Society, Worcester, Massachusetts
MWM	Worcester Art Museum

LIBRARY SYMBOLS

MWiW	Williams College
MWiW-C	Williams College, Chapin Library
N	New York State Library
NCanHi	Ontario County Historical Society, New York
Nc-Ar	North Carolina State Department of Archives and History
Nh	New Hampshire State Library
NhD	Dartmouth College
NHi	New York Historical Society
NjHi	New Jersey Historical Society
NjN	Newark Public Library
NjP	Princeton University
NN	New York Public Library
NNA	American Geographical Society
NNMM	Metropolitan Museum of Art
OCHP	Historical and Philosophical Society of Ohio
OC*l*W	Western Reserve University
OC*l*WHi	Western Reserve Historical Society
P	Pennsylvania State Library
PHi	Historical Society of Pennsylvania
PP	Free Library of Philadelphia
PPAmP	American Philosophical Society, Philadelphia
PPAmSwM	American Swedish Historical Foundation, Philadelphia
PPL	Library Company of Philadelphia
PPRF	Rosenback Foundation, Philadelphia
PRO	Public Record Office, London
PU	University of Pennsylvania
RHi	Rhode Island Historical Society
RP	Providence Public Library
RPJCB	John Carter Brown Library, Providence, Rhode Island
ScC	Charleston Library Society
ViU	University of Virginia
VtHi	Vermont Historical Society
VtU	University of Vermont

1 [1774]

Description [A Map of the Whole Navigation.] At lower right corner below neat line: PROTRACTED BY B: ROMANS. Great Britain, Spain, and the eastern bulge of Africa are shown at both ends of the map, which is drawn to Mercator's projection. The geography is sketchy except along the tracks of the voyages in the South Pacific and Indian Oceans. The map title is taken from the title page of the book.

Size 7¼″ x 17¼″.   *Scale* None (1″ = c. 1500 miles).

Published in John Hawkesworth, comp., *A New Voyage, Round the World, 1,* opp. 1.

Reference Philip L. Phillips, *Notes on Bernard Romans,* p. 76.

2 [1777]   *State* I (see also Map 3)

Description Above upper neat line across top: THE PRESENT STATE OF EUROPE & AMERICA / OR / THE MAN IN THE MOON TAKING A VIEW OF THE ENGLISH ARMADA. This is a caricature portraying the position of England sending her forces to subdue America with the French enemy close at hand. After the title page of the pamphlet is an "Explanation of the Frontispiece." East and west are reversed. No identifying numerals are given on the map.

Size 2⅜″ x 4⅛″.   *Scale* None (greatly condensed east and west).

Published in *The Plea of the Colonies,* front.

3 [1777]   *State* II (see also Map 2)

Description The numerals listed in the "Explanation" are now engraved on the map at the points indicated.

Published in *The Plea of the Colonies,* front.

4 [1784]   *State* I (see also Map 7)

Description On a decorative ribbon at upper center: THE WORLD. At bottom center: AGREEABLE TO THE LAST DISCOVERIES IN THE SOUTH SEAS. This is the first Morse map of two hemispheres. N. ZELAND appears thus. MOGULS is inscribed on Arabia.

Size 2⅝″ x 3⅞″.   *Scale* None (diam. sphere = 1 ¹¹⁄₁₆″).

Published in Jedidiah Morse, *Geography Made Easy,* 1st ed., front.

5 1778

Description Across top above neat line: A NEW MAP OF THE WORLD, DRAWN FROM THE LATEST DISCOVERIES, AND BEST AUTHORITIES. In lower left corner: E. RUGGLES JUNR. SCULPT. Below bottom neat line at center: PRINTED AND SOLD AT POMFRET, IN THE STATE OF CONNECTICUT, BY THE AUTHOR. *1788.* This map, by Edward Ruggles, Jr., was advertised in the *Norwich* (Conn.) *Packet,* during the latter half of 1788, beginning on August 14, as follows: "Just published, and to be sold at this office, an elegant and accurate map of the world on a plan of six feet in length which is much larger than any yet extent [sic]; with great improvements from the latest discoveries, including those of Capt. Cook. Carefully examined and approved by several gentlemen." The map is rectangular in form, with the world shown in two hemispheres and the corners filled in with allegorical figures and decorations. It is engraved on nine plates. At the upper center is a dedication to George Washington.

Below the neat line at the lower right appears the following note: AS THIS IS THE FIRST WORK OF THE KIND, THE AUTHOR EVER PUBLISHED: AND AS HE EXECUTED THE DIFFERENT ARTS HIMSELF, WITHOUT ANY EXPERIENCE, AND HAS TOOK UNWEARIED PAINS TO RENDER THE WORK / ACCURATE AND USEFUL TO COMMUNITY; HE FLATTERS HIMSELF, THAT THE CANDID PUBLIC, WILL OVERLOOK WHAT ERRORS THEY DISCOVER IN IT; AND CONSIDER THEY ARE UNAVOIDABLE. Late discoveries are featured and the track of Capt. Cook's last voyage is indicated. Salem, New Jersey, is shown rather prominently.

Size 38″ x 71″.   *Scale* None (diam. sphere = 35″).

Published Separately.

References Evans 21213; Carl I. Wheat, *Mapping the Transmississippi West, 1,* 149, no. 214.

Locations CtY, MWA, NHi.

6 1790   *State* I (II post-1799, see below, Description)

Description At lower left corner, reading diagonally: TO / GEORGE WASHINGTON / PRESIDENT

BIBLIOGRAPHY OF MAPS AND CHARTS

OF THE UNITED STATES OF AMERICA / THIS / MAG-NETIC ATLAS / OR / VARIATION CHART / IS HUMBLY INSCRIBED BY / JOHN CHURCHMAN. At bottom center: PUBLISH'D ACCORDING TO ACT OF CONGRESS *1790*. This map is drawn in the form of concentric gores of a northern hemisphere joined together at the parallel of 60° North Latitude and separated radially from there to the equator. At the lower right corner appears a diagram of: CHORDS, SIGNES, SEGANTS AND TANGENTS. An advertisement of proposals to print the map appeared in the *New-York Packet* for May 26, 1789, and also on the verso of the cover of the (Philadelphia) *American Museum* for June, 1789.

This map was re-engraved and used as Plate I in John Churchman's *The Magnetic Atlas*, New York, 1800. The title page identifies this as the third edition, an edition having appeared in London in 1794. "Plate I" is now engraved at the upper left corner and, "Published 1st July 1800 for the Author J. Churchman," under the bottom neat line at center. The dedication to George Washington is not given.

Size 23⅞" x 23⅞". *Scale* None (1" = 8° latitude at the equator).

Published in John Churchman, *An Explanation of the Magnetic Atlas*, front.

Reference Philip I. Phillips, *Virginia Cartography*, pp. 58–59.

7 [1790] *State* II (see also Map 4)

Description In lower right corner has been added: DOOLITTLE SCULP. N.H.

Published in Jedidiah Morse, *Geography Made Easy*, 2d ed., front.

8 [1790]

Description [Plate to shew figure of the earth.] Below bottom neat line at right: DOOLITTLE SC. N HAVEN. Above top neat line at left: NO. II. This is a map designed to illustrate the curvature of the earth. A figure at the top of the globe is shown sighting on three ships sailing around it to the left. A large island is shown off the west coast of Africa parallel to Madagascar. A land south of Africa is labeled ZEALAND. The title is taken from the "Directions to the Bookbinder . . . ," on the verso of the dedication. The globe and enclosing neat lines occupy the upper two-thirds of the page.

Size 4" x 2¾". *Scale* None (diam. sphere = 1⅝").

Published in Jedidiah Morse, *Geography Made Easy*, 2d ed., opp. p. 15.

9 [1790]

Description [Map of the World.] The title page of this edition of Workman's *Elements* lists this map, but the Readex Microprint edition of Evans states that: "No copy located has the map of the world."

Size Unknown. *Scale* Unknown.

Published in Benjamin Workman, *Elements of Geography*, 2d ed.

Reference Evans 23091.

10 [1790]

Description On decorated ribbon at upper center: WORLD. Two hemispheres are shown. N. ZEELAND appears, also OWHYHEE and OTAHIETEE (see also Map 27).

Size 2⅝" x 4". *Scale* None (diam. sphere = 1 11/16").

Published in Benjamin Workman, *Elements of Geography*, 3d ed., front.; ibid., 4th, 5th, 6th, and 7th eds.

11 [1791]

Description This is a re-engraving of Map 8. The globe now is in the center of the page with the neat lines enclosing the area of the full page. No engraver's name is given and the "No. II" has been omitted at the upper left.

Size 6⅛" x 3⅛". *Scale* None (diam. sphere = 2 1/16").

Published in Jedidiah Morse, *Geography Made Easy*, 3d ed., opp. p. 13.

12 [1791]

Description In decorative ribbon at upper center: THE WORLD. At bottom center: AGREEABLE TO THE LAST DISCOVERIES IN THE SOUTH SEAS. GREENLAND is inscribed from Alaska to Baffin's Bay. Only one of the Great Lakes is indicated, and the contour of Alaska is very poorly shown. This is the second Morse map of two hemispheres.

Size 3¼" x 6⅛". *Scale* None (diam. sphere = 2⅛").

Published in Jedidiah Morse, *Geography Made Easy*, 3d ed., front.

13 [1792]

Description Four diagrams are given on plate: FIG. 2. at lower right is a terrestrial globe mounted on a stand. EUROPE and parts of AFRICA and ASIA are shown. GEOGRAPHY appears at top center; at lower right corner: SMITHER SCULP; at upper right corner: PLATE CCXI.

Size 5¼" x 3¼" (FIG. 2. only). *Scale* None.

Published in Thomas Dobson, *Encyclopaedia*, 7, opp. 660.

2

14 [1792]

Description Six diagrams are given on the plate, four of them showing portions of the earth's surface: FIG. *1.* at upper left (2¹³⁄₁₆″ diam.); FIG. *2.* at upper right (2½″ diam.); FIG. *3.* at lower left (3¾″ diam.); FIG. *4.* at right center (2¾″ diam.). All the continents are indicated on one or more of the hemispheres. California is shown as an island. At upper center: GEOGRAPHY, and at upper right: PLATE CCIX.

Size 8⅝″ x 6¾″ (of plate).   *Scale* None.

Published in Thomas Dobson, *Encyclopaedia,* 7, opp. 650.

15 [1792]

Description A "Universal Dial" incorporating a "terrestrial globe" is shown as FIG. *10* at the lower right corner. PLATE CLIX is given at upper right corner, and DIALING at top center. AFRICA, EUROPE, ASIA, and AMERICA are indicated on the globe.

Size 5″ x 3½″.   *Scale* None (diam. sphere = 1⅛″).

Published in Thomas Dobson, *Encyclopaedia,* 5, opp. 792.

16 [1792]

Description At upper center: MAP OF THE WORLD, / COMPREHENDING THE LATEST DISCOVERIES. At lower right corner: W. BARKER SCULPT. At upper right corner: PLATE CCXIV. At upper center above title: GEOGRAPHY. Captain Cook's last voyage is shown with his Alaskan discoveries. ZAARA OR THE DESART appears for the Sahara in Africa.

Size 8″ x 14⅛″ (of plate).   *Scale* None (diam. sphere = 6⅝″).

Published in Thomas Dobson, *Encyclopaedia,* 7, foll. 662.

17 [1792]

Description At upper center: A MAP OF THE WORLD / IN THREE SECTIONS / DESCRIBING THE POLAR REGIONS TO THE TROPICS / IN WHICH ARE TRACED THE TRACTS [sic] OF / LORD MULGRAVE AND CAPTAIN COOK / TOWARDS THE NORTH & SOUTH POLES / AND THE / TORRID ZONE OR TROPICAL REGIONS / WITH THE / NEW DISCOVERIES IN THE / SOUTH SEA. At lower right corner: W. BARKER SCULPT. At top center above title: GEOGRAPHY. At upper right corner: PLATE CCXIII. The world is shown in three sections: two circumpolar projections and the region between the tropics with parallel meridians. Above the upper left section is its title: THE SOUTH POLE TO THE TROPIC OF CAPRICORN / IN WHICH ARE TRACED THE SEVERAL ATTEMPTS OF CAPT. COOK TO DISCOVER A SOUTHERN CONTINENT IN *1773, 74,* & *75.* Above the upper right section: THE NORTH POLE TO THE TROPIC OF CANCER. / DESCRIBING THE TRACT [sic] OF THE HONBLE. CAPT. PHIPPS NOW LORD MULGRAVE IN *1773.* At the lower section in the center: TORRID ZONE OR TROPICAL REGIONS OF THE WORLD / IN WHICH ARE LAID DOWN / THE NEW DISCOVERIES IN THE PACIFIC OCEAN OR SOUTH SEA. DIEMENS / LAND *1618* and CARPENTARE / *1620* appear on the north coast of Australia; SHIP LION *1622* and I. EDENS *1619.*, on the southwest coast. ANTIPODES OF LONDON is inscribed south of NEW ZEELAND. JUAN FERNANDE, off the west coast of South America, and HALLIFAX appear thus. NOVA SCOTIA extends east from the Great Lakes. ZAARA OR THE DESART appears thus in Africa. GIOLO appears for Gilolo in the East Indies.

Size 9⁵⁄₁₆″ x 17⁵⁄₁₆″ (of plate).   *Scale* None (diam. sphere = 6¹³⁄₁₆).

Published in Thomas Dobson, *Encyclopaedia,* 7, foll. 662.

18 [1792]

Description At top center of plate: THE / SIX DAYS WORK / OF THE / CREATION; on panel 3 at left center: SEPERATION [sic] OF THE EARTH FROM YE WATERS; on panel 4 at right center: THE CREATION OF THE SUN MOON AND STARS; at top: ENGRAVED FOR THE AMERICAN EDITION OF MAYNARDS JOSEPHUS. The two center panels, no. *3* measuring 3½″ x 2⅝″ and no. *4,* 3½″ x 2¹¹⁄₁₆″, are maps, as they represent the earth, showing the ground masses of Asia, Africa, and Europe. The engraving is by Amos Doolittle.

Size 12⅝″ x 8″ (of plate).   *Scale* None.

Published in Flavius Josephus, *The Whole Genuine and Complete Works,* opp. p. 7.

19 [1793]

Description In ornamented circle at upper center: THE / WORLD / FROM THE BEST / AUTHORITIES. Above the title and ornaments: PUBLISHED BY THOMAS & ANDREWS. At bottom center: ENGRAVED FOR MORSES GEOGRAPHY BY A DOOLITTLE N. HAVEN. GR. BRITAN and NEW BRITAN (Labrador) appear thus. Lake Huron is omitted, but the other Great Lakes are shown. Several islands are given north and northwest of the Azores. ZAARA OR THE DESART appears in Africa, ABASSIA for Abyssinia, and ST. DAMINGO for San Domingo. This is the third Morse map of two hemispheres.

Size 8″ x 15⅛″.   *Scale* None (diam. sphere = 7″).

Published in Jedidiah Morse, *The American Universal Geography,* 1, front.

3

20 [¹794]

Description In decorated ribbon at top center: THE WORLD. At bottom center: TANNER SCULPT. N. ZEELAND appears and also BOTANY BAY. Hawaii and Tahiti are not named. The "F" for "France" and "E" for "Europe" are superimposed. MOGULS EMPIRE is inscribed across the two Indian peninsulas.

Size 2⁹⁄₁₆″ x 3¹³⁄₁₆″. *Scale* None (diam. sphere = 1¹¹⁄₁₆″).

Published in Donald Fraser, *The Young Gentleman* and *Lady's Assistant*, 2d and 3d eds.

21 [¹794] *State* I (see also Map 32)

Description In decorative ribbon at top: THE WORLD. In lower right corner: DOOLITTLE SC. Outside top neat line at center: PUBLISHED BY THOMAS AND ANDREWS BOSTON. Inside a double circle above the title is a four-petal flower that in this state is obscured by shading. This is the fourth Morse map of two hemispheres.

Size 3¼″ x 5¹¹⁄₁₆″. *Scale* None (diam. sphere = 2¼″).

Published in Jedidiah Morse, *Geography Made Easy*, 4th ed., front.

22 [¹794]

Description In lower left corner: A / GENERAL CHART OF THE / GLOBE, / SHEWING THE COURSE OF THE GULPH STREAM, / AND / VARIOUS TRACKS TO AND FROM THE / EAST INDIES, CHINA, EUROPE &C: / BY / CAPTN: / THOS: TRUXTUN [sic]. This is a chart on Mercator's projection. Eight different lines lettered from "A" to "H" show Truxton's courses between various points. The Gulf Stream is shown and also an odd train of very large lakes northwest of Lake Superior. NOOTKA OR K. GEORGES SD., CROSS SOUND, and P. WILLIAMS SD are all left indefinite.

Size 18¹⁄₁₆″ x 35 ³⁄₁₆″. *Scale* None (1″ = c. 690 miles).

Published in Thomas Truxton, *Remarks, Instructions, and Examples*, front.

Reference Lloyd A. Brown, "The River in the Ocean," p. 82.

23 [¹795] *State* I (II and III post-1799, see below, Description)

Description In oval at lower left: A CHART / OF THE / WORLD, / ACCORDING TO / MERCATORS PROJECTION, / SHEWING THE LATEST DISCOVERIES / OF CAPT. COOK. Below oval: WILLIAM BARKER SCULP. Above top neat line: ENGRAVED FOR CAREY'S AMERICAN EDITION OF GUTHRIE'S GEOGRAPHY IMPROVED. The three voyages of Capt. Cook are traced. The mouth of the Coppermine River is shown in 72° North Latitude instead of about

67° 30′. A fictitious inland sea or strait connects Hudson's Bay and Ungava Bay. DIEMEN'S LAND is inscribed on the northern coast of Australia. This map appears in the Sept. 9, 1800, edition of *Carey's General Atlas* with the figure "2" at upper right corner. Both Barker's signature and the inscription above top neat line have been eliminated in State III in the 1814 edition.

Size 14¼″ x 18⁷⁄₁₆″. *Scale* None (1″ = c. 20° latitude).

Published in Mathew Carey, *Carey's General Atlas*, no. 2; idem, *The General Atlas for Carey's Edition of Guthrie's Geography Improved*, no. 2.

24 [¹795] *State* I (II post-1799, see below, Description)

Description At top within spread of neat lines: A MAP OF THE DISCOVERIES MADE BY CAPTS. COOK & CLERKE IN THE YEARS *1778* & *1779* BETWEEN THE EASTERN COAST OF ASIA / AND THE WESTERN COAST OF NORTH AMERICA, WHEN THEY ATTEMPTED TO NAVIGATE THE NORTH SEA. / ALSO MR HEARN'S DISCOVERIES TO THE NORTH WESTWARD OF HUDSON'S BAY, IN *1772*. Following title: J. T. SCOTT SCULP. Above top neat line: ENGRAVED FOR CAREY'S, AMERICAN EDITION OF GUTHRIE'S GEOGRAPHY IMPROVED. NIPHON is given for Japan, and NORTHERN ARCHIPELAGO appears between Siberia and Alaska. In the 1800 edition of *Carey's General Atlas* "45" appears in upper right corner.

Size 8¹³⁄₁₆″ x 11¾″. *Scale* None (1″ = c. 9° latitude).

Published in Mathew Carey, *Carey's American Atlas*, no. 24; idem, *Carey's General Atlas*, no. 45; idem, *The General Atlas for Carey's Edition of Guthrie's Geography Improved*, no. 45.

25 [¹795] *State* I (II post-1799, see below, Description)

Description In oval at upper center: A / MAP OF THE / WORLD / FROM THE BEST AUTHORITIES. Below oval: THACKARA & VALLANCE SC. Above oval: ENGRAV'D FOR CAREY'S EDITION OF GUTHRIE'S NEW SYSTEM OF GEOGRAPHY. The three voyages of Captain Cook are traced. The world is shown in two hemispheres. It appears again in *Carey's General Atlas*, Sept. 9, 1800, with the figure "1" added at upper right corner; and also in *Carey's General Atlas*, 1814, with the inscription above the title removed and the number "1" remaining at the upper right corner.

Size 11⅝″ x 20⅜″. *Scale* None (diam. sphere = 9¹¹⁄₁₆″).

Published in Mathew Carey, *Carey's General Atlas*, no. 1; idem, *The General Atlas for Carey's Edition of Guthrie's Geography Improved*, no. 1.

26 [1795] *State* I (see also Maps 30 and 37)

Description In oval at lower left: CHART / OF THE / WORLD / ON / MERCATORS PROJECTION. Below oval to right: H. SC. Above top neat line at center: ENRAVED FOR MORSE'S ELEMENTS OF GEOGRAPHY. Below bottom neat line at center: PUBLISHED BY THOMAS & ANDREWS, BOSTON. ITALY is inscribed on the Balkan peninsula. This is the first Morse chart of the world.

Size 4⁹⁄₁₆″ x 5¹⁵⁄₁₆″. *Scale* None (1″ = c. 55° latitude).

Published in Jedidiah Morse, *Elements of Geography*, 1st ed., front.

27 [1795]

Description In rectangle at upper center: THE WORLD. This map appears to be copied from Map 10. SOCIETY IS, NEW ZEALAND, and BEHRING STR. appear.

Size 2⁵⁄₁₆″ x 3⅝″. *Scale* None (diam. sphere = 1¹¹⁄₁₆″).

Published in Charles Smith, *Universal Geography Made Easy*, front.

28 [1796]

Description Across top above neat line: A GENERAL CHART: / EXHIBITING THE DISCOVERIES MADE BY CAPTN. JAMES COOK IN THIS AND HIS TWO PREECEEDING [sic] VOYAGES; WITH THE TRACKS OF THE SHIPS UNDER HIS COMMAND. At lower right corner below neat line: ROLLINSON. At upper right corner above neat line: ENGRAV'D FOR COOK'S VOYAGE. OCTAVO EDITION. This is a chart drawn on the Mercator projection. The EXPLANATION for the ship track lines is given at the lower right corner.

Size 16¼″ x 23″. *Scale* None (1″ = c. 800 miles).

Published in James Cook and James King, *Voyage to the Pacific Ocean,* New York, 1796, opp. p. XXXIV.

Location NHi (in their copy of [*Atlas for Winterbotham's History of America*]).

29 [1796]

Description [Eastern Hemisphere.] This is a topographical map showing Europe, Africa, and Asia, with the major countries of Asia named. Thirteen numbered locations are identified in two references lists given at the lower left and right. COBI appears thus twice. The letter "N" of OCEAN, at the left, indicating the Atlantic, is given north of Ireland. A re-engraved version of this map was used in the 1799 edition of the work (see Map 43).

Size 5¾″ x 6¼″. *Scale* None (diam. sphere = 5⅝″).

Published in Constantin F. C. Volney, *The Ruins,* opp. p. 29.

30 [1796] *State* II (see also Maps 26 and 37)

Description The name CHINA has been inscribed on that section of Asia. ITALY is still inscribed on the Balkan Peninsula.

Published in Jedidiah Morse, *Elements of Geography*, 2d ed., front.

31 [1796]

Description In oval at lower left: CHART / OF THE / WORLD / ON / MERCATORS PROJECTION. Beneath oval: DOOLITTLE SCULP: NEW-HAVEN. Above top neat line: PUBLISHED BY THOMS [sic] & ANDREWS, BOSTON. WEST R is shown flowing from present-day North Dakota to a NOOTKA SOUND shown in the mainland. MC. KENSES R appears for the Mackenzie. This is the second Morse chart of the world.

Size 7⁹⁄₁₆″ x 10″. *Scale* None (1″ = 35° latitude).

Published in Jedidiah Morse, *The American Universal Geography,* 3d ed., *1,* opp. 786.

32 [1796] *State* II (see also Map 21)

Description The shading lines have been removed from the four-petal flowers in the double circle above the title, and the petals appear white. The outline of shading around the continents has been recut.

Published in Jedidiah Morse, *Geography Made Easy,* 5th ed., front.

33 [1796]

Description In oval at upper center: MAP / OF THE / WORLD / FROM THE BEST / AUTHORITIES. Below oval: DOOLITTLE SCULP: At bottom center: ENGRAVED FOR MORSE'S UNIVERSAL GEOGRAPHY, PUBLISHED BY THOMAS & ANDREWS, BOSTON. CHRISTMAST I in the Pacific and TIOPIC OF CANCER where it crosses the Sahara are shown thus. The east coast of NEW / HOLLAND is inscribed NEW SOUTH WALLS. The east coast of New Guinea is not defined, and a large island of New Britain is indicated. This is the fifth Morse map of two hemispheres.

Size 7¼″ x 13¾″. *Scale* None (diam. sphere = 6¹¹⁄₁₆″).

Published in Jedidiah Morse, *The American Universal Geography,* 3d ed., *1,* front.

34 [1797]

Description In center at top: ATLANTIC HEMISPHERE: / WITH IT'S ICES, IT'S CURRENTS, &

5

ITS TIDES, IN THE MONTHS OF JANUARY & FEBRU-ARY. At upper left corner: PLATE. II. At upper right corner: VOL. I. PAGE *118*. At bottom center: PUBLISHED BY J. NANCREDE, NO. *49*, MARLBOROH. STREET, BOSTON. At lower right on edge of globe: S. HILL. SC. BOSTON. The several currents and their directions are noted by arrows. On some copies the imprint at the bottom of the map has been trimmed off, but the map in other respects is the same.

Size 7½" x 6¼". *Scale* None (diam. sphere = 6").

Published in Jacques Saint Pierre, *Studies of Nature*, opp. p. 118; idem, *Vindication*, opp. p. 54.

35 [1797]

Description At upper center: A GENERAL CHART OF THE WORLD ON MERCATOR'S PROJECTION, / EXHIBITING ALL / THE NEW DISCOVERIES AND ALL THE TRACKS OF THE DIFFERENT CIRCUM-NAVIGA-TORS. ENGRAVED FOR SPOTSWOOD'S & NANCREDE'S EDITION OF MALHAM'S NAVAL GAZETTEER. Below neat line at right corner: J NORMAN SC. The Great Lakes region is much distorted. The R OF THE WEST is indicated as rising near WOOD L and flowing from Minnesota to the Pacific. A NEW SEA appears in the center of Labrador. SANCTA FE is shown thus in the latitude of New York. The OHIO R is shown twice: once in its proper place and once in place of the Missouri. The East Indies are especially distorted, the Celebes, Java, and Luzon being shown very poorly. This map is copied from the map of similar title engraved by S. J. Neele in the London, 1795 edition.

Size 13" x 17⁹⁄₁₆". *Scale* None (1" = c. 21° latitude).

Published in John Malham, *The Naval Gazetteer, 1,* opp. title page.

36 [1798]

Description Top and bottom center: THE / WORLD. Bottom right: J. T. SCOTT SCULP. PHILADA.

Size 2⁷⁄₁₆" x 3⅞". *Scale* None (diam. sphere = 1¹¹⁄₁₆).

Published in John Gibson, *Atlas Minimus*, no. 1.

37 1798

Description A new plate has been made, copying Map 30 in size and scale, but with a number of place names added, notably: TBIBET [sic], PHILADELPHIA, NOOTKA SOUND, CHARLESTON, PERU, BRAZIL, MOROCCO, and CONGO. Some additional islands are also shown: OWHYHEE, JUAN FERNANDES, BERMUDAS, MADEIRA, and ST. HELENA.

The engraver's mark, "H. Sc," below the oval in left lower corner is omitted, and *1798* has been added to the publisher's imprint beneath bottom neat line. ITALY is still inscribed on the Balkan peninsula. (See also Maps 26 and 30.)

Published in Jedidiah Morse, *Elements of Geography*, 3d ed., front.

38 1798 *State* I (II post-1799, see below, Description)

Description At upper center: A NEW MAP OF THE WORLD; WITH THE / LATEST DISCOVERIES. / *1798*. At bottom center: ENGRAVED FOR MORSE'S ABRIDGEMENT OF GEOGRAPHY. / PUBLISHED BY THOMAS & ANDREWS, BOSTON. NEW SOUTH WALES denotes the entire eastern section of NEW / HOL-LAND; VAN DIEMENS LAND is a peninsula; NUYTS LAND appears in the southwest corner of the Australian continent; and a large island called NEW / BRITAIN appears just east of New Guinea. OWHYHEE / WHERE CAPT. COOK WAS KILLED appears thus. DRAKES HARB. appears for San Francisco. LONG ISLAND is shown east of Cape Cod. This is Morse's sixth map of two hemispheres. This map was re-engraved for the 7th ed. of Morse's *Geography Made Easy*, Boston, 1800. "R. St. Lawrence" and "Bohama Is" appear thus in this later state, and the date does not appear in the title.

Size 5¹¹⁄₁₆" x 10⁵⁄₁₆". *Scale* None (diam. sphere = 5¹¹⁄₁₆").

Published in Jedidiah Morse, *Geography Made Easy*, 6th ed., front.

39 [1798]

Description On shaded oval tablet at upper left: GENERAL CHART / ON MERCATORS PROJECTION. Below tablet: ROLLINSON SCULPT. Above top neat line at center: ENGRAVED FOR PAYN'S [sic] UNIVER-SAL GEOGRAPHY PUBLISHED BY LOW & WILLIS NEW YORK. DRAKES HARB. and WEST R running into NOOTKA SOUND are shown. Capt. Cook's last voyage is traced, as well as some FORMER TRACKS OF J COOK SHEWING THE NON EXISTANCE OF A TERRA AUSTRALIS OR SOUTHERN CONTINENT.

Size 7" x 9¾". *Scale* None (1" = c. 35° latitude).

Published in John Payne, *A New and Complete Universal Geography, 1,* opp. V.

40 [1798]

Description In oval at upper center: THE / WORLD / FROM THE BEST / AUTHORITIES. In oval below title: ROLLINSON SCT. At bottom center: ENGRAVEVD [sic] FOR PAYNE'S UNIVERSAL GEOGRA-PHY PUBLISHED BY LOW & WILLIS NEW YORK. The two hemispheres are shown on the globular projection. NEW GUINEA OR PANEAAS is given for Papua; CAPE CIRCUMCISION is shown directly south of Africa; MAGELHANIE appears north of Patagonia; and DAVISS / LAND is given in the South Pacific.

Size 8³⁄₁₆″ x 15″ (over plate). *Scale* None (diam. sphere = 7″).

Published in John Payne, *A New and Complete Universal Geography, 1,* front.

41 [¹798]

Description At top center within upper section of two-part plate: GEOGRAPHICAL CIRCLES ZONES &C. &C. At lower right (of upper portion): PLATE III. Below dividing neat line at center: MARINER'S COMPASS with diagram of a compass. At lower right in lower section: PLATE IV; at lower left: GEO. BONNOR SCULPT. The upper section of this page shows a hemisphere with the five world zones indicated and with crude representations of the Western Hemisphere and part of Europe and Africa.

Size 4⅛″ x 6⅞″ (on plate: 8⅞″ x 6⅞″). *Scale* None (diam. sphere = 3″).

Published in [W. Williams], *First Principles of Geography,* foll. p. 11.

42 [¹799]

Description At upper center: A NEW MAP / OF THE / WORLD / WITH THE LATEST / DISCOVERIES. The map is in two hemispheres. California begins north of CAPE MENDOZINO.

Size 5¹¹⁄₁₆″ x 10½″. *Scale* None (diam. sphere = 5″).

Published in Joseph Scott, *The New and Universal Gazetteer, 1,* at leaf Oo¹.

43 [¹799]

Description [Eastern Hemisphere.] At lower right under references eight through thirteen: JONES SC. In the references at the lower left, the following spelling changes are noted: *3* R. JOURDAN, not R Jordan; *5* BAHARAN ISLANDS, not Baharen Islands; *7* ECHATANIA, not Echatana. At the left, the letter "N" of OCEAN, indicating the Atlantic, is given south of Ireland. This is a re-engraving of Map 29, and is probably the work of Benjamin JONES.

Size 5¾″ x 6¼″. *Scale* None (diam. sphere = 5⅜″).

Published in Constantin F. C. Volney, *The Ruins,* Philadelphia, 1799, opp. p. 1.

44 1717 *State* I (see also Maps 45, 46, 48, and 49)

Description [A new chart of North America.] At bottom center: ENGRAVEN AND PRINTED BY FRA DEWING BOSTON NEW ENGLAND *1717*. This is the first known general map of the eastern North American continent printed in America. It shows the full length of the Atlantic seaboard from Newfoundland south to Florida, and the interior west to the Mississippi River, including the Great Lakes. While it may serve to some extent as a general chart of the Atlantic coast, Captain Southack states as his purpose, just above a long list of references at the lower right, that: . . . READING HIS EXCELLENCY ROBT HUNTER ESQR GOVERNOUR OF NEW YORK &C. / HIS SPEECH TO THE GENERAL ASSEMBLY OF THE SD COLONY OF THE 5th OF JUNE *1716* (warning of French designs on the American West). HAS BIN THE OCCASION OF MY DRAWING THIS CHART . . . A succession of newly constructed French forts across this area bears out this warning. A dedication to Governor SAMUEL SHUTE of MASSACHUSETTS BAY and the COUNCIL AND REPRESENTATIVES / IN GENERAL COURT ASSEMBLED on 7TH OF NOVEMBER, *1716,* is given in a decorative cartouche at the lower left, signed by the author, CYPRIAN SOUTHACK. A further explanation of symbols is given in the lower left corner.

Size 27¼" x 30⅞". *Scale* 1" = c. 65 miles.

Published Separately. Reproduced separately, with "Notes" by John Carter Brown Library, Providence, 1942; ibid., *The French and Indian War,* no. 3.

References Clara E. LeGear, "The New England Coasting Pilot of Cyprian Southack"; see also Mrs. LeGear's account of Capt. Southack in *DAB.*

Location RPJCB.

45 1717 *State* II (see also Maps 44, 46, 48, and 49)

Description The following title has been inserted in manuscript at upper center on the Public Record Office copy: "A new chart / of the English Empire in / North America." Many other changes and additions have been made on various parts of this copy of the map. "Mary Land" has been removed and replaced in manuscript on the Delmarva Peninsula by "Mair / land"; "Virginia" has been removed and replaced in manuscript directly under the southern extreme of Lake Michigan.

Published Separately.

Location PRO.

46 [1721] *State* III (see also Maps 44, 45, 48, and 49)

Description An issue of this date was advertised in *The Boston News-Letter* for April 10–13, 1721. This map may carry some of the changes indicated upon the Public Record Office, State II, copy.

Published Separately.

Location No copy located.

47 1730

Description [Part of North America.] The following advertisement appeared in *The New-York Gazette,* September 21–28, 1730:

"This is to give Notice, That the Mercator Chart Drawn by Phillip Cockrem, extending from the Lat. of 9 Degrees. to the Lat. of 43 Degrees North; Easterly to the Island of Barbados, Westerly to the Entrance of Massisipi [sic]: is now entirely finished and printed on fine Royal Paper, and are to be seen and sold at the House of Phillip Cockrem in Princess-Street, near Smith Street in New-York; the Price being Twenty Shillings each, New-York Money."

The map is also listed in the October 16–26 issue of the *Gazette* as being available: ". . . at John Macklennan's at the Sign of the Blue Anchor on the Dock New York."

Size Unknown. *Scale* Unknown.

Published Separately.

References [Rita S. Gottesman], *The Arts and Crafts in New York 1726–1776,* p. 17; Gerald D. McDonald, "A Gift of *The New-York Gazette,*" p. 498.

Location No copy located.

48 1746 *State* IV (see also Maps 44, 45, 46, and 49)

Description At top left center the following title has been added: A NEW CHART OF THE / BRITISH EMPIRE IN / NORTH AMERICA / WITH THE DISTINCT COLONIES GRANTED / BY LETTERS PATENT FROM CAPE CANSO / TO ST MATTHIAS RIVER / *1746.* At bottom left center the date has been changed to *1746.* This map was advertised in the *Boston Weekly News-Letter,* August 15, 1746: "To Be Sold, by William Price," and noted the addition of the "Account of taking the strong City of Louisbourg, &c.," given at the upper right.

Published Separately.

Reference Philip L. Phillips, *A List of Maps of America,* p. 571.

Location DLC.

49 [1754?] *State* V (see also Maps 44, 45, 46, and 48)

Description NEW FORT / FRENCH BUILT *1754* is shown on the legendary R. ST. JEROM (actually a combination of the Wabash and the lower Ohio rivers), and a new river has been added emptying into it from the south. A tributary of the ST. JEROM is now labeled the OHIO RIVER. HALLI-FAX (founded 1749) has been noted thus on the NOVA SCOTIA coast, the letters TIA of the Province have been moved to the right, and a historical note concerning the failure of the French expedition under the Duke d'Anville in 1746 has been inserted.

Published Separately.

Location PHi.

50 [1759]

Description [Land Carte . . . der englischen Provinzen in Nord America . . .] This is a rough topographic map indicating some of the more important forts, towns, and rivers of northeastern North America. The title is taken from the text under the map.

Size 4⅝" x 7". *Scale* 1" = 140 miles.

Published in Anton Armbruster, *Neu-Eingerichteter Americanischer Geschicts-Und Haus Calendar.*

51 [1790]

Description In oval at upper left: A / GENERAL MAP OF / NORTH / AMERICA / FROM THE BEST / AUTHORITIES. In the lower right corner: SCOT. At upper right in the border: PLATE XIV. MEXICO C is placed just outside the lower neat line. The Olympic Peninsula is indicated as an island extending south to the RIVER OF THE WEST. A large WESTERN / SEA is shown in modern

British Columbia and Washington. San Francisco Bay is marked: HR. WHERE SR. / FRANCIS DRAKE / WAS 5 WEEKS. A range of mountains, called BARE / MTS at southern end, is shown along the east bank of the MISSISSIPPI from the Illinois River to the St. Croix. The map was engraved by Robert Scot.

Size 7" x 8⅝". *Scale* None (1" = c. 6° 40' latitude).

Published in Thomas Dobson, *Encyclopaedia, I,* opp. 538; Jedidiah Morse, *The history of America,* 1st ed., front; ibid., 2d and 3d eds.

52 [1790]

Description In oval vignette at upper left: NORTH / AMERICA. Philadelphia, New York, and Boston are located but not named. THE LAKES indicates an odd configuration for the Great Lakes. OREGON R, THE ARCTIC CONTINENT, and GROENLAND appear.

Size 3¹⁵⁄₁₆" x 2¹¹⁄₁₆". *Scale* None (1" = c. 25° latitude).

Published in Benjamin Workman, *Elements of Geography,* 3d ed., opp. p. 64; ibid., 4th, 5th, 6th, and 7th eds.

53 1795

Description [A general Chart of the Coast of North America . . . Certification by Osgood Carleton, Boston, 1795.] This chart is listed on the letterpress cover title but is missing in two known copies of the *Pilot.*

Size Unknown. *Scale* Unknown.

Published in William Norman, *A Pilot for the West-Indies.*

Location No copy located.

54 [1795]

Description In rectangle at upper left: NORTH / AMERICA. This was copied from Map 52. GROENLAND and THE ARCTIC CONTINENT still appear. The northern Pacific Coast and a number of place names have been added. The configurations are the same.

Size 3¾" x 2⅜". *Scale* None (1" = 24½° latitude).

Published in Charles Smith, *Universal Geography Made Easy,* opp. p. 125.

55 [1796]

Description In oval at lower center: A / GENERAL MAP OF / NORTH AMERICA / FROM THE BEST / AUTHORITIES. Below title inside oval: DOOLITTLE SCULP:. Above top neat line at center: PUBLISHED BY THOMAS & ANDREWS, BOSTON. NORWEST TERI-

TORY appears thus along the east bank of the Mississippi above the Ohio. ACANSIS R appears for the Arkansas. HEADS OF THE / MISSISSIPPI & R / OF THE WEST appear among the Minnesota Lakes. KANSES appears for the Kansas River. IOWA / TOWN is shown in modern Iowa. *3 MARYS* appears for the Tres Marias off the Mexican coast. THE SEA appears at the mouth of the Coppermine River, but no Northwest Passage is indicated. This is the first Morse map of North America.

Size 7⅜" x 8¾". *Scale* None (1" = 10° latitude).

Published in Jedidiah Morse, *The American Universal Geography,* 3d ed., *1*, opp. 128.

56 [1796] *State* I (see also Map 57)

Description In oval at lower left: A / GENERAL MAP / OF / NORTH AMERICA / DRAWN FROM THE BEST SURVEYS / *1795.* In oval below title: SCOLES SC. Below bottom neat line at center: PUBLISHED BY SMITH, REID, & WAYLAND. Two lakes appear in the present United States west of the Rockies. JUAN DE FONCA'S INLET appears thus, as well as ST. [sic] FRANCISCO with the Bay indicated. STONY MOUNTAINS appears for the Canadian Rockies. Maine is not named and is given a very squat shape, with the St. Croix River running west by south. The states of the United States are tabulated, with Roman numeral references to fifteen of them appearing at right center.

Size 14⅛" x 18". *Scale* None (1" = c. 5° latitude).

Published in William Winterbotham, [*Atlas*].

57 [1796] *State* II (see also Map 56)

Description The imprint below bottom neat line at center has been changed to: PUBLISHED BY JOHN REID N. YORK.

Published in John Reid, *The American Atlas,* [1796?] (with cover title *The Atlas for Winterbotham's History of America. 1796*), no. 1; idem, *The American Atlas,* 1796, no. 1.

References Baltimore Museum of Art, *The World Encompassed,* no. 206; Carl I. Wheat, *Mapping the Transmississippi West, 1,* 150, no. 233.

58 [1797]

Description In oval at upper left: A / CORRECT CHART / OF THE EAST COAST OF / NORTH AMERICA / ENGRAVED FOR / MALHAM'S NAVAL GAZETTEER. Below bottom neat line at center: PUBLISH'D SEPTR *1796* BY SPOTSWOOD AND NANCREDE BOSTON. At right corner: B CALLENDER SCULPT BOSTON. This is a chart on Mercator's

projection showing the coast from Sadel Bay in Labrador to the west coast of Florida. The ALONKIN Indians are located west of Quebec. INDIANA is shown east of KENTUCKE and southwest of PENSYLVANIA. This map is copied from the one engraved by S. J. Neele in the London, 1795 edition.

Size 9⁹⁄₁₆" x 7³⁄₁₆". *Scale* 1" = 85 leagues.

Published in John Malham, *The Naval Gazetteer, 1,* opp. 30.

59 [1797]

Description In oval at upper right: A / CORRECT CHART / OF THE WEST COAST OF / NORTH AMERICA / FROM / BHERING'S STRAITS TO NOOTKA SOUND / ENGD. FOR MALHAMS NAVAL GAZETTEER. Below bottom neat line at center: PUBLISH'D SEPR *1796* BY SPOTSWOOD AND NANCREDE BOSTON; At right: B CALLENDER SCULPT BOSTON. This is a chart on Mercator's projection; it is copied from the one engraved by S. J. Neele in the London, 1795 edition.

Size 7¼" x 9⅜". *Scale* None (1" = c. 5½° latitude).

Published in John Malham, *The Naval Gazetteer, 1,* opp. 30.

60 1797

Description In oval at lower left: A NEW MAP / OF / NORTH AMERICA / SHEWING ALL THE / NEW DISCOVERIES / *1797.* Below bottom neat line at right: HILL, SC. Outside top neat line at center: ENGRAVED FOR MORSE'S GAZETTEER OF AMERICA. The Arctic shore line is indicated with a dotted line and the COPPERMINE / R named. Dotted lines indicate a waterway across southern Greenland. IOVA / TOWN appears in modern Iowa. KANSEZ appears as an Indian town. ILLINOISE R appears thus. *3* NARIAS appears thus for the Tres Marias. CHANNEL OF ST. BARBARA appears along the southern coast of modern California. CUMBERLAND R appears. This is the second Morse map of North America.

Size 7⁹⁄₁₆" x 9". *Scale* None (1" = 10° latitude).

Published in Jedidiah Morse, *The American Gazetteer,* front. Reproduced in U.S. Bureau of the Census, *A Century of Population Growth,* front.

Reference Carl I. Wheat, *Mapping the Transmississippi West, 1,* 151–52, no. 244.

61 [1798]

Description At upper left: NORTH / AMERICA. Below bottom neat line at right: ENGRAV'D BY F.

SHALLUS. Above top neat line at center: *5*. The boundaries of old French Canada on Gibson's 1792 map still appear south of Lake Superior.

Size 3⅝" x 2½". *Scale* None (1" = c. 24½° latitude).

Published in John Gibson, *Atlas Minimus*, no. 5.

62 1798

Description In oval in lower left corner: A MAP / OF / NORTH AMERICA / FROM THE LATEST / DISCOVERIES / *1798*. Above top neat line at center: PUBLISHED BY THOMAS & ANDREWS BOSTON *1798*. This map shows the COPPERMINE / R and indicates a northwest passage by sea. Many names are given along the northwest coast. SIR FRANCIS DRAKES HAR., NEW YEARS HARB., and MONTERRY *1603*, are all shown on the California coast. ENTRANCE OF / JUAN DE FUCA is shown with an indefinite bay behind it. The RIVER OF THE WEST flows into this bay. This river becomes the OREGON R further east and originates in a small lake south of WENNIPEG / L near the HEADS OF THE / MISSISIPPI. This is the third Morse map of North America. See also Map 63.

Size 6" x 7 9/16". *Scale* None (1" = c. 12.3° latitude).

Published in Jedidiah Morse, *Geography Made Easy*, 6th ed., opp. p. 76.

63 1798

Description The map is a re-engraving of Map 62 upon a new plate with a few minor corrections and two dots (which have been placed by the engraver to identify the second plate) under *1798* inside the oval. KANSES appears now instead of Kansez; MONTAGUE I instead of Montague, off Prince Williams Sound in Alaska; and IOVA / TOWN and the *3* NARIAS still appear thus. A comma has been added after THOMAS & ANDREWS above the top neat line.

Size 5 15/16" x 7⅜". *Scale* None (1" = 12.3° latitude).

Published in Jedidiah Morse, *An Abridgement of the American Gazetteer*, front.

64 [1799?]

Description At upper right: A / NEW CHART / OF THE / N.W. COAST OF AMERICA, / WITH PART OF THE COAST OF CALIFORNIA; / INCLUDING THE SANDWICH ISLANDS AND THE PRINCIPAL HARBOURS / AS SURVEYED BY GEORGE VANCOUVER ESQ. / REVISED AND CORRECTED BY OSGOOD CARLETON ESQR TEACHER OF MATHEMATICS BOSTON / BOSTON PUBLISHED AND SOLD BY W. NORMAN MAP CHART AND BOOKSELLER. This is a fine, detailed chart giving much topographic detail along the immediate coast from COOKS INLET in Alaska south to Cape ST. LUCAS in Lower California. Many soundings are given in the insets. The chart is dedicated TO THE / MERCHANTS AND UNDERWRITERS / OF THE / UNITED STATES OF AMERICA . . . BY . . . THE PUBLISHER.

Size 48¾" x 40½". *Scale* None (1" = c. 75 miles).

Insets [a] At right center below dedication: A SURVEY / OF / PORT CHALMERS. Size: 8⅞" x 8½". Scale: 1" = 1 1/16 miles.

[b] Cutting marginal degree line below [a]: PORT SN DIEGO. Size: 6¾" x 4⅛". Scale: 1" = 3 miles.

[c] At left of [b]: ENTRANCE / OF / PORT FRANCISCO. Size: 6¼" x 7 3/16". Scale: 1" = 2 miles.

[d] Below [c] at right margin: BAY OF TRINADAD. Size: 4⅞" x 4¼". Scale: 1" = ½ mile.

[e] At left of [d]; A SUPVEY [sic] / OF / PORT STEWART. Size: 4⅞" x 3½". Scale: 1" = ⅝ mile.

[f] At left center: ENTRANCE / OF / COLUMBIA RIVER. PT ADAMS is identified. Size: 5⅝" x 8⅝". Scale: 1" = 1⅓ leagues.

[g] At left below [f]: GRAYS HARBOUR. PT BROWN is noted. Size: 7½" x 6⅞". Scale: 1" = 2 1/7 leagues.

[h] At left of [g]: PORT DISCOVERY. Size: 7½" x 5¼". Scale: 1" = 2 1/7 leagues.

[i] At lower left corner: A CHART / OF THE / SANDWICH ISLANDS / AS SURVEYED BY / GEORGE VANCOUVER ESQ. The islands are identified and some topographical details noted. Size: 15¼" x 17". Scale None.

[j] In lower left corner of [i]: A SURVEY / OF / PORT CHATHAM. Size: 6⅜" x 5¼". Scale: 1" = 1⅗ leagues.

Published Separately.

Location RPJCB.

65 1799

Description In oval at lower left: A MAP OF / NORTH AMERICA / FROM THE LATEST / AUTHORITIES / *1799*. Below bottom neat line at center: ENGRAVED FOR PAYNES GEOGRAPHY PUBLISHED BY I LOW NEW YORK. At right corner: SCOLES SCULP. RICHMOND / BAY is an arm of HUDSONS / BAY; the *3* MARYS are off the west coast of Mexico; and PENSILVA / NIA is given thus.

Size 7¼" x 8 9/16". *Scale* None (1" = c. 9° latitude).

Published in John Payne, *A New and Complete System of Universal Geography*, *4*, opp. 11.

66 [1799]

Description In oval at lower left: A NEW MAP / OF / NORTH AMERICA / SHEWING ALL THE /

NEW DISCOVERIES. The R OF THE WEST and ORE-GON R system is shown extending eastward to the modern Dakotas. N. W. TERRITORY is indicated. A dashed line is given from SLAVE LAKE north to THE SEA.

Size 7¹¹⁄₁₆″ x 9¼″.   *Scale* None (1″ = c. 10° latitude).

Published in Joseph Scott, *The New and Universal Gazetteer, 1,* leaf I².

CANADA

67 [1711]

Description [Chart of the St. Lawrence River and the Gulf of St. Lawrence.] This chart was prepared by Cyprian Southack for the ill-fated 1711 British expedition against Quebec, commanded by Sir Hovenden Walker. Fifty copies were published for the use of the ships of the fleet.

Size Unknown.　*Scale* Unknown.

Reference Clara E. LeGear, "The New England Coasting Pilot of Cyprian Southack," p. 142.

Location No copy located.

68 1720

Description Above top neat line: THE HARBOUR AND ISLANDS OF CANSO PART OF THE BOUNDARIES OF NOVA SCOTIA. The outer bottom neat line is broken at center by: ENGRAVEN AND PRINTED BY FRA: DEWING. BOSTON 1720. Many soundings are given. A number of houses are indicated including those of FRENCH INTRUDERS. NO SCALE FOR BETWEEN YE FRENCH / SHORE ISLAND MADAM & CANSO / ISLAND ... The route of Capt. Thomas Smart in the *Squirrel* in September, 1718, is noted with a PRICT LINE. A fishing scene is shown at the lower right. The dedication signed by CAPTAIN / CYPRIAN / SOUTHACK to Richard Phillips, Governor of Nova Scotia, is given in a cartouche at the lower left. This map was advertised in the *Boston News-Letter*, April 14–18, 1720, as "Drawn by Capt. Cyprian Southack."

Size 17⅝" x 25⅛".　*Scale* 1" = c. ⅝ English mile.

Published Separately.

References William Dunlap, *A History of the Arts of Design*, 3, 265; Clara E. LeGear, "The New England Coasting Pilot of Cyprian Southack," p. 143.

Location PRO.

69 [1733]

Description [Map of Louisbourg and its Harbour.] Eleven references are printed directly under the map, which appears at the top left of the page. A defensive wall is shown being built along the land side of the peninsula on which Louisbourg is located. The map was drawn under the direction of a recently returned mariner, John Gardner, whose affidavit is given in part on the page preceding the map.

Size 2½" x 2¾".　*Scale* None (1" = c. 1¼ miles).

Published in *New-York Weekly Journal*, December 24, 1733, no. VIII, [4].

References Clarence S. Brigham, *Journals and Journeymen*, p. 41; [Rita Gottesman], *The Arts and Crafts in New York 1726–1776*, p. 395.

70 [1745]

Description Across top above frame line: PLAN OF THE TOWN AND HARBOUR OF LOUISBURG. There are eight numbered and two lettered references in an EXPLANATION below the PLAN. A paragraph above the title and another below the table of explanations also discuss and explain the map. It is probably a woodcut with some type inset.

Size 4" x 4¹¹⁄₁₆".　*Scale* 1" = 4 furlongs.

Published in *New-York Weekly Post Boy*, June 10, 1745. Reproduced in Louis E. De Forest, ed., *Louisbourg Journals, 1745*, opp. p. 204; Society of Colonial Wars, *Annual Register of Officers and Members of the Society of Colonial Wars*, Appendix, p. I.

Reference Clarence S. Brigham, *Journals and Journeymen*, p. 46.

71 1745

Description Above top neat line: A PLAN OF CAPE BRETON, & FORT LOUISBOURGH, &C. Below reference table at lower right inside neat lines: JULY 30 ENGRAV'D BY AUTHORITY / 1745. In the lower right corner is a table of nine references. The map itself shows the Isle of Canso and the vicinity between latitudes 43½° to 49° North and longitudes 58° to 64° West. ACADIE with MICMAQUES below is marked below NEW / SCOTLAND. The SHOALES OF ACADIE are also shown thus. I. CAPE BRETON is marked 240 MILES CIRCUMFERENCE. This has the appearance of being an early engraving by Thomas Johnston. The term: BY AUTHORITY, is unusual for an American map, however.

Size 12½" x 9⁷⁄₁₆". *Scale* None (1" = c. 35 miles).

Inset In lower left corner, a view of Louisbourg fort and harbour. There is no title. The positions of the defending batteries are shown as well as the English battery at the west gate. Size: 4" x 9⁷⁄₁₆". Scale None (1" = c. ½ mile).

Published Separately.

Reference [Henry E. Huntington Library and Art Gallery], *A Catalogue of Maps of America*, p. 27.

Location CSmH.

72 [1745] *State* I (see also Maps 73 and 74)

Description Type set across top of map above neat line: A PLAN OF THE TOWN AND HARBOUR OF LOUISBOURGH, &C. White letters in dark strip below neat line at top center: J. TURNER SC. The map is printed on a left-hand page, sidewise, with top at left. To left at top of page outside the neat line of the map, appears the magazine page number: 272, and at center: HISTORICAL CHRONICLE. Ten numbered and two lettered references are explained at the top of the opposite page. The geography follows the inset on the Gridley map as engraved by Peter Pelham (see Map 75). This is a woodcut map with some type probably set in and is better made than most such maps of this period. Anchors show the location of the French fleet, but these are not mentioned in the explanation. No detail of the town is shown, but merely the fortifications and the relative location of the center of the town. It was engraved by James Turner.

Size 4⅛" x 6½". *Scale* 1" = 4 furlongs.

Published in *American Magazine & Historical Chronicle*, 2 (1745), opp. 273.

73 [1745] *State* II (see also Maps 72 and 74)

Description The title across top above the neat line has been changed to read: PLAN OF THE HARBOUR AND FORTIFICATIONS / OF LOUISBOURG ON CAPE-BRETON, WITH THE SAILORS SONG ON TAKING OF THEM. There is no change in the woodcut as used in the *American Magazine & Historical Chronicle* for June, 1745. The ten numbered and two lettered references are now explained below the woodcut. The type and type ornaments, which are used between the two columns of the explanation and beneath it, are identical with those used in State I. This second appearance of Turner's woodcut appears to be in the form of a broadside featuring a song of the victorious sailors. Unfortunately only the title, the map, and the explanation of the map remain on the only copy located. The broadside

was undoubtedly issued by Gamaliel Rogers and Daniel Fowle, the printers of the *American Magazine & Historical Chronicle*.

Published Separately.

Location CSmH (bound into: Thomas Prince, *Extraordinary Events the Doing of God*, opp. p. 6).

74 [1745] *State* I (see also Map 79)

Description [Draught of the City of Louisburg.] At upper center: J. TURNER SC:. This is a slightly smaller version of the James Turner map of Louisbourg which appeared originally in the *American Magazine & Historical Chronicle* in June, 1745, and again in a broadside published during that same year. The scale is the same. Like the other two, it has ten numbered and two lettered references, here given in an "Explanation" directly under the map. Less area east and west of Louisbourg is shown, five anchors indicate the anchorage of the French fleet instead of four as in the earlier version, and a smaller battle scene is pictured at the right. This is a woodcut as are the others. See also Maps 72 and 73.

Size 3⅞" x 4⅞". *Scale* 1" = 4 furlongs.

Published in *Boston Evening-Post*, July 8, 1745.

75 1746

Description At top left center: A PLAN OF THE CITY AND FORTRESS OF LOUISBOURG / WITH A SMALL PLAN / OF THE HARBOUR. At lower right corner above neat line: P PHELHAM FECIT *1746*. SOLD BY J SMIBERT IN QUEEN STREET BOSTON N: E. It was advertised in the *Boston Weekly News-Letter*, September 4, 1746, as ". . . Done in Metzotinto on Royal-Paper by Mr Pelham, from the Original Drawing of Richard Gridley, Esq; Commander of the Train of Artillery at the Siege of Louisbourg . . ." There are 43 lettered references to the map in a table at the left. At the upper right is a long dedication to WILLIAM SHIRLEY by RICHARD GRIDLEY, dated Boston, February 5, 1745. The inset map was copied in some contemporary publications.

Size 17⅞" x 21⅜". *Scale* 1" = c. 300 feet.

Insets [a] At upper center is the inset: PLAN OF THE HARBOUR noted in the above title. Twelve references are given in the EXPLANATION OF THE HARBOUR at the lower left corner. VII is given out of order. Size: 6¾" x 9". Scale: 1" = c. ⅓ mile.

[b] At lower right: THE PROFILE. This is a cross section of the outer fortification. Nine references

are given just above. Size: 5¼″ x 1½″. Scale: None.

Published Separately. Reproduced in Massachusetts Historical Society, *Prints, Maps and Drawings*, no. 8

References George F. Dow, *The Arts & Crafts in New England*, p. 28; David M. Stauffer, *American Engravers*, *1*, 305; ibid., *2*, 409.

Locations MHi, MWM, RPJCB.

76 1746

Description In cartouche at upper left: A / CHART / OF / CANADA RIVER / FROM YE ISLAND OF ANTICOSTY AS FAR UP AS QUEBECK, YE ISLANDS, / ROCKS, SHOALS, & SOUNDINGS AS THEY APPEAR AT LOW WATER. Below cartouche and scale: ENGRAVEN, PRINTED AND SOLD BY THOS: JOHNSTON BOSTON NEW ENGLAND. / *1746*. Many place names are noted along the CANADA or St. Lawrence River. Eleven lettered references and four special symbols are explained in the cartouche following the title. The LADY MOUNTAINS and the LEWIS MOUNTAINS are shown in profile just south of the river. It was advertised in the *Boston Weekly News-Letter*, August 7, 1746, as "New Engraven" and described as "A Correct French Draft of the River of Canada." It was offered again in the *Boston Gazette*, July 16, 1759.

Size 17¼″ x 38″. *Scale* 1″ = 3 French leagues.

Published Separately.

References George F. Dow, *The Arts & Crafts in New England*, pp. 28, 31; David M. Stauffer, *American Engravers*, 2, 252; U.S. Library of Congress, *Report 1904*, p. 185.

Locations DLC, MWA.

77 [c. 1750] *State* I (see also Maps 86, 88, and 92)

Description In highly decorated cartouche at lower right: TO HIS / EXCELLENCY EDWD CORNWALLIS ESQ: / GOVERNOUR &C OF HIS MAJESTYS PROVINCE / OF NOVA SCOTIA IN AMERICA — &C — / THIS CHART OF THE COASTS OF NOVA-SCOTIA / AND PARTS ADJACENT, IS HUMBLY PRESENTED / BY YOR. EXCELLENCYS MOST OBEDIENT / AND DEVOTED HUMBLE SERVANT / JAMES TURNER. At bottom center beneath scale: ENGRAVED PRINTED & SOLD BY JAMES TURNER NEAR THE TOWN HOUSE BOSTON NEW ENGLAND. The chart indicates that Edward Cornwallis, governor for three years following the summer of 1749, when he founded Halifax, tried at that early date to encourage emigration from New England to Nova Scotia. It follows in coastal delineation "A New Chart of the Coast of New England, Nova Scotia . . . ," *Gentleman's Magazine*, *16* (January, 1746 [see note p. 8], but

usually placed in the bound volumes between pages 72 and 73 of the February number), which in turn is a re-engraving by Thomas Jefferys of Jacques N. Bellin's map of this region, which appeared in Pierre Charlevoix, *Histoire de la Nouvelle France* in 1744. The boundary between the Provinces of Nova Scotia and Sagadahoc starts at the mouth of the St. Croix River and extends indefinitely north. Very little topographic detail is given.

Size 19¼″ x 18⅛″. *Scale* 1″ = 60 miles.

Insets [a] At upper left corner: THE SITUATION OF / HALIFAX / DRAUGHT OF THE / HARBOUR &C. Includes from the harbor's mouth to the coves at the top of BEDFORD BAY. Soundings are given up to the head of the BAY. Size: 6³⁄₁₆″ x 3⅛″. Scale: 1″ = 2 miles.

[b] Along top border to right of [a]: PLAN OF HALIFAX. There are ten lettered references. This is taken from the official survey of the original settlement as planned in 1749. The building of St. Paul's Church was actually commenced in 1750 on the spot originally intended for and shown here as the Government House. Size: 3⅝″ x 4⅛″. Scale: None (1″ = c. 15 miles).

[c] Along top border to right of [b]: PLAN OF QUEBEC. There are eight lettered references. Size: 2⅜″ x 2″. Scale: 1″ = 3000 feet.

[d] Along top border at right of [c]: CITY & PORT / OF LOUISBOURG. There are fifteen lettered references. Soundings are given in the harbor. The fortifications of the CITY are shown and the English batteries raised in 1745. Size: 2½″ x 3⁷⁄₁₆″. Scale: 1″ = ⅘ mile.

[e] Along top border at right: VIEW OF / BOSTON CI. OF N E / PLANTED *1630*. This is a fine miniature view of the city where Turner was then in business. Size: 1½″ x 3⅛″.

Published Separately.

References John Carter Brown Library, *Report, 1946*, pp. 36–41; Lawrence C. Wroth and Marion W. Adams, *American Woodcuts and Engravings*, pp. 21–22, no. 16, and cartouche, p. 24.

Locations MWA, RPJCB.

78 [1758]

Description [Plan of the Harbour of Louisburg.] The eleven lettered references in English upper case are explained in German beneath the map.

Size 3¾″ x 6¼″. *Scale* 1″ = 5 furlongs.

Published in Anton Armbruster, *Neu-eingerichteter Americanischer Geschichts-Calendar 1759*.

79 [1758] *State* II (see also Map 74)

Description "J. Turner Sc" has been now removed at upper center.

Published in *Boston Evening-Post,* July 24, 1758.

80 [1758]

Description Below neat line at base of map proper: AN EXACT PLAN OF THE HARBOUR OF / LOUISBOURG. Eleven lettered references are given just below the title.

Size 4⁵⁄₁₆″ x 2¼″.   *Scale* 1″ = c. 1 mile.

Published in *The New-York Pocket Almanack for 1759.*

81 [1758]

Description In explanation above top neat line: [Plan of Louisbourg]. This is a map of Louisbourg and the harbor with eleven lettered references given in an "Explanation of the Plan . . ." noted at the top. It is quite similar to the map appearing in the Weatherwise almanacs of this same year (see Map 83). FURLONGS is in upper case.

Size 4″ x 6⅜″.   *Scale* 1″ = 4¾ furlongs.

Published in John Nathan Hutchins, *Hutchins's Almanack, for 1759.*

82 [1758]

Description Across top above neat line: PLAN OF LOUISBOURG. Following the title: 215. There are ten numbered and two lettered references explained in the text on the same page below the map. This is a woodcut much like the James Turner woodcut in the *American Magazine & Historical Chronicle,* June, 1745 (see Map 72).

Size 5⅛″ x 3¾″.   *Scale* 1″ = 2¾ furlongs.

Published in *New American Magazine,* 8 (1758), 215.

83 [1758]

Description Type set above top neat line: AN EXACT PLAN OF THE HARBOUR OF LOUISBOURG. ENGRAV'D FOR WEATHERWISE'S ALMANACK, FOR 1759. This is a woodcut map with inset type for references and scale designations. Eleven lettered references are explained at the bottom of the opposite page. It is very probably the same map that appears in the same *Almanack* published in New York by Hugh Gaine, [1758]. Though the title and the top neat line of the copy examined (at the American Antiquarian Society) are missing, there are several slight differences in the type insets. The scale designation FURLONGS is no longer on a straight line but wavers, and the number "7" in the scale now touches the scale marking. Another map that is very similar to those listed here is that appearing in *Hutchins's Almanack,* New York, [1758]. No

copy has been located of the Weatherwise *Almanack* listed by Evans (no. 8281) giving the following imprint: "Philadelphia, W. Dunlap, for G Noel, Bookseller, in New-York [1758]." This also probably carried a copy of the Louisbourg map. See also Map 81.

Size 3¾″ x 6¼″.   *Scale* 1″ = 5 furlongs.

Published in Abraham Weatherwise [pseud.], *Father Abraham's Almanack for 1759;* ibid., Printed at Philadelphia for Daniel Henchman, Boston [1758].

84 [1759]

Description At top of page and left end of map: PLAN OF THE CITY OF QUEBECK. This is a wood engraving very much like that in the *New-York Gazette,* December 10, 1759 (see Map 85). In this PLAN there are no trees at the lower left corner and the "F" reference is given at the extreme left, not immediately at the end of the lower city wall as in the other. Nine letter references are given on the page opposite.

Size 3″ x 5¼″.   *Scale* None.

Published in Roger More [pseud.], *Poor Roger, 1760, The American Country Almanack for 1760;* Abraham Weatherwise [pseud.], *Father Abraham's Almanac for 1761.* Reproduced in Justin Winsor, ed., *Narrative and Critical History,* 5, 534, 543–44.

85 [1759]

Description Above map: A PLAN OF THE CITY AND HARBOUR OF QUEBEC. This is a woodcut of the City showing the attack by the English under Wolfe. Nine lettered "References to the PLATE" are given just under the map. See also Map 84.

Size 3⅞″ x 5⅞″.   *Scale* None.

Published in *New-York Gazette,* December 10, 1759, p. 2.

86 1759   *State* II (see also Maps 77, 88, and 92)

Description The title now reads: . . . THIS MAP OF THE PROVINCE OF NOVA-SCOTIA . . . In imprint at bottom center under scale the address now reads: IN ARCH STREET PHILADELPHIA 2D. EDITION 1759. This map was advertised for sale by James Turner in the (Philadelphia) *Pennsylvania Journal* of October 11, 1759. Turner died in December of that year. The length of the scale line, which is now enclosed in a rectangular box, has been increased from 100 to 150 miles. Many topographical changes and additions have been made throughout the map. The New England coastline from Boston north to Point Escoudet has been completely re-engraved. The boundary between Nova Scotia and Sagadahoc is now definitely shown as extending from the mouth of the St. Croix River directly north to the St. Lawrence River. The provinces of SAGADAHOC and MAIN [sic] are shown. JEFFERY LEDGE is noted off C. ANN. Many topographical features have been inserted both in New England and Canada.

Published Separately. Reproduced in William I. Morse, *The Land of New Adventure*, front.

Reference Eugenie Archibald, *Catalogue of the William Inglis Morse Collection*, p. 108.

Locations CaNSHD, CtY.

87 [1760]

Description [Quebec and vicinity.] This woodcut combines the elements of a map with a non-perspective view. Below the bottom neat line there are printed, in German, explanations for ten lettered references given in Roman capitals. These references are also given, in English, on the Tobler copy. The map shows both banks of the St. Lawrence from the western part of the Island of Orleans and the Montmorency Falls to above the city. The location of the English batteries that fired upon the city are indicated.

Size 5³⁄₁₆″ x 7¾″.   *Scale* None (1″ = c. 1 mile).

Published in Christoph Saur, *Der Hoch-Deutsch Americanische Calender 1761*; John Tobler, *The Pennsylvania Town and Country-Man's Almanack 1761*.

88 1760 *State* III (see also Maps 77, 86, and 92)

Description The imprint at bottom center under scale now reads: SOLD BY ANDREW HOOK IN PHILADELPHIA 2D. EDITION *1760*. Traces of the previous James Turner imprint are still evident. PHILADELPHIA 2D. EDITION *17* remains the same.

Published Separately.

Location CSmH, MiU-C.

89 [1775]

Description In rectangular cartouche at left center: A MAP / OF THE / PRESENT SEAT OF WAR / ON THE BORDERS / OF / CANADA. Below cartouche at left: AITKEN SCULP. Above neat line at left: FOR THE PENNA MAGAZINE P. *463*. This map shows the key waterway leading from Lake George to the St. Lawrence River with the primary geographical features, forts, and the names of some of the landowners in the area. It was engraved by Robert Aitken.

Size 6¹⁄₁₆″ x 15¼″.   *Scale* 1″ = 10 English miles.

Published in (Philadelphia) *Pennsylvania Magazine, 1* (1775), opp. 463.

90 [1775]

Description In rectangle at upper left: A PLAN / OF / QUEBEC, / METROPOLIS OF / CANADA / IN / NORTH AMERICA. Below bottom neat line at right: AITKEN SCULP. Above top neat line: ENGRAV'D FOR THE PENNSYLVANIA MAGAE. At right: P. *563*. The plan shows the primary buildings and fortifications of the City and its immediate environs. A list of seventeen REFERENCES is given at the left, under the title. It was engraved by Robert Aitken.

Size 4³⁄₈″ x 6¹⁵⁄₁₆″.   *Scale* None (1″ = c. 300 yards).

Published in (Philadelphia) *Pennsylvania Magazine, 1* (1775), opp. 563.

91 [1775]

Description Below bottom neat line: PLAN OF THE TOWN & FORTIFICATIONS OF MONTREAL OR VILLE MARIE IN CANADA. Below bottom neat line, above title, at right: AITKIN [sic] SC. Above top neat line at center: ENGRAV'D FOR THE PENNSYLVANIA MAGAZINE. At right *P: 517*. This is a detailed PLAN showing the primary buildings and gardens of the City. An article entitled "A Description of the Town and Island of Montreal . . ." begins on p. 517. It was engraved by Robert Aitken.

Size 6⁹⁄₁₆″ x 9⁹⁄₁₆″.   *Scale* 1″ = 90 French toises.

Inset At upper right corner is a: VIEW OF THE TOWN &C OF MONTREAL. Size: 2¹¹⁄₁₆″ x 4¼″. Scale: None (1″ = c. 50 yards).

Published in (Philadelphia) *Pennsylvania Magazine, 1* (1775), opp. 517.

92 1776 *State* IV (see also Maps 77, 86, and 88)

Description The imprint at lower center has been altered to read: PRINTED AND SOLD BY R. AITKEN IN PHILADELPHIA 2D EDITION *1776*. This map was advertised in the (Philadelphia) *Pennsylvania Packet and Daily Advertiser*, January 1, 1776, as follows:

"This Day is Published, and to be sold by R. Aitken, Bookseller, Opposite the London Coffee-House, Printed on a large sheet of Demy Paper, (Price Two Shillings) A Correct Map . . . in which may be seen the march of Col. Arnold, from Casco-Bay to Quebec, by way of Kennebec river . . ."

No other changes are apparent.

Published Separately.
Reference Evans 15121.
Locations CtY, DLC, PHi.

[1778] see Map 147.

93 [1790]

Description At upper left corner in decorated shell: CHART / OF THE / COAST OF AMERICA / FROM / CAPE FORCHU TO LIVERPOOL B. / FROM THE LATEST SURVEYS. Below title decorations: BOSTON / PUBLISHED AND SOLD BY / MATTW. CLARK. Above and to right of title: NO. 3. The map bears an engraved inscription, signed by Osgood Carleton when the map was sold singly, stating that it was examined and compared WITH HOLAND'S & DES BARR'S, etc., and found accurate. Many soundings and place names are given along the coast. This and Map 95 are pasted together in the Library of Congress copy.

Size 16¼" x 24½". *Scale* None (1" = c. 5° latitude).

Published in Matthew Clark, [*A Complete Chart*], no. 3; separately.

94 [1790]

Description In upper left corner: CHART / OF THE COAST OF AMERICA / FROM CHARLOTTE BAY TO PORT HOWE / FROM THE LATEST SURVEYS. Beneath title: BOSTON PUBLISHED AND SOLD BY M CLARK / J SEYMOUR SCULP. In extreme upper left corner: NO. 2. The map bears an engraved inscription, signed by Osgood Carleton when the map was sold singly, stating that it was examined and compared with DES BARRES and others and found accurate. HALLIFAX HARBOUR is given, but the town is not indicated. See also Map 96.

Size 16" x 23¾". *Scale* None (1" = c. 5° latitude).

Published in Matthew Clark, [*A Complete Chart*], no. 2; separately.

95 [1790]

Description At lower center in decorated rectangle: CHART / OF THE COAST OF / AMERICA / FROM MOUSE HARBR. TO MAHONE BAY. In rectangle below title: FROM THE LATEST SURVEYS / PUBLISHED & SOLD BY M CLARK. Below rectangle and decorations: JOSH. SEYMOUR SCULP. In upper right corner: NO. 4. The map bears an engraved inscription, signed by Osgood Carleton when the map was sold singly, stating that it was examined and compared with DES BARRS, etc., and found accurate. ST. CROIX RIVER is outside the neat lines at the upper left. Charts three and four are

pasted together in the Library of Congress copy. See also Map 93.

Size 17" x 24⅞". *Scale* None (1" = c. 5° latitude).

Published in Matthew Clark, [*A Complete Chart*], no. 4; separately.

96 [1790]

Description In the upper right corner: CHART / OF THE COAST OF / AMERICA / FROM PORT HOWE TO C BRETON / FROM THE LATEST SURVEYS. Below title: BOSTON / PUBLISHD & SOLD BY M CLARK / J SEYMOUR SCULP. In lower right corner: NO. 1. The map bears an engraved inscription, signed by Osgood Carleton when the map was purchased singly, stating that it was examined and compared with: DES BARRES & OTHER GOOD AUTHORITIES and found accurate. LOISBOURGH is noted thus; also LABRAS DOR. In the Library of Congress copy, charts one and two are pasted together (see also Map 94).

Size 25" x 16". *Scale* None (1" = c. 5° latitude).

Published in Matthew Clark, [*A Complete Chart*], no. 1; separately.

97 [1790]

Description At upper center: A MAP SHEWING THE COMMUNICATION OF THE LAKES / AND THE RIVERS BETWEEN LAKE SUPERIOR AND SLAVE LAKE / IN NORTH AMERICA. Below bottom neat line at right: TIEBOUT S. The STRAIT OF / JUAN DE FUCA is named in latitude 48°, but no inlet is shown. The routes from Hudson Bay via both Nelson's River and York River are shown. North of Slave Lake, the river is drawn straight north to the NORTH SEA — HERE THE / WATER EBBS & FLOWS. West of Slave Lake appears: SO FAR POND and a communication is dotted to COOKS RIVER. Close to the coast appears: SO FAR COOK. The area shown extends from Prince Williams Sound to Lake Superior and from the Arctic to the Mississippi River at latitude 43°. The map was engraved by Cornelius Tiebout.

Size 7¾" x 8⅞". *Scale* None (1" = c. 3½° latitude).

Published in *New York Magazine; or Literary Repository*, *1* (1790), opp. 677.

98 [1791]

Description [Chart of the Bay of Fundy from Machias Bay to 64° 35' West Longitude.] The marginal degree line is omitted on the right side. The Atlantic coast of Nova Scotia is shown also from Cape Sable to GAMBIER HAR.

Size 20¾" x 16⅝". *Scale* None (1" = c. 8¾ miles).

Published in John Norman, *The American Pilot*, [1791], no. 9; ibid., 1792, no. 9; ibid., 1794, no. 9; William Norman, *The American Pilot*, 1794, no. 9.

99 [1791] *State* I (see also Map 107)

Description [Chart of the Streights (sic) of Belle Isle.] The coast of Newfoundland is shown from CAPE RAY to EXPLOITS BAY. The lettering in STREIGHTS OF BELLE ISLE and NEWFOUNDLAND is open, i.e. unshaded.

Size 20⅝″ x 16½″. *Scale* None (1″ = c. 18½ miles).

Published in John Norman, *The American Pilot*, [1791], no. 10; ibid., 1792, no. 10; ibid., 1794, no. 10; William Norman, *The American Pilot*, 1794, no. 10.

100 [1792] *State* I (see also Maps 102 and 106)

Description At upper right: A CHART / OF THE / BANKS OF NEWFOUNDLAND, / DRAWN / FROM A GREAT NUMBER OF / HYDROGRAPHICAL SURVEYS, / CHIEFLY FROM THOSE OF / CHABERT, COOK AND FLEURIEU, / CONNECTED AND ASCERTAINED BY / ASTRONOMICAL OBSERVATIONS. Below title and scale: LONDON PRINTED FOR & SOLD BY ROBERT SAYER NO. 53 IN / FLEET STREET AS THE ACT DIRECTS 25 OF MARCH 1785. PRICE 5 s. This chart is copied from the similar chart in Thomas Jefferys' *American Atlas* and the *North American Pilot*, 1777, but it is cut off slightly on the east and extended five degrees west. The engraver had before him an impression from a later state of the plate than the one used in above atlases, and the English imprint given above has been copied on the American plate by the engraver. At lower right is a table giving the: ASTRONOMICAL OBSERVATIONS ON WHICH THIS CHART IS GROUNDED. At right center is shown the: OUTER / BANK / OR / FALSE BANK ATS THE FLEMISH / CAP. On the Sayer Chart "ats" appears in italics contrasting with the following words; here the last four words are in similar letters. Two plates are used.

Size 19¼″ x 32⅝″. *Scale* 1″ = 10 nautic leagues.

Published in John Norman, *The American Pilot*, 1792, no. 11.

101 1794 *State* I (see also Map 103; III post-1799, see Map 103, Description)

Description At lower center: THE / BRITISH POSSESSIONS / IN / NORTH AMERICA / FROM THE BEST AUTHORITIES / BY SAMUEL LEWIS 1794. This is a topographical map indicating also the main political boundaries. Canada, including Newfoundland, is shown as far as the western end of Lake Superior. This map may have also been issued with the date "1795" and/or "1796" but no existing copies have thus far been located.

Size 15 1/16″ x 17⅛″. *Scale* 1″ = 115 American miles.

Inset At upper left [Hudson's and Baffin's bays.] Given here is the fictitious NEW SEA in the interior of Labrador that appears in the inset of the John Mitchell's "A map of the British and French dominions in North America . . . , London. 1755." Size: 8 1/16″ x 10⅝″. Scale: None (1″ = c. 85 American miles).

Published in Mathew Carey, *The General Atlas for Carey's Edition of Guthrie's Geography Improved*, no. 23; some copies of *Carey's American Atlas*, no. 1.

102 [1794] *State* II (see also Maps 100 and 106)

Description The English imprint does not appear. The erasure of the imprint is poorly done.

Published in John Norman, *The American Pilot*, 1794, no. 11; William Norman, *The American Pilot*, 1794, no. 11.

103 [1796] *State* II (see also Map 101; III post-1799, see below, Description)

Description The following imprint has been added above the top neat line: ENGRAVED FOR CAREY'S AMERICAN EDITION OF GUTHRIE'S GEOGRAPHY IMPROVED. This map was used later in the September 9, 1800, edition of *Carey's General Atlas* with the figure "23" added at the upper right corner.

Published in Mathew Carey, *Carey's General Atlas*, no. 23; some copies of *Carey's American Atlas*, no. 1.

104 [1796] *State* I (see also Map 105)

Description [Map of the City of Quebec.] Sabin states that the Pl. 2 at the upper left corner of our State II was "afterwards marked," thus indicating this earlier state of the plate.

Size Unknown. *Scale* Unknown.

Reference Sabin 82379.

Location No copy located.

105 [1796] *State* II (see also Map 104)

Description In oval at lower right: MAP / OF THE CITY OF / QUEBEC. Below bottom neat line at center: PUBLISHED BY C. SMITH N. YORK. At upper left corner: PL. 2. At the lower left is a table of 25 lettered and five numbered references. All the letters are used except "J" and "U"; "H" appears twice—once in error instead of "U." Sabin states the "Pl. 2" was "afterwards marked" thus indicating another, earlier, state of the plate.

Size 7⁹⁄₁₆″ x 8¹⁄₁₆″. *Scale* 1″ = 1500 feet.

Published in *The Monthly Military Repository, 1,* foll. 72. Reprinted in Charles Smith, *The American War,* opp. p. 14.

Reference Sabin 82379.

106 [1798] *State* III (see also Maps 100 and 102)

Description The outlines of some of the banks and the marginal degree line have been recut. CROSS ISLAND north of Cape Breton is shaded across its entire area.

Published in William Norman, *The American Pilot,* 1798, no. 9.

107 [1798] *State* II (see also Map 99)

Description The lettering in STREIGHTS OF BELLE ISLE and NEWFOUNDLAND has been shaded.

Published in William Norman, *The American Pilot,* 1798, no. 8.

108 [1777]

Description [The Theatre of War in North America, with a polymetric table shewing the distances and roads of the principal places, towns, forts, rivers, &c. Being a complete map of the Thirteen United States, divided by different colours, and all that hath been heretofore comprehended under the name of the British colonies in North-America.] The title is taken from an advertisement which appeared in the (Philadelphia) *Pennsylvania Evening Post*, July 10, 1777, p. 363, and also July 19, 1777, p. 384. The advertisement begins: "Just published, and now selling by John Norman engraver . . . (Price Three Dollars) . . ." It goes on to state: "N.B. This map is engraved from a very late copy done in England on a new and accurate plan, calculated for the use of the officers in the British army." The "copy" referred to is probably the map: "The Theatre of War in North America, with the Roads and A Table of the Distances," published in London by Robert Sayer and John Bennett in March, 1776. The map was also advertised in the (Philadelphia) *Pennsylvania Journal*, July 16, 1777.

Size Unknown. *Scale* Unknown.

Published Separately.

References David M. Stauffer, *American Engravers*, 2, 390, no. 2369; Harry B. Weiss, "John Norman, Engraver, Publisher, Bookseller," p. 6.

Location No copy located.

109 [1784] *State* I (see also Map 110)

Description In cartouche at lower right: A / NEW AND CORRECT MAP / OF THE / UNITED STATES / OF / NORTH AMERICA / LAYD DOWN FROM THE LATEST OBSERVATIONS AND / BEST AUTHORITIES AGREEABLE TO THE PEACE OF / *1783* / HUMBLY INSCRIBED TO HIS EXCELLENCY THE / GOVERNOR AND COMPANY / OF THE STATE OF CONNECTICUT / BY THEIR / MOST OBEDIENT / AND VERY HUMBLE SERVANT / ABEL BUELL. This map was advertised as "now published, and ready for subscribers" in the (New Haven) *Connecticut Journal* of March 31, 1784. It was referred to in the advertisement as "the first ever compiled, engraved and finished by one man, and an American." MUSCLE SHOALS appears here for the first time on an American printed map. (Thomas Hutch-

ins showed this name on his map of 1778, printed in England.) The map is largely transcribed from John Mitchell and Lewis Evans but is an important landmark in the history of American engraving. Its crudity and many errors, of commission as well as omission, were doubtless largely due to Buell's efforts to publish the map before his competitors were able to issue theirs. The territory claimed by Connecticut is featured on this map extending west of the east branch of Susquehannah River between parallels of 41° and about 42° 02' latitude to the Missisippi River. More data and notes are given on this tract than any other area west of the mountains. BUFFALOW LOW LANDS is shown in the Pennsylvania lands at the head of TOBYS R. In the northwest corner of the map a small lake is shown as the source of a stream running northwest marked: ORIGAN OR RIVER OF THE WEST. West of the Falls of St. Anthony appears the note: UNBOUNDED PLAINS / SUPPOSED TO EXTEND / TO THE SOUTH SEA. The elaborate cartouche is interesting and in it an American flag is shown on a printed map for the first time. The most important use of this map was undoubtedly in the Spanish foreign office in 1785–86. Diego de Gardoqui the Spanish envoy to the United States sent over two copies of the southwest sheet with his dispatch of July 25, 1785.

Size 42$\frac{15}{16}$" x 48$\frac{1}{8}$". *Scale* 1" = 35 English miles.

Published Separately. Reproduced in Isaac N. P. Stokes and Daniel C. Haskell, *American Historical Prints*, pl. 28.

References Philip L. Phillips, *Notes on Bernard Romans*, pp. 33–34; Lawrence C. Wroth, *Abel Buell*, pp. 63–70; ibid., rev. ed., pp. 73–82.

Location NN.

110 [1784?] *State* II (see also Map 109)

Description The following imprint has been added below Buell's name in the cartouche at lower right: NEWHAVEN PUBLISHED ACCORDING TO ACT OF ASSEMBLY. This, the second state, is the one that is usually seen.

Published Separately. Reproduced by *American Heritage*, separately and in reduced form, from the copy belonging to the New Jersey Historical Society, 1962; in Robert M. Lunny, *Early Maps of North America*, p. 43.

Locations   BM, CtHi, CtY, NHi, NjHi, PRO.

111 [1784]

Description   In rectangular scroll at top center: THE / UNITED STATES / ACCORDING TO THE DEFINITIVE TREATY OF PEACE SIGNED AT PARIS, SEPTR. 3D. *1783* . . . BY WM. MCMURRAY, LATE / ASST. GEOGR. TO THE U.S. In lower right corner: R. SCOT SCULP. The publication of this map was announced in the (Philadelphia) *Pennsylvania Packet, and Daily Advertiser,* of December 10, 1784, for Monday, December 13. The following note appears at the left center in oval: THE LINES SINGLY COLOURED N.W. / OF THE OHIO ARE THE DIVISIONS OF THAT / COUNTRY INTO TEN NEW STATES, BY A RE- / SOLVE OF CONGRESS OF APRIL 23D. *1784.* On a scroll between the title and the signature is a long note referring generally to the many surveys used in forming the map and claiming use of the best that had been made. Along a line drawn from Green Bay to the Mississippi River is engraved: ALL N. W. OF THIS LINE IS TAKEN FROM CARVER, COMPARED WITH LATER TRAVEL. At a mountain along the Cumberland River appears the note: MUSCLE SHOALS SEEN FROM YS ROCK. Muscle Shoals is named 100 miles southwest from there. The Cumberland and the Tennessee, or Cherokee, rivers empty into the Ohio River independently. The ten states of the Northwest Territory are indicated but not named. SAGADAHOC is shown between the Kennebec River and the St. Croix. The fictitious islands shown by Charlevoix appear in Lake Superior. MT. JULIET appears on the PLEIN R southeast of Lake Michigan. WHITE BEAR LAKE is shown as the source of the Mississippi with HEAD BR. OF / ORIGAN adjacent. BUFFALOE SWAMP appears in north central Pennsylvania. Grand Traverse Bay is not shown in Michigan but GRAND TRAVERSE appears across the mouth of the GREEN OR PUANS B.

Size   26⅝" x 37¾".   *Scale*   1" = 50 miles.

Inset   At lower right a map inscribed: N. AMERICA (at upper left), showing what was known of North America outside of the United States. Size: 12½" x 11³⁄₁₆". Scale: None (1" = c. 145 miles).

Published   Separately. A reproduction of a portion of this map appears in Louis C. Karpinski, *Bibliography of the Printed Maps of Michigan,* pl. 23.

References   Evans 20476; Philip L. Phillips, *Notes on Bernard Romans,* p. 33; idem, *The Rare Map of the Northwest 1785,* pp. 26–27.

Locations   CtY, DLC, MiU-C, MWA, RPJCB.

112 [1784]   *State* I (see also Maps 114 and 116)

Description   In cartouche at lower right: A / MAP / OF THE / UNITED STATES / OF / AMERICA. The cartouche contains a ribbon, carried in the beak of an eagle and in the hands of a figure, inscribed with the motto: PER ASPERA AD ASTRA. PENSYLVANIA appears thus; also, the ARCANSES Indian tribe. R OF THE WEST appears starting at a lake in Minnesota. In many respects this map follows the delineation of Abel Buell, especially in the contour of Michigan and the Great Lakes, and in many of the names. This is the first Morse map of the United States.

Size   5½" x 5⅜".   *Scale*   1" = 5⅛° latitude.

Published in Jedidiah Morse, *Geography Made Easy,* 1st ed., opp. p. 24.

113 [1784]   *State* I (see also Map 115)

Description   In decorative cartouche at lower left: A MAP OF THE / UNITED STATES / OF N. AMERICA. Below bottom neat line at right: PHILADA. ENGRAVED BY H. D. PURSELL FOR F. BAILEY'S POCKET ALMANAC. This is the first known published map to show the Jeffersonian States in the West and it is the only known American map upon which the names of those states are engraved. The proposed district of WASHINGTON is shown west of Virginia and Maryland. APPALACHIAN MTS. is partially erased and is followed by ALLEGHENY MOUNTAINS. A number of Indian tribes are given. The HEAD OF THE OREGON WHICH RUNS W / TO THE PACIFIC OCEAN is shown. The map also shows traces of changes and erasures on the plate. A re-engraving appeared in Johann David Schöpf, *Reise Durch Einige Der Mittlern Und Südlichen Vereinigten Nordamerikanischen Staaten,* opp. p. [1]. There are several differences between the Pursell original and this copy, among them being: FALLS NIAGARA appears here but only "Niagara" on the Schöpf copy; I. ROYAL appears as "L Royal"; and CHIPPEWAY as "Chippeways."

Size   5¼" x 6¹⁵⁄₁₆".   *Scale*   None (1" = 4° latitude).

Published in Francis Bailey, *Bailey's Pocket Almanac 1785,* front; used as frontispiece in 1787 issue of *Bailey's Pocket Almanac;* separately. Reproduced in Thomas Jefferson, *The Papers of,* Julian P. Boyd, ed., 6, opp. 605. Reproductions of the Schöpf re-engraving are given in the following: Louis C. Karpinski, *Bibliography of the Printed Maps of Michigan,* foll. p. 352; Justin Winsor, ed., *Narrative and Critical History,* 7, 529.

References   Evans 18338 & 19488; Library Company of Philadelphia, *Annual Report 1960,*

Buell, A New and Correct Map of the United States, 1784,
State II (No. 110)

p. 46; Edward B. Mathews, "Bibliography and Cartography of Maryland," p. 356; Philip L. Phillips, *A List of Maps of America*, p. 865; idem, *The Rare Map of the Northwest 1785*, p. 27; Alice W. Spieseke, *The First Textbooks*, pp. 64–65.

Locations DLC, MH (as separates).

114 [1785] *State* II (see also Maps 112 and 116)

Description The engraver's signature has been added below bottom neat line at right: A DOOLITTLE SC. Advertisements in the (Portsmouth) *New-Hampshire Gazette* for October 20, and November 3, 1785, mention this map. It was included in some copies of the *Almanack* at an extra price. The same map had been sold singly before ("for more than it will now cost with the Almanac," according to the advertisement of November 3).

Published in Nathan Ben Salomon, [pseud.], *An Astronomical Diary or Almanack for 1786*; separately.

References Albert C. Bates, "Check List of Connecticut Almanacs, 1709–1850," p. 138; Evans 19108.

115 [1787] *State* II (see also Map 113)

Description The following has been erased after PURSELL under neat line at lower right: "for F. Bailey's Pocket Almanac."

Published in [John M'Culloch, comp.], *Introduction to the History of America*, front.; Benjamin Workman, *Elements of Geography*, 2d ed., opp. p. 57. Reproduced in Alice W. Spieseke, *The First Textbooks*, opp. p. 64.

Reference Evans 20471. See also Spieseke, above, pp. 64–65.

116 [1790] *State* III (see also Maps 112 and 114)

Description Above top neat line at left now appears: NO. IV. Some names of rivers and places have been added, notably: KENTUCKY, PITSBURG, MARIETTA, PATOMACK R, JAMES R, AND SAVANNAH R.

Published in Jedidiah Morse, *Geography Made Easy*, 2d ed., opp. p 37. Reproduced by U.S. Geological Survey, 1938, and issued by the U.S. Constitution Sesquicentennial Commission.

117 [1790] *State* I (see also Maps 120 and 140; IV post-1799, see Map 140, Description)

Description In oval at lower right: THE / UNITED STATES / OF / AMERICA. Above top neat line at left: LONGITUDE WEST FROM LONDON. Longitude is given both from London (top) and from Philadelphia (bottom). Very little detail is noted. SAGADAHOC appears as a separate division. WESTERN TERRITORY includes modern Wisconsin, Illinois, Ohio, etc. SOUTHERN TERRITORY is inscribed over Kentucky and Tennessee. KENTUCKY appears with a north and south eastern boundary line, but Tennessee is not shown. The bottom marginal degree line is broken to include part of East and West Florida below the southern boundary of Georgia. The degrees are indicated on the inside of the lower neat line. MEREDN. OF / PHILADA. is marked on the 75° West Meridian (the only one drawn through the map) and every fifth degree is numbered below. The compass rose is badly oriented about NNW by North.

Size 6¹¹⁄₁₆″ x 8¾″. *Scale* 1″ = 200 miles.

Published in John M'Culloch, *A Concise History*, front. (Library of Congress 2d copy, fragment); Benjamin Workman, *Elements of Geography*, 3d ed.

Reference Alice W. Spieseke, *The First Textbooks*, pp. 69, 83–84, 95.

118 [1791]

Description At left below center: A / MAP / OF THE / UNITED STATES / OF / AMERICA. Above top neat line at left: ENGRAVED FOR MORSES GEOGRAPHY. The longitude legend reads: LONGITUDE WEST FROM LONDON, but the meridians are marked with reference to Philadelphia. The zero meridian is laid down where the 75° West from London should be, and traces of the erasure of "75" still appear. Pennsylvania's northern boundary is shown even with the northern boundary of Massachusetts. Kentucky is given a straight north and south border on the east. ADELPHIA is shown for Marietta. TWIG-TWEES indicates a large territory in modern central Indiana. Rhode Island is not named. MASSACHUSETS BAY appears for the state. TAMASSEE appears as a town in western North Carolina. Some fictitious islands called I PHILIP, I MAURIPAS, PONCHARTRAIN I, HOCKQUART I, and I BEAUHARNOT appear in Lake Superior (following Bellin and Charlevoix). This is the second Morse map of the United States.

Size 8¹⁄₁₆″ x 9½″. *Scale* None (1″ = c. 170 miles).

Published in Jedidiah Morse, *Geography Made Easy*, 3d ed., opp. p. 37.

119 [1791] *State* I (see also Map 138)

Description In circle at lower right: THE / UNITED STATES / OF / AMERICA / LAID DOWN / FROM THE BEST AUTHORITIES / AGREEABLE TO THE PEACE OF / 1783. Between marginal degree line and bottom neat line at lower right corner: BOSTON / PUBLISHED & SOLD BY I. NORMAN / NO. 75 NEWBURY STREET. This map was advertised in the *Boston Gazette* of March 21, 1791, and in a Baltimore paper, July 4, 1791. Many soundings are shown, especially around New England and Nova Scotia. Surveyed townships inscribed: LANDS BELONGING TO MESS. GORHAM & PHELPS appear in western New York. The 7 RANGES are shown west of the Ohio River. A small log cabin is drawn on the Scioto River and marked: HURRICAN TOMS. FIFTY TOWNSHIPS SOLD BY / LOTTERY & LYING BETWEEN THE / RIVERS PENOBSCOT & SCHODIC in present Maine (here marked PART / OF / MASSACHUSETTS) are shown divided into north, middle, and east divisions. The TRUE ST. CROIX is shown leading northeast about parallel to the coast from the northeast corner of Passamaquoddy Bay, and the engraved Maine boundary runs to the mouth of the St. Lawrence River. A colored line cuts across near the Restigouche River on the Library of Congress copy. NEW BRUNSWICK is inscribed across the ambitious northeast boundary line. New England is shown in great detail, as is also the eastern coast line itself. In the Northwest Territory the lands of the Ohio Company are located and, also: the DONATION LANDS FROM THE COMMONWEALTH OF VIRGINIA; General Clark's grant of 150,000 acres; the Army Lands at the lower end of present Illinois; and the Wabash Company, the New Jersey Company, and the Illinois Company Lands. In Lake Superior appear the fictitious islands of Charlevoix and Bellin. GRAND TRAVERSE B does not appear in Michigan but this name appears near the mouth of GREEN OR PUAN'S B. The Wisconsin River appears as OUISIONSING R. White Bear Lake is shown as the source of the Mississippi. A small note west of the Falls of St. Anthony reads: IMMENSE PLAINS WEST. Little detail in Kentucky is shown; MERCER and LOUISVILLE are the only towns marked. ROCK 15 F HIGH is located on the Cumberland River, northeast of Muscle Shoals on the Cherokee River. These two rivers are shown emptying into the Ohio River independently.

Size 32¼" x 45". *Scale* 1" = 45 miles.

Inset At upper center in rectangle with title at upper right: A MAP / OF THE / LAKES AND RIVERS / BETWEEN / LAKE SUPERIOR / AND THE / NORTH SEA. Size: 8⅝" x 6¾". Scale: None (1" = c. 250 miles).

Published Separately.

References Evans 23250 & 23638; Philip L. Phillips, *A List of Maps of America*, p. 864.

Locations CtY, DLC, MiU-C, NHi, PPAmP.

120 [1793] *State* II (see also Maps 117 and 140; IV post-1799, see Map 140, Description)

Description SOUTHERN TERRITORY still appears over Kentucky and Tennessee. IROQUOIS now is given in southeastern Michigan. The R. FABINE is shown in the central extreme west among numerous additional names of tributaries to the Mississippi. NEW WINDSOR appears in northeastern Georgia. Other additions also appear. On pp. 3–4 of Workman's *Elements*, 4th ed., appears: "The map of the United States has been much improved, by the addition of near one hundred words, in names of cities, rivers . . ." In a following "Note" it states that: "the improvements in the map, are made by an eminant [sic] teacher of geography in this city." On p. 4 of Workman's *Elements*, 7th ed. (see Map 140), the teacher is identified as William Waring.

Published in Benjamin Workman, *Elements of Geography*, 4th ed., opp. p. 83; ibid., 5th ed.

121 1794

Description [A Map of the United States shewing or containing the boundaries or division lines of the different and respective states (with their respective divisions into counties &c) . . . Compiled from best authorities. By Reading Howell. Philadelphia, Feb. 26th 1794. 56th Pennsylvania District Copyright, issued to Reading Howell, as author, 26 February 1794.]

Size Unknown.   *Scale* Unknown.

Published Separately.

Reference Evans 27142.

Location No copy located.

122 [1794]

Description In oval cartouche at left below center: A / MAP / OF THE / UNITED STATES / OF / AMERICA. Below cartouche: A DOOLITTLE SC. N. HAVEN. Outside top neat line at center: PUBLISHED BY THOMAS & ANDREWS, BOSTON. Below bottom neat line: ENGRAVED FOR THE ABRIDGEMENT OF MORSE'S AMERICAN UNIVERSAL GEOGRAPHY. This, Morse's third map of the United States, is very similar to his second (see Map 118) and is little more than that map re-engraved. All the items noted for the second map appear on this third map. Also, Rhode Island is named, MASSACHUSETTS BAY appears thus as the State name, and the fictitious island of Ponchartrain is left out of Lake Superior. On this map R ST CROUIX in Minnesota appears thus. FLL OF ST MARY appears at the Sault.

Size 7¹¹⁄₁₆" x 9⅛".   *Scale* None (1" = c. 2½° latitude).

Published in Jedidiah Morse, *Geography Made Easy*, 4th ed., opp. p. 67; ibid., 5th ed., opp. p. 67.

123 1795 *State* I (see also Maps 132, 133, and 137; V post-1799, see Map 133, Description)

Description At right center: A MAP / OF THE / UNITED STATES: / COMPILED CHIEFLY FROM / THE STATE MAPS, / AND / OTHER AUTHENTIC INFORMATION, / BY / SAML. LEWIS / *1795*. Below bottom neat line at right corner: W. HARRISON JUNR. SCULPT. The northeast boundary line runs across the St. John River to the St. Lawrence divide. The lower shore of Lake Erie is a half degree further south than the lower end of Lake Michigan. The tract sold by New York to Pennsylvania is shown separated from both states. AN EXTENSIVE HIGH PLAIN is shown centrally in the upper portion of the lower peninsula of Michigan. Okefenokee Swamp is shown as AKENFONOGA on the main map and as OKENFONOKA on the inset. The fictitious islands of Charlevoix and Bellin in Lake Superior are prominently repeated here.

Size 24¼" x 35⅛". *Scale* None (1" = c. 57 miles).

Inset Inside neat lines at lower right: [Map of the Florida peninsula]. *Size:* 9" x 11⅛". Scale: Same as main map.

Published Separately.

Locations MH, MiU-C.

124 [1795]

Description In oval at lower right: A / MAP / OF THE / UNITED / STATES. / OF / AMERICA. Above top neat line: ENGRAVED FOR MORSE'S ELEMENTS OF GEOGRAPHY, PUBLISHED BY THOMAS & ANDREWS, BOSTON. R OF THE WEST appears below WOOD LAKE. The Kentucky eastern border is shown as a straight north and south line west of the Sandy River. PENSYLVANIA is spelled thus and its western boundary is shown as a winding line. The northeastern boundaries of Maine reach Chaleur Bay, and NOVASCOTIA is inscribed thus across them. The western boundary of North Carolina is shown as a straight north and south line. This is the fourth Morse map of the United States.

Size 4⅝" x 5⁵⁄₁₆". *Scale* None (1" = c. 5° latitude).

Published in Jedidiah Morse, *Elements of Geography*, 1st ed., opp. p. 74; ibid., 2d ed., opp. p. 74.

125 [1795]

Description At lower right: A / MAP / OF THE / UNITED STATES. The map is similar in geographical outline to Map 134 with the northern portion of Maine cut off and the lower end of Lake Michigan placed further south than the

southern shore of Lake Erie. Scott's map of the Northwest Territory in the same *Gazetteer* (Map 674) and in his *Atlas* shows the end of Lake Michigan almost a full degree north of Lake Erie's southern shore! MASSACHUSETTS is spelled thus. The Erie triangle is shown as part of Pennsylvania. AN EXTENSIVE HIGH PLAIN is printed across the upper portion of the lower Michigan peninsula.

Size 10¾" x 14⅝". *Scale* None (1" = c. 100 miles).

Published in Joseph Scott, *An Atlas of the United States*, no. 1; idem, *The United States Gazetteer*, front.

126 [1795]

Description In oval at lower right: THE / UNITED STATES / OF / AMERICA. Below neat line at lower right corner: SCOLES SC. Longitude is shown from both Greenwich and Philadelphia. SAGADAHOC appears northeast of a narrow PROVINCE OF MAIN. WASHINGTON is shown prominently. KENTUCKY is shown as half of the SOUTHERN TERRITORY. The false islands shown earlier by Bellin appear in LAKE SUPERIOR. L ST JOHN is shown north of Quebec. This is very similar to Benjamin Workman's "Map of the United States" (see Map 117); see also the Tanner engraving of a map of the same title (Map 139).

Size 6⅜" x 8⁹⁄₁₆". *Scale* 1" = 220 miles.

Published in Charles Smith, *Universal Geography Made Easy*, opp. p. 133.

127 [1796] *State* I (see also Maps 128, 129, and 130; V post-1799, see Map 130, Description)

Description At the upper left: A MAP / OF THE / UNITED STATES / EXHIBITING POST ROADS & DISTANCES / BY / ABRAHAM BRADLEY JUNR. / THE FIRST SHEET COMPREHENDING THE / NINE NORTHERN STATES, WITH PARTS OF VIRGINIA / AND THE TERRITORY NORTH OF OHIO. This is the earliest known section of Bradley's "Map of the United States . . . ," the best map of the new nation to appear up to this time. Abraham Bradley, Jr., was associated with the Post Office Department for a period of forty or more years and his maps became the official maps of that Department. This northeast section of the larger Bradley map may have been issued and sold separately as, thus far, no complete copy of this first State has been found. It carries its own title (though referring to the larger map) and has its own scale and a table of explanation which differs in some regards from the overall table. At the lower left, between the OHIO RIVER and CULPEPER CH [sic], are the words PART OF VIRGINIA. No rectangular townships are drawn in north central Maine or in western New York, nor are the Seven Ranges shown in eastern Ohio. The OHIO RIVER and the Kanawha are shown breaking through the neat line at the lower left with the figure "39," denoting the thirty-ninth latitude, appearing between them.

Size 17⅜" x 21½". *Scale* 1" = 40 miles.

Published Separately(?).

References Evans 30122; U.S. Library of Congress, Division of Maps, *An Account of the Activities, 1939,* pp. 163–64.

Locations BM, DLC.

128 1796 *State* II (see also Maps 127, 129, and 130; V post-1799, see Map 130, Description)

Description At lower center: MAP / OF THE / UNITED STATES, / EXHIBITING THE / POST-ROADS, THE SITUATIONS, CONNECTIONS & DISTANCES OF THE POST-OFFICES / STAGE ROADS, COUNTIES, PORTS OF ENTRY AND / DELIVERY FOR FOREIGN VESSELS, AND THE PRINCIPAL RIVERS. / BY / ABRAHAM BRADLEY JUN. Just under title appears W: HARRISON JUNR. SC:. Below bottom neat line at right corner W. BARKER SCULP. PHILADA. The upper right sheet has at the lower left, below the neat line: DEPOSITED AS THE A[C]T DIRECTS APRIL 25, 1796. At the right below the neat line: J. SMITHER SCULP. There are also a number of changes on the sheet itself: the first two words of "Part of Virginia" have been omitted; the SEVEN RANGES OF / TOWNSHIPS are now indicated in eastern Ohio, and townships are also indicated by rectangular grids in western NEW YORK State and in MAINE; the course of the OHIO RIVER has been modified southward at the lower left and it no longer breaks through the neat line; the latitude marking "39" has been omitted; NEW BRUNSWICK has been extended at the upper right, and ST. JOHN's has been added outside the neat line; and the Meridian of Washington has been added.

This is the first known issuance of the complete Bradley MAP / OF THE / UNITED STATES as only the northeast sheet has thus far been discovered of State I (Map 127). The complete map now consists of: the upper right sheet; another measuring about 19⅛" x 25¾" that covers the southern states and bears the main title; a smaller sheet, 15¼" x 15¼" to the neat lines, covering the territory north of 39° and west of Gallipolis; and an engraved table entitled: PROGRESS OF THE MAIL ON THE MAIN LINE at the lower right corner. This last section is, in fact, a postal timetable showing the route of the mail carriers from Brewer, Maine, south along the Eastern Seaboard to Charleston, South Carolina, with all the various stopping stations noted as well as times of arrivals and departures. When the original upper right sheet (Map 127)

is joined to the complete map (State II), the left marginal neat lines are trimmed off, and the lower portion ends along latitude 39° with irregularities near the GALLIPOLIS corner. Reaching the POTOWMAC RIVER, the map follows its course skirting the District of Columbia until the 38° line is reached. The lower marginal line ends at the two degree mark.

Size 34¹⁄₁₆" x 36¾". *Scale* 1" = 38 miles.

Published Separately.

References Evans 30123; John Carter Brown Library, *Report, 1956,* pp. 59–61; Louis C. Karpinski, *Bibliography of the Printed Maps of Michigan,* pp. 193–94; Isaac N. P. Stokes, *The Iconography of Manhattan Island, 6,* 49–50; Isaac N. P. Stokes and Daniel C. Haskell, *American Historical Prints,* pp. 71–72; U.S. Library of Congress, Division of Maps, *An Account of the Activities, 1939,* pp. 163–64.

Locations DLC, MH (untrimmed upper right sheet).

129 1796 *State* III (see also Maps 127, 128, and 130; V post-1799, see Map 130, Description)

Description Above the upper neat line at left: DEPOSITED AS THE ACT DIRECTS SEPTEMBER 26TH. 1796. South of TENNASSEE appears: UNITED STATES TERRITORY. GEOR / GIA is given on two lines thus.

Published Separately.

Locations CtY, DLC, MiU-C, RPJCB.

130 [1796?] *State* IV (see also Maps 127, 128, and 129; V post-1799, see below, Description)

Description In GEOR / GIA appears a dashed line and the words: ALL WEST IS CLAIMED BOTH BY THE U. S. AND BY GEORGIA. To the table of signs east of SOUTH CAROLINA are added the following words: POST ROADS DISCONTINUED. Roads have been added: in MAINE and NEW HAMPSHIRE, from NORTH NARMOUTH [sic] to SANDWICH via FAYBERG; in VERMONT, from BURLINGTON to WINDSOR; in PENNSYLVANIA, from LEWISBERG to HUNTINGTON; in NEW JERSEY, from LITTLE EGG HARBOR to DELAWARE RIVER opposite PHILADELPHIA; and in VIRGINIA, from CULPEPPER CH to FAUQUER CH. Later states of this map appeared after 1800, State V being published in 1804.

Published Separately.

Location DLC.

131 [1796] *State* I (II post-1799, see below, Description)

Description At lower right: THE / UNITED STATES / OF / AMERICA. Below title: W. BARKER

SCULP. PHILADELPHIA. Bellin's fictitious islands in Lake Superior are still shown. KENTUCKY and TENNESSEE are named but Vermont is not. PAMTICOE SD. is so shown. MUSCLE SHOALS is given. The northeast border crosses the St. John River and goes up to a mountain range indicated just south of the St. Lawrence. CHICAGO appears in the lower end of Lake Michigan. This map was reissued in the 1801 edition of *Carey's American Pocket Atlas* with many additional names of places, among them: Penobscot, Machias, Salem, Newark, Rome, Hudson, Goshen, Reading, Tyoga River, Genesee River, and Norfolk.

Size $9^{13}/_{16}''$ x $12^{7}/_{16}''$. *Scale* $1'' = 150$ miles.

Published in Mathew Carey, *Carey's American Pocket Atlas,* foll. p. 4.

132 [1796] *State* II (see also Maps 123, 133, and 137; V post-1799, see Map 133, Description)

Description Above the inset map has been added: ENGRAVED FOR AND SOLD BY MATTHEW [sic] CAREY PHILADELPHIA.

Published in Mathew Carey, *The General Atlas for Carey's Edition of Guthrie's Geography Improved,* no. 24; the early issues of *Carey's General Atlas,* no. 24; separately.

Location MWA (as separate).

133 [1796] *State* III (see also Maps 123, 132, and 137; V post-1799, see below, Description)

Description This map may be identified by the uneven depth of the shading lines in Chesapeake Bay, Albemarle Sound, and Lake George (both New York and Florida). In the earlier state, these shading lines are even in depth, while in the later state the depth has usually been increased close to the shores. This map was used later in the Sept. 9, 1800, edition of *Carey's General Atlas* with the figure "24" added at upper left corner.

Published in later issues of Mathew Carey, *Carey's General Atlas,* no. 24.

134 [1796] *State* I (see also Maps 135, 136, and 143)

Description In oval at lower right: AN / ACCURATE MAP / OF THE / UNITED STATES / OF / AMERICA. / ACCORDING TO THE TREATY OF PEACE OF / 1783. In oval below title: A. ANDERSON SCULP. Maine is shown as: MAIN and SAGADAHOCK, and the northeast boundary line does not extend north as far as the St. John River. The southern end of Lake Michigan is shown about a half degree further south than the southern shore of Lake Erie. The elevated plane is omitted from the interior of the lower Michigan Peninsula.

The Seven Ranges north of the Ohio are shown, though not extending far enough north. Lands of the Illinois Company, New Jersey Company, Wabash Company, and Ohio Company are indicated. Pennsylvania is shown without the tract purchased from New York. New Jersey is shown as: JERSEY. Okefenokee Swamp is shown as: OAQUAPHENOGAW. New York State is shown including the Erie triangle.

Size $14^{1}/_{16}''$ x $17^{13}/_{16}''$. *Scale* None $(1'' = $ c. 110 miles).

Published Separately.

Locations MH, RPJCB.

135 [1796] *State* II (see also Maps 134, 136, and 143)

Description The following imprint has been added below neat line: PUBLISHED BY SMITH, REID AND WAYLAND.

Published in William Winterbotham, [*Atlas*].

136 [1796] *State* III (see also Maps 134, 135, and 143)

Description The imprint below bottom neat line has been changed to read: PUBLISHED BY JOHN REID, N. YORK.

Published in John Reid, *The American Atlas* [1796?], no. 3; ibid., 1796, no. 3.

137 [1797] *State* IV? (see also Maps 123, 132, 133; V post-1799, see Map 133, Description)

Description [Map of the United States: compiled chiefly from the state maps, and other authentic information, by Sam'l Lewis. Engraved for and sold by Matthew Carey. Philadelphia: (1797).] This may be State IV of the 1795 map by Samuel Lewis (see Map 123).

Published Separately.

Reference Evans 32378.

Location No copy located.

138 [1797?] *State* II (see also Map 119)

Description The title now reads: A / NEW MAP / OF THE / UNITED STATES / OF / AMERICA. Just below this is a certificate of correctness by: OSGOOD CARLETON. The imprint in the lower right corner now reads: BOSTON PUBLISHED AND SOLD BY W. NORMAN BOOK & CHART-SELLER. The inset at upper center is now replaced by: A TABLE EXHIBITING THE LENGTH BREADTH AND POPULATION OF EACH STATE . . . A TABLE OF THE POST ROADS & DISTANCES is given at the bottom right. Parts of the Eastern coastline have been redrawn and some place names and soundings have been removed. Other place names have been relettered and still others added. Some names have also been added in the West. A few major roads have been indicated. PENSYLVANIA is still shown thus. FEDERAL CITY / OF WASHINGTON is given as is TENNESSEE. CANADA is now lettered north of the RIVER ST LAURENCE. WESTERN / TERRITORY is noted on the Old Northwest.

Published Separately.

Location MHi.

139 [1797]

Description In oval at lower right: THE / UNITED STATES / OF / AMERICA. In oval below title: B. TANNER, SCULPT. Below bottom neat line: PUBLISH'D BY C. SMITH. NEW YORK. The boundary between Kentucky and Virginia is shown as a north and south line. Peconic Bay on Long Island is too long and the island, too wide. Staten Island is too large. CAPE HATTARAS is shown thus. ALBAM appears as a village in western Georgia. NEW WINDSOR appears in northern Georgia. ANAPOLIS appears thus in Nova Scotia. See also Map 126.

Size 6½" x 8½".   *Scale* 1" = 200 miles.

Published in Charles Smith, *American Gazetteer;* also found inserted in the *Monthly Military Repository, 1,* foll. p. 8.

Reference Philip L. Phillips, *A List of Maps of America*, p. 872.

140 [1797]   *State* III (see also Maps 117 and 120; IV post-1799, see below, Description)

Description TENNASSEE [sic] appears west of North Carolina beyond the Cumberland Mountains and "Southern Territory," which previously appeared over that area, has been erased. In the fourth state of the map, appearing in M'Culloch's *A Concise History*, 3d ed., "Ohio" appears and "Louisiana" is lettered along the western extreme, running north and south.

Published in John M'Culloch, *A Concise History of the United States*, 2d ed., front.; Benjamin Workman, *Elements of Geography*, 7th ed., opp. p. 71.

Reference Alice W. Spieseke, *The First Textbooks*, pp. 83–84, 95.

141 1798

Description In oval at lower right: A MAP OF / THE UNITED STATES / OF / AMERICA. Above top neat line: ENGRAVED FOR MORSE'S ELEMENTS OF GEOGRAPHY. Below bottom neat line: PUBLISHED BY THOMAS & ANDREWS, BOSTON, *1798*. EAST FLORIDA and the north bank of the St. Lawrence River extend beyond the neat line; several states are not indicated; PENSYLVANIA is spelled thus; and INDIANA is inscribed in western Virginia. Only one dotted border line is shown, this running through the center of Lake Erie. *187 FEET* is inscribed at upper end of the Niagara River. NIAGARA FORT is named but there is no mention of the Falls. BIG BONES is inscribed in a bend of the Ohio River. This is the fifth Morse map of the United States.

Size 5¼" x 5⅝".   *Scale* 1" = 70 [marine leagues].

Published in Jedidiah Morse, *Elements of Geography*, 3d ed., opp. p. 74.

142 [1799]

Description In oval at lower right: THE / UNITED STATES / OF / AMERICA. Below bottom neat line: ENGRAVED FOR PAYNES GEOGRAPHY PUBLISHED BY. J. LOW NEW YORK. The map shows mainly drainage features, but also some orographical data and cities. TENNESSEE [sic] appears without an eastern boundary.

Size 9⁹⁄₁₆" x 12³⁄₁₆".   *Scale* 1" = 150 miles.

Published in John Payne, *A New and Complete Universal Geography*, 4 (1799), opp. 50.

143 [Before 1800?]   *State* IV (see also Maps 134, 135, and 136)

Description The publisher's imprint below the bottom neat line has been erased.

Published Separately.

Locations MH, RPJCB.

144 [1677] *State* I (see also Map 145)

Description In a rectangle at upper right: A MAP OF / NEW-ENGLAND, / BEING THE FIRST THAT WAS EVER HERE CUT, AND DONE BY / THE BEST PATTERN THAT COULD BE HAD, WHICH BEING IN / SOME PLACES DEFECTIVE, IT MADE THE OTHER LESS EXACT: / YET DOTH IT SUFFICIENTLY SHEW THE SCITUATION OF / THE COUNTRY, AND CONVENIENTLY WELL THE / DISTANCE OF PLACES. This is the first known map printed in English America. It was probably designed for William Hubbard's *Narrative* by the author, and the wood block engraved by the book's printer, John Foster. The title speaks of a "PATTERN" but no definite source map has yet been identified. The book was reprinted in London later the same year and with it came another issue of the same map which, due to one of the over twenty-five differences in spelling and style between it and the former, has come to be called the "Wine Hills" version. There has been much controversy regarding the priority of the so called "White Hills" and "Wine Hills" maps. One theory is that both woodcuts were prepared by one individual, probably John Foster in Boston, and that the "Wine Hills" version, the rough original, was sent hurriedly to London when it was completed, while the other, corrected copy was retained and used in Boston. Others point out that there are sufficient differences between the two to argue that they were cut by different individuals. The "White Hills" map, they say, was cut first and a proof of either the uncorrected copy or the finished copy was used in London by another engraver to cut the London "Wine Hills" map, thus accounting for the errors and differences in style that exist between them. Dr. Randolph G. Adams has pointed out (see reference below) that no "Wine Hills" map has been found that was originally bound into the Boston edition of Hubbard. While the "Wine Hills" map may have been cut in America, it was probably printed in England. It also, in providing the town symbol between SEACONK and PLIMOUTH, follows State II of the "White Hills" map.

Size 11½" x 15¼". *Scale* 1" = 15 miles.

Published in William Hubbard, *A Narrative of the Troubles with the Indians in New-England,* foll. p. 132. Reproduced in Sinclair Hamilton, *Early American Book Illustrators and Wood Engravers 1670–1870,* pl. 2; idem, "John Foster and the 'White Hills' Map," opp. p. 180; Richard B. Holman, "John Foster's Woodcut Map of New England," in *Printing & Graphic Arts, 8* (1960), no. 3.

References Randolph G. Adams, "William Hubbard's 'Narrative,' 1677. A Bibliographical Study"; Emerson D. Fite and Archibald Freeman, *A Book of Old Maps,* pp. 165–66; David M. Stauffer, *American Engravers,* 2, no. 1010; Roderick Stinehour, "But there are more Questions," letter in *Printing & Graphic Arts, 8* (1960), 125; Thomas W. Streeter, *Americana-Beginnings,* pp. 19–22; Lawrence C. Wroth and Marion W. Adams, *American Woodcuts and Engravings 1670–1800,* no. 3; see also reproductions above, under Published.

145 [1677] *State* II (see also Map 144)

Description A town symbol has been added between SEACONK and PLIMOUTH.

Published in William Hubbard, *A Narrative of the Troubles with the Indians in New-England,* foll. p. 132. Reproduced in Samuel A. Green, *Ten Fac-simile Reproductions Relating to New England,* p. 12; Massachusetts Historical Society, *Prints, Maps and Drawings 1677–1822,* no. 1. Henry Stevens published separates of both American and English issues of the map, [London, 1872].

Reference Roderick Stinehour, "But there are more Questions," letter in *Printing & Graphic Arts, 8* (1960), 125.

146 [1760]

Description [Plan of the country.] This is a small woodcut map with thirty-seven letter and number references. Most of the lettering is inset type. The references are identified in a table on the opposite page. The area shown includes from Philadelphia to Lake Erie, and from the mouth of the St. Lawrence to Louisbourg. The title is from the opposite page.

Size 3⅝" x 5⅞". *Scale* None (1" = c. 125 miles).

Published in Thomas More, [pseud.], *Poor Thomas Improved; Being More's Country Almanack for 1761.*

147 [1778]

Description Below bottom neat line: A CHOROGRAPHICAL MAP OF THE NORTHERN DEPARTMENT OF NORTH AMERICA / DRAWN FROM THE LATEST AND MOST ACCURATE OBSERVATIONS. At lower left corner below neat line: ENGRAVED PRINTED AND SOLD AT NEW HAVEN. The map is oriented peculiarly, north being toward the lower left-hand portion. The configurations follow Capt. Samuel Holland's "The Provinces of New York, and New Jersey; with part of Pensilvania [sic] . . ." [London, 1775], the upper sheet of which bears the following title above the neat line: "A chorographical Map of the Country between Albany . . . and Les Trois Riviéres . . ." The map features and identifies various townships and grants made throughout the area by the several governments; these are explained in a boxed note at the upper left corner. The neat lines are broken at left center for the St. Lawrence River. This map was advertised in the June 5, 1778, (New London) *Connecticut Gazette.*

Size 21½" x 25". *Scale* 1" = 12 miles.

Published Separately. A re-engraving by H. Klockhoff was published by Covens and Mortier, Amsterdam, 1780. Reproduced in *The Documentary History of the State of New-York, 4,* opp. [530] (this was copied from an original in the Office of the State Engineer and Surveyor in New York which has since been reported lost); Pierre Pouchot, *Memoir upon the Late War in North America, between the French and English, 1755–60, 2,* opp. 68; Vermont, *Records of the Governor and Council of the State of Vermont, 7,* opp. 430 (see also p. 435).

References Philip L. Phillips, *Notes on Bernard Romans,* pp. 88–91; Willard O. Waters, comp., "American Imprints, 1648–1797 in the Huntington Library," no. 426.

Locations BM, CSmH (title trimmed off), CtHT, RPJCB.

148 [1785]

Description [Accurate map of the Four New-England States.] The only probable copy of this map located to date has a section, measuring 13" x 18", missing at the lower right corner. Apparently the title and imprint were on that part of the map. Subscriptions were advertised in the (Boston) *Independent Chronicle* on February 17 and March 31, 1785. Publication was announced as being distributed to subscribers at the "Map Office." The latter advertisement also stated that the accuracy of the map was "Attested by John Leach, Surveyor, and Teacher of the Mathematics in Boston," who had also checked them against the best British and Ameri-

can maps of the same area. On April 14, 1785, it was again advertised in the *Chronicle,* this time as "This Day is published," and referred to as "The great New Map." Twelve plates were used in printing it. John Norman, who together with John Coles was the publisher, also did the engraving. POKEPSEY is shown thus. THE DEVILS BELT / COMMONLY CALLED / LONG ISLAND SOUND appears. WEKAPAUG BROOK THE / TRUE W BOUNDS OF THE / NARRAGANSET COUNTY appears as a note in the ocean between JUDITH and WATCH POINT. The River St. Croix is shown emptying into the eastern side of Passamaquoddy Bay. The SCHODICK R is shown entering this Bay at the northwest corner. The title was taken from the "Subscription List . . ." noted in References, below.

Size 60½" x 61½". *Scale* 1" = 7 English miles.

Published Separately.

References Evans 19144; "Subscription list for a map of the 'Four New England States' 1785 From an Original List of Subscribers in the Society's Collections."

Location MWA.

149 [1789] *State* I (see also Map 153)

Description In cartouche at lower right: A MAP OF THE / NORTHERN AND MIDDLE / STATES; / COMPREHENDING THE WESTERN TERRITORY / AND THE BRITISH DOMINIONS IN / NORTH AMERICA. / COMPILED FROM THE BEST AUTHORITIES. Below bottom neat line: DELINEATED & ENGRAV'D FOR MORSES GEOGRAPHY BY AMOS DOOLITTLE NEWHAVEN. In the preface Morse states: "The Map of the northern states was compiled principally by the Engraver, from the best maps that could be procured." An EXPLANATION of certain signs, letters, and numbers appears in the likeness of an open book at the upper left corner. NOVA SCOTIA is shown for all of New Brunswick and Nova Scotia. The northeastern border runs straight north across the St. Johns River to a point on the highlands dividing the St. Lawrence River basin from that of the Restigouche. Maine is divided into the PROVINCE / OF / MAIN and SAGADAHOCK. The district around Lake Champlain is badly drawn. The river between Montreal and Lake Ontario is shown IROQUIS OR CATARAQUAY R. BUFFALOE SWAMP is shown in the north central mountains of Pennsylvania. Delaware and Maryland are distorted. PATOWMAC RIVER is given for Potomac. AN HIGH PLAIN is shown in north central Michigan. HEAD OF / ORIGAN is shown 3° south of Lake of the Woods. Northern Minnesota is inscribed FULL OF MERSHES & LAKES. The fictitious islands of Bellin and Charlevoix in Lake Superior are shown. IROQUOES appears north of Lake Ontario. GRAND

TRAVERS is inscribed across the entrance to GREEN B.

Size 12½″ x 15⅞″. *Scale* None (1″ = c. 1° 40′ latitude).

Published in Jedidiah Morse, *The American Geography*, 1st ed., opp. p. 33.

150 1789

Description In cartouche at lower right: A / NEW MAP OF THE STATES / OF PENSYLVANIA NEW JERSEY / NEW YORK CONNECTICUT / RHODE ISLAND MASSACHUSETS / AND NEW HAMPSHIRE INCLUDING / NOVA SCOTIA AND CANADA / FROM THE LATEST AUTHORITIES. Above top neat line: ENGRAVED FOR GORDON'S HISTORY OF THE AMERICAN WAR. Below bottom neat line at right: C. TIEBOUT SCULPT. N. YORK.–*1789*. This map was copied from Map 149. IROQUOES still appears north of Lake Ontario, also IROQUIS OR CATARAQUAY R on the upper St. Lawrence, MIEMI F. & R. for Maumee, and CEDER PT. The EXPLANATION of symbols used appears at extreme right center. Above the Lake of the Woods, in place of Doolittle's open book, is the inscription: KRIS / OR / CHRISTINAUX.

Size 10⅝″ x 15⅞″. *Scale* None (1″ = c. 1° 40′ latitude).

Published in William Gordon, *History of the Rise of the United States*, 1st ed., 2, front.; ibid., 2d ed., 2, front.

151 [1791] *State* I (see also Map 157; III post-1799, see Map 157, Description)

Description In oval at bottom center: CHART / FROM NEW YORK TO TIMBER ISLAND / INCLUDING / NANTUCKET SHOALS / FROM THE LATEST SURVEYS. In oval below title: PRINTED & SOLD BY J NORMAN NO 75 NEWBURY STR BOSTON. The neat line is broken at the lower left corner by Manhattan Island. Measurement is taken over the end of the Island. This chart is shaped like an inverted "T." Six plates were used to print it. The borders on the topmost plate do not match those of the one below it on the left side. A certification under the title reads: I HAVE CAREFULLY EXAMINED THIS CHART AND FIND IT TO AGREE WITH / HOLLANDS SURVEYS THE SHOALS BY ONE WELL AUTHENTICATED BY BRH PILOTS / OSGOOD CARLETON / TEACHER OF NAVIGATION AND / OTHER BRANCHES OF THE MATHEMATICS. The right extension of the "T" shows GEORGES BANK and seems to have been added to a finished chart of reversed "L" shape. This sheet appears to be attached over finished border lines on one copy examined; the other was cut at this point. This right plate contains the inset map of PLYMOUTH BAY. The 1791 edition of the *Pilot* has this right extension bound in as a separate chart, no. 7 (see Map 152). The complete border of neat line and marginal

degree line is omitted from one side of four of the plates that form an edge of the complete chart. The first plate is the top plate, which may be omitted, leaving a finished chart—except that without it the TIMBER ISLAND of the title will not be shown. The second plate, showing the coast to Newbury and Ipswich Bay, has its own finished neat line and marginal degree line across the top.

Size 42″ x 74½″. *Scale* 1″ = 4 nautical miles.

Inset In rectangle at lower right: PLYMOUTH / BAY. Some soundings are given. Size: 6¾″ x 5¹⁄₁₆″. Scale: None (1″ = c. 8 nautical miles).

Published in John Norman, *The American Pilot* [1791], no. 6; ibid., 1792, no. 7; William Norman, *The American Pilot*, 1794, no. 7.

152 [1791]

Description At upper center: GEORGES BANK. In the 1792 edition of the *Pilot*, the chart is usually attached to and forms a "T" shaped extension to the CHART / FROM NEW YORK TO TIMBER ISLAND (Map 151). In some copies of the 1792 edition, however, it is also inserted as a separate chart.

Size 16″ x 20½″. *Scale* None (1″ = 4 nautical miles).

Inset In rectangle at lower right: PLYMOUTH / BAY. Size: 6¾″ x 6⅛″. Scale: None (1″ = c. 8 nautical miles).

Published in John Norman, *The American Pilot*, [1791], no. 7.

153 [1793] *State* II (see also Map 149)

Description Above top neat line has been added: PUBLISHED BY THOMAS & ANDREWS BOSTON. New Brunswick and Nova Scotia are now shown separately. The "A" of the original Nova Scotia was not erased and it now appears after New Brunswick, making: NEW BRUNSWICKA. The names WASHINGTON COUNTY and HANCOCK COUNTY and the representation of a mountain range replace "Sagadahock." St. Clair's defeat has been represented with BATTLE GROUND NOV. *4, 1791*. IROQUOIS now appears in present southern Ontario instead of "Iroquoes" and for the upper St. Lawrence IROQUOIS OR CATARAQUAY R in place of "Iroquis or Cataraquay R."

Published in Jedidiah Morse, *The American Universal Geography*, 1st ed., *1*, opp. 309.

154 [1794]

Description In upper left corner of border: *1279 / 1369 / 1459*. Above border at upper right corner: ELIZA COLLES SCUL. This is a section of a large indexed topographical map intended to cover the United States and possibly more. It includes a portion of southern Canada, some of Northern Vermont and New Hampshire, and a small part of northeast New York and northwest Maine. The indexing is done by means of many letters on the map which refer to explanations in the text of the book. The map sections are supplied loose and are not bound with the alphabetical references, alphabetical indexes, or directions for use of the maps which comprise the book that the maps were made to accompany. The middle number of the three at upper left corner, *1369*, identifies this section of the main map. The lesser number above this, *1279*, identifies the section just north of this and the greater number below, *1459*, identifies the section just south. There is an upper border consisting of three marginal degree lines showing longitudes from Paris, London, and Philadelphia. Above these is another border line with the scale attached. Inside the extreme left border line are marginal scale lines showing GRATEST [sic] LENGTH OF DAYS AND NIGHTS and degrees of latitude. Only five different sections of the complete map are known, with the references and indexes for them (see also Maps 155, 156, 309, and 358).

Size 14⅞" x 20". *Scale* 1" = 10 miles.

Published with Christopher Colles, *The Geographical Ledger.*

References Christopher Colles, *A Survey of the Roads 1789*, 1961, pp. 77–81; Lloyd W. Griffen, "Christopher Colles," pp. 178–82.

Location DLC.

155 [¹794]

Description In upper left corner: *1459 / 1549 / 1639*. Above border at upper right corner: ELIZA COLLES SCULP. This is one section of a large topographical map intended to cover the entire United States and possibly more. It includes the lower Hudson River Valley, Connecticut, Rhode Island, and part of Massachusetts. The northern edge of this map matches the southern edge of Map 156 and the western edge matches Map 309. The multiple margin lines are similar to the other Colles maps accompanying the *Geographical Ledger;* for a description see Map 154. Long Island is noted as NASSAU ISLAND.

Size 14⅝" x 20⁹⁄₁₆". *Scale* 1" = 10 miles.

Inset In lower right corner: [Hook of Cape Cod]. CRAB / BANK and NANTUKKET [sic] I are also noted. Size: 8⅝" x 7¾". Scale: same as larger map.

Published with Christopher Colles, *The Geographical Ledger.* Reproduced in Christopher Colles, *A Survey of the Roads 1789*, 1961, p. [80].

References see Map 154.

Locations DLC, NHi.

156 [¹794]

Description In upper left corner of border: *1369 / 1459 / 1549*. This is one section of a large indexed topographical map intended to cover the entire United States and possibly more. It shows an area extending from Central Vermont and New Hampshire to south of Boston, and from the Hudson River to the Atlantic Coast. The upper edge of this map matches the lower edge of Map 154; the lower edge matches the top of Map 155, the western edge, Map 358. The multiple margin lines are similar to the other Colles maps accompanying *The Geographical Ledger;* for a description see Map 154.

Size 14½" x 20". *Scale* 1" = 10 miles.

Published with Christopher Colles, *The Geographical Ledger.*

References see Map 154.

Locations DLC, NN.

157 [¹794] *State* II (see also Map 151; III post-1799, see below, Description)

Description Roads have been added in Massachusetts north of Boston, such as that between NEWBURY and ROWLEY. This chart was published again in William Norman's *American Pilot* of 1803 with considerable recutting. The letters in COAST OF NEW ENGLAND are shaded and beadlike decorations are added to them. The top plate containing TIMBER ISLAND and the right plate showing "Georges Bank" are omitted, giving the chart a shortened reversed "L" shape. The lower left portion of the 1803 edition has been extended by the addition of another small plate (measuring 6⅜" x 16⅝") to show the southern coast of Long Island from Longitude 72° 49' West and the entrance to New York Harbor with Paulus Hook.

Published in John Norman, *The American Pilot*, 1794, no. 7; William Norman, *The American Pilot*, 1794.

158 [¹797]

Description At lower right: MAP / OF THE / NORTHERN PART / OF THE / UNITED STATES / OF/ AMERICA / BY / ABRAHAM BRADLEY JUNR. Below bottom neat line at right: B CALLENDER SCP. At center: ENGRAVED FOR MORSE'S AMERICAN GAZETTEER. STATIN I appears thus; also, the INDIAN BOUNDARY BY GEN. WAYNE'S TREATY 1795. Numerous reservations are indicated beyond this line, including CHICAGO. CAYOGA joins the Muskingham River but the PORTAGE is inscribed. The Western Reserve is inscribed: NEW CONNECTICUT. WAYNE CO. appears in Michigan and NEW GNADENHUTTEN on a Huron River which flows into Lake St. Clair. The five proposed new states of the Ordinance of 1789 are indicated with Roman numerals, approximating very closely Wisconsin, Michigan, Illinois, Indiana, and Ohio. CINCINNATUS appears for Cincinnati. LAKE SUPERIOR and QUEBECK are inscribed above the top neat line.

Size 8⅜" x 15⅝".   *Scale* None (1" = c. 100 miles).

Published in Jedidiah Morse, *The American Gazetteer,* opp. "New England." Reproduced in U.S. Bureau of the Census, *A Century of Population Growth,* opp. p. 16.

159 [1798] *State* I (II post-1799, see below, Description)

Description The title appears in a simple cartouche at upper center: A CHART / OF THE / COAST OF NEW ENGLAND / FROM THE / SOUTH SHOALS TO CAPE SABLE / INCLUDING / GEORGES BANK / FROM / HOLLAND'S ACTUAL SURVEYS. Below title: PUBLISHED AND SOLD BY W NORMAN / NO 75 NEWBURY STREET / BOSTON. Four plates are used. At upper right and left are a number of shore line contours. Soundings are given along the coast and near rocks; ledges and other features are indicated. This chart, somewhat recut, is also used in William Norman's *American Pilot* of 1803. In this later state, the mainland in the inset map contacts the lower border of the inset with a shaded shore line. In the 1798 map the shore line is unshaded for a short distance here.

Size 40½" x 33⁵⁄₁₆".   *Scale* None (1" = c. 8½ miles).

Inset At upper left: A PLAN OF / BOSTON HARBOUR / FROM HOLLANDS / ACTUAL SURVEYS. Size: 9⁷⁄₁₆" x 11¹¹⁄₁₆". Scale: None (1" = c. 350 rods).

Published in William Norman, *The American Pilot,* 1798, no. 6.

MAINE

160 [1720]

Description Capt. Cyprian Southack advertised in the *Boston News-Letter*, April 10–13, 1721, and the several issues following:

". . . Map of Casco Bay, with the Harbour Islands, Adjacents [sic] Rocks, Shoals, Channel ways &c. Very large Scale . . . Eight shillings for one."

Dunlap (cited below) states that Francis Dewing engraved a map of Casco which was printed the same year as his engraving of Canso Harbor (see Map 68). An English printed map engraved by Emanual Bowen "The Harbour of Casco Bay and Islands Adjacent. By Capt. Cyprian Southicke [sic]" is also dated 1720. This map or chart was included in the *English Pilot. Fourth Book*, London, 1721, and the editions following. No copy of the Dewing map, if such exists, has thus far been discovered; the Bowen engraving could be a copy of such a map; or both could have been engraved individually from separate copies of a Southack original map. Southack at this time was advertising three maps: his large map of North America (see Map 44), the Casco, and the Canso maps, all as separates. Two of these survive today and carry Dewing's name as engraver.

Size Unknown.   *Scale* Unknown.

Published Separately.

References William Dunlap, *A History of the Arts of Design*, 3, 295; Clara E. LeGear, "The New England Coasting Pilot of Cyprian Southack," p. 143.

Location No copy located.

161 [1753]   *State* I (see also Map 162)

Description In decorative cartouche at lower right: A TRUE COPPY FROM AN ANCIENT / PLAN OF E HUTCHINSON'S ESQR: & FROM JOSE HEATH / IN *1719*. & PHINS: JONES'S SURVEY IN *1731*. & FROM / JOHN NORTH'S LATE SURVEY IN *1752*. ATTESTR: THOS JOHNSTON. This map was issued as a broadside by the proprietors of Brunswick Township in 1753 with a letterpress section quoting extracts from various conveyances demonstrating the limits of the claim of the Plymouth Company. The engraving was the work of Thomas Johnston. It includes the area from Norridgwock

Town to Cape Elizabeth and Falmouth Neck to Pemaquid Point.

Size 11⅝" x 8⅝".   *Scale* 1" = 8 miles.

Published Separately. Reproduced in Francis Baylies, *An Historical Memoir of the Colony of New Plymouth*, Addition, 2, pt. 5, 36; as a Massachusetts Historical Society, *Special Publication* (Boston, 1912); in Alexander O. Vietor, "Printed Maps," pl. 278 (B).

References Brunswick Township, Maine, Prop. of, *An Answer to the Remarks of the Plymouth Co.*; Worthington C. Ford, *Broadsides, Ballads, Printed in Massachusetts 1639–1800*, no. 966; Plymouth Co., *Remarks on the Plan*; Robert W. G. Vail, *Old Frontier*, no. 464; Joseph Williamson, *Bibliography of Maine*, no. 1670; Lawrence C. Wroth, "The Thomas Johnston Maps of the Kennebec Purchase."

Locations CtY, MeHi, MHi, MWA, PRO, RPJCB.

162 [1753] or [1754]   *State* II (see also Map 161)

Description ATKINS BAY in the Kennebeck River about a mile from the mouth on its western side has been named.

Published Separately.

Locations CtY, DLC, MeHi.

163 1754

Description In cartouche at lower right: TO HIS / EXCELLENCY WILLIAM SHIRLEY . . . THIS PLAN OF KENNEBECK, & SAGA / DAHOCK RIVERS, & COUNTRY ADJACENT, (WHEREON / ARE DELINEATED YE BOUNDARIES OF SEVERAL AN- / -CIENT GRANTS) BEING TAKEN FROM ACTUAL SURVEYS / MADE BY JOSEPH HEATH ESQ. MR: PHINEAS JONES / JOHN NORTH ESQR: & MR: EPHRAIM JONES IS / . . . INSCRIBED BY . . . THOS: JOHNSTON. In lower left corner of cartouche: BOSTON / NOVEMR: 20, / *1754*. At lower center: ENGRAV'D PRINTED & SOLD BY THOMAS JOHNSTON BRATTLE STREET BOSTON NEW ENGLAND *1754*. Twenty six lines of script are engraved under the inset map at the upper left. Two columns of script extend about halfway down the map at the upper right explaining lines drawn on the main map. The script refers to colored lines not always found on the map.

Although this map may seem to be a personal publishing venture of Thomas Johnston's, he was actually reimbursed by the Plymouth Company, at least for the large copper plates used in making it.

Size 31⅜″ x 21⅞″.   *Scale* 1″ = 4 miles.

Insets [a] At upper left corner with note in script at upper left of inset containing title: . . . A GENERAL / VIEW OF THE PRINCIPAL RIVERS TO YE NORTH & WEST OF THE / MASSACHUSETTS . . . Size: 8⁹⁄₁₆″ x 7¾″. Scale: 1″ = 50 miles.

[b] At center is an enlarged inset plan of: FORT HALLIFAX. Size: 2¾″ x 2½″. Scale: 1″ = c. 100 feet.

[c] At left is an enlarged inset plan of: FORT WESTERN. Size: 3″ x 3¾″. Scale: 1″ = c. 70 feet.

[d] At right center is an enlarged plan of: FORT FRANKFORT. Size: 3″ x 3″. Scale 1″ = c. 100 feet.

Published Separately.   Re-engraved by Thomas Kitchin and published in London by Andrew Miller in 1755; copy in Public Record Office (NAC-Me-12). Reproduced in Massachusetts Historical Society *Prints, Maps and Drawings 1677-1822*, no. 13; by idem, as a *Special Publication*, Boston, 1912; in Alexander O. Vietor, "Printed Maps," pl. 280.

References Brunswick Township, Maine, Prop. of, *An Answer to the Remarks of the Plymouth Co.*; George F. Dow, *Arts and Crafts in New England*, pp. 29–30; William Dunlap, *A History of the Arts of Design*, 3, 312; William Goold, "Col. Arthur Noble, of Georgetown," p. 124; Justin H. Smith, *Arnold's March from Cambridge to Quebec*, p. 305; Lawrence C. Wroth, "The Thomas Johnston Maps of Kennebec Purchase."

Locations CtHi, MHi.

164 [178–?]

Description At upper right: PLAN OF PART / OF THE / DISTRICT OF MAIN. This map shows the various surveyed ranges and townships and seems to have been made especially to locate the surveys of a 40 mile square tract on the Kennebec River just north of CARRIGTONKA [sic] / FALLS, and an irregular tract, divided into MIDDLE, NORTH, and EAST divisions that extends from just back of the coast north and northeast of TRENTON to the St. Croix lakes. The conflicting boundaries of the township surveys with the claims of the BROWN, the PLYMOUTH Company, and the WALDO PATENT are shown. Bangor Township, incorporated in 1791, is actually No. 1 of the second range north of the WALDO PATENT, but has no name indicated. The boundary lines between Cumberland, Lincoln, and Hancock Counties are shown as they were before Ken-

nebec County was formed. JONES'S / PLANTN. appears just east of present Augusta (which is not shown). FRAK FORT appears near the Kennebec south of PITS / TOWN. No St. Croix River is shown. The PASSAMAGUADDY [sic] R. is shown coming from the direction of St. Johns. The SCOODIC R appears leading from the St. Croix lakes to PASSAMAQUADDY / BAY. The engraving is well done.

Size 13½″ x 15⅝″.   *Scale* 1″ = 12 miles.

Published Separately.

Reference Philip L. Phillips, *A List of Maps of America*, p. 383.

Location DLC.

165 [1790]

Description In cartouche at upper left: CHART / OF THE COAST OF AMERICA FROM C. ELIZ / TO MOUSE HARBOUR FROM THE LATEST SURVEYS. In cartouche below title: BOSTON / PUBLISHED AND SOLD BY M. CLARK / JOSH. H SEYMOUR / SCULP. In extreme upper left corner: NO. 5. The chart bears an engraved inscription, which was signed by Osgood Carleton when the chart was sold singly, stating that it was examined and compared with DES BARR's, etc., and found accurate. Just below the cartouche at left center are four lines of profiles: THE MAKING OF THE LAND ON THE COAST OF NEW ENGLAND.

Size 16¼″ x 25″.   *Scale* None (1″ = c. 5° latitude).

Published in Matthew Clark, [*A Complete Chart*], no. 5.

166 [1791] *State* I (II post-1799, see below, Description)

Description [A chart of the Coast of America from Wood Island to Good Harbour from Hollands surveys.] The marginal degree line is omitted at the bottom. The neat line is broken at upper right to show Englishman Bay. Two plates are used. The title is taken from State II, which appears in the 1803, William Norman, *American Pilot*, with the above title added at upper left.

Size 20½″ x 32⅝″.   *Scale* None (1″ = c. 4½ miles).

Published in John Norman, *The American Pilot*, [1791], no. 8; ibid., 1792, no. 8; 1794, no. 8; William Norman, *The American Pilot*, 1794, no. 8; ibid., 1798, no. 7.

167 [1793]

Description [Map of part of Maine.] No copy of the *Description of the Situation*, so far as is known, contains a copy of the map mentioned on page three of the text.

Size Unknown.   *Scale* Unknown.

Published in [Benjamin Lincoln?], *A Description of the Situation.*

Reference Robert W. G. Vail, *Old Frontier,* no. 952.

168 [¹793]

Description In oval at lower right: THE / DISTRICT OF MAIN / FROM THE LATEST SURVEYS / O. CARLETON DELIN. The northeastern border begins at a point low down on the ST. JOHNS RIVER and runs across the Restigouche to the HIGH LANDS between that river and the St. Lawrence. The RIVER ST CROIX, PASSAMAQUADY B and SCOODIE R are all shown inaccurately. MOUSEHEAD LAKE is given for Moosehead; MASA / CHUSETS, for the State; and DISTRICT / OF / MAINE is inscribed on the map instead of MAIN as in the title.

Size 10⅝″ x 7¹⁵⁄₁₆″.   *Scale* 1 ″ = 45 English miles.

Published in Jedidiah Morse, *The American Universal Geography,* opp. p. 345.

169 [¹795]   *State* I (II post-1799, see below, Published)

Description At upper left: THE / PROVINCE / OF / MAINE, / FROM THE BEST AUTHORITIES / BY SAMUEL LEWIS, *1794.* Beneath title: W. BARKER SCULP. Above top near line: ENGRAVED FOR CAREY'S AMERICAN EDITION OF GUTHRIE'S GEOGRAPHY IMPROVED. The map indicates topographical features, the primary road into the province, and gives some place names. West of the Pleasant River are shown the SKUTTOCK HILLS. The northeastern corner is located in accordance with the claims of Maine on the highlands about 65 miles north of the St. John River. The northeastern corner is shown south of the highlands separating the St. Lawrence water shed from the CONNECTICUT and AMORISCOGGIN rivers. Machias Bay is given as MECHIAS.

Size 14³⁄₁₆″ x 9⁷⁄₁₆″.   *Scale* 1″ = 27 American miles.

Published in Mathew Carey, *Carey's American Atlas,* no. 2; idem, *Carey's General Atlas,* no. 27 (the same map appears in the September, 1800 edition of this atlas with the number "27" added at upper right corner); idem, *The General Atlas for Carey's Edition of Guthrie's Geography Improved,* no. 27.

170 [¹795]

Description In cartouche at lower right: AN ACCURATE / MAP, / OF THE / DISTRICT OF MAINE / BEING PART OF THE COMMONWEALTH OF / MASSACHUSETTS: / COMPILED PURSUANT TO AN ACT OF THE / GENERAL COURT, / FROM ACTUAL SURVEYS OF THE SEVERAL TOWNS &C. / TAKEN BY THEIR ORDER: / EXHIBITING, THE BOUNDARY LINES OF THE DISTRICT / . . . BY OSGD. CARLETON. In cartouche below title: BOSTON PUBLISHED AND SOLD BY O. CARLETON & J. NORMAN / SOLD ALSO BY WM. NORMAN NO. 75 NEWBURY STREET. This is a fine, detailed map showing political boundaries down to towns, and also roads, rivers, islands, lakes, mills, falls, iron works, and public buildings. A table of twelve symbols is given at lower center, and a column of eight explanations to lettered references appears at left center. Distances from Boston are given for each town and also distances from the county seat. All orographical features are omitted excepting a definite range of mountains along the boundary line with Canada. The following note appears at bottom left center: NB AS THE SURVEYS OF SOME TOWNS WERE NOT SO FULL AS OTHERS THE ROADS & STREAMS OF THOSE TOWNS / HAVE BEEN UNAVOIDABLY DISCONTINUED. Longitude is given: EAST OF WASHINGTON. The ST. CROIX R is shown as the upper portion of the CHAPENETTACOOK OR PASSAMAQUADDY RIVER just below LAKE UMQUEMENKEEG. The river empties into the SCODIC whose mouth is shown at the northwestern corner of PASSAMAQUADY [sic] / BAY. The NORTH BRANCH OF / PASSAMAQUADDY R. appears on the northern side of a string of lakes continuous with the St. Croix River. From the source of this branch the U.S. boundary line is run north across the St. John's River to the mountain ridge shown as the boundary of Quebec Province.

Evans dates this "[1795]" as Carleton was only selling maps in 1795. The William L. Clements Library copy is printed on paper watermarked "1794." Other references give various dates from 1790–1799.

Size 53⅝″ x 38½″.   *Scale* 1″ = 6 miles.

Published Separately.

References Evans 28391; David M. Stauffer, *American Engravers,* 2, 389; U.S. Library of Congress, *Report 1904,* p. 185; Willard O. Waters, "American Imprints 1648–1797 in the Huntington Library," no. 668; Joseph Williamson, *Bibliography of the State of Maine,* no. 5816.

Locations CSmH, DLC, MH, MHi, MiU-C, MWA, NHi, PPL, RPJCB.

171 1795

Description In cartouche at upper left: A / MAP / OF THE / DISTRICT OF MAINE / DRAWN FROM THE LATEST SURVEYS / AND OTHER BEST / AUTHORITIES, / BY OSGOOD CARLETON. Below cartouche:

DOOLITTLE SC. NEW HAVEN. Above top neat line: ENGRAVED FOR JUDGE SULLIVAN'S HISTORY OF THE DISTRICT OF MAINE. PUBLISHED BY THOMAS & ANDREWS. BOSTON. *1795*. A straight line of hills is shown, close to the St. Lawrence and running northeast, as the national boundary. The present St. Croix is shown as the Scoodic, and St. Croix is the name applied to the most easterly river emptying into Passamaquoddy Bay. Six land grants are shown with lettered references to the grantees.

Size 20½" x 16⁷⁄₁₆".   *Scale* 1" = 18 English statute miles.

Inset At lower right: A / MAP / OF THOSE PARTS OF THE COUNTRY MOST / FAMOUS FOR BEING HARASSED BY THE / INDIANS . . . Size: 8" x 7½". Scale: 1 = 11 English miles.

Published in James Sullivan, *The History of the District of Maine*, front. Partially reproduced in Charles O. Paullin, *Atlas of Historical Geography*, pl. 44A.

References Evans 29589 (lists the inset map as a separate); Joseph Williamson, *Bibliography of the State of Maine*, no. 9608.

172 [c. 1795]

Description At lower right corner: A / NEW MAP / OF THE / DISTRICT OF MAINE / TAKEN FROM THE / ORIGINAL MAP COMPILED BY / OSGOOD CARLETON ESQ. / . . . WITH ADDITIONS CORRECTIONS & IMPROVEMENTS. Beneath title: BOSTON PUBLISHED & SOLD BY I. NORMAN ENGRAVER. This follows the Carleton-Norman large map (see Map 170) and does not indicate the newly discovered large lake north of Moosehead Lake which is shown on the Carleton-Callendar & Hill map (see Map 179). The St. John's River in New Brunswick is quite different from that shown on either of the large maps and its general course is not as correct; the course of the Aroostook River is shown more accurately.

Size 24⁷⁄₁₆" x 19⁹⁄₁₆".   *Scale* None (1" = c. 13' latitude).

Published Separately.

Location MWA.

173 [1795] *State* I (II post-1799, see below, Description)

Description At upper left: MAINE. The map shows five counties (no boundaries, however) and five towns. The northeastern corner follows Samuel Lewis' map (see Map 169). The northwestern corner is shown definitely upon the highland ridge between the St. Lawrence basin and the coastal water shed. MACHIAS B. is so spelled. This map was reprinted with changes

in Scott's *The New and Universal Gazetteer, 3*. George T., Thomas T., Camp Bello I., and Belfast are now shown.

Size 7⁷⁄₁₆" x 6¹⁄₁₆".   *Scale* 1" = 44 miles.

Published in Joseph Scott, *An Atlas of the United States*, [no. 2]; idem, *The United States, Gazetteer*, opp. "Maine." Reproduced in Joseph Scott, *Atlas of the United States 1795–1800*, [no. 8].

174 [1796] *State* I (II post-1799, see below, Description)

Description At upper left: PROVINCE / OF / MAINE. Below scale: ENGRAVED BY A. DOOLITTLE NEW HAVEN. The SPYE RIVER is shown running south into the ST. JOHNS R. In this first state no double line wagon roads are shown. It was republished in the 1801, 2d ed., of *The Pocket Atlas* with a number of additions, among them: Campo Bello, Prospect, Passconaquoddi B.; HALLOWELL has been changed to Hallowellhook.

Size 7⁷⁄₁₆" x 5¹¹⁄₁₆".   *Scale* 1" = 50 miles.

Published in Mathew Carey, *Carey's American Pocket Atlas*, opp. p. 23.

175 [1796]

Description At lower right: A / MAP OF THE / DISTRICT OF MAINE / WITH / NEW BRUNSWICK & / NOVA SCOTIA. At bottom, left of center: DOOLITTLE SCULPT. Above top neat line: ENGRAVED FOR MORSE'S UNIVERSAL GEOGRAPHY: PUBLISHED BY THOMAS & ANDREWS BOSTON. Chaleur Bay almost makes an island of the Gaspe Peninsula. CAPE BRETON appears for the Cape, but CAPE BRITON is inscribed on the Island. MOSE HEAD LAKE appears for Moosehead. Five counties are shown in Maine with their boundaries.

Size 6⅞" x 9⅛".   *Scale* 1" = 58 miles.

Published in Jedidiah Morse, *The American Universal Geography*, I, opp. 379.

176 [1796]

Description In rectangle at upper left: THE / PROVINCE / OF / MAINE, / FROM THE BEST AUTHORITIES / *1795*. The SKULLOCK HILLS are shown west of the Pleasant River. MECHIAS B appears again. This map is copied from Map 169.

Size 14⁵⁄₁₆" x 9⁹⁄₁₆".   *Scale* 1" = 28 American miles.

Published in John Reid, *The American Atlas*, [1796?], no. 5; ibid., 1796, no. 5; William Winterbotham, *[Atlas]*. Reproduced in U.S. Bureau of the Census, *Heads of Families at the First Census Maine*, front.

177 [c. 1798]

Description At lower left corner: AN ACCU-RATE PLAN / OF *189126* ACRES OF LAND ON PENOB / SCOT RIVER BEING THE PURCHASE FROM THE / PENOBSCOT INDIANS BY GOVERNMENT ON EACH / SIDE SAID RIVER TOGETHER WITH TWO GORES OF LAND / ONE ON EACH SIDE DRAWN FROM THE ORIGINAL BY / OSGOOD CARLETON. This map describes a tract just northeast of present day Bangor extending eleven miles north on both sides of the Penobscot River. The townships are divided in quarters and the acreages given. The engraving is rather crudely done in the John Norman manner on a plate that had been previously used for a piece of music. Traces of the erased musical notes appear over the face of the map. On the Harvard College Library copy, along the lower left boundary of the survey, is the following MSS note (among others): "North line of Bangor. Within this line is the Township of Bangor incorporated the 25th of February 1791."

Size 15⅝" x 19¾₆". *Scale* None (1" = c. 1⅔ miles).

Published Separately.

Reference The New England Historical and Genealogical Register, 55 (1901), 54.

Location MH.

178 1799

Description In oval at upper left: THE / PROVINCE / OF / MAINE / FROM THE BEST AUTHOR-ITIES / *1799*. Above top neat line: ENGRAVED FOR PAYNE'S GEOGRAPHY. The border line runs across the St. John River to 48° 15′ North Latitude. MT. DESART I. appears so. This is a reduced copy of Map 176.

Size 10⅝" x 7⁵⁄₁₆". *Scale* 1" = 35 miles.

Published in John Payne, *A New and Complete Universal Geography, 4,* opp. 253.

179 [Before 1800?] *State* I (II post-1799, see below, Description)

Description At lower right: MAP / OF THE / DISTRICT OF MAINE / MASSACHUSETTS / COMPILED FROM ACTUAL SURVEYS / MADE BY ORDER OF THE / GENERAL COURT, / AND UNDER THE INSPECTION OF AGENTS OF THEIR APPOINTMENT / BY OSGOOD CARLETON. Below title: DRAWN BY G. GRAHAM. ENGRA'D BY J. CALLENDER & S. HILL BOSTON. The St. Croix River is not named on this map. On the second state of this map the following imprint has been added below the neat line at the lower right corner: "Boston: Published by B. & J. Loring, 1802."

Size 53¹⁄₁₆" x 36⅜". *Scale* 1" = 6 miles.

Published Separately.

Locations Clerk of Courts Office, Ellsworth, Maine, MHi, MWA.

NEW HAMPSHIRE

180 [c. 1784]

Description At upper left: A / TOPOGRAPHICAL MAP / OF THE / STATE OF NEW HAMPSHIRE / SURVEYED UNDER THE DIRECTION / OF / SAMUEL HOLLAND ESQR. The line between Maine and New Hampshire is marked: EAST BOUNDARY LINE BETWEEN THE STATE OF NEW HAMPSHIRE AND MAIN [sic]. Townships and their boundaries are shown. Major roads are given as are a number of land grants and patents. DARTH. COLL. and HANOVER appear. This map is apparently taken from the second state of Samuel Holland's "A Topographical map of the Province of New Hampshire . . . , London, 1784."

Size 21⁷⁄₁₆″ x 15⁵⁄₁₆″.   *Scale* None (1″ = c. 6′ 30″ latitude).

Published Separately.

Reference MSS. list of known maps of New Hampshire to 1800, in Map Room, Dartmouth College, Hanover, New Hampshire.

Location MH.

181 1784 *State* II (I published outside U.S., see below, Description)

Description Across top above neat line: AN ACCURATE MAP OF THE STATE AND PROVINCE OF NEW-HAMPSHIRE IN NEW ENGLAND, TAKEN FROM ACTUAL SURVEYS / OF ALL THE INHABITED PART, AND FROM THE BEST INFORMATION OF WHAT IS UNINHABITED, TOGETHER WITH THE ADJACENT COUNTRIES, WHICH EXHIBITS THE THEATRE OF THIS WAR IN THAT PART OF THE WORLD, BY COL. BLANCHARD, AND THE REVD. MR. LANGDON. Beneath title at center above neat line: ENGRAVED BY THOMAS JEFFERYS, GEOGRAPHER TO HIS MAJESTY. Dedication in elaborate cartouche at center: TO HIS EXCELLENCY / JOHN HANCOCK ESQ. GOV. / AND THE HONOURABLE COUNCIL OF THE / COMMONWEALTH OF THE MASSACHUSETS / AND THE HONOURABLE COUNCIL OF THE / STATE OF NEWHAMPSHIRE / THIS MAP OF THE PROVINCE OF NEW HAMPSHIRE IS HUMBLY INSCRIBED, BY / YOUR MOST OBLIGED & MOST OBEDT. SERVTS. / SAMUEL LANGDON. At lower left in cartouche: BOSTON / 21ST 1784 / WITH MANY ADDITIONS, BY ABEL SAWYER JUNR. This map is one of the rare few printed from a plate originally engraved in England but brought to this country and partially re-engraved here. In the first state the title begins: "An accurate Map of His Majesty's Province of New-Hampshire in New England, taken . . . ," the balance of the title being the same as above. The dedication in the first state reads: "To the Right Honourable / Charles Townshend, / His Majesty's Secretary at War, & / One of His Majesty's most Honourable / Privy Council, &c. / This map . . . Servts. / Joseph Blanchard, / Samuel Langdon." At left in the cartouche: "Portsmouth, / New Hampshire, / 21. Octr. 1761." The notes given in the cartouche at bottom right remain the same in the second state except that an additional sentence has been added in the third paragraph following, "for their churches": BUT NOW A D *1783* THE GREATER PART OF THE NEW TOWNS ARE WELL SETTLED. The first state appeared in Thomas Jefferys' *A General Topography of North America and the West Indies.*

The area actually encompassed by the map extends from Quebec south to Boston and from Montreal and Albany on the west to Penobscot Bay and the Atlantic Coast. Most of the notes, place names, and boundary lines given on the first state have been retained here and many more added. Corrections have been made in a number of places. Counties in Vermont, New Hampshire, and Maine are indicated and many more townships have been added. STATE OF / NEW / HAMPSHIRE is given under the dedication at center.

Size 30″ x 27″.   *Scale* 1″ = 10 miles.

Inset At upper right corner, title across top, within neat lines: A GENERAL MAP OF THE RIVER ST. LAWRENCE ABOVE MONTREAL TO LAKE ONTARIO / WITH THE ADJACENT COUNTRY ON THE WEST FROM ALBANY & LAKE CHAMPLAIN. This remains unchanged from State I. SCHENECTADI is given thus in both states and is given: SCHENECTADA on both states of the main map. Size: 7″ x 7½″. Scale: 1″ = 35 miles.

Published Separately. Reproduced as one of a series published by the U.S. Geological Survey for the U.S. Constitution Sesquicentennial Commission, Washington, D.C., 1938.

References Massachusetts Historical Society, *Proceedings*, 2d Ser., *18*, 232; U.S. Library of Congress, *Report 1915*, p. 86.

Locations CtY, DLC, ICN, MH, MWA, NHi, RPJCB.

182 [1791]

Description [Bellows or Great Falls.] This is a woodcut map showing the Bellows or Great Falls on the Connecticut River. It accompanies, "A Description of the surprising Cataract, in the great River Connecticut" (pp. 253–55).

Size 2¾" x 1¾". *Scale* None (1" = 200 yards).

Published in *American Museum, 9* (1791), 254.

183 1791 *State* I (II post-1799, see below, Description)

Description In oval scroll at upper right: A / NEW MAP / OF / NEW HAMPSHIRE, / BY / JEREMY BELKNAP. / *1791*. Below title, outside scroll: ENGRAV'D BY S. HILL. This is a topographical map showing many details. The boundaries of five counties are given and many portages are indicated but no roads. The LINE OF MASON'S PATENT *1787* is noted; Lake MEMFRIMAGOG is shown mostly in Quebec. The degrees and minutes are indicated on a marginal degree line just inside an outer neat line and they are numbered with figures engraved outside this outer neat line. This map appeared again in the Dover, 1812, and Boston, 1813, editions of Belknap's *History* with *42000* ACRES TO DARTMOUTH COLLEGE, on the northern boundary, changed to "40960" acres.

Size 14⅝" x 10". *Scale* 1" = 12 miles.

Published in Jeremy Belknap, *History of New-Hampshire, 2,* front.

Reference Evans 23166.

184 1793

Description Across top of map below neat line: PLAN OF THE TOWN OF STRATHAM. At bottom center and right: JULY *17*TH. *1793* BY / PHINEHAS MERRILL. This is a detailed map showing the houses with the owners' names, the roads, and also a number of topographical features. The TOWN boundary lines are shown but no property lines or surveys are indicated.

Size 9½" x 7⅜". *Scale* 1" = 200 rods.

Published Separately. Reproduced in Alexander O. Vietor, "Printed Maps," pl. 279 (C).

Location CtY, MiU-C.

185 [1795] *State* I (II post-1799, see below, Published)

Description In rectangle at upper left: THE STATE OF / NEW HAMPSHIRE. / COMPILED CHIEFLY FROM ACTUAL SURVEYS. / BY SAMUEL LEWIS, *1794*. Below scale: SMITHER SCULPT. This is a topographical map indicating primary roads, county boundaries, and towns. At right center: N.B. THE WHITE HILLS APPEAR MANY / LEAGUES OFF AT SEA LIKE WHITE CLOUDS: JUST / RISING ABOVE THE HORIZON. It also shows the HEAD of the SOUHEGON River in a lake close to five hills in Massachusetts. *42000* ACRES / TO DARMOUTH [sic] / COLLEGE appears at the northwest corner.

Size 17¹¹⁄₁₆" x 11⅛". *Scale* 1" = 11 American miles.

Published in Mathew Carey, idem, *Carey's American Atlas,* no. 3; idem, *Carey's General Atlas,* no. 26 (the same map appears in the September, 1800 edition of this *Atlas* with the number "26" added at upper left corner); idem, *The General Atlas for Carey's Edition of Guthrie's Geography Improved,* no. 26.

186 [1795] *State* I (II post-1799, see below, Description)

Description At upper left: NEWHAMPSHIRE. Five counties are shown with their boundaries, as well as main roads and a number of towns. COCHOCHO R. appears for the Cocheco. The ASHUELOT R. is given thus. This map was republished in Scott's *The New and Universal Gazetteer, 4.* This second state has been slightly retouched to compensate for the wear of the plate. It may be identified by the addition of some dots east of the hatchings for the hills in the southwest corner and the same on the easternmost White Hills. Here the road from Charlestown runs south to the marginal degree line, whereas on the first state this road fades out before the degree line is reached.

Size 7½" x 6⅛". *Scale* 1" = 24 miles.

Published in Joseph Scott, *An Atlas of the United States;* idem, *The United States Gazetteer,* opp. "New-Hampshire." Reproduced in Joseph Scott, *Atlas of the United States 1795–1800,* [no. 11].

187 [1796] *State* I (II post-1799, see below, Description)

Description At upper left: THE STATE OF / NEW HAMPSHIRE, / BY SAML. LEWIS. Below scale: ENGRAVED FOR M. CAREY. Below bottom neat line at right: SEYMOUR SCULP. PLUMB I. appears so. This first state has no roads shown and no mountains along the Canadian border line. State II, with these added details, is found in the 1801 edition of the Mathew Carey's *American Pocket Atlas,* opp. p. 20.

Size 7⁹⁄₁₆" x 5¾". *Scale* 1" = 26 American miles.

Published in Mathew Carey, *Carey's American Pocket Atlas,* opp. p. 18.

188 [1796]

Description At upper right: A / MAP OF THE STATES / OF / NEW HAMPSHIRE / AND / VERMONT / BY J. DENISON. Beneath title: DOOLITTLE SCULPT. Above top neat line: ENGRAVED FOR MORSE'S UNIVERSAL GEOGRAPHY: PUBLISHED BY THOMAS & ANDREWS BOSTON. No boundary line is drawn between Maine and New Hampshire. Five counties are shown in New Hampshire and eleven counties in Vermont. DART: COL: appears.

Size 7⅜" x 9⅛".   *Scale* 1" = 25 miles.

Published in Jedidiah Morse, *The American Universal Geography*, 3d ed., *1*, opp. 348.

189 1796

Description In oval at upper left: THE STATE OF / NEW HAMPSHIRE, / COMPILED CHIEFLY FROM / ACTUAL SURVEYS. / *1796*. In oval below title: B. TANNER, SCULPT. Below bottom neat line: PUBLISHED BY JOHN REID, NEW-YORK. This map is copied from Map 185; it also has the note beginning: NB. THE WHITE HILLS APPEAR . . . , and shows the HEAD of the SOUHEGON River in a lake close to five hills. CHARLSTOWN and ASHVELOT appear thus.

Size 17¾₁₆" x 10¹⁵⁄₁₆".   *Scale* 1" = 11 American miles.

Published in John Reid, *The American Atlas*, [1796?], no. 4; ibid., 1796, no. 4; William Winterbotham, [*Atlas*]. Reproduced in U.S. Bureau of the Census, *Heads of Families at the First Census New Hampshire*, front.

190 1799 *State* I (II post-1799, see below, Description)

Description In oval at upper left: THE STATE OF / NEW HAMPSHIRE / COMPILED CHIEFLY FROM / ACTUAL SURVEYS. / *1799*. Above top neat line: ENGRAVED FOR PAYNES GEOGRAPHY. Below bottom neat line at left: A. ANDERSON DEL. At right: C. TIEBOUT SC. This is a topographical map. CHARLSTOWN [sic] and the HEIGHT OF LAND north of the Connecticut River are noted. A later state appeared in 1810 with the following notation: "Engrav'd for the New Encyclopedia. Pubd. by E. Low, N. Y." There is a separate copy of this second state in the Library of Congress.

Size 11⁹⁄₁₆" x 7⁵⁄₁₆".   *Scale* 1" = 17 miles.

Published in John Payne, *A New and Complete Universal Geography*, *4*, opp. 229.

191 [1763]

Description [Plan of ye Town of Pownall.] The title is taken from Dunlap in his biographical note on the engraver Thomas Johnston. He gives the date "1763" for the map.

Size Unknown. *Scale* Unknown.

Published Separately.

Reference William Dunlap, *A History of the Arts of Design, 3,* 312.

Location No copy located.

1784   see Map 181.

192 1789 *State* I (see also Map 193)

Description Under decorated arms of Vermont at lower right: A / TOPOGRAPHICAL MAP / OF THE / STATE OF VERMONT, / FROM ACTUAL SURVEY. / MOST HUMBLY DEDICATED / TO HIS EXCELLENCY THOMAS CHITTENDEN ESQR. GOVERNOR / AND COMMANDER IN CHIEF; / THE HONORABLE THE COUNCIL, / AND THE / HONORABLE THE REPRESENTATIVES OF SAID STATE; / BY THEIR / MOST OBEDIENT AND DEVOTED HUMBLE SERVANT / WILLIAM BLODGET. Below title: BENNINGTON STATE OF VERMONT. JANY 1ST. 1789. Under line below title: NEW HAVEN: / ENGRAV'D AND PRINTED FOR WILLIAM BLODGET, BY / AMOS DOOLITTLE AT HIS HOUSE IN COLLEGE-STREET / 1789. This is a large, detailed map showing county and township boundaries, roads, and many place names. Above the scale at right center is a table explaining ten conventional signs used in the map. Contested lines are especially marked. The following appeared in the (New York) *Daily Advertiser,* March 5, 1789, and issues following: "This day is published a new map of the State of Vermont from actual survey . . . Dedicated to . . . Thomas Chittenden . . . By William Blodgett [sic] . . . Very elegantly executed by an American artist."

Size 38" x 29⅞".   *Scale* 1" = 4⅓ miles.

Published Separately.

References Evans 21696; Phillis Kihn, "William Blodget, Map Maker," pp. 42–43.

Location MHi.

193 1789[?] *State* II (see also Map 192)

Description A number of additions have been made to the map. The words: CHARLESTON / FOMERLY [sic] NO. 4, have been inserted opposite the boundary between Springfield and Rockingham. The town names: SKEENSROR'O and HAMPTON are given in the portion of New York adjacent to Rutland County, and the name: CORNWELL in the town west of Middlebury. To the right of CORNWELL is: ESQR / TALMIENS', a symbol for a meeting house, and a road extends from this building into Shoreham Township. The parallel of 45° North Latitude has now been extended from the eastern shore of Lake Champlain to the inner neat line. The word SWAMP is introduced in Cornwell Township.

Published Separately.

Reference U.S. Library of Congress, *Report 1940,* p. 127.

Location BM, CtHi, MWA.

194 1793

Description In decorated oval at lower right: A / MAP / OF THE / STATE / OF / VERMONT / BY / J. WHITELAW / 1793. Beneath oval: CALLENDER SCP. BOSTON. The counties and their boundaries are given but the townships are indicated by name only. No roads are shown; CAVENDISH AND SWANTON appear thus. According to Evans, this map "was also sold separately at Anthony Haswell's Printing Office in Bennington."

Size 13⅞" x 10⅛".   *Scale* 1" = 12½ miles.

Published in Samuel Williams, *The Natural and Civil History of Vermont,* front.; separately.

References Evans 26478 and 28094.

195 [1795] *State* I (II & III post-1799, see below, *Description*)

Description In cartouche at lower right: VERMONT / FROM ACTUAL SURVEY. In cartouche below title: DELINEATED & ENGRAVED BY AMOS DOOLITTLE N.H. Above top neat line: ENGRAVED FOR CAREY'S AMERICAN EDITION OF GUTHRIE'S GEOGRAPHY IMPROVED. Vermont is shown divided into seven counties and the townships are also shown and named. The following appear thus: SEXTONS R, SLOWE, WETHERSFIELD, ST ALBIONS, BRATTEBORO', and FAIRLLEE. Carey advertised a map of Vermont for sale in the (Philadelphia) *Gazette the United States,* May 8, 1794; no copy has thus far been located although it may have been a prior separate publication of this map. The second state was used in the September, 1800 edition of *Carey's General Atlas* with the figure "25" added at the upper right corner. In State III the Carey imprint has been erased and an extra neat line added outside the heavy line, thus making a three-part neat line. Much of the lake shore and many of the hills have been re-engraved.

Size 14⅝" x 11⅞".   *Scale* 1" = 10½ miles.

Published in Mathew Carey, *Carey's American Atlas,* no. 4; idem, *Carey's General Atlas,* no. 256; idem. *The General Atlas for Carey's Edition of Guthrie's Geography Improved,* no. 25.

196 [1795]   *State* I (II post-1799, see below, Description)

Description   At lower right: STATE / OF / VERMONT / DRAWN AND ENGRAVED. County boundaries, primary settlements, roads, and some topographical features are noted. VERMONT is engraved in old English letters in the title. The line between Orange and Chittenden counties does not cross the Black River. The second state appeared in Scott, *The New and Universal Gazetteer, 4,* with the words "drawn and engraved" removed from the title. The central parts of Lake Champlain, filled with parallel hatching lines in State I, are unshaded in the later State.

Size 7½" x 6⁹⁄₁₆".   *Scale* 1" = 22 miles.

Published in Joseph Scott, *An Atlas of the United States;* idem, *The United States Gazetteer,* opp. "Vermont." Reproduced in Joseph Scott, *Atlas of the United States 1795–1800,* [no. 19].

197 [1796]   *State* I (II post-1799, see below, Description)

Description   In lower right: VERMONT, / FROM ACTUAL SURVEY. Below bottom neat line at right: SEYMOUR SC. Below scale: ENGRAVED FOR M. CAREY. The counties are outlined but not named; most of the township names appear but they are not outlined. This map was republished in the 1801 edition of Carey's *American Pocket Atlas* with additions and corrections. In the first state the 2° LONG at the top appears over the first "A" in Canada and the 3° between the second "A" and the "D." This is corrected in State II so the 2° comes between the first "A" and the "N" and the 3° over the "D." No wagon roads are shown on State I and no east and west county divisions

north of Charlotte on the west side and Thetford on the east. No lakes are shown east of Lake Memphramagog and no hills indicated north of the Canada border.

Size 7⁹⁄₁₆" x 5¾".   *Scale* 1" = 24 American miles.

Published in Mathew Carey, *Carey's American Pocket Atlas,* opp. p. 13.

198 [1796]   *State* I (see also Map 199)

Description   In oval at lower right: VERMONT / FROM THE LATEST / AUTHORITIES. In oval beneath title: PUBLISHED BY J. REID NEW YORK. Below oval: ROBERTS SC. This map is copied from Map 195, and shows the State divided into seven counties and then into townships. The Ottauquechee River is shown as the WATERGUECHEC R.

Size 16⅝" x 13½".   *Scale* 1" = 10 miles.

Published in John Reid, *The American Atlas,* [1796?], no. 7; ibid., 1796, no. 7; William Winterbotham, [*Atlas*]. Reproduced in Vermont, Secretary of State, *State Papers of Vermont, 1,* attached to front end paper.

199 1796   *State* II (see also Map 198)

Description   The date *1796* has been added below AUTHORITIES in oval at lower right. No original copy of this map with this date added has thus far been discovered. It may have been added at the time of the preparation of the facsimile noted below.

Published   Separately (?). Reproduced in U.S. Bureau of the Census, *Heads of Families at the First Census Vermont,* front.

200 1796   *State* I (II post-1799, see below, Description)

Description   Surrounded by rural view at lower right corner: A CORRECT MAP / OF THE / STATE OF VERMONT / FROM ACTUAL SURVEY; / EXHIBITING THE COUNTY AND TOWN LINES, RIVERS, LAKES, PONDS, / MOUNTAINS, MEETINGHOUSES, MILLS, PUBLIC ROADS. &C. / BY / JAMES WHITELAW ESQR: SURVEYOR GENERAL. / *1796* / WITH PRIVILEGE OF COPY RIGHT. Beneath view at lower right: ENGRAVED BY AMOS DOOLITTLE NEW HAVEN *1796.* This was issued as an official map of the State with the cartographer retaining copyright privileges. Considerable detail is shown including the dates of most of the grants of the townships. A table showing the sixteen conventional characters used is given above the scale. Below the scale and just above the cartouche at the lower right is a NOTE giving information concerning the sources of the data incorporated into the map. It was republished a number of times during the next century: in 1810, 1821, 1838, and 1851. The copy dated September, 1810, contained plate changes engraved by James Wilson. The following broadside was issued prior to publication: *Proposals for Publishing by Subscription a Correct Map of the State of Vermont*, Ryegate, Vermont, October 27, 1795, with a list of subscribers. Two editions of the *Proposals* exist; the text is the same in both.

Size 44¾" x 30¼".   *Scale* 1" = 4 miles.

Published Separately.

References Evans 29887 and 31626; Marcus A. McCorison, *Vermont Imprints*, nos. 368, 417, and 1238.

Locations BM, CtY, DLC, MH, MHi, MWA, NhD, VtHi, VtU.

[1796] see Map 188.

201 1799

Description In oval at lower right: VERMONT / FROM THE LATEST / AUTHORITIES / *1799*. Below bottom neat line at center: ENGRAVED FOR PAYNE'S UNIVERSAL GEOGRAPHY, PUBLISHED BY J. LOW, NEW YORK. At lower right corner: TIEBOUT SCULP. At lower left corner: A. ANDERSON DEL. The map shows county and township boundaries. BENNINTON / COUNTY, and FISH BLADDER / I. in Lake Champlain appear so. Topographical features are shown. This map is very similar to those in John Reid's *American Atlas* and the Carey atlases.

Size 9¹⁄₁₆" x 7⁷⁄₁₆".   *Scale* 1" = 18 miles.

Published in John Payne, *A New and Complete Universal Geography*, 4, opp. 229.

MASSACHUSETTS

202 [1775] *State* I (see also Maps 203 and 204)

Description An impression of this state of the ". . . Map of the Seat of Civil War . . . ," once owned by Mr. Isaac N. P. Stokes, differs slightly from the second state now in the Stokes Collection at the New York Public Library. Notes concerning the differences were lost.

Size Unknown.   *Scale* Unknown.

Published Separately.

Reference Isaac N. P. Stokes and Daniel C. Haskell, *American Historical Prints*, p. 48.

Location No copy located.

203 [1775] *State* II (see also Maps 202 and 204)

Description Below bottom neat line at left: TO THE HONE. JNO. HANCOCK ESQRE, PRESIDENT OF YE CONTINENTAL CONGRESS, / THIS MAP OF THE SEAT OF CIVIL WAR IN AMERICA, IS RESPECTFULLY INSCRIBED / BY HIS MOST OBEDIENT HUMBLE SERV-ANT B: ROMANS. This map shows principal settle-ments, roads, some topographical features, and the political boundary lines. Above the top neat line are twenty-five lettered references to the main map and an asterisk reference to BUNKERS HILL. It was advertised in the (Philadelphia) *Pennsylvania Gazette*, August 23, 1775: "Boston. Romans's Maps . . . This Map of Boston, &c. is one of the most correct that has ever been pub-lished. The draught was taken by the most skill-ful draughtsman in all America, and who was on the spot at the engagements of *Lexington* and *Bunker's Hill* . . . They may be had im-mediately, of *Nicholas Brooks*, who is the printer of said Map . . . Price plain, *Five Shill-ings*—coloured, *Six Shillings* and *Six Pence* . . ."

Size 15⅞" x 17¹¹⁄₁₆".   *Scale* (on left mar-ginal line) 1" = 5 miles.

Insets [a] At upper right: PLAN OF / BOSTON / AND ITS / ENVIRONS / 1775. There are twelve numbered REFERENCES in the lower left corner of this inset. Size: 3½" x 2⅞". Scale: 1" = 2 miles.
[b] View under bottom neat line at right: A VIEW OF THE LINES THROWN UP, ON BOSTON NECK: BY THE MINISTERIAL ARMY. There is a list of

seven numbered REFERENCES to the view at the left. Size: ⅞" x 7⅜".

Published Separately.

References Evans 14444 (gives Robert Ait-ken as the printer); Samuel A. Green, *Ten Fac-simile Reproductions Relating to Various Sub-jects*, pp. 29–30; Philip L. Phillips, *Notes on Bernard Romans*, pp. 81–82; Isaac N. P. Stokes and Daniel C. Haskell, *American Historical Prints*, p. 48 (refers to two states).

Locations DLC, MHi, MiU-C, NHi, NN, PHi (2), PPL, RPJCB.

204 [1775] *State* III (see also Maps 202 and 203)

Description Symbols used in indicating: POST ROADS, ROADS NOT POST ROADS, COUNTY ROADS, TOWNSHIP LINES, and PROVINCE LINES have been engraved in margin outside right neat line.

Published Separately.

Locations CtY, PPL, RPJCB.

205 [1776?]

Description In circle at upper right corner: A MAP OF / FORTY MILES NORTH THIRTY MILES / WEST AND TWENTY FIVE MILES SOUTH / OF / BOS-TON / INCLUDING AN ACCURATE DRAFT OF / THE HARBOUR AND / TOWN. There are 32 numbered REFERENCES explained in a type set tabulation printed on the same sheet below the engraved map. References to the main map are given at the left. PUTNAMS CAMP is inscribed at BUNKERS HILL. The roads from Charleston to Lexington, to Concord, and back to Cambridge are the only ones shown on the map. The map ap-parently dates from immediately after the Bunker Hill, Lexington, and Concord actions from the showing of those points on the map. Longitude is shown from London. The ap-pearance of the map is very American.

Size 11⅝" x 16¹¹⁄₁₆".   *Scale* None (1" = c. 2⅔ miles).

Inset At lower right: BOSTON TOWN. There are 24 lettered REFERENCES to streets and build-ings on the inset map which are explained be-low the inset. Soundings are also indicated. Size: 5⅜" x 4⅛" (over scroll enclosed title). Scale: None (1" = c. ⅕ mile).

45

BIBLIOGRAPHY OF MAPS AND CHARTS

Published Separately.

Location RPJCB.

206 1789

Description In oval at upper left: CHART / OF THE / COAST OF AMERICA / FROM / CAPE COD / TO / CAPE ELIZABETH / FROM THE LATEST SURVEYS. Below oval: PRINTED FOR & SOLD BY MATTW. CLARK BOSTON OCTR. *1789*. In extreme upper left corner: NO. 6. The chart bears an engraved inscription (which was signed by Osgood Carleton when the chart was sold singly) stating that it was examined and compared with HOLAND'S / AND DES BARR'S, etc., and found accurate. There are five profiles at upper right: AGAMANTICUS HILL (three different views), BONABEAG HILLS, and CAPE ANN. In the Library of Congress copy of Clark's [*Chart*], charts nos. 5 and 6 are pasted together.

Size 17″ x 23¾″.   *Scale* 1″ = 1.9 nautic leagues.

Insets [a] At lower right [Boston Harbor]. The top neat line is broken by: CASHES / LEDGE. Soundings are given. Size: 6″ x 8″. Scale: 1″ = 2 miles.
[b] Below [a], [Coast from Nahant Point to Cape Ann]. Scale is also given here for insets [a], [b], and [c]. Soundings indicated. Size: 2⅞″ x 12¼″. Scale: 1″ = 2 miles.
[c] At right of [a]: PORTSMOUTH / HAR. Size: 2⅛″ x 4¼″. Scale: 1″ = 2 miles.
[d] Below [c]: NEWBURY HAR. Scale is given here for insets [d] and [e]. Size: 2⅛″ x 4¼″. Scale: 1″ = 0.8 miles.
[e] Below [d]: IPSWICH HAR. Size: 2⅛″ x 4¼″. Scale: 1″ = 0.8 miles.

Published in Matthew Clark, [*A Complete Chart*], no. 6.

207 1789

Description In oval at upper left: CHART / OF THE / COAST OF AMERICA / FROM / GEORGE'S BANK TO RHODE ISLAND / INCLUDING / NANTUCKET SHOALS &C / FROM THE LATEST SURVEYS. Below oval: J. NORMAN SC. / PRINTED FOR & SOLD BY MATTHEW CLARK BOSTON OCTR *1789*. At upper right corner: NO. 7. The chart bears an engraved inscription (which was signed by Osgood Carleton when the chart was sold singly) stating that it was examined and compared with DES BARR'S, etc., and found accurate. On this map there is another note given just below the title: THIS IS A TRUE AND ACCURATE / CHART OF NANTUCKET / SHOALS. There are five horizontal silhouettes shown across the top of the chart: SANCOTY HEAD on Nantucket Island, SANDY POINT, CAPE POGE on Martha's Vineyard, GAY HEAD, and CAPE COD.

In the Library of Congress copy of Clark's [*Chart*] this and Map 330 are pasted together.

Size 16⅜″ x 24⅝″.   *Scale* 1″ = 1.9 nautic leagues.

Inset At lower right: PLYMOUTH BAY. Soundings are given. Size: 4⅜″ x 4⅝″. Scale: Unfinished (1″ = c. 2½ nautic miles).

Published in Matthew Clark, [*A Complete Chart*], no. 7.

208 [1789]

Description In tablet at upper left: A MAP / OF THE / SEAT OF THE LATE WAR / AT BOSTON / IN THE / STATE OF MASSACHUSETTS. This is a well executed map showing roads, towns, and streams. Mileages from BOSTON and CHARLES TOWN are indicated along the roads to WORCESTER. Stauffer states that it was engraved by James Trenchard.

Size 6¾″ x 10⅛″.   *Scale* None (1″ = c. 6 miles).

Published in *Columbian Magazine, 3* (Philadelphia, 1789), opp. 385.

Reference David M. Stauffer, *American Engravers, 2,* 542.

209 [1791]

Description At upper right: A MAP OF CAPE COD, / AND THE PARTS ADJACENT. Above top neat line at extreme right: MASSA. MAG. The area shown includes CAPE / ANNE on the north to NANTUKKET I. on the south. Narragansett Bay is included at the left. The shoreline is given in outline only, very few land features being shown. The map accompanies a letter describing a proposal for a canal from Barnstable Bay to Buzzards Bay at Sandwich (see pp. 25–27).

Size 12⅝″ x 10⅝″.   *Scale* None (1″ = c. 9 miles).

Published in *Massachusetts Magazine, 3* (Boston, 1791), opp. 25.

210 1791 *State* I (see also Map 221; III post-1799, see Map 221, Description)

Description Lower left: A CHART / OF / NANTUCKET SHOALS / SURVEYED BY / CAPT. PAUL PINKHAM. / Below title: BOSTON / PUBLISHED & SOLD BY JOHN NORMAN NO. 75 NEWBURY STREET FEB. *16*TH. *1791* / ACCORDING TO ACT OF CONGRESS. PRICE ONE DOLLAR. In the upper left are two certificates, one by nine pilots and navigators, the other by PELEG GOFFIN JUNR. Both are dated SEPR. *1*ST. *1790*. Ship channels are indicated by dotted lines.

46

Size 19¹⁵⁄₁₆″ x 30⅝″. *Scale* 1″ = 2½ miles.

Published in John Norman, *The American Pilot,* 1792, no. 1; William Norman, *The American Pilot,* 1794, no. 1.

211 [1793]

Description In scroll at lower right corner: A MAP / OF THE COUNTY / OF / WORCESTER, / BY / CHARLES BAKER ESQR & / CAPN. JOHN PEIRCE OF SAID / COUNTY. Below scroll: SEYMOUR SC. This is a political map of the County giving the townships and their boundaries. Ponds and rivers are indicated and also the: COUNTRY ROAD, OR POST ROAD, but no towns or settlements are located. The engraver was probably Joseph H. Seymour. STATE OF RHOAD ISLAND is given thus at the left.

Size 14¹⁄₁₆″ x 12¼″. *Scale* 1″ = 4 miles.

Published in Peter Whitney, *The History of the County of Worcester,* front.

Reference Evans 26481.

212 [1794?]

Description [Map of the Colony of Plymouth.] The volume containing this map was being readied for publication in 1794.

Size Unknown. *Scale* Unknown.

Published in Peres Fobes, *A History of the Ancient Colony of Plymouth.*

Reference Massachusetts Historical Society, *Collections,* 1st Ser., *3* (1794); reprinted, 1810, p. 176.

Location No copy located.

213 [1795] *State* I (II post-1799, see below, Description)

Description In lower left corner: THE STATE OF / MASSACHUSETTS. / COMPILED FROM THE BEST AUTHORITIES / BY SAMUEL LEWIS. Above top neat line: ENGRAVED FOR CAREY'S AMERICAN EDITION OF GUTHRIES GEOGRAPHY IMPROVED BY J T. SCOTT. This map shows the hills, streams, county boundaries, main roads, and towns. Errors have been corrected in ALMSBURY, MARSHFIELD PT., and PROVINCE T. Norfolk County is not shown. The same map appears in the September, 1800 edition of *Carey's General Atlas* with the number "28" added at upper right corner.

Size 14⅛″ x 18½″. *Scale* 1″ = 11 American miles.

Published in Mathew Carey, *Carey's American Atlas,* no. 5; idem, *Carey's General Atlas,* no. 28; idem, *The General Atlas for Carey's Edition of Guthrie's Geography Improved,* no. 28.

214 [1795]

Description In elaborate cartouche at lower left: AN ACCURATE / MAP / OF / THE COMMONWEALTH OF / MASSACHUSETTS / EXCLUSIVE OF THE DISTRICT OF MAINE / COMPILED PURSUANT TO AN ACT OF THE GENERAL COURT / FROM ACTUAL SURVEYS OF THE SEVERAL TOWNS, &C. TAKEN BY THEIR ORDER . . . BY OSGOOD CARLETON. In cartouche below line: BOSTON / PUBLISHED AND SOLD BY O CARLETON AND I NORMAN / SOLD ALSO BY W NORMAN NO 75 NEWBURY STREET. This is a detailed political and topographic map showing counties, townships, roads, rivers, and many other features. An EXPLANATION of symbols is given at lower center. The outer neat line is broken through at right center. At the lower left corner: NB: AS THE SURVEYS OF SOME TOWNS WERE NOT SO FULL AS OTHERS THE ROADS AND STREAMS OF THOSE TOWNS HAVE BEEN UNAVOIDABLY DISCONTINUED. The watermark of the William L. Clements Library copy is dated "1794." This map is similar to that by Osgood Carlton which Evans dates [1795] (see Map 170).

Size 34½″ x 46½″. *Scale* 1″ = c. 4 miles.

Published Separately.

References Maine Historical Society, *Collections,* 7 (1879), 17; Jedidiah Morse, *The American Universal Geography,* p. 393; *New England Historical and Genealogical Register,* 55 (1901), 54; David M. Stauffer, *American Engravers,* 2, 51; U.S. Library of Congress, *Report 1906,* p. 46.

Location BM, MiU-C, PPL.

215 [1795]

Description [A New Map of that Part of Massachusetts State, which includes the Proposed Canal, from Connecticut River, to the Waters that surround the Town of Boston. Boston, 1795.]

Size Unknown. *Scale* Unknown.

Published Separately.

Reference Evans 29183.

Location No copy located.

216 [1795] *State* I (II post-1799, see below, Description)

Description At lower left: MASSACHUSETTS. Counties are shown but the boundaries between Berkshire and Hampshire, and between Norfolk and Suffolk are omitted. CHICKOBEE R. appears for Chicopee and SPRINGFIELD instead of West Springfield. This map was reissued for Scott's *The New and Universal Gazetteer,* 3. The second state has been retouched very little, but may be identified by the course of the road from Springfield; in the 1800 issue it runs directly to Boston while in this first state it goes from Springfield to Charlestown.

Size 6″ x 7¼″.   *Scale* 1″ = 30 miles.

Published in Joseph Scott, *An Atlas of the United States*, no. 5; idem, *The United States Gazetteer*, opp. "Massachusetts." Reproduced in Joseph Scott, *Atlas of the United States 1795–1800*, [no. 10].

217 [1796] *State* I (II post-1799, see below, Description)

Description At lower left: MASSACHUSETTS. Below bottom neat line at right: W. BARKER SCULP. PLUMB I and CAPE CODD / BAY appear thus. This map was republished in the 1801 edition of *Carey's American Pocket Atlas* with some additions to the plate. State I has no roads shown north or west of Springfield except those extending northwest and southwest from Concord. No roads are shown through Haverhill and Groton, or to Gloucester. No dotted division lines are shown.

Size 5¹³⁄₁₆″ x 7⁹⁄₁₆″.   *Scale* 1″ = 27 miles.

Published in Mathew Carey, *Carey's American Pocket Atlas*, opp. p. 27.

218 [1796]

Description In oval at upper right: A MAP OF / MASSACHUSETTS, / FROM THE BEST AUTHORITIES / BY / J. DENISON. In oval below title: S. H. SC. Above top neat line: PUBLISHED BY THOMAS & ANDREWS, BOSTON. This note appears beneath the scale at right: THE SURVEY'S OF THE EASTERN / COUNTIES, COULD NOT BE / OBTAINED SEASONABLY TO / COMPTETE [sic] THIS MAP. Plymouth, Bristol, and Barnstable counties are left practically blank. The PROPOSED CANAL is indicated near SANDWICH. The map was engraved by Samuel Hill.

Size 7⅜″ x 9¹³⁄₁₆″.   *Scale* 1″ = 16 miles.

Inset At lower left: BERKSHIRE, & HAMPSHIRE / COUNTIES CONTINUED. Size: 3⅛″ x 2″. Scale: 1″ = 16 miles.

Published in Jedidiah Morse, *The American Universal Geography*, 3d ed., *1*, opp. 393.

219 1796

Description In oval at lower left: THE STATE OF / MASSACHUSETTS / FROM THE BEST INFORMATION / 1796. Below bottom neat line: PUBLISH'D BY J. REID NEW YORK. WEST SPANGFIELD is given for Springfield; BELERICA for Billerica; METHAM for Methuen; CHICKOPEE R. for the Chicopee. This map appears to be copied from Map 213.

Size 14½″ x 17¹¹⁄₁₆″.   *Scale* 1″ = 10½ American miles.

Published in John Reid, *The American Atlas*, [1796?], no. 6; ibid., 1796, no. 6; William Winterbotham, [*Atlas*]. Reproduced in U.S. Bureau of the Census, *Heads of Families at the First Census Massachusetts*, front.

220 1797

Description In cartouche near upper center: A / CHART / OF / GEORGE'S BANK, / INCLUDING / CAPE COD, NANTUCKET AND THE SHOALS LYING ON THEIR COAST, / WITH DIRECTIONS FOR SAILING OVER THE SAME &C. / SURVEYED BY / CAPT: PAUL PINKHAM. In cartouche below title: ENGRAV'D BY AMOS DOOLITTLE NEWHAVEN / 1797. In lower right corner: ENGRAV'D & PRINTED FOR / EDMUND M. BLUNT / PROPRIETOR OF / AMERICAN COAST PILOT / 1797. This is a very detailed chart with many small navigational notes. At the far right there is a long explanation TO THE PUBLIC which describes the area in detail. A CERTIFICATE, signed by six captains and testifying to the accuracy of the chart, is given at the lower right. Phillips (see References) indicates New Haven as the place of publication. Blunt was in business in Newburyport in 1797.

Size 24¼″ x 32¹³⁄₁₆″.   *Scale* 1″ = 2 leagues.

Published Separately.

References Evans 32693; Philip L. Phillips, *A List of Maps of America*, p. 758.

Locations DLC, MWA.

221 1798 *State* II (see also Map 210; III post-1799, see below, Description)

Description John Norman has been changed to: WM NORMAN in the imprint beneath the title. The outlines of Nantucket Island and Martha's Vineyard have been recut and the names of these islands and part of the title of the chart have been emphasized by shading. This chart was republished in William Norman's *American Pilot*, 1803, with "Wm. Norman" changed yet again to "J. Norman."

Published in William Norman, *The American Pilot*, 1798, no. 1.

222 1799

Description In oval at lower left: THE STATE OF / MASSACHUSETTS / FROM THE BEST INFORMATION. / 1799. Below bottom neat line at left: ANDERSON DEL. At center: ENGRAVED FOR PAYNE'S GEOGRAPHY. PUBLISHED BY I. LOW, NEW-YORK. At right: TIEBOUT SC. Some topographical features are shown as well as roads, county names, and boundaries. The Berkshire County boundary is not shown and Norfolk County is not shown at all. Provincetown is on an island. This is a reduced copy of Map 219. MALDER is still spelled with an "r" but "Saltsbury" has been corrected to SALISBURY.

Size 7⁷⁄₁₆" x 9⁵⁄₁₆".   *Scale* 1" = 20 American miles.

Published in John Payne, *A New and Complete Universal Geography*, 4 (1799), opp. 235.

223 [Before 1800?]

Description At lower left: A / NEW MAP / OF

THE / STATE OF MASSACHUSETTS / FROM THE / ORIGINAL MAP COMPILED / BY / OSGOOD CARLETON ESQR. / FROM THE ACTUAL SURVEYS THAT WERE MADE AGREABLE TO AN ACT OF THE GENERAL COURT. Below title: BOSTON PUBLISHED & SOLD BY I. NORMAN ENGRAVER. This is copied from Map 214 with some detail omitted. The southwestern corner of the state breaks thru the marginal degree line at left center. Two plates are used. POWNAL and WHITTINGHAM are given thus.

Size 17½" x 26⅜".   *Scale* None (1" = c. 7 miles).

Published Separately.

Location PHi.

49

BOSTON

224 1722 *State* I (see also Maps 225–26 and 228–34)

Description In upper right corner: THE TOWN OF / BOSTON / IN / NEW ENGLAND / BY / JOHN BONNER / 1722. Below bottom neat line: ENGRAVEN AND PRINTED BY FRA. DEWING. BOSTON NE. 1722. This is well known as the earliest and most important engraved plan of Boston. The plate was added to and the map republished again and again (at least nine times) over a period of 47 years. After that it continued to live as the basis for other maps of Boston until Osgood Carleton's survey was published in 1796 and 1797. The practice of reissuing this map with the addition of statistical dates, new streets, docks, buildings, etc., has been of invaluable assistance to historians. The Phelps Stokes collection in the New York Public Library contains the only known impression of the earliest recorded state of this map; it is probably the only known state that may be ascribed to the year 1722 as in this one alone there is no reference to William Price. Price is not mentioned among the sellers in the advertisement of May 14, 1722, in the *Boston News-Letter*. On this impression, the scale and tables of statistics at lower left have been added in manuscript. On the later states they appear engraved in the hand of Francis Dewing. The MSS population note gives "15000" instead of "12000" as later engraved.

Size 16¹³⁄₁₆″ x 23¼″.   *Scale* None (1″ = c. 469 feet).

Published Separately. Reproduced in Isaac N. P. Stokes and Daniel C. Haskell, *American Historical Prints*, opp. p. 26; Walter M. Whitehill, *Boston A Topographical History*, p. 23.

References George F. Dow, *The Arts & Crafts in New England, 1704–1775*, p. 27; Nathaniel B. Shurtleff, *A Topographical and Historical Description*, p. 92; Isaac N. P. Stokes, *Iconography of Manhattan Island, 1*, 254; ibid., *4*, 975; see also reproductions above, under Published.

Location NN.

225 [c. 1725] *State* II (see also Maps 224, 226, and 228–34)

Description The author's name has been embellished with scrolls. Below bottom neat line at right has been added: SOLD BY CAPT JOHN BONNER AND WILLM. PRICE AGAINST YE TOWN HOUSE WHERE MAY BE HAD ALL SORTS OF PRINTS, MAPPS, &C. Between a new scale and reference table at lower left has also been added: BOSTON, N. ED / PLANTED AN. DOM. 1630. A second neat line has been drawn inside the original on the left side. The fortification and the nearby inn have been erased and re-engraved so they now appear similarly inside the new neat line. A covered gateway is shown in the wall and it is marked: FORTIFICATION. The shore line of Boston Neck now extends past the fortification wall to the inner neat line. "Dorchester Flatts" has been erased, and in the lower left corner a new SCALE OF ½ A MILE appears above the new Boston imprint given above along with four columns containing eleven (upper case) lettered references to churches, eight (lower case) lettered references to public buildings, dates of 8 GREAT FIRES, and dates of 6 GENLL SMALL POX epidemics. DAVIES L is now shown and named toward present Louisbourg Square; Margaret Lane now appears but without name. Three lanes: Gray's, Tilley's, and Gridley's, that were shown on the earlier state are now named. Two sloops, one rowboat, and a canoe are now engraved in the Charles River. HUDSON'S POINT and 23 names of wharfs have been added. The Ayer Collection in the Newberry Library contains a unique example of this state. The earliest advertisement of the map by William Price seems to be April 26, 1725, in the *Boston Gazette,* and it may be inferred that his name was added to the plate about that time.

Published Separately.

Reference Justin Winsor, *Memorial History of Boston, 2*.

Location ICN.

226 [c. 1725] *State* III (see also Maps 224–25 and 228–34)

Description The title CAPT has been added before the author's name and AETATIS SUAE 80 below the date. These additions to the title in honor of the aging Capt. Bonner seem to have been added during the last half of 1725 or the first month of 1726. The Price imprint was probably added when he began to advertise the map in April, 1725. Capt. Bonner died January

30, 1725/26. The Massachusetts Historical Society possesses the only known impression of this state. When this impression belonged to Mr. William Taylor in 1835, it was re-engraved and published by George G. Smith and its correctness certified by Stephen P. Fuller. This copy has often been mistaken as an original but may be recognized by the error in Capt. Bonner's age which read "AEtatis Suae 6o," even if the Fuller and Smith imprints have been removed. The advertisement "where may be had all Sorts of Prints, Mapps, &c," is omitted from the copy. This Smith copy is reproduced in Arthur Gilman's *The Story of Boston*, opp. p. 187. Sections from this reproduction are reproduced and discussed in Justin Winsor's *Memorial History of Boston*.

Published Separately. Reproduced in Massachusetts Historical Society, *Prints, Maps and Drawings 1677–1822*, no. 4; see also above, Description.

Location MHi.

227 [1728]

Description In oval at lower left center with large supporting figures and surmounted by governor's arms is this dedication: TO / HIS EXCELLENCY / WILLIAM BURNET ESQR. / THIS PLAN OF / BOSTON IN NEW ENGLAND / IS HUMBLY DEDICATED / BY HIS EXCELLENCYS / MOST OBEDIENT AND / HUMBLE SERVANT / WILL BURGISS. In cartouche below figures: BOSTON N ENGD. PLANTED AD. MDCXXX. In lower right corner: ENGRAVEN BY THOS IOHNSON BOSTON / N. E. The date 1728 is assigned by Winsor and Shurtleff because Burnet was actively governor only that year and nothing indicating a later date is shown on the map. Reference tables to twelve churches, eight other public buildings, and the dates of eight great fires are given. The boundary lines of eight companies are marked; ROXBURY FLATS is inscribed on both sides of the Neck; a pond is shown on the Common; the garden on the line of present Beacon Street is named BANISTERS / GARDENS; and Winter Street is shown WINER.

Size 10¼" x 14¼". *Scale* 1" = 5½ miles.

Published Separately. Reproduced in Nathaniel B. Shurtleff, *A Topographical and Historical Description*, A. Williams and Co., 1871, opp. p. 32; ibid., by Request of the City Council, 1871, opp. p. 22; Walter M. Whitehill, *Boston A Topographical History*, p. 25; the Boston Athenaeum published a collotype facsimile (prepared by The Meriden Gravure Co.) in 1951.

References Massachusetts Historical Society, *Proceedings* (1st. Ser.), *6* (1862–63), 37; Nathaniel B. Shurtleff, *List of the Printed Maps of Boston*, pp. 3–4; Justin Winsor, *Memorial History of Boston*, 2; see also reproductions above, under Published.

Locations DLC, MBAt, NNMM (Halsey Collection).

228 1732 *State* IV (see also Maps 224–26 and 229–34)

Description The old title has been completely removed and an entirely new one re-engraved below the upper neat line at left: A NEW PLAN OF YE GREAT TOWN OF BOSTON IN NEW ENGLAND IN AMERICA / WITH THE MANY ADDITIONALL BUILDINGS & NEW STREETS, TO THE YEAR, *1732*. In an ornate cartouche at upper left now appears a dedication to Governor Jonathan Belcher signed: WILLIAM PRICE, and beneath Price's name in the cartouche: T. JOHNSON SCULP. Below this cartouche now appears a long advertisement: PRINTED FOR & SOLD BY WM PRICE AT YE KINGS HEAD & LOOKING GLASS, IN / CORNHILL, NEAR THE TOWN HOUSE IN BOSTON, WHERE IS SOLD . . . BY WHOLESALE OR / RETAIL AT REASONABLE RATES. The whole appearance of this map has been changed as the old title and Bonner's name have been erased from the plate. The bottom imprint with Dewing's signature, the original date, and the joint advertisement of Bonner and Price has been covered with a heavy outer neat line which has been added all around the map, a short distance outside the old neat line at top, bottom, and right. The inner neat line has been moved out about ⅜" on the left side. The following note has been added below the title at right of cartouche: BOSTON THE METROPOLIS OF NEW ENGLAND . . . THIS TOWN HATH BEEN SETTLED *102* YEARS, ITS NUMBER OF HOUSES ABOUT *4000* AND INHABITANTS ABOUT *18000*. IN IT ARE 2 CHURCHES OF ENGLAND / *8* CONGREGATIONAL MEETING HOUSES, *1* FRENCH, *1* ANABAPTIST, *1* IRISH, *1* QUAKERS MEETING HOUSE . . . IN THE YEAR *1723* / WERE BUILT IN NEW ENGLAND ABOVE *700* SAIL OF SHIPS . . . WHICH MAY IN SOME MEASURE SHEW THE GREAT / TRADE OF THIS FLOURISHING TOWN AND COUNTRY. Governor Belcher was commissioned on January 8, 1729–30. This dates the first state with the new dedication as not before 1730. In the above note on the succeeding state of the plate (Map 229) appears: THIS TOWN HATH BEEN SETTLED *103* YEARS. The *3* of the *103* has obviously been changed from a *2* to a *3* without erasure by adding a lower curl. This indicates a 1732 state for this map.

Size 17¼" x 23⅞". *Scale* 1" = 469 feet.

Published Separately.

References Samuel G. Drake, *The History and Antiquities of Boston*, p. 820; Justin Winsor, *Memorial History of Boston*, 2.

Location No copy located.

229 1733 *State* V (see also Maps 224–26, 228, and 230–34)

Description The date at end of title has the last two digits erased from the plate. "33" is inserted in manuscript. The engraver's signature has been erased below Price's name in the cartouche, but traces of the erasure of "T. JOHNSON SCULP" still remain. Eight wards are indicated with numbers. The latest date among the statistics is *1731*. A single row of sixteen trees now appears along the edge of the Common. A fence is indicated on each side of the road outside the fortification, and BOSTON NECK appears on this road. An impression of this state belonged to the Rev. Dr. Thomas Prince and in 1821 a MSS copy was made by G. A. Ward (probably George Atkinson Ward), which is now in the Essex Institute, Salem. An impression belonging to David Pulsifer of Boston was examined and described by Justin Winsor and by Samuel G. Drake.

Published Separately.

References Boston. Engineering Dept., *List of Maps of Boston published between 1600 and 1903*, p. 18; Nathaniel B. Shurtleff, *A Topographical and Historical Description*, p. 92; Justin Winsor, *Memorial History of Boston*, 2.

Location RPJCB. MSS copy in MSaE.

230 1739 *State* VI (see also Maps 224–26, 228–29, and 231–34)

Description The date at the end of the title has two digits, *39*, inserted in manuscript. Appended to the note at right of cartouche below the title now appears: IN THE YEAR, / *1735* THIS TOWN WAS DIVIDED INTO *12* WARDS . . . IN EACH WARD IS A MILITARY COMPANY . . . ALSO ONE / OVERSEER OF THE POOR CHOSEN YEARLY IN MARCH. At lower left has been tabulated: THE NAMES OF THE *12* WARDS. To the second column of the table of explanations has been added: THE WARDS MILITARY COMPANIES DIS / TINGUISH'D BY THE PRICKT LINE THUS—FROM NO. *1* TO *12*———. Below the right end of the scale appears: NOTE THE FIRST LETTER OF NAME OF THE STREET IS SET TO THE BOUNDS OF EACH STREET. On the map such letters have been added. A second row of thirteen trees has been added along THE MALL. The WORK-HOUSE has been pictured over the "h" identifying the BRIDEWELL. The individual dwellings and shops engraved by Francis Dewing for the original map have not been added to (except for churches and other public buildings) as the town has grown. In this state of the plate the edges of the various streets between the old individual buildings shown have been bordered with crosshatched banks which gives a solidly built up appearance. The latest date among the statistics is *1738*. In the note under the title the age of the town is still left as *103* years and the number of Churches of England is given as two, although TRINITY CHURCH with the date *1734* has been shown in addition to KINGS CHAPPEL and CHRIST CHURCH which were previously on the plate. Nine Congregational Meeting Houses are now listed. "Davies L" which crossed the present State House lot toward Louisburg Square is discontinued. JACKSON'S STILL HOUSE is now pictured.

Published Separately.

Location BM.

231 1743 *State* VII (see also Maps 224–26, 228–30, and 232–34)

Description The date at end of title now reads *1743*. All the digits of the date are now engraved, the last two apparently at a later date than the *17*. To the advertisement of William Price below the cartouche has been added: ALSO FLUTES, HAUTBOYS & VIO / LINS, STRINGS, MUSICAL BOOKS / SONGS, SPECTACLES, / & PROSPECT / GLASSES &C. In the note under the title the age of the town still appears as *103* years. The number of inhabitants is changed to *20000*, the Churches of England to three, and the number of Congregational Meeting Houses to ten. Faneuil Hall (T) now appears as part of the Town Dock, Hollis Street is continued to the edge of Roxbury Flats, and PLEASANT STREET is added there. The latest date among the statistics is now *1742*.

Published Separately. Reproduced in John G. Palfrey, *History of New England, 4*, front. (from an impression that belonged to Mr. Charles Deane).

Reference Nathaniel B. Shurtleff, *A Topographical and Historical Description*, p. 92.

Locations CtY, DLC, MB, NN.

232 [1754?] (see also Maps 224–26, 228–31, and 233–34)

Description In the *Boston Weekly News-Letter* for May 30, 1754, and for several issues following, William Price advertised: "A New Prospect and Plan of Boston." Col. Lawrence C. Martin, former Chief of the Map Division of the Library of Congress, has suggested that the advertisement may signify an issue at this time, bearing this date.

Published Separately.

Location No copy located.

233 1760 *State* VIII (see also Maps 224–26, 228–31, and 234)

Description The date at end of title now

reads: *1760*. The "60" has been noted in manuscript. The latest date appearing in the statistics is *1760*.

Published Separately. Reproduced in *The Month at Goodspeed's*, 14 (1942–43), 168–69.

Reference see reproduction above, under Published.

Location MH.

234 1769 *State* IX (see also Maps 224–26 and 228–33)

Description The date at end of title now reads *1769*. All four digits are engraved on the plate. To the note giving Boston data, below the title at right of the cartouche, has been added the line: BOSTON WAS FIRST SETTLED IN YE YEAR *1630*. In the body of this note the age of the Town is given as *139* years. The name of "Clarks Wharfe" has been changed to HANDCOCK'S WHARFE. / ESQR. HANCOCK SEAT is pictured on Beacon Street with the marginal reference "U" which is appended to the table. MARKET DAYS TUESDAY, THURSDAY AND SATURDAYS appears below the marginal reference to Faneuil Hall. TEMPLE STREET and MIDDLECOT STREET are added.

Published Separately. Reproduced in Bostonian Society, *Publications*, 9, front. (original owned by the City of Boston); Walter M. Whitehill, *Boston A Topographical History*, p. 45; Justin Winsor, *Memorial History of Boston*, 2, LVI (from an impression that belonged to Mr. Charles Deane).

Locations City of Boston, DLC, MiU-C, NN.

235 [¹775]

Description At lower left: PLAN / OF / BOSTON. At upper left corner: FIG. I. There are sixteen lettered references on the main map and twenty on the inset map. Tables of explanation for these references are given on the page opposite in the *Almanack*. This is the same as Map 240, but from a different wood-cut.

Size 3⅛″ x 5¹³⁄₁₆″.　*Scale* None (1″ = ⅖ mile).

Inset At upper right [Plan of the vicinity of Boston]. This extends from Winter Hill on the north to Roxbury Hill on the south. FIG. 2 is noted at the upper left. Size: 2⅜″ x 2½″. Scale: None (1″ = c. 2 miles).

Published in John Nathan Hutchins, *Hutchin's Improved: being an Almanack for 1776*.

236 [¹775]

Description At left center: PLAN OF / BOSTON. 25 lettered and three numbered references are explained in a table on the verso of the map

This is a woodcut map. Some of the reference markings seem to be type inserts and others cut. The lines of the American investment of Boston are indicated.

Size 5³⁄₁₆″ x 3¹⁄₁₆″.　*Scale* None (1″ = c. 2 miles).

Published in *The New-York and Country Almanack 1776*.

237 [¹775]

Description In rectangle at upper center: EXACT PLAN / OF / GENERAL GAGE'S LINES / ON BOSTON NECK / IN / AMERICA. Below bottom neat line at right: AITKEN SCULP. Above top neat line at right: ENGRAV'D FOR THE PENNSYLVA. MAGAZINE. There are 30 reference numbers on the map with a table of explanation on the opposite page of the magazine where this note appears, referring to the map: "This is a true state this day, July 31, 1775." The fortifications and entrenchments are shown in detail.

Size 11⅝″ x 8⅞″.　*Scale* 1″ = 280 feet.

Published in *Pennsylvania Magazine*, 1 (1775), opp. 358.

238 [¹775]

Description In decorated rectangle at lower left: A NEW AND CORRECT / PLAN OF THE TOWN / OF / BOSTON, / AND / PROVINCIAL CAMP. Below title, outside the rectangle: AITKEN SCULP. Above top neat line at right: ENGRAV'D FOR THE PENNSYLVA. MAGAZINE. Some of the hills or knolls on the peninsula are shown. CORPS HILL appears thus, also HANCOKS WHARF, MINOTS T, and LIBERTY T. Two ISLAND WHARFS are shown.

Size 10⅜″ x 7⅜″.　*Scale* None (1″ = ¼ mile).

Inset At lower right [Map of the country around Boston]. Shown are the Provincial Lines from Cambridge to Winter Hill and Gen. Gage's Lines from Pierponts Mill and Roxbury Hill to Boston Neck. Size: 4¼″ x 4⅜″. Scale: 1″ = 2 miles.

Published in *Pennsylvania Magazine*, 1 (1775), opp. 291.

239 [¹775]

Description In cartouche at upper right: A NEW PLAN / OF / BOSTON HARBOUR / FROM AN ACTUAL / SURVEY. Below bottom neat line at right corner: CLOWNES SCULP. Above top neat line at center: ENGRAV'D FOR THE PENNSYLVA. MAGAZINE. Six lettered references and a note about the burning of Charlestown appear beneath the cartouche. The engraver is Caleb Lownes.

Size $10\frac{5}{16}$" x $7\frac{1}{4}$". *Scale* 1" = $1\frac{3}{4}$ miles.

Published in *Pennsylvania Magazine, 1* (1775), opp. 241.

240 [1775]

Description At lower left: PLAN / OF / BOSTON. At upper left: FIG. *1*. The sixteen lettered references on the main map and 20 on the inset are explained in the tables on the opposite page. This is the same as Map 235, but from a different wood-cut.

Size 3" x $5\frac{9}{16}$". *Scale* None (1" = $\frac{2}{5}$ mile).

Inset At upper right [Plan of the vicinity of Boston]. FIG. 2 is noted at upper left. Size: $2\frac{7}{16}$" x $2\frac{1}{2}$". Scale: None (1" = c. 2 miles).

Published in Benjamin West, *Bickerstaff's New-England Almanac for 1776*.

241 1781

Description Outside neat line on left side: PLAN OF THE TOWN OF BOSTON, WITH THE / ATTACK ON BUNKERS-HILL, IN THE PENINSULA OF CHARLESTOWN, / THE *17*TH of JUNE, *1775*. At lower right corner: J. NORMAN SC. Lists of the major fires, the twelve wards, and the eleven REFERENCES are given at the lower right. CHARLESTOWN IN FLAMES is pictorially portrayed.

Size $11\frac{3}{8}$" x $6\frac{1}{4}$". *Scale* None (1" = c. $\frac{1}{4}$ mile).

Published in *An Impartial History of the War in America, 1*, opp. 257.

Reference John Carter Brown Library, *Report, 1937*, pp. 20–23.

242 [1784]

Description At lower right: PLAN OF THE TOWN / OF / BOSTON. Above top neat line at left. GEOGL. GAZR.; at center: BOS. MAG. NO. XII; at right: PAGE *1*ST. This map is based very largely upon Map 241. The Charlestown Peninsula and the reference concerning Boston in the lower right corner have been omitted here.

Size 9" x $5\frac{7}{8}$". *Scale* None (1" = c. 1000 feet).

Published in the *Geographical Gazetteer* (eight pages issued as a supplement to the *Boston Magazine*), October, 1784.

References Massachusetts Historical Society, *Proceedings*, 2d Ser., *18* (1904), 329 (ascribes this to J. Norman); Philip L. Phillips, *A List of Maps of America*, p. 152; Nathaniel B. Shurtleff, *A Topographical and Historical Description*, p. 96.

243 [1789]

Description At lower right: PLAN OF THE TOWN / OF / BOSTON. This map is a re-engraving of Map 242 with corrections and additions to date. ELIOT STREET (between Orange and Pleasant streets), laid out in 1788, is shown.

Size $9\frac{1}{8}$" x $5\frac{5}{8}$". *Scale* None (1" = c. 1000 feet).

Published in *The Boston Directory*.

References Boston. Engineering Dept., *List of Maps of Boston Published Between 1600 and 1903*, pp. 79–80; idem, *List of Maps of Boston Published Subsequent to 1600*, pp. 33–34; Massachusetts Historical Society, *Proceedings*, (1st ser.) *6* (1862), 38; Nathaniel B. Shurtleff, *A Topographical and Historical Description*, p. 96; Justin Winsor, *The Memorial History of Boston*, *3*.

244 [1789]

Description At lower right: PLAN OF THE TOWN / OF / BOSTON. This is apparently a re-engraving of Map 243 which has been copied in most details. N BATTERY appears in a horizontal position instead of vertically. HARVARD and BENNET streets on Boston Neck are named, as is ALLENS L. GREEN ST is also marked GREEN LANE. Green Lane had been erased from the plate of Map 243. STILL H SQ appears instead of Distill H Sq.

Size $9\frac{1}{8}$" x $6\frac{1}{8}$". *Scale* None (1" = c. 1000 feet).

Published in *The Boston Directory*. Reproduced in *The Boston Directory*, Boston, 1789 (reproduction published by the Sampson and Murdock Company, Boston, 1930).

245 [1791]

Description At bottom center: PLAN & ELEVATION OF THE TONTINE CRESCENT, NOW ERECTING IN BOSTON. At lower right: S. HILL, SC. At upper right: MASSA. MAG. *1794*. The "Description of the Plate" on the opposite page gives details concerning the CRESCENT, which measured 480 feet in length. It was located on the south side of Franklin Place. The Massachusetts Historical Society had its quarters here for 39 years, moving in 1833. The engraving was made by Samuel Hill.

Size $5\frac{3}{8}$" x $10\frac{5}{8}$" (size of plate). *Scale* None (1" = 48 feet).

Published in *Massachusetts Magazine, 6* (1794), opp. p. 67. Reproduced in Massachusetts Historical Society, *Proceedings* (1st Ser.), *1* (1795–1835), opp. 67.

246 1796

Description At bottom center: A PLAN / OF BOSTON, / FROM ACTUAL SURVEY; / BY OSGOOD CARLETON. / *1796*. In scroll beneath title: S. HILL. SC. Above neat line at bottom center: PUBLISHED BY JOHN WEST, NO. 75, CORNHILL, BOSTON. There are eight numbered REFERENCES on the map identified in a table at right of the title. This map is described by N. B. Shurtleff and by Justin Winsor as being drawn in 1795 after a new survey by Osgood Carleton. Both these authorities ascribe the engraving to Joseph Callender, not to Samuel Hill, and say it appeared in West's second *Boston Directory* of 1796. Mr. Julius H. Tuttle, former Librarian of the Massachusetts Historical Society, advised that the copies in the Boston Athenaeum, Boston Public Library, Massachusetts State Library, and Massachusetts Historical Society were all engraved by Samuel Hill. He thought it possible that Callender was working in Hill's shop and did the actual engraving, but applied Hill's imprint, and that Mr. T. C. Amory or Dr. Shurtleff was aware of this.

Size 14⅚₆″ x 8⁵⁄₁₆″.   *Scale* 1″ = 47 yards.

Published in John West, *Boston Directory;* ibid., 1798 and 1800 editions; separately.

References Evans 30164; Massachusetts Historical Society, *Proceedings* (1st Ser.), *6* (1862), 38; Nathaniel B. Shurtleff, *List of the Printed Maps of Boston*, p. 4; idem, *A Topographical and Historical Description*, p. 96; Dorothea N. Spear, *Bibliography of American Directories*, p. 46; Justin Winsor, *The Memorial History of Boston, 3,* IX.

247 [1796]

Description At upper right: A PLAN / OF THE / ACTION AT BREEDS HILL * ON THE *17*TH. OF JUNE *1775*. BETWEEN THE AMERICAN FORCES, / AND / THE BRITISH TROOPS. / * ERRONEOUSLY CALLED BUNKERS HILL. Below bottom neat line at right corner: D. MARTIN SCULPT; below bottom neat line at center: PUBLISH'D BY C. SMITH N. YORK; at upper right corner: PL. *1*. This is a reduced copy of the map in Charles Stedman's *The History of the Origin, Progress, and Termination of the American War*, London, 1794. A discussion of the action that this PLAN illustrates begins on p. 9. British landing places are shown as well as the positions occupied by both sides during the battle. The engraver is David Martin.

Size 9⅟₁₆″ x 8½″.   *Scale* 1″ = 275 yards.

Published in *The Monthly Military Repository, 1*, opp. 9; Charles Smith, *The American War*, opp. p. 4. Reproduced in James F. Hunnewell, *Bibliography of Charlestown, Massachusetts and Bunker Hill*, foll. p. 16; see also ibid., entry no. 15, p. 18.

248 1797   *State* I (II post-1799, see below, Description)

Description In oval at upper left: AN / ACCURATE PLAN / OF THE TOWN OF / BOSTON, / AND ITS VICINITY: / EXHIBITING A GROUND PLAN OF ALL THE STREETS, LANES, / ALLEYS, WHARVES, AND PUBLIC BUILDINGS IN BOSTON; . . . FROM THE ACTUAL SURVEYS / OF THE PUBLISHER: ALSO, PART OF CHARLESTOWN AND CAM / BRIDGE, FROM THE SURVEYS OF SAMUEL THOMPSON, ESQR. AND / PART OF ROXBURY AND DORCHESTER, FROM THOSE OF MR. / WITHERINGTON [SIC] . . . BY OSGOOD CARLETON / TEACHER OF MATHEMATICS / IN BOSTON. In oval below title: I. NORMAN SC. Beneath oval: PUBLISH'D & SOLD BY O. CARLETON SOLD ALSO BY WM. NORMAN NO. 75 NEWBURY STREET. Below last imprint at left: PUBLISHED AS THE ACT DIRECTS MAY *16. 1797*. At upper right under the compass rose: BOSTON NEW STATE-HOUSE / LAT. *42°, 23′* NORTH / LONG. / *71°03′* W. OF GREENWICH IN ENGLAND / *6 10′* E. OF THE CITY OF WASHINGTON. The only streets shown are on the Boston Peninsula. The public buildings are named. The flats and channels between Boston, Charlestown, Cambridge, Roxbury, and Dorchester are shown with the two bridges and causeway. The boundary lines between Boston and these towns are accurately shown, and also the bounds of twelve wards in Boston. This plate was cut down and the map reissued in 1800 under the title: "A New Plan of Boston from Actual Surveys by Osgood Carleton With Corrections Additions & Improvements," showing only the peninsula. The surveyor is Matthew Withington (not Witherington).

Size 41″ x 37⅜″.   *Scale* 1″ = 21 rods.

Published Separately. Reproduced in Justin Winsor, *Memorial History of Boston, 4,* opp. 26.

References Boston. Engineering Dept., *List of Maps of Boston published between 1600 and 1903*, p. 84; Massachusetts Historical Society, *Proceedings* (1st Ser.), *17* (1879–80), 365; *New England Historical & Genealogical Register, 55* (1901), pp. 52–55; Isaac N. P. Stokes and Daniel C. Haskell, *American Historical Prints*, p. 78.

Locations MH, MWA.

1789   see Map 330.

249 [1794]

Description [Western Narragansett shore.] Above neat line at upper right: PLATE IX. P. 345. Below bottom neat line at right corner: DOOLIT-TLE SC. This is a map of part of the western shore of Narragansett Bay, indicating: MR. THEO. WHALES RESIDENCE FROM *1680* TO *1715*.

Size 5⅞″ x 3⅝″.   *Scale* 1″ = 2½ miles.

Published in Ezra Stiles, *A History of Three of the Judges.*

250 [1795] *State* I (II post-1799, see below, Description)

Description In oval at upper right: THE STATE OF / RHODE-ISLAND; / COMPILED, FROM THE / SURVEYS AND OBSERVATIONS OF / CALEB HARRIS,/ BY / HARDING HARRIS. Below oval: J. SMITHER SCULP. Townships and county boundaries, the main roads, drainage, principal hills, and towns are indicated. It shows QUICKSAND POND mostly in Rhode Island. COLLEGE is shown in Providence. The map appears in the September, 1800 edition of *Carey's General Atlas* with the number "29" added at the upper right corner.

Size 13⁵⁄₁₆ x 9⁵⁄₁₆.   *Scale* 1″ = 4½ miles.

Published in Mathew Carey, *Carey's American Atlas*, no. 7; idem, *Carey's General Atlas*, no. 29; idem, *The General Atlas for Carey's Edition of Guthrie's Geography Improved*, no. 29.

251 1795

Description In decorated oval at upper right: A / MAP / OF THE STATE OF / RHODE ISLAND; / TAKEN MOSTLY FROM SURVEYS / BY / CALEB HARRIS. In oval below title: HARDING HARRIS / DELINEAVT. Below oval: SAML. HILL SCULPT. BOSTON. Below bottom neat line at center: ENGRAVED FOR CARTER & WILKINSON, PROVIDENCE. *1795*. This is a fine political map of the State showing also a few topographical features. Just below the cartouche at the upper right is the ARMS OF RHODE ISLAND, and a table of REFERENCES appears at the lower right. Both townships and counties are indicated. Major roads are given.

Size 21⁵⁄₁₆″ x 15⅞″.   *Scale* 1″ = 2½ miles.

Published Separately.

References [Howard M. Chapin], "Chronological Check List of Maps of Rhode Island," p. 97; Evans 28803; Harvard University, *A Catalogue of the Maps and Charts*, p. 192.

Locations BM, MB, MH, MWA, NHi, RHi, RPJCB.

252 [1795] *State* I (II post-1799, see below, Description)

Description At lower right: RHODE ISLAND. Three counties are named and bounded. This map shows QUICK SAND P. mostly in Rhode Island and PAUTUCKET R. for the Pawtucket. PATUXET is given for the Pawtuxet River and village. This map was reissued in Scott's *The New and Universal Gazetteer*, 4, with a number of place names added including, "Chapman P.," "Fairfield P.," and, "South Ferry."

Size 7¼″ x 6⅛″.   *Scale* 1″ = 7½ miles.

Published in Joseph Scott, *An Atlas of the United States*, no. 6; idem, *The United States Gazetteer*, opp. "Rhode Island." Reproduced in Joseph Scott, *Atlas of the United States 1795–1800* [no. 16].

253 [1796] *State* I (II post-1799, see below, Description)

Description At lower right: RHODE ISLAND. Below bottom neat line at right: W. BARKER SCULP: PHILADA. QUICKSAND P. is almost all in Rhode Island. This map was reissued in the 1801 edition of *Carey's American Pocket Atlas* with the addition of numerous double line delineations of wagon roads. None are indicated in the first state.

Size 7⁹⁄₁₆″ x 5¹³⁄₁₆″.   *Scale* 1″ = 8½ miles.

Published in Mathew Carey, *Carey's American Pocket Atlas*, opp. p. 34.

254 1796

Description In oval at upper right: THE STATE OF / RHODE ISLAND, / FROM THE / LATEST SURVEYS. / *1796*. Beneath oval: B. TANNER, DELT. & SCULPT. Below bottom neat line: ENGRAVED FOR THE AMERICAN EDITION OF WINTERBOTHAM'S AMER-

56

ICA. PUBLISHED BY JOHN REID. N YORK. This map shows QUICKSAND PD wholly in Massachusetts.

Size 16⅞" x 12⅞". *Scale* 1" = 4¼ miles.

Published in John Reid, *The American Atlas*, [1796?], no. 8; ibid., 1796, no. 8; William Winterbotham, *[Atlas]*. Reproduced in U.S. Bureau of the Census, *Heads of Families at the First Census Rhode Island*, front.

[1796]   see Map 287.

255   [1799]

Description   At lower right: RHODE ISLAND. Below bottom neat line at center: ENGRAVED FOR PAYNE'S GEOGRAPHY PUBLISHED BY J. LOW, N. YORK. At right: W. BARKER. SCULP. PHILADA. Drainage features, roads, and county and township bounds are shown.

Size 9½" x 7⁵⁄₁₆". *Scale* None (1" = c. 6½ miles).

Published in John Payne, *A New and Complete Universal Geography*, 4, opp. 258.

CONNECTICUT

256 [1732–33]

Description [Draught showing the old eastern boundary of New York and the section of the Oblong taken out of Connecticut.] The map is a very crude representation of the boundary changes and the "Equivalent Lands." The advertisement sets forth the justice of the claims of Hauly & Co. *v.* Eyles & Co. The map was printed from a wooden block with type insets.

Size 4¹¹⁄₁₆″ x 3⅜″.   *Scale* None (1″ = c. 19 miles).

Published in *New-York Gazette*, January 30 to February 6, 1732/33, "Advertisement" supplement dated February 5, p. 2.

Reference Edmund Thompson, *Maps of Connecticut before 1800*, p. 28.

257 1766 *State* I (see also Map 258)

Description At upper left: TO THE RIGHT HONOURABLE / THE / EARL OF SHELBURN [sic] / HIS MAJESTY'S PRINCIPAL / SECRETARY OF STATE / FOR THE SOUTHERN DEPARTMENT / THIS PLAN OF THE COLONY OF CONNECTICUT IN / NORTH-AMERICA / IS HUMBLY DEDICATED BY HIS LORDSHIP'S / MOST OBEDIENT HUMBLE / SERVT. / MOSES PARK / NOVR. *24, 1766*. This is a detailed map of Connecticut showing some topographical features. It was prepared under the sponsorship of the Colony of Connecticut and was originally requested by the British government in 1764 in its effort to better the overall postal service in America. The surveys for the map were conducted by Asa Spalding, Moses Park, and Samuel Mott. A manuscript copy of the map was sent to England, November 13, 1765. This, printed, map is dated: NOVR. *24. 1766*, and was offered for sale in New London, January 1, 1768. The misspelling of Lord Shelburne's name in this first state of the map indicates that it may have been published in America. An EXPLANATION is given in a decorative cartouche at the lower right corner. The full scale is given as ENGLISH MILES *60* TO A DEGREE.

Size 21″ x 28¾″.   *Scale* 1″ = 4¼ miles.

Published Separately.

References Thompson R. Harlow, "The Moses Park Map, 1766," pp. 33–37; William

Smith, *An Examination of the Connecticut Claim to Lands in Pennsylvania*, p. 74; Edmund Thompson, *Maps of Connecticut before 1800*, pp. 34–35.

Location MiU-C.

258 [1766?] *State* II (see also Map 257)

Description There are at least ten differences between the first and second states, among them the following: the line "60 to a degree" appearing under the scale of miles has been erased from the plate; an "E" has been added to the name "Shelburne" in the title; at New Haven has been added the notation LAT. *41: 10* N. / LON. *55: 24* W. (Note that this is an error of nearly 20 degrees in longitude. It was followed on several later maps.); the CONNECTICUT R. is now named.

Published Separately.   Reproduced in Thompson R. Harlow, "The Moses Park Map, 1766," cover.

Reference U.S. Library of Congress, *Report 1941*, pp. 111–12; see also Map 257, References.

Locations CtY, CtHi, DLC, RPJCB.

259 [1774?] *State* I (see also Map 264)

Description [Capt. Parkers Chart of Saybrook Bar.] This "Chart" was published as part of an attempt by the communities on the Connecticut River to make the River more accessible from Long Island Sound. Money for the engraving of the plates, done by Abel Buell, probably in 1774, as well as the other expenses involved was raised by a lottery authorized by the Assembly in 1772. The title is taken from State II.

Size Unknown.   *Scale* Unknown.

Published Separately.

References William D. Love, "The Navigation of the Connecticut River," pp. 395–96; Edmund Thompson, *Maps of Connecticut before 1800*, pp. 36–37; James H. Trumbull, *List of Books Printed in Connecticut 1709–1800*, no. 1061; Lawrence C. Wroth, *Abel Buell*, pp. 50–55; ibid., rev. ed., pp. 57–62.

Location No copy located.

260 [1774]

Description [Map showing Continuation West of the Latitudes of the Connecticut Coast Line.] A rough engraving showing Provost Smith's alternative interpretations of the grant to Lord Saye and Sele under which Connecticut might claim lands beyond their usually recognized boundary lines. It is referred to in the text (in note below pp. 31 and 32) as "The annexed Plan, which is only a rough Sketch for marking out the Places referred to in this Work. Those Places, however, and the general Course of the Coast, are laid down from the best Maps." The arc shown extends from Cape Cod to the Susquehanna River.

Size 5⅞" x 10" (size of plate). *Scale* None (1" = c. 45 miles).

Published in William Smith, *An Examination of the Connecticut Claim to Lands in Pennsylvania,* opp. p. 31. Reproduced in *Pennsylvania Archives,* Ser. 2, *18.*

Reference Evans 13629.

261 [1777] *State* I (see also Maps 262 and 263)

Description In ornate cartouche at lower right: CONNECTICUT / AND PARTS ADJACENT. Below neat line at lower right: ENGRAVED PRINTED AND SOLD AT NEW HAVEN. This is a political and topographical map showing numerous communities in the State. The coastline is shown as a single line in contrast to State III (?) (see Map 263) which has added depth contour lines. The authorship of the map has been attributed to Bernard Romans on the basis of newspaper advertisements which appeared in the (New London) *Connecticut Gazette and the Universal Intelligencer,* October 31, 1777, and the *Boston Gazette and Country Journal,* November 17, 1777. WESTBURY is located south of WATERBURY; SOUTHBURY is given east of the NAUGATUCK RIVER and south of WOODBURY.

Size 20¾" x 23⅝". *Scale* 1" = 5 miles.

Published Separately.

References Evans 15585; Philip L. Phillips, *Notes on Bernard Romans,* p. 86; Edmund Thompson, *Maps of Connecticut before 1800,* pp. 40–41; Alexander O. Vietor, "Printed Maps," p. 440.

Location RPJCB.

262 [1777?] *State* II? (see also Maps 261 and 263)

Description This intermediate state of Map 261 is thought to exist, as a Dutch copy of it was published in 1780 with the incorrect location of Southbury, east of the Naugatuck River, eliminated. The Dutch version has the same title as the original, adding that it was published: "at Amsterdam / bÿ Cóvens and Mortier / and / Cóvens Junior"; "H. Klockhoff, Sculp. 1780." Chatham Township, found on neither State I nor State III (?), has been added. Several names given on State I are not given here: Judaea in Litchfield County; Stanwich in Fairfield County (the town symbol is given, however); and the Oil Mill near Colchester.

Published Separately.

Reference Edmund Thompson, *Maps of Connecticut before 1800,* p. 42.

Location No copy located. (Cóvens and Mortier issue: CtY, DLC, MH.)

263 [1777?] *State* III? (see also Maps 261 and 262)

Description Depth contours have been added along the coast, and on the rivers and lakes. WESTBURY is now north of WATERBURY; the incorrect location of SOUTHBURY east of the NAUGATUCK RIVER has been eliminated, and the nearby streams redrawn. FIRE ISLAND INLET, MUDDY BR, and STONY BR have been added.

Published Separately.

Reference Edmund Thompson, *Maps of Connecticut before 1800,* pp. 40–41.

Location CSmH.

264 [c. 1784] *State* II (see also Map 259)

Description At upper left center: CAPT. PARKERS / CHART, / OF / SAYBROOK BAR. Dedication in cartouche at upper left corner: TO THE HONBLE / GOVENOR [sic] & / COMPANY, OF THE COLONY OF / CONNECTICUT IN NEW ENGLAND THIS MAP / IS HUMBLY DEDICATED BY YOUR HONOURS / MOST OBEDIENT HUMBLE SERVT / ABNER PARKER / *1771.* This is a large scale chart of the mouth of the Connecticut River giving landmarks for following the channels. In a rectangle at the extreme left center are the: DIRECTIONS TO FIND YE CHANNEL. State II is identified by the location of the GOVERNOR'S HOUSE which was the home of Matthew Griswold, Governor of Connecticut from 1784 to 1786. The CHART must then be dated 1784 or after.

Size 26¾" x 39⅜" (size of plate). *Scale* 1" = c. ⅓ mile.

Published Separately. Reproduced in Connecticut, *The Public Records of the Colony of Connecticut from May, 1768, to May, 1772, 13,* opp. 503 (copy of tracing made from engraved map); E. Harold Hugo and Thompson R. Harlow, *Abel Buell a Jack of all Trades,* p. [4];

Alexander O. Vietor, "Printed Maps," pl. 282 (B); Lawrence C. Wroth, *Abel Buell,* opp. p. 52; ibid., rev. ed., opp. p. 57.

References see Map 259.

Location CtHi.

265 [1789]

Description Above top neat line: FROM NEW YORK (*4*) TO STRATFORD. This map shows, in three vertical strips, the road from HORSE NECK (Cos Cob—36 ½ miles from New York), through STAM FORD, Darien (shown but not named), and MIDDLE SEX, to about three miles west of Norwalk.

Size 7⅛" x 4½". *Scale* None (1" = 4⁄7 mile).

Published in Christopher Colles, *A Survey of the Roads.* Reproduced in ibid., 1961, p. 124.

266 [1789]

Description Above top neat line: FROM NEW YORK (*5*) TO STRATFORD. This map shows, in two vertical strips, the road from two miles west of NOR WALK, (48½ miles from New York), through Norwalk and over SAGATUCK BRIDGE, to about four miles west of Fairfield.

Size 7" x 4½". *Scale* None (1" = 4⁄7 mile).

Published in Christopher Colles, *A Survey of the Roads.* Reproduced in ibid., 1961, p. 125.

267 [1789]

Description Above top neat line: FROM NEW YORK (*6*) TO STRATFORD. This map shows, in two vertical strips, the road from three miles east of the Saugatuck River (59 miles from New York), through FAIR FIELD to the outskirts of Old Fairfield (close to west edge of present Bridgeport).

Size 7" x 4½". *Scale* None (1" = 4⁄7 mile).

Published in Christopher Colles, *A Survey of the Roads.* Reproduced in ibid., 1961, p. 126.

268 [1789]

Description Above top neat line: FROM NEW YORK (*7*) TO STRATFORD. This map shows, in two vertical strips, the road from the western border of OLD FAIR FIELD (67 miles from New York), through present Bridgeport and STRATFORD, to the ferry across the Housatonic River a mile east of Stratford.

Size 7" x 4½". *Scale* None (1" = 4⁄7 mile).

Published in Christopher Colles, *A Survey of the Roads.* Reproduced in ibid., 1961, p. 127.

269 [1789]

Description Above top neat line: FROM STRATFORD (*15*) TO POUGHKEEPSIE. This map shows, in three vertical strips, the road from STRATFORD, through NORTH STRATFORD, and about seven miles further northwest.

Size 7" x 4½". *Scale* None (1" = 4⁄7 mile).

Published in Christopher Colles, *A Survey of the Roads.* Reproduced in ibid., 1961, p. 135.

270 [1789]

Description Above top neat line: FROM STRATFORD (*16*) TO POUGHKEEPSIE. This map shows, in three vertical strips, the road from eight and one half miles south of NEW TOWN (12 miles from Stratford), to four miles west.

Size 7" x 4½". *Scale* None (1" = 4⁄7 mile).

Published in Christopher Colles, *A Survey of the Roads.* Reproduced in ibid., 1961, p. 136.

271 [1789]

Description Above top neat line: FROM STRATFORD (*17*) TO POUGHKEEPSIE. This map shows, in three vertical strips, the road from five miles east of Danbury (25 miles from Stratford), through DAN BURY, and into DUTCHESS COUNTY, YORK STATE [sic], eight miles northwest of Danbury.

Size 7" x 4½". *Scale* None (1" = 4⁄7 mile).

Published in Christopher Colles, *A Survey of the Roads.* Reproduced in ibid., 1961, p. 137.

1789 see Map 330.

272 [1792] *State I (see also Map 273)*

Description In cartouche at lower right: A / NEW AND CORRECT MAP OF / CONNECTICUT / ONE OF THE UNITED STATES OF / NORTH AMERICA / FROM ACTUAL SURVEY / HUMBLY DEDICATED BY PERMISSION TO HIS EXCELLENCY / SAMUEL HUNTINGTON ESQUIRE / GOVERNOR AND COMMANDER IN CHIEF OF SAID / STATE / BY HIS MOST HUMBLE SERVANT / WILLIAM BLODGET. Below cartouche: JOEL ALLEN SCRIPT. ET SCULPT. The map was issued undated. MONTAUK POINT is inscribed vertically outside the neat line at lower right and the top of Long Island is shown just projecting beyond the neat line there. Pictorial references indicate churches, academies, distilleries, different kinds of mills, etc. Great attention is given to delineation of rivers and several new names of streams appear but many communities shown by Romans are omitted. The position of New

Haven is given as LAT. *41° 10′ N. / LONG. 55. 24 W.*

Size 27¼″ x 33¹⁵⁄₁₆″. *Scale* 1″ = 3¼ miles.

Published Separately.

References Evans 24125; Phyllis Kihn, "William Blodget," pp. 43–48; David M. Stauffer, *American Engravers*, *1, 7*; ibid., *2, 10*; Edmund Thompson, *Maps of Connecticut before 1800*, pp. 44–46.

Location CtHi.

273 1792 *State* II (see also Map 272)

Description An imprint has been added below bottom neat line at right center: MIDDLETOWN PRINTED FOR THE PUBLISHER MARCH *1792*. The longitude of New Haven has been corrected to *73. 14*. Three streams have been added in HEBRON. The word FALLS has been added in Suffield on the Connecticut River.

Published Separately.

Reference Evans 24124; see also Map 272, References.

Locations CtY, MWA, NHi, NN.

274 [1794] *State* I (see also Map 284; III post-1799, see Map 284, Description)

Description With decorations in lower right corner: CONNECTICUT / FROM THE BEST / AUTHORITIES. Below title under decorations: DELINEATED AND ENGRAVED BY A DOOLITTLE N. HAVEN. Mathew Carey advertised a map of Connecticut for sale in the (Philadelphia) *Gazette of the United States*, May 8, 1794. The three trees shown in the Carey atlas map (Map 284) and its later states, marking a lower New York corner, do not appear. The disputed oblong is indicated between New York and Connecticut. The southwest corner is shown east of the mouth of the Byram River. STAT [sic] MASSACHUSETTS is given above the northern boundary line.

Size 11¹¹⁄₁₆″ x 14½″. *Scale* 1″ = 7¼ miles.

Published Separately.

Reference Harvard University, *A Catalogue of the Maps and Charts*, p. 192.

Location MH (2 copies).

275 [1794]

Description At top center: CITY OF NEW HAVEN; above top neat line at right corner: PLATE V P. *126;* below bottom neat line at right corner: DOOLITTLE SC. This plan indicates the home of Colonel John Dixwell, one of the Regi-

cides, and his burial place. YAL: COLL: and the homes of several prominent individuals are also noted.

Size 5⅞″ x 3½″. *Scale* 1″ = 55 rods.

Published in Ezra Stiles, *A History of Three of the Judges*.

276 [1794]

Description At top center: GRAVES OF THE JUDGES / IN NEW-HAVEN. At top left corner: NO. 3. This map is on the same plate with Maps 278 and 280. It measures 6¹³⁄₁₆″ x 8¾″ over the neat lines and gives: PLATE IV. P. *114*, at upper left corner. Other maps in the book carry the name of Amos Doolittle as engraver.

Size 2⅞″ x 5¾″. *Scale* 1″ = 8 feet.

Published in Ezra Stiles, *A History of Three of the Judges*.

277 [1794]

Description At upper center: GUILFORD; above top neat line at right corner: PLATE III P. *80;* below top neat line: NO. 2. This map is on the same plate with Maps 282 and 283. It measures 5¹³⁄₁₆″ x 3⅝″ over the neat lines and carries below the bottom neat line at the right corner: DOOLITTLE SC. Several residences and buildings in Guilford about 1661 are located and identified.

Size 3⁵⁄₁₆″ x 2⁵⁄₁₆″. *Scale* 1″ = c. 23 rods.

Published in Ezra Stiles, *A History of Three of the Judges*.

278 [1794]

Description At right center: HADLEY. At upper right corner: NO. 2. This map is on the same plate with Maps 276 and 280. It measures 6¹³⁄₁₆″ x 8¾″ over the neat lines and carries: PLATE IV. P. *114* at upper left corner. A number of residences are indicated in the town. Other maps in the same book carry the name of Amos Doolittle as engraver.

Size 6¹³⁄₁₆″ x 2⅞″. *Scale* 1″ = 78 rods.

Inset At top: HADLEY. A smaller scale map. Size: 1¾″ x 2¼″. Scale: None (1″ = c. 23 rods).

Published in Ezra Stiles, *A History of Three of the Judges*.

279 [1794]

Description At upper center: HADLEY; above neat line at right corner: PLATE VIII P. *202;* below bottom neat line at right corner: DOOLITTLE SC. The REVD JOHN RUSSELS residence, as well as several others nearby, is indicated.

Size 5⅝" x 3½". *Scale* 1" = c. 140 rods.

Inset At top: MR. RUSSELS HOUSE. THE JUDGES CHAMBER *1665* is indicated. Size: 2" x 2¼". Scale: None.

Published in Ezra Stiles, *A History of Three of the Judges.*

280 [1794]

Description At top center: LODGMENTS OF THE JUDGES IN & ABOUT NEW HAVEN / FROM *1661* to *1664*. At upper left corner: PLATE IV. P. *114*. / NO. *1*. This map is on the same plate, measuring 6$^{13}/_{16}$" x 8¾" over the neat lines, with Maps 276 and 278. Other maps in this book carry the name of Amos Doolittle as engraver.

Size 3$^{15}/_{16}$" x 5¾". *Scale* 1" = 5½ miles.

Published in Ezra Stiles, *A History of Three of the Judges.*

281 [1794]

Description At lower left: MAP OF NEW-HAVEN / AND ITS ENVIRONS. Below upper neat line near right corner: PLATE I. P *29*. The map shows only a conventional representation of the town indicating its location. Topographical features are shown, and also the stopping places of the judges. Other plates in this book carry the name of Amos Doolittle as the engraver.

Size 6⅞" x 9$^{1}/_{16}$". *Scale* 1" = ⅘ mile.

Published in Ezra Stiles, *A History of Three of the Judges.*

282 [1794]

Description At top center (of small map): MILFORD. Below bottom neat line at right corner: DOOLITTLE SC. This map is on the same plate with Maps 277 and 283. It measures 5$^{13}/_{16}$" x 3⅝" over the neat lines and carries above the top neat line at the right corner: PLATE III P. *80*. MR. TOMKINS residence is indicated as THE JUDGES CELL FOR 2 YS. Several other residences are located as well.

Size 2⅝" x 2⅜". *Scale* 1" = c. 23 rods.

Published in Ezra Stiles, *A History of Three of the Judges.*

283 [1794]

Description [The Second Harbor of the Judges.] Beneath top neat line at left corner: NO. *1*. This map is on the same plate, measuring 5$^{13}/_{16}$" x 3⅝" over the neat lines with Maps 277 and 282. It carries above the top neat line at the right corner: PLATE III P. *80*, and below the bottom neat line at the right corner: DOOLITTLE SC. The title is taken from the location on Map 280.

Size 5$^{13}/_{16}$" x 1¼". *Scale* 1" = 8 rods.

Published in Ezra Stiles, *A History of Three of the Judges.*

284 [1795] *State* II (see also Map 274; III post-1799, see below Description)

Description Added above top neat line: ENGRAVED FOR CAREY'S AMERICAN EDITION OF GUTHRIE'S GEOGRAPHY IMPROVED. Above the northern boundary and below marginal degree line, now appears: STATE OF / VERMONT [sic] / STATE OF / MASSACHUSETTS. The *3* TREES marking a lower New York corner have been engraved on the plate and named. The CROTON River at the left is now named and HIGH LANDS appears just above it. PLUMB I and GULL'S I appear off the end of Oyster Pond PT. Further changes to the plate were made as it was used later, including an extra neat line (making a triple line) and shadow lines around the letters of Connecticut in the title. The same map was used in the 1800 edition of *Carey's General Atlas* with the number "30" added at the upper left corner.

Published in Mathew Carey, *Carey's American Atlas,* no. 6; and, in *Carey's General Atlas,* no. 30; idem, *The General Atlas for Carey's Edition of Guthrie's Geography Improved,* no. 30.

285 [1795] *State* I (see also Map 293)

Description At lower right: CONNECTICUT. The counties are given as well as the roads, rivers, and towns.

Size 6" x 7¼". *Scale* 1" = 13½ miles.

Published in Joseph Scott, *An Atlas of the United States,* no. 7; idem, *The United States Gazetteer,* opp. "Connecticut." Reproduced in Joseph Scott, *Atlas of the United States 1795–1800,* no. 4.

286 [1796] *State* I (II post-1799, see below, Description)

Description At lower right: CONNECTICUT. Below bottom neat line at right: W. BARKER SCULP. This map shows the *3* TREES at the lower left. The southwest corner is shown east of the mouth of the Byram River. No roads appear on this first state and only two of the latitude and longitude figures, *73°* and *2°*, are followed by the degree symbol. The map was reissued in the 1801 edition of *Carey's American Pocket Atlas* with the addition of important roads, and with all the latitude and longitude figures properly marked.

Size 5⅝" x 7½". *Scale* 1" = 15 miles.

Published in Mathew Carey, *Carey's American Pocket Atlas,* opp. p. 40.

287 [1796]

Description In oval at lower right: RHODE-ISLAND / AND / CONNECTICUT. / H HARRIS / DELINVT; beneath oval: HILL SC; above top neat line: PUBLISHED BY THOMAS & ANDREWS, BOSTON. The OBLONG-CEEDED TO NEW YORK MAY *14*TH. *1731* is shown. YALE COLLEGE LANDS are noted at upper left. The map was drawn by Harding Harris.

Size 7⁹⁄₁₆″ x 13³⁄₁₆″.   *Scale* 1″ = 10½ miles.

Published in Jedidiah Morse, *The American Universal Geography,* 3d ed., *1*, opp. 433.

288 [1796]   *State* I (see also Maps 289 and 290)

Description In oval at lower right: CONNECTICUT / FROM THE BEST / AUTHORITIES. In oval below title: B. TANNER, DEL. & SCULPT. Below bottom neat line: ENGRAVED FOR THE AMERICAN EDITION OF WINTERBOTHAMS HISTORY OF AMERICA, PUBLISHED BY JOHN REID. This map shows the OBLONG, an area in dispute between Connecticut and New York, and is copied from Map 284. The boundary line is shown following the BYRAM R. from LONG ISLAND SOUND to the line east of the *3* TREES. PART OF / VERMONT is at the upper left.

Size 13¹³⁄₁₆″ x 17″.   *Scale* 1″ = 7 miles.

Published in John Reid, *The American Atlas,* [1796?], no. 9; William Winterbotham, [Atlas].

289 1796   *State* II (see also Maps 288 and 290)

Description "Part of / Vermont" has been omitted at upper left.

Published in John Reid, *The American Atlas,* 1796, no. 9 (DLC cop. 3 & 4).

290 1796   *State* III (?) (see also Maps 288 and 289)

Description The date: *1796.* has been added below: AUTHORITIES in oval at lower right. No original copy of this map with this date added has thus far been discovered. It may have been added at the time of the preparation of the facsimile noted below.

Published Separately(?). Reproduced in U.S. Bureau of the Census, *Heads of Families at the First Census Connecticut,* front.

291 1797

Description In cartouche at lower right corner: A CORRECT MAP OF / CONNECTICUT / FROM ACTUAL SURVEY. At bottom of same cartouche: ENGRAVED BY A. DOOLITTLE NEW HAVEN / *1797*. Above top neat line: ENGRAVED FOR DR: TRUMBULL'S HISTORY OF CONNECTICUT. On this map, LISBON and FRANKLIN are transposed, although they are shown correctly by Doolittle earlier.

Size 12⅞″ x 16¼″.   *Scale* 1″ = 6½ miles.

Published in Benjamin Trumbull, *A Complete History of Connecticut,* opp. p. 1.

References Evans 32492; Edmund Thompson, *Maps of Connecticut before 1800,* pp. 52–53; U.S. Library of Congress, *Report 1916,* p. 66.

292 1799

Description In oval at lower right: A NEW MAP OF / CONNECTICUT / FROM THE BEST / AUTHORITIES. / *1799*. Below bottom neat line at left: A. ANDERSON, DEL. At center: ENGRAVED FOR PAYNES GEOGRAPHY, PUBLISHED BY J. LOW, N. YORK. Some topographical features as well as county and township boundaries, courthouses, and settlements with churches are shown. This map was copied from Map 288 including Benjamin Tanner's mistake of following the Byram River too far along the southwestern boundary.

Size 7⁷⁄₁₆″ x 9¼″.   *Scale* 1″ = 12 miles.

Published in John Payne, *A New and Complete Universal Geography,* 4, opp. 270.

293 [1799]   *State* II (see also Map 285)

Description Most of the lines have been re-cut and the degrees of latitude are now marked in the marginal degree lines. Many towns and some streams and roads have been added, including: SHARON, NEWTON, SUFFIELD, POMFRET, E. HADDAM, and LYME; also, the word "Road" is omitted from "POST ROAD" between New Haven and New London.

Published in Joseph Scott, *The New and Universal Gazetteer,* *1*, opp. "Connecticut."

294 [1747]

Description In ornamental cartouche at right center: MAP NO. I. Below cartouche: EN-GRAVED & PRINTED BY JAMES TURNER NEAR THE TOWN HOUSE BOSTON. On page four of the text of the *Bill* (see below) is stated: "This map . . . is copied from part of Popple's large Map of the English Colonies in America, except the red, blue, green and yellow Colours, and the Notes, which are added . . ." Henry Popple's "A Map of the British Empire in America . . ." had been published in London in 1733. A note following the title contains a listing of old Dutch names and their English equivalents. The area shown extends from Boston to Cape Hatteras. This is one of three maps, all engraved by James Turner, included in a *Bill* filed in the Court of Chancery, April 17, 1745, by the Board of General Proprietors concerning their claims to lands in the Newark-Elizabeth area of the Province of New Jersey. Both this map and Map 397 may have been adapted for publication by Lewis Evans. Evans is apparently the author of Map 398.

Size 15⅜" x 12⅞".   *Scale* None (1" = c. 33 miles).

Published in Board of General Proprietors of Eastern Division of New Jersey, *A Bill in the Chancery of New-Jersey*, foll. p. 124.

References William P. Cumming, *The South-east in Early Maps*, no. 266; Benjamin Franklin, *The Papers of*, 3, 32, 144–45; George J. Miller, "The Printing of the Elizabethtown Bill," pp. 10–12.

295 1749 *State* I (see also Maps 296 and 297)

Description At top center in slightly orna-mented cartouche: A MAP OF PENSILVANIA, NEW-JERSEY, NEW-YORK, / AND THE THREE DELAWARE COUNTIES: BY LEWIS EVANS. MDCCXLIX. In upper left corner: PUBLISHED BY LEWIS EVANS / MARCH 25 1749 ACCORDING TO / ACT OF PARLIAMENT. Be-low bottom neat line at right: L. HEBERT. SCULPT. This detailed topographical map shows the area extending from Lake Ontario to THE FALSE CAPE on the Delaware shore. Evans himself provides the following information concerning the map in this legend in the lower left corner: I HAVE

OMITTED NOTHING IN MY POWER TO RENDER THIS MAP AS COMPLETE AS POSSIBLE. AND THO' NO DISTANCE COULD BE TAKEN BUT BY ACTUAL / MEN-SURATION (THE WOODS BEING YET SO THICK) I CAN DECLARE IT TO BE MORE EXACT THAN COULD BE WELL EXPECTED; BUT THE MERIT IS FAR / FROM BEING MY OWN. TO FILL THOSE PARTS, WHERE OUR SETTLEMENTS AND DISCOVERIES HAVE NOT YET EX-TENDED TO, I HAVE INTRODUCED SEVL. / USEFUL REMARKS IN PHYSICS & COMMERCE. THE GENEROSITY OF SEVL. GENTM. EXPECIALLY MESSS. NICHS. SCULL, JOSEPH REEVES, GEO. SMITH, / JOHN LYDIUS, & NICHS. STILWIL, IN FURNISHING ME WITH THEIR DRAUGHTS & DISCOVERIES DEMANDS MY THANKS AND ACKNOWLEDGMENT. / I HAVE BEEN ASSISTED WITH THE DRAUGHTS OF MANY OTHER GENT. THAT I HAD NOT IMMEDIATE ACQUAINTANCE WITH, AMONGST WHICH THE / MS. & PRINTED MAPS OF THE NORTH-ERN NECK, MR. LAWRENCE'S NEW DIVISION LINE OF JERSEY & MR. NOXON'S MAP OF THE THREE LOWER / COUNTIES WERE NOT THE LEAST REMARKABLE. THE COLLECTIONS OF ISAAC NORRIS AND JAMES ALEXANDER ESQS. WERE OF SINGULAR SER- / VICE TO ME, AS CONTAINING VARIETY OF DRAUGHTS NOT TO BE MET WITH ELSEWHERE. AND THE GREATEST PART OF NEW YORK PROVINCE IS / OWING TO THE HONOURABLE CADWALLADER COLDEN ESQR. The USEFUL REMARKS IN PHYSICS AND COMMERCE re-ferred to above are provided in long legends en-graved on various places on the face of the map. They give information on climate, navigation of bays and rivers, and many other related sub-jects. The note, at the upper left, on the prog-ress of storms: ALL OUR GREAT STORMS BEGIN TO LEEWARD: THUS A NE STORM SHALL BE A DAY SOONER IN VIRGINIA THAN BOSTON . . . , is con-sidered to be the first recorded statement that our storms travel in an easterly direction.

Thomas Pownall, on page 45 of his *Topo-graphical Description*, states that this map was "printed at Philadelphia 1749," and, although Evans (no. 6316) definitely lists it as from the New York press of James Parker, Dr. Lawrence C. Wroth, in an appendix (VI, page 153) of his *An American Bookshelf 1755*, produces evidence to substantiate Pownall's statement. The en-graver is evidently the Lawrence Hebert or Her-bert who advertised as working in Philadelphia in 1748 and 1751.

Size 25⁹⁄₁₆" x 18¹⁵⁄₁₆".   *Scale* 1" = 15½ miles.

Published Separately. Reproduced in Lawrence H. Gipson, *Lewis Evans*, p. 223; *Pennsylvania Archives*, 3d Ser., Appendix; Henry N. Stevens, *Lewis Evans His Map of the Middle British Colonies*, opp. p. 58.

References Evans 6316; Thomas Pownall, *A Topographical Description*; Henry N. Stevens, *Lewis Evans His Map of 1752*; Lawrence C. Wroth, *An American Bookshelf 1755*, pp. 148-55; see also reproductions above, under Published.

Locations BM, DLC, MdHi, MH, PHi, RPJCB.

296 1752 *State* II (see also Maps 295 and 297)

Description Under Lewis Evans' name in upper left corner: THE SECOND EDITION. JULY 1752. The name HEATH still appears just west of Trenton, in New Jersey. The name EASTON appears here. Richard Peters wrote Thomas Penn, May 3, 1753, that some impressions of this state were sent him before this name was added. Evans has made some changes in the place names near the entrance to Delaware Bay, attempting to straighten out the confusion regarding Cape Hinlopen which was caused by the attempted arbitrary allocation of this name by Lord Chancellor Hardwick to the intersection of the southern Delaware line with the Atlantic coast. The northern boundary line of Pennsylvania, shown at latitude 42° on the map of 1749, still remains lettered THE BOUNDS OF PENSILVANIA BY PATENT, but a new dotted line, at about 42° 44', appears with: THE ROYAL PATENT GRANTING MR. PENN 3 DEG. OF LAT. & A DECREE IN / CHANCERY DETERMINING HIS SOUTHERN LIMITS WILL PROBABLY EXTEND / THE NORTHERN BOUNDS OF PENSILVANIA TO THIS LATITUDE.

The southern boundary line of Pennsylvania, which appears as a dotted line in the 1749 map, is now emphasized with an additional black line and this note: NB. THE BLACK LINE SHEWS THE / TRUE LIMITS, ACCORDING TO A DE- / CREE IN CHANCERY, MAY 15. 1750. The western and southern bounds of the Delaware counties have been added in dotted lines. In the top left corner, the southern shore of Lake Ontario has been extended through the engraved lettering as far as the left degree line. A dotted line has been added, extending from near the junction of the East and West Branches of the Susquehanna River eastward to Viskill on the East Branch of the Delaware River. With this is noted: RELEASED BY THE INDIAN HUTTOONGALIACS FROM THE KITTATINNI MS. TO THIS LINE / AUG. 22. 1749. Other place names and new counties have been added and the bounds of certain counties considerably altered.

Published Separately.

References U.S. Library of Congress, *Report 1929*, pp. 150-51; Lawrence C. Wroth, *An American Bookshelf 1755*, pp. 154-55.

Location DLC.

297 1752 *State* III (see also Maps 295 and 296)

Description This map has the same title as State II but is a later impression containing additional names and roads north and east of Trenton in New Jersey, notably: SUNBURY, BELMONT, POMFRET, SIDNEY, HAMBDEN, and REDDING. The name "Heath" has been removed just west of Trenton. Correspondence between Richard Peters and Thomas Penn indicates that these corrections were made before 1753.

Published Separately. Reproduced in Lawrence H. Gipson, *Lewis Evans*, p. 227; Henry N. Stevens, *Lewis Evans His Map of 1752*, opp. p. 4.

References U.S. Library of Congress, *Report 1930*, p. 174; see also reproductions above, under Published.

Locations CSmH, DLC, MdHi.

298 1755 *State* I (see also Map 299)

Description In cartouche at upper center: A GENERAL MAP OF THE / MIDDLE BRITISH COLONIES, IN AMERICA; / VIZ VIRGINIA, MÀRILAND, DÈLAWARE, PENSILVANIA, / NEW-JERSEY, NEW-YORK, CONNECTICUT, AND RHODE ISLAND: / OF AQUANISHUONÎGY, THE COUNTRY OF THE CONFEDERATE INDIANS; / COMPREHENDING AQUANISHUONÎGY PROPER, THEIR PLACE OF RESIDENCE, / OHIO AND TÏIUXSOXRÚNTIE THEIR DEER-HUNTING COUNTRIES; / COUXSAXRÁGE AND SKANIADARÂDE, THEIR BEAVER-HUNTING COUNTRIES; / OF THE LAKES ERIE, ONTÁRIO AND CHAMPLAIN, / AND OF PART OF NEW-FRANCE: / WHEREIN IS ALSO SHEWN THE ANTIENT AND PRESENT SEATS OF THE INDIAN NATIONS. / BY LEWIS EVANS. 1755. At left of cartouche: ENGRAVED BY JAS. TURNER IN PHILADELPHIA. In lower right corner: PUBLISHED ACCORDING TO ACT OF PARLIAMENT, BY LEWIS EVANS, JUNE 23. 1755. AND / SOLD BY R. DODSLEY, IN PALL-MALL, LONDON, & BY THE AUTHOR IN PHILADELPHIA. This is one of the landmarks of American cartography and the best known of Lewis Evans' maps. It shows an area extending from Montreal and the lower end of Lake Huron to the North Carolina border and from the Falls of the Ohio to Narragansett Bay. Of special interest is the description of the Ohio Country, the accuracy of this part of the map being remarkable for this period. Thomas Hutchins pays a tribute to Evans by using his work verbatim as late as 1778. The map itself was republished many times, with and without credit to Evans, in England, France, and Germany as late as 1814. In the upper left corner is a dedication: TO THE HONOURABLE THOMAS POWNALL ESQR; in the lower right corner are three tables of distances; at lower center is this inscription: FOR A PARTICULAR MAP OF VIRGINIA THE READER IS / REFERRED TO THAT BY FRY AND JEFFERSON, PUBLISH'D BY MR. / JEFFERYS NEAR CHARING-CROSS LONDON, IN *1751*. The map referred to is Joshua Fry and Peter Jefferson's "A Map of the most inhabited part of Virginia . . . ," London, [1755]. There are many important geographical and topographical notes and great care has been used to show the lands claimed by the different Indian tribes, especially the Confederate Nations. The BUFFALOE SWAMP and GREAT SWAMP are shown as on Map 422. A state previous to the one described here may have been issued with the inset showing the Illinois Country omitted (see Gipson, *Lewis Evans,* p. 65, footnote 25). The engraver was James Turner.

Size 19⅜" x 25⁵⁄₁₆".   *Scale* 1" = 36 English miles.

Inset In cartouche at upper left: A SKETCH / OF THE REMAINING PART / OF OHIO R. &C. This shows the Illinois country. Size: 6⅜" x 5³⁄₁₆". Scale: 1" = 100 English miles.

Published in Lewis Evans, *Geographical, Historical, Political, Philosophical and Mechanical Essays;* some copies of ibid., 2d ed. Reproduced in Henry N. Stevens, *Lewis Evans His Map of the Middle British Colonies,* London, 1920, No. II, foll. p. 58.

References Baltimore Museum of Art, *The World Encompassed,* no. 255; Evans 7411–13; Hazel S. Garrison, "Cartography of Pennsylvania," pp. 270–74; Lawrence H. Gipson, *Lewis Evans,* pp. 55–72; Charles O. Paullin, *Atlas of Historical Geography,* p. 13 (Jeffery's 1758 reprint used for plate); *Pennsylvania Archives,* 2; Philip L. Phillips, *A List of Maps of America,* p. 575; U.S. Library of Congress, *Report 1930,* p. 174; Justin Winsor, ed., *Narrative and Critical History,* 5, 83; Lawrence C. Wroth, *An American Bookshelf 1755,* pp. 115–60.

299 1755 *State* II (see also Map 298)

Description The words: THE LAKES CATARAQUI have been added just north of LAKE ONTARIO. This map was advertised in the (Philadelphia) *Pennsylvania Gazette,* March 11, 1756, and later issues. In 1776, the plate for this was considerably altered in London, and the title changed to read, "A Map of the / Middle British Colonies in North America / First Published by Mr. Lewis Evans, of Philadelphia, in 1755; / with the addition of New England, . . . By T.

Pownall MP. / . . . London. / March 25th. 1776." With an extension showing New England, the map appeared thus in Thomas Pownall, *A Topographical Description.* Numerous alterations are made in the western portion of the map including the route of Christopher Gist in 1750–51 and an alternate course for the lower reach of the Ohio River. The alterations are all explained in the text.

Published in some copies of Lewis Evans, *Geographical, Historical, Political, Philosophical and Mechanical Essays,* 2d ed.; Separately. Reproduced in *Pennsylvania Archives,* 3d Ser., Appendix; Lawrence H. Gipson, *Lewis Evans,* p. 231; Henry N. Stevens, *Lewis Evans His Map of the Middle British Colonies,* foll. p. 58, nos. XIIIa, XIIIb (extension); accompanying Ethyl Corporation, *Lewis Evans.*

References See reproductions above, under Published.

Locations DLC, PHi.

300 [1771] *State* I (see also Maps 301 and 305)

Description [A map of part of Pennsylvania & Maryland intended to shew, at one view, the several places proposed for opening a communication between the waters of the Delaware & Chesopeak Bays.] Beneath scale at left: J. SMITHER SCULP. At upper right: PLATE VII, FIG. I. There is no neat line. Figure two, on the same plate at the left, is a perspective drawing of a machine for cutting files. The map accompanies "An Abstract of Sunday Papers and Proposals for Improving the Inland Navigation of Pennsylvania and Maryland . . . ," in the *Transactions* of the American Philosophical Society. The "Abstract" and map were the result of the work of the Committee for American Improvements which had been appointed by the Society to investigate the best roads and canals connecting the navigable waters of the Susquehanna and Delaware rivers. The Committee had been especially active during 1769, and on March 2, 1770, a manuscript map with the above title was presented to the Society by W. T. Fisher (i.e., Thomas Fisher). On May 18 Fisher and Mathew Clarkson were asked to begin work preparing the material for publication. On November 2, 1770, the "Abstract of Canal Papers [were] read & ordered to be printed. Fisher's map ordered to be engraved."

Size 12½" x 13⅛" (map area only). 12½" x 16¾" (entire plate).   *Scale* 1" = 7¾ miles.

Published in American Philosophical Society, *Transactions, I* (1771), foll. 292.

References American Philosophical Society,

Early Proceedings from 1744 to 1838; David M. Stauffer, *American Engravers, 2,* 492.

301 1772 *State* II (see also Maps 300 and 305)

Description The same map, with no changes, was also issued as a broadside with a page headed: REMARKS., and dated at bottom right: PHILADELPHIA, JANUARY 20, 1772. The perspective drawing of the file cutting machine is usually trimmed off the broadside printing.

Size 12½″ x 19¾″. *Scale* 1″ = 7¾ miles.

Published Separately.

Location PPAmP, PL.

[1774] see Map 260.

302 [1777]

Description [Map of New Jersey and Pennsylvania, with Part of Maryland and Virginia, wherein the Delaware and Cheasapeak (sic) bays, are accurately laid down.] This map was advertised in the (Philadelphia) *Pennsylvania Journal* of March 12, 1777, by John Norman.

Size Unknown. *Scale* Unknown.

Published Separately.

Reference Harry B. Weiss, "John Norman," p. 6.

Location No copy located.

303 [1777] *State* II (see also Map 327)

Description [A Map of the present Seat of War, including the States of New York and Connecticut, with part of New Jersey, and extending northward as far as Crown Point. Also shewing the passage of the ships into the Sound, by the east end of Long-Island.] This title is taken from an advertisement by John Norman in the (Philadelphia) *Pennsylvania Journal,* March 12, 1777. This is probably an enlarged and improved state of Map 327.

Size Unknown. *Scale* Unknown.

Published Separately.

Reference Harry B. Weiss, "John Norman," p. 6.

Location No copy located.

304 [1778]

Description Below bottom neat line at left: A CHOROGRAPHICAL MAP OF THE COUNTRY ROUND PHILADELPHIA. Below bottom neat line at right: BY B-ROMANS. The Romans imprint as given on this map means he engraved it as well as drew

it. It is dated by advertisements in the (Hartford) *Connecticut Courant* for June 2, 1778, and the *New London Gazette* and the (New London) *Connecticut Gazette* for June 5, 1778, announcing publication. Valley Forge is indicated by a cluster of tents and inscribed: GRAND AMERICAN WINTER CAMP JANUARY 1778. The TRACKS of the armies of Generals Washington and Sir William Howe are shown. The map was copied and republished by Cóvens and Mortier in Amsterdam, about 1780.

Size 11⅞″ x 13⅛″. *Scale* 1″ = 12½ miles.

Published Separately. Reproduced in *The Month at Goodspeed's, 10* (1938–39), 138–39.

References Philip L. Phillips, *Notes on Bernard Romans,* pp. 91–92; James H. Trumbull, *List of Books Printed in Connecticut 1709–1800,* no. 1064.

Locations CtHi, PP, RPJCB.

305 [1789] *State* III (see also Maps 300 and 301)

Description TURKEY PT. has been added near the mouth of the ELKE RIVER. A previously unnamed island near the head of Chesapeake Bay is now labeled PURSUSEY ISL. This is probably modern Spesutie Island. The date at the bottom has been removed.

Size 12⅜″ x 13⅛″. *Scale* 1″ = 7¾ miles.

Published in American Philosophical Society, *Transactions,* 2d ed. corrected, *1* (1789), opp. 367.

Locations MiU-C, PPAmP.

306 [1790]

Description In oval at top center: CHART / OF THE / COAST OF AMERICA / FROM / CAPE MAY / TO / MACHAPUNGO; beneath oval: BOSTON PUBLISHED & SOLD BY MATTHEW CLARK; in upper left corner: NO. 10. The chart bears an engraved inscription, which was signed by Osgood Carleton when sold singly, stating that it was examined and compared with the best charts and found accurate. In the Library of Congress copy of Clark's [*Chart*], this and Map 307 are pasted together.

Size 16⅞″ x 24¾″. *Scale* None (1″ = c. 6 miles).

Published in Matthew Clark, [*A Complete Chart*], no. 10; separately.

307 [1790]

Description In oval at upper left center: CHART / OF THE / COAST OF AMERICA / FROM /

NEW YORK HARBOUR / TO / CAPE MAY; in oval below title: BOSTON PUBLISHED & SOLD BY MATTHEW CLARK; at upper left corner: NO. 9. The chart bears an engraved inscription, which was signed by Osgood Carleton when sold singly, stating that it was examined and compared with the best charts and found accurate. SANDY HOOK is shown as an island. In the Library of Congress copy of Clark's, [Chart], this and Map 306 are pasted together.

Size 17⅜" x 24⅛". *Scale* None (1" = c. 6 miles).

Published in Matthew Clark, [*A Complete Chart*], no. 9; separately.

308 [1791]

Description Near right center: A CHART / FROM / NEW YORK / TO / WHIMBLE SHOALS. A certificate testifying to the charts' accuracy appears under the title, signed by Osgood Carleton. This chart was engraved on three plates. The upper one has been reduced and the degree and neat lines on the right recut to match the plate below it.

Size 38" x 20⅛". *Scale* 1" = 8⅓ nautical miles.

Published in John Norman, *The American Pilot*, [1791], no. 5; ibid., 1792, no. 6; ibid., 1794, no. 6.

309 [1794]

Description In upper left corner of border *1458 / 1548 / 1638*. This is one section of a large indexed topographical map intended to cover the entire United States and possibly more. It includes parts of Ulster and Orange counties in southern New York, north-western New Jersey, and north-eastern Pennsylvania. The indexing is done by means of many letters on the map which are used as references, and are explained in the text of the book. The map sections are supplied loose and are not bound with the alphabetical references, alphabetical indexes, or directions for use of the maps which comprise the book that the maps were made to accompany. The middle number of the three at the upper left corner, *1548*, identifies this section of the main map. The lesser number above this, *1458*, identifies the section just north of this and the greater number below, *1638*, identifies the section just south. The adjoining map on the east of this section is identified as number *1549*. These adjoining map sections all match each other's adjacent edges. There is an upper border consisting of three marginal degree lines showing longitude from Paris, London, and Philadelphia. Above these is another border line with the scale attached. Inside the

extreme left border line are marginal scale lines showing: GREATEST LENGTH OF DAYS AND NIGHTS and degrees of latitude. (See also Maps 154–56 and 358.)

Size 14¾" x 20⅝". *Scale* 1" = 10 miles.

Published with Christopher Colles, *The Geographical Ledger and Systematized Atlas.*

References Christopher Colles, *A Survey of the Roads 1789*, 1961, pp. 77–81; Lloyd W. Griffen, "Christopher Colles," pp. 178–82.

Location DLC.

310 [1794] *State* I (II post-1799, see below, Description)

Description In rectangle at lower right corner: A NEW AND ACCURATE CHART / OF THE / / BAY OF CHESAPEAK / INCLUDING DELAWARE BAY / WITH ALL THE SHOALS, CHANNELS, ISLANDS, ENTRANCCS [sic], SOUNDINGS, & SAILING / MARKS AS FAR AS THE NAVIGABLE PART OF / THE RIVERS PATOWMACK PATAPSCO & N EAST / DRAWN FROM SEVERAL DRAUGHTS MADE BY THE MOST EXPERIENCED NAVIGATORS / CHIEFLY FROM THOSE OF ANTHONY SMITH PILOT OF ST MAPYS [sic] / AND COMPARED WITH THE LATEST SURVEYS OF / VIRGINIA AND MARYLAND. In rectangle below the title: BOSTON PRINTED & SOLD BY W. NORMAN AT HIS SHOP NO. 75 NEWBURY STREET. There is a certificate signed by Osgood Carleton at center and many notes about currents, tides, and soundings. Minute sailing directions are also given. Four plates are used. This chart was republished in William Norman's *American Pilot*, Boston, 1803. ST. MAPYS in the title has been corrected to "St. Marys" in this later state.

Size 41" x 33". *Scale* 1" = 5½ miles.

Published in William Norman, *The American Pilot*, 1794, no. 6; ibid., 1798, no. 5.

311 [1796]

Description [The Susquehanna River and surrounding areas.] Below neat line at lower right corner: W. BARKER, SCULP. Shown here are the primary rivers and roads of an area extending from OSWEGO FT. on the north to CHESAPEAK BAY, and from New York City to the western Pennsylvania border.

Size 7⅝" x 8¼". *Scale* None (1" = c. 45 miles).

Published in [Jonathan W. Condy], *A Description of the River Susquehanna*, opp. p. 60.

References Samuel Breck, *Sketch of the Internal Improvements already made by Pennsylvania*, p. 44; Evans 30338; Sabin 93935.

312 [1798]

Description At lower left: A MAP OF / PENN-SYLVANIA / DELAWARE / NEW JERSEY & / MARY-LAND, / WITH THE PARTS ADJACENT; below bottom neat line at right corner: THACKARA SC; above top neat line at center: ENGRAV'D FOR R P'S HISTY. OF PENNA. This is a topographical map showing also political boundaries and major roads. CAPE INLOPEN OR / CAPE JAMES, CAPE HIN-LOPEN OR / FENWICKS ISLAND, FEDERAL CITY, and THE RAPID ANN R. appear thus. TERRITORIES OF PENNSYLVANIA / NOW / DELAWARE appears on that State.

Size 12 3/16" x 15 1/8". *Scale* 1" = 28 miles.

Published in Robert Proud, *The History of Pennsylvania*, 2, front.

313 1798

Description On decorated scroll at lower left: A / MAP OF THE MIDDLE / STATES, SHEWING THE / SITUATION OF THE GENESEE / LANDS & THEIR CONNECTION / WITH THE ATLANTIC COAST / *1798*. This map shows only the water routes, including many of the Finger Lakes, which are unnamed. A road is shown from the lakes to Ft. Niagara and Lake Erie. Charles Williamson was the agent of the Pultney Estate in New York. A view of Fort Oswego in the same book was drawn by Simeon DeWitt and engraved by Gideon Fairman.

Size 10 1/4" x 9 5/8". *Scale* None (1" = c. 35 miles).

Published in [Charles Williamson], *Description of the Genesee Country*, foll. p. 37.

References Evans 35033; Robert W. G. Vail, *Old Frontier*, no. 1182.

314 [1799] *State* I (see also Maps 315 and 316)

Description At lower right: A / MAP / OF THE / MIDDLE STATES OF NORTH AMERICA. The Macomb, Totten, and Crosfield & Morris tracts are named and located. The counties of Ontario and Steuben in New York are shown with their ranges of townships. The PENNSYLVANIA LINE is shown. Only a few main roads, states, and other prominent names and waterway features are given. COLUMBIA / OR THE / FEDERAL CITY is shown south of the Potomac River. There are sixteen lettered references on the map but no table of explanation for them.

Size 14 5/8" x 15 9/16". *Scale* None (1" = 35 miles).

Published in [Charles Williamson], *Description of the Settlement of the Genesee Country*, front.

References Evans 36727; Robert W. G. Vail, *Old Frontier*, no. 1221.

315 [1799] *State* II (see also Maps 314 and 316)

Description The title remains the same but seventeen REFERENCES have been added at the upper left as well as further geographical details.

Published in [Charles Williamson], *Description of the Settlement of the Genesee Country*.

Reference Robert W. G. Vail, *Old Frontier*, no. 1221.

316 1799 *State* III (see also Maps 314 and 315)

Description In lower right corner the full title now reads: A / MAP / OF THE / MIDDLE STATES OF NORTH AMERICA, / SHEWING THE POSITION OF THE GENESEO / COUNTRY COMPREHENDING THE COUNTIES OF / ONTARIO & STEUBEN AS LAID OFF IN TOWN— / SHIPS OF SIX MILES SQUARE EACH. Below title and scale: MAVERICK SCULPT:—*65* LIBERTY STREET N.Y. The engraver is probably Peter Rushton Maverick.

Published in [Charles Williamson], *Description of the Settlement of the Genesee Country*, front.; idem, *Observations on the Proposed State Road*, opp. title page.

References Philip L. Phillips, *A List of Maps of America*, p. 869; Robert W. G. Vail, *Old Frontier*, nos. 1221 and 1265.

317 [1724] *State* I (see also Map 318)

Description At top center: A MAP OF THE COUNTRY OF THE FIVE NATIONS / BELONGING TO THE PROVINCE OF NEW YORK AND OF / THE LAKES NEAR WHICH THE NATIONS OF FAR INDIANS / LIVE WITH PART OF CANADA TAKEN FROM THE MAP OF THE / LOUISIANE DONE BY MR. DELISLE IN *1718*. Cadwallader Colden was at this time Surveyor-General of the Province of New York. A map answering the description of this engraved map was drawn by Colden and sent to Lord John Carteret accompanying a letter from Governor William Burnet dated December 16, 1723. This map was first engraved to form the frontispiece of Colden's 1724, *Papers*. No author's, draughtsman's, or engraver's name appears on the map, nor does a place of execution. The impression is faint. It has been claimed to be the first map engraved in New York but no definite evidence is available. The country shown extends from Lake Michigan to below Quebec and from the eastern end of Lake Superior to New Jersey. The main water routes with the portages are shown. DETROIT OR TUSACKRONDE appears, and IAGARA for Niagara. Along the right side appears a note: N. B. THE TUSCARORAS / ARE NOW RECKON'D A SIXTH / NATION . . . AND YE NECARIAGES . . . SEVENTH . . . THE CHIEF TRADE . . . IS AT YE / ONONDAGES RIVERS MOUTH / WHERE THEY MUST ALL / PASS TO GO TOWARDS / CANADA. It was advertised by William Bradford in his *New-York Gazette*, February 20–27, 1727. The Guillaume de L'Isle map mentioned in the title was his, "Carte de la Louisiane et du cours du Mississipi, Paris, 1718."

Size 8⅜″ x 13¾″.   *Scale* 1″ = 80 miles.

Published in Cadwallader Colden, *Papers Relating to an Act of New York for Encouragement of the Indian Trade*, front; idem, *History of the Five Indian Nations*, but not as an integral part of book; separately. Reproduced in *Photostat Americana*, 2d Ser., no. 55, opp. p. 1.

References George Brinley, *Catalogue of the American Library*, nos. 3384, 3446; *Documents Relative to the Colonial History of New-York*, 5, 704; Louis C. Karpinski, *Bibliography of the Printed Maps of Michigan*, p. 141; Isaac N. P. Stokes, *Iconography of Manhattan Island*, *1*, 255; ibid., *3*, 862; ibid., *6*, 259; Robert W. G. Vail, *Old Frontier*, no. 342.

[1732–33] see Map 256.

318 [1735] *State* II (see also Map 317)

Description Title now reads: . . . LIVE WITH PART OF CANADA & RIVER ST. LAWRENCE. The title and note at right are now enclosed in double line borders. The longitude degree designations at the top are changed, as is also the configuration of the portion of the Atlantic coast that is shown. More than 50 new place names have been added such as, OSWEGO, LAKE ST CLAIR, PEKEPSEY, HIGH LANDS, and IERSEY. The knowledge gained during ten years of Colden's surveys shows in these additions. The only changes to the waterways and coastlines were made inside the province of New York and in New York harbor. The shape of the harbor was greatly improved but the corrections to the upstate rivers and lakes do not improve the map very much. Niagara now appears as ONIAGRA. William Bradford advertised this reissue in the *New-York Gazette*, August 25–September 1, 1735. The University of Virginia's copy is found inserted opp. p. 1 in a copy of the 1727 edition of Colden's *Papers* (i.e. *The History of the Five Indian Nations*).

Published Separately.

References Cadwallader Colden, *The History of the Five Indian Nations*; Isaac N. P. Stokes, *Iconography of Manhattan Island*, *1*, 255; ibid., *3*, 862; ibid., *6*, 260; idem and Daniel C. Haskell, *American Historical Prints*, p. 23.

Locations ICN, NHi, NN, ViU.

319 [1751]

Description At center: THE / GREAT NINE PARTNERS TRACT. This is a map made up of type inserts and metal line material showing the bounds of the original grant, reaching from the east bank of the Hudson River to the Connecticut line near Crown Elbow. The "N" in the direction sign is reversed.

Size 6¹³⁄₁₆″ x 4⅛″.   *Scale* None (1″ = c. 7 miles).

Published in John Bard, *A Letter to the Proprietors*, foll. p. 22.

Reference Robert W. G. Vail, *Old Frontier*, no. 448.

320 1755 *State I (see also Map 321)*

Description At bottom right: A PROSPECTIVE PLAN OF THE BATTLE FOUGHT NEAR LAKE GEORGE ON THE 8TH OF SEPTEMBER *1755*, BETWEEN *2000* ENGLISH WITH *250* / MOHAWKS UNDER THE COMMAND OF GENERAL JOHNSON AND *2500* FRENCH AND INDIANS UNDER THE COMMAND OF GENERAL DIESKAU / IN WHICH THE ENGLISH WERE VICTORIOUS, CAPTIVATING THE FRENCH GENERAL WITH A NUMBER OF HIS MEN, KILLING *700* AND PUTTING THE REST TO FLIGHT. Above dedication cartouche at lower left: S. BLODGET DEL. and THOS. JOHNSTON SCULP:. The PLAN is actually in two parts: at left center is a view of the first engagement of the battle with reference numbers one through five; at right center is a somewhat larger view of the second engagement with reference numbers six through thirty-nine. The numbers are explained in the accompanying pamphlet, noted below. A dedication to Governor William Shirley is given in a cartouche at the lower left. Samuel Blodget, the author, was present at the battle as a sutler. The pamphlet and plan were republished, the plan with some changes, by Thomas Jefferys in London in 1756.

Size 13⅝″ x 17¾″.   *Scale* None.

Insets [a] At upper center and left is a plan of: HUDSONS RIVER. Size: 2¹³⁄₁₆″ x 14¼″. Scale: 1″ = 15 miles FOR YE LENGTH OF YE RIVER; 1″ = 4 miles FOR YE WEDTH OF YE RIVER.

[b] At upper right center: FORT / WILLIAM / HENRY. Size: 1⅝″ x 2¼″. Scale: None (1″ = c. 500 feet).

[c] In upper right corner: FORT / EDWARD. Size: 2¾″ x 3⁷⁄₁₆″. Scale: None (1″ = c. 180 feet).

Published with Samuel Blodget, *A prospective-Plan of the Battle near Lake George* (some copies were apparently issued with "Plan" inserted). Reproduced in Isaac N. P. Stokes and Daniel C. Haskell, *American Historical Prints*, pl. 16; an edition of 125 copies was issued in Boston in 1902, according to Evans.

References Samuel Blodget, *The Battle Near Lake George in 1755 a Prospective Plan from Edition Published in London in 1756 with Note by Henry N. Stevens*; Evans 7363; Samuel A. Green, *Ten Fac-simile Reproductions Relating to New England*, pp. 33–35; Massachusetts Historical Society, *Proceedings*, 2d Ser., 5 (1889–1890), 416–18; David M. Stauffer, *American Engravers*, 2, 251; Robert W. G. Vail, *Old Frontier*, no. 473; see also reproductions above, under Published.

Locations MB, MWiW, NHi, NN, RPJCB.

321 1755 *State II (see also Map 320)*

Description Trees have been added around FORT / EDWARD on Inset [c].

Published with Samuel Blodget, *A Prospective Plan of the Battle near Lake George*. Reproduced in Samuel A. Green, *Ten Fac-simile Reproductions Relating to New England*, foll. p. 36; Massachusetts Historical Society *Proceedings*, 2d Ser., 5 (1889–1890), opp. 416.

References See reproductions above, under Published.

Location MHi.

322 1756

Description In ornate cartouche at upper left: TO HIS / EXCELLENCY WILLIAM SHIRLEY ESQR: . . . THIS PLAN / OF HUDSONS RIVR: / FROM ALBANY TO FORT / EDWARD, (& YE ROAD FROM THENCE TO LAKE GEORGE AS SURVEY'D) LAKE GEORGE, THE / NARROWS, CROWN POINT, PART OF LAKE CHAMPLAIN WITH ITS SOUTH BAY, / AND WOOD CREEK ACCORDING TO YE BEST ACCOUNTS FROM YE FRENCH GENLS; PLAN; / & OTHER OBSERVATIONS (BY SCALE NO; *1*) & AN EXACT PLAN OF FORT EDWARD / & WILLIAM HENRY (BY SCALE NO 2) & YE WEST END OF LAKE GEO; & OF YE / LAND DEFENDED ON Y 8TH, OF SEPT; LAST & OF OUR ARMY'S INTRENCHMENT AFTERWARD / BY SCALE 3) & SUNDRY PARTICULARS RESPECTING YE LATE ENGAGEMENT WITH YE DIS- / TANCE & BEARING OF CROWN POINT AND WOOD CREEK FROM NO: *4* BY / YOUR MOST DEVOTED HUMBLE SERVT; / TIMO; CLEMENT / SURVR:. Just below cartouche at right: HAVERL: FEB: *10 1756*. At left center in Fort Edward inset: ENGRAV'D & PRINTED BY THOMAS JOHNSTON BOSTON NEW-ENGLAND APRIL *1756*. This plan was published shortly after Map 320. In Timothy Clement's petition to the Massachusetts authorities for compensation, he states:

"I have hear Gentlemen Laid to your vew a Plan of what I surveyed, with sum farther intelligence of the Laying of the Lakes and of their Distance: Which I took from the French Plans: Which we Took on the 8th of Septr. from the french Generall . . ."

At the lower left is a small scale diagram giving the bearings of Crown Point and Wood Creek (at Fort Anne) from Mohawk Hill and from the Connecticut River a little below NO. *4* (modern Charlestown, N.H.).

Size 17⅜″ x 26¾″.   *Scale* 1″ = 3½ miles.

Insets [a] Below cartouche at left center: FORT EDWARD. An outline plan showing the primary buildings of the Fort. THE WAGON ROAD leads from the Fort to the right. Size: 6½″ x 9⅜″. Scale: 1″ = 6 rods.

[b] At upper right: FORT WILLIAM HENRY. An outline plan of the Fort with a view of the several phases of the Battle of Lake George and the entrenchments. Size: 10¾" x 7⅜". Scale: (of Fort) 1" = 6 rods; (of surrounding area) 1" = 15 rods.

Published   Separately. Reproduced separately by Mr. Howe Fisher, 1932 (Williams College copy); in Justin Winsor, ed., *Narrative and Critical History, 5*, 586a (a rough sketch of the American Antiquarian Society copy.)

References   Evans 7390; Massachusetts Archives, 75, 422–23 (Timothy Clement's Petition, March 31, 1756); Robert W. G. Vail, *Old Frontier*, no. 473.

Locations   MH,   MWA,   MWiW,   NHi, RPJCB.

323   [1760]

Description   Above neat line across top: A MAP OF THE COUNTRY BETWEEN CROWN-POINT AND F. EDWARD. This is a topographical map showing the roads and trails connecting the several forts of this area. The references are explained on the page following.

Size   5½" x 3½".   *Scale*   1" = c. 10 miles.

Published   in Roger More, [pseud.], *Poor Roger; 1761*.

324   [1762]

Description   At lower center: PLAN / OF NIAGARA / WITH THE ADJACENT COUNTRY / SURRENDRED / TO THE ENGLISH ARMY / UNDER THE COMMAND / OF SR. WILLM. JOHNSON BART. / ON THE 25TH. OF JULY *1759*. In cartouche at lower left: TO THE / HONBLE. SIR WILLM. JOHNSON BART. / ENGRAVED AND PUBLISHED BY / MICHAEL & SON GODHART DEBRULS, / IN NEW-YORK NORTH AMERICA. This is a detailed, topographical map of the country around the mouth of the Niagara River. It is engraved on two plates. There are sixteen lettered references to the main map explained in a table below the title. The entrenchments and disposition of the troops are shown. This was advertised in the (New York) *American Chronicle*, April 19, 1762, and the *New-York Mercury*, May 3, 1762, as being prepared for delivery on June 28 next. Michael De Bruls, or Michelson Godhart, was actively engraving in New York from 1757 to 1763.

Size   12¾" x 34¼".   *Scale*   1" = 100 fathoms.

Inset   At lower corner: PLAN / AND REFERENCES / OF / FORT NIAGARA. Below table of references at lower right: LAID DOWN BY GEORGE DEMLER INGENIER. Size: 9⁹⁄₁₆" x 14⅜". Scale: 1" = 25 fathoms.

Published   Separately.

References   [Rita S. Gottesman], *The Arts and Crafts in New York 1726–1776*, pp. 9–10; David M. Stauffer, *American Engravers, I*, 31.

Location   NHi.

325   [1762]

Description   [A Plan of Part of Lake Champlain, and the large New Fort at Crown-Point, mounting 108 Cannon, built by General Amherst; Done from an actual Survey taken by Francis Miller. With References and Explanations of the different Plans.] This title is taken from an advertisement appearing in the *Boston News-Letter*, May 20, 1762. Also noted is that: "On the same sheet are Perspective Views of Quebec and Montreal." The map was also advertised in the *Boston Gazette*, June 7, 1762.

Size   Unknown.   *Scale*   Unknown.

Published   Separately.

References   George F. Dow, *Arts & Crafts in New England*, p. 31; David M. Stauffer, *American Engravers, 2*, 252.

Location   No copy located.

326   [before 1769]

Description   [Western Shore of Lake Champlain.] In a letter of August 10, 1769, to the Earl of Hillsborough, Governor Henry Moore of New York states: ". . . As some Townships were supposed to be laid out on the west side of Lake Champlain (altho' there was no foundation for such a supposition than a Map printed in the Province of Connecticut) . . ." No identification of this map has thus far been made.

Size   Unknown.   *Scale*   Unknown.

Published   Separately.

Reference   *Documents Relative to the Colonial History of the State of New-York, 8*, 178–79.

Location   No copy located.

327   [1776]   *State* I (see also Map 303)

Description   [A Map of the present Seat of War, with the Harbours of New-York and Perth-Amboy.] This map was advertised by John Norman in the (Philadelphia) *Pennsylvania Gazette*, October 9, 1776. The title is taken from the advertisement. The (Philadelphia) *Pennsylvania Journal* of March 12, 1777, advertised what was probably this map, enlarged to include New York, Connecticut, and parts of New Jersey (see Map 303).

Size Unknown.   *Scale* Unknown.

Published Separately.

References David M. Stauffer, *American Engravers, 1,* 192; Harry B. Weiss, "John Norman," p. 6.

Location No copy located.

328 1778

Description [Map of Ticonderoga, Mount Independence and the adjacent country.] This is a detailed topographical map showing roads, types of woods, and the various military and naval positions incident to the siege of Ticonderoga in 1777. On page 52 of the *Proceedings* is an "Explanation of the Draught annexed," listing the references on the map. The title is taken from page 28. The scale is noted as not having been determined from survey "but taken from view."

Size 12¼" x 10⅛".   *Scale* 1" = c. ½ mile.

Published in Arthur St. Clair, *Proceedings of a General Court Martial for the Trial of Maj. Gen. St. Clair,* opp. p. 52. Reproduced in New-York Historical Society, *Collections, 13* (1880), opp. 172.

Reference Evans 16141: see also Reproduction above, under Published.

329 [178–?]

Description Across top just below neat line: A MAP OF TOTTIN [sic] & CROSFIELDS [sic] PURCHASE & THE WATERS ADJACENT / IN THE STATE OF NEW YORK. A map of the purchase made by Joseph Totten and Stephen Crossfield in 1771. The area is divided into townships and over it is engraved "OR JESSUPS PATENT." The property, upon which £2,000 had been advanced when the Revolution began, was actually purchased for Edward and Ebenezer Jessup who fled to Canada and fought for Great Britain. A number of other patents are also shown such as the T & C patent, Military "Artilley Patent," etc.

Size 9⁵⁄₁₆" x 7¹⁵⁄₁₆".   *Scale* 1" = 12 miles.

Published Separately.

Location NHi.

330 1789

Description In oval at upper left: CHART / OF THE / COAST OF AMERICA / FROM / NEW YORK / TO / RHODE ISLAND / FROM THE LATEST SURVEYS; beneath oval: J. NORMAN SC. / PRINTED FOR AND SOLD BY MATTW CLARK / BOSTON OCTBR. 1789; in upper left corner: NO. 8. This chart carries an engraved inscription stating that it was ex-

amined by Osgood Carleton and found to be true and accurate. The signature is engraved and dated October 17, 1789. There is another note that the chart is true and accurate over the name of THOS BARNARD. There are four horizon silhouettes at top center: BLOCK ISLAND, HIGHLAND OF NEVERSINK, EAST END OF LONG ISLAND, and another of LONG ISLAND. In the Library of Congress copy of Clark's [*A Complete Chart*] this and Map 207 are pasted together.

Size 16⅞" x 25¼".   *Scale* 1" = 6½ miles.

Inset At lower right corner: [Chart of Hell Gate.] Size: 5⅜" x 6". Two scales: 1" = 2⅔ nautic miles, and 1" = 7½ fathoms.

Published in Matthew Clark, [*A Complete Chart*], no. 8.

331 [1789]

Description Above top neat line: FROM NEW YORK (1) TO STRATFORD. The engraved title page of Colles', *A Survey,* carries the imprint "C. Tiebout Sculpt," and the engraving of the maps is generally attributed to Cornelius Tiebout. A scale for the maps is engraved on the title page of 1" = 4⁄7 of a mile. A table of "References" gives eight conventional signs to indicate churches, taverns, blacksmith shops, bridges, etc., along the roads. This map shows, in three vertical strips, the road from FEDERAL HALL in New York City twelve miles up Manhattan Island past Fort Washington.

Size 7" x 4½".   *Scale* None (1" = 4⁄7 mile).

Published in Christopher Colles, *A Survey of the Roads.* Reproduced, ibid., 1961, p. 121; Isaac N. P. Stokes, *The Iconography of Manhattan Island, 5,* pl. 51B.

332 [1789]

Description Above top neat line: FROM NEW YORK (2) TO SLRATFORD [sic]. This map shows, in two and one half vertical strips, the road from just north of Ft. Washington across the top of Manhattan Island, over KINGS BRIDGE, across BRUNKS RIVER, through EAST CHESTER, and through NEW ROCHELL [sic].

Size 7" x 4½".   *Scale* None (1" = 4⁄7 mile).

Published in Christopher Colles, *A Survey of the Roads.* Reproduced, ibid., 1961, p. 122.

333 [1789]

Description Above top neat line: FROM NEW YORK (3) TO STRATFORD. This map shows, in three vertical strips, the road from just northeast of

New Rochelle (24 miles from New York), through RYE, across BUYRUM [sic] BRIDGE about two miles into Connecticut.

Size 7" x 4⅝". *Scale* None (1" = ⁴⁄₇ mile).

Published in Christopher Colles, *A Survey of the Roads*. Reproduced, ibid., 1961, p. 123.

334 [1789]

Description Above top neat line: FROM NEW YORK (*8*) TO POUGHKEEPSIE. This map shows, in three vertical strips, the road FROM G PAGE 2, just across Kings Bridge from Manhattan Island, to a point two miles north of DOBBS'S [sic] / FERRY.

Size 6⅞" x 4⁷⁄₁₆". *Scale* None (1" = ⁴⁄₇ mile).

Published in Christopher Colles, *A Survey of the Roads*. Reproduced, ibid., 1961, p. 128.

335 [1789]

Description Above top neat line: FROM NEW YORK (*9*) TO POUGHKEEPSIE. This map shows, in three vertical strips, the road from two miles north of Dobbs Ferry (27 miles north of New York), through TARRY TOWN, to a point just across the CROTON RIVER.

Size 7" x 4½". *Scale* None (1" = ⁴⁄₇ mile).

Published in Christopher Colles, *A Survey of the Roads*. Reproduced, ibid., 1961, p. 129.

336 [1789]

Description Above top neat line: FROM NEW YORK (*10*) TO POUGHKEEPSIE. This map shows, in two vertical strips, the road from a point just northwest of the Croton River (40 miles from New York), to a point about two miles south of Peekskill.

Size 6¹⁵⁄₁₆" x 4⁷⁄₁₆". *Scale* None (1" = ⁴⁄₇ mile).

Published in Christopher Colles, *A Survey of the Roads*. Reproduced, ibid., 1961, p. 130.

337 [1789]

Description Above top neat line: FROM NEW YORK (*11*) TO POUGHKEESIE [sic]. This map shows, in three vertical strips, the road from about two miles south of Peekskill (49 miles from New York), through PEEKS KILL and CONTINENTAL / VILLAGE, to about six miles south of Fishkill.

Size 7" x 4½". *Scale* None (1" = ⁴⁄₇ mile).

Published in Christopher Colles, *A Survey of the Roads*. Reproduced, ibid., 1961, p. 131.

338 [1789]

Description Above top neat line: FROM NEW YORK (*12*) TO POUGHKEEPSIE. This map shows, in two vertical strips, the road from about six miles south of FISH KILL (61 miles north of New York), through FISH KILL, to a point two and one half miles north.

Size 6¾" x 4⁷⁄₁₆". *Scale* None (1" = ⁴⁄₇ mile).

Published in Christopher Colles, *A Survey of the Roads*. Reproduced, ibid., 1961, p. 132.

339 [1789]

Description Above top neat line: FROM NEW YORK TO (*13*) POUGHKEEPSIE. This map shows, in two vertical strips, the road from two and one half miles north of Fishkill (70½ miles north of New York), to within two miles of Poughkeepsie.

Size 7" x 4½". *Scale* None (1" = ⁴⁄₇ mile).

Published in Christopher Colles, *A Survey of the Roads*. Reproduced, ibid., 1961, p. 133.

340 [1789]

Description Above top neat line: FROM POUGHKEEPSIE (*14*) TO ALBANY. This map shows, in one large and two smaller vertical strips, the road from one point about a mile and one half directly south and a second point two and one half miles southeast of Poughkeepsie (the first 80 miles from New York and the second 69½ miles from Stratford), through POUGH KEEPSIE to about four and one half miles south of "Staatsborough, the modern Staatsburg." 74 [miles] TO ALBANY appears at Poughkeepsie. SEE PAGE 20 appears at lower right and SEE PAGE 21 at upper right corner.

Size 7" x 4½". *Scale* None (1" = ⁴⁄₇ mile).

Published in Christopher Colles, *A Survey of the Roads*. Reproduced, ibid., 1961, p. 134.

341 [1789]

Description Above top neat line: FROM STRATFORD (*18*) TO POUGHKEEPSIE. This map shows, in three vertical strips, the road from eight miles northwest of Danbury, Conn. (38½ from Stratford), thirteen miles further to half a mile past BROWNELLS Tavern.

Size 7" x 4½". *Scale* None (1" = ⁴⁄₇ mile).

Published in Christopher Colles, *A Survey of the Roads.* Reproduced, ibid., 1961, p. 138.

342 [1789]

Description Above top neat line: FROM STRATFORD (*19*) TO POUGHKEEPSIE. This map shows, in two vertical strips, the road from half a mile west of Brownells Tavern (51½ miles from Stratford), to within a quarter mile of "Somes's" Tavern.

Size 7" x 4½".   *Scale* None (1" = 4/7 mile).

Published in Christopher Colles, *A Survey of the Roads.* Reproduced, ibid., 1961, p. 139.

343 [1789]

Description Above top neat line: FROM STRATFORD (*20*) TO POUGHKEEPSIE. This map shows, in two vertical strips, the road from SOMES's Tavern (60½ miles from Stratford), nine miles to SWARTWOUTS Tavern. SEE PAGE *14* appears at this point referring to the continuation of this road at the lower right corner of Map 340.

Size 7" x 4½".   *Scale* None (1" = 4/7 mile).

Published in Christopher Colles, *A Survey of the Roads.* Reproduced, ibid., 1961, p. 140.

344 [1789]

Description Above top neat line: FROM POUGHKEEPSIE (*21*) TO ALBANY. This map shows, in three vertical strips, the road from a point 2½ miles north of Poughkeepsie (88 miles from New York), through STAATSBOROUGH and RHYNBECK / FLATS, to a point 19 miles north-by-east of Poughkeepsie.

Size 7" x 4½".   *Scale* None (1" = 4/7 mile).

Published in Christopher Colles, *A Survey of the Roads.* Reproduced, ibid., 1961, p. 141.

345 [1789]

Description Above top neat line: FROM POUGHKEEPSIE (*22*) TO ALBANY. This map shows, in three vertical strips, the road from a point 19½ miles north-by-east of Poughkeepsie (100½ miles from New York), through RED HOOK, to a point 31½ miles north-north-west of Poughkeepsie.

Size 7" x 4½".   *Scale* None (1" = 4/7 mile).

Published in Christopher Colles, *A Survey of the Roads.* Reproduced, ibid., 1961, p. 142.

346 [1789]

Description Above top neat line: FROM POUGHKEEPSIE (*23*) TO ALBANY. This map shows, in three vertical strips, the road from 31½ miles north-north-west of Poughkeepsie (113 miles from New York), past CLAVERACK M[eeting] H[ouse], to 45 miles north-north-west of Poughkeepsie.

Size 7" x 4¾".   *Scale* None (1" = 4/7 mile).

Published in Christopher Colles, *A Survey of the Roads.* Reproduced, ibid., 1961, p. 143.

347 [1789]

Description Above top neat line: FROM POUGHKEEPSIE (*24*) TO ALBANY. This map shows, in three vertical strips, the road from a point 45 miles north-west of Poughkeepsie (126 miles from New York), through KENDER HOOK, to a point 57 miles north-north-west of Poughkeepsie.

Size 7" x 4½".   *Scale* None (1" = 4/7 mile).

Published in Christopher Colles, *A Survey of the Roads.* Reproduced, ibid., 1961, p. 144.

348 [1789]

Description Above top neat line: FROM POUGHKEEPSIE (*25*) TO ALBANY. This map shows, in three vertical strips, the road from a point 17 miles south-by-east of Albany (139 miles from New York), to a point 4½ miles south-east of Albany.

Size 7" x 4½".   *Scale* None (1" = 4/7 mile).

Published in Christopher Colles, *A Survey of the Roads.* Reproduced, ibid., 1961, p. 145.

349 [1789]

Description Above top neat line: FROM ALBANY TO (*26*) NEWBOROUGH. This map shows, in two vertical strips, the road from 4½ miles south-east of Albany (151½ miles from New York), across the NORTH RIVER and through ALBANY, to a point 4 miles down the west side of the river.

Size 7" x 4½".   *Scale* None (1" = 4/7 mile).

Published in Christopher Colles, *A Survey of the Roads.* Reproduced, ibid., 1961, p. 146.

350 [1789]

Description Above top neat line: FROM ALBANY (*27*) TO NEWBOROUGH. This map shows, in three vertical strips, the road from 4 miles to

75

17 miles down the west side of the Hudson River from Albany.

Size 7" x 4½". *Scale* None (1" = 4/7 mile).

Published in Christopher Colles, *A Survey of the Roads.* Reproduced, ibid., 1961, p. 147.

351 [1789]

Description Above top neat line: FROM ALBANY (*28*) TO NEWBOROUGH. This map shows, in three vertical strips, the road from a point 17 miles down the west side of the Hudson or North River from Albany, past KONYNS Tavern (at 19½ miles), KOOKSACHKE M[eeting] H[ouse] (at 22 ½ miles), and VALKENBUR GHS Tavern (at 29 miles), to a point 29½ miles from Albany.

Size 7" x 4½". *Scale* None (1" = 4/7 mile).

Published in Christopher Colles, *A Survey of the Roads.* Reproduced, ibid., 1961, p. 148.

352 [1789]

Description Above top neat line: FROM ALBANY (*29*) TO NEWBOROUGH. This map shows, in three vertical strips, the road from 29½ miles south of Albany, into ULSTER County, to 42 miles down the west side of the Hudson River from Albany.

Size 7" x 4½". *Scale* None (1" = 4/7 mile).

Published in Christopher Colles, *A Survey of the Roads.* Reproduced, ibid., 1961, p. 149.

353 [1789]

Description Above top neat line: FROM ALBANY (*30*) TO NEWBOROUGH. This map shows, in three vertical strips, the road from 42 miles south of Albany, through WEST CAMP, over ESOPUS CR. (at 45½ miles), to a point 54 miles south-by-west of Albany.

Size 7" x 4⅞". *Scale* None (1" = 4/7 mile).

Published in Christopher Colles, *A Survey of the Roads.* Reproduced, ibid., 1961, p. 150.

354 [1789]

Description Above top neat line: FROM ALBANY (*31*) TO NEWBOROUGH. This map shows, in two vertical strips, the road from 54 miles from Albany, through KINGS TON (at 56 miles), across ROUNDOUT KILL (at 58 miles), to a point 63 miles down the west side of the Hudson from Albany.

Size 7" x 4½". *Scale* None (1" = 4/7 mile).

Published in Christopher Colles, *A Survey of the Roads.* Reproduced, ibid., 1961, p. 151.

355 [1789]

Description Above top neat line: FROM ALBANY (*32*) TO NEWBOROUGH. This map shows, in three vertical strips, the road from 63 miles down the west side of the Hudson from Albany, over KLEYN SOPUS CR. (at 65½ miles), to 75 miles from Albany.

Size 7" x 4½". *Scale* None (1" = 4/7 mile).

Published in Christopher Colles, *A Survey of the Roads.* Reproduced, ibid., 1961, p. 152.

356 [1789]

Description Above top neat line: FROM ALBANY (*33*) TO NEWBOROUGH. This map shows, in three and a half vertical strips, the road from a point 75 miles down the west side of Hudson from Albany, past LATTIMORE'S FERRY (at 78 miles), to NEWBOROUGH.

Size 7" x 4½". *Scale* None (1" = 4/7 mile).

Published in Christopher Colles, *A Survey of the Roads.* Reproduced, ibid., 1961, p. 153.

357 [1792] *State* I (see also Map 360)

Description Above top neat line at center: 1ST. SHEET OF DE WITT'S STATE-MAP OF NEW-YORK. Below bottom neat line at right corner: C. TIEBOUT SCULP. N YORK. Political boundaries are given and the various surveys of this area, extending from Oswego to the Pennsylvania boundary and from Seneca Lake to OTSEGO LAKE, are shown in detail. Some topographical features are noted as are the primary roads. Evans cites the copyright, issued October 26, 1792. Jedidiah Morse mentions ". . . De Witt's [map] of part of New York . . ." in the preface of his *American Gazetteer.* The scale is given below the neat line at the lower left. Simeon De Witt was Surveyor-General of New York for a period of fifty years beginning in 1784. His "A Map of the State of New York," engraved by Gideon Fairman, was published in 1802.

Size 19⅝" x 22¾". *Scale* 1" = 6 miles.

Published Separately.

References Evans 24265; Jedidiah Morse, *American Gazetteer,* p. IV; Philip L. Phillips, *A List of Maps of America,* p. 508.

Location DLC.

358 [1794]

Description In upper left corner of border:

1368 / 1458 / 1548. This is one section of a large, indexed, topographical map intended to cover the whole U.S. and possibly more. It includes most of central New York State. The indexing is done by means of many letters on the map used as references and explained in the text of the book. The map sections are supplied loose and are not bound with the alphabetical references, alphabetical indexes, or directions for use of the maps which comprise the book that the maps were made to accompany. The middle number of the three at upper left corner, *1458,* identifies this section of the main map. The lesser number above this, *1368,* identifies the section just north of this and the greater number below, *1548,* identifies the section just south. The adjoining map on the east of this section is identified as number *1459.* These adjoining map sections all match the other's adjacent edges. There is an upper border consisting of three marginal degree lines showing longitude from Paris, London, and Philadelphia. Above these is another border line with the scale attached. Inside the extreme left border line are marginal scale lines showing: GREATEST LENGTH OF DAYS AND NIGHTS and degrees of latitude. (See also Maps 154–56 and 309.)

Size 14¾″ x 19¹⁵⁄₁₆″. *Scale* 1″ = 10 miles.

Published with Christopher Colles, *The Geographical Ledger and Systematized Atlas.*

References Christopher Colles, *A Survey of the Roads,* 1961, pp. 77–81; Lloyd W. Griffen, "Christopher Colles and His Two American Map Series."

Locations DLC, NHi.

359 1794

Description In oval cartouche at upper left: A / PLAN / OF THE / CITY / OF / ALBANY / SURVEYED / AT THE REQUEST OF THE / MAYOR ALDERMAN / AND / COMMONALTY / BY / SIMEON DE WITT / MDCCXCIV. Below oval at left: HUTTON SCULPT. ALBY. This is a detailed plan of the city with an EXPLANATION at lower left center identifying ten numbered locations. Several estates within the city limits are shown and the names of the owners given. The engraver is Isaac Hutton.

Size 20″ x 15½″. *Scale* 1″ = 400 feet.

Insets [a] Under cartouche: *1* COURT HOUSE, LAT *42° 39′.* A profile sketch of the building. Size: 2⅛″ x 2¼″.

[b] Under [a]: *2* PRISON. A front view of the building. Size: 2¾″ x ⅜″.

Published Separately. Reproduced as inset map on John Bradt's "Map . . . of Albany," Neale & Pate, New York, 1843; John D. Hatch, "Isaac Hutton, Silversmith," p. 32.

References John Carter Brown Library, *Report, 1956,* pp. 58–59; U.S. Library of Congress, *Report 1907,* p. 45; see also reproductions above, under Published.

Locations DLC, NHi, NN, RPJCB.

360 [1794?] *State* II (see also Map 357)

Description At lower right is added: TOWN OF MIDDLETOWN. The river and creek system is shown in: 230400 ACRES CEDED TO MASSACHUSETS and in: WILLIAM S. SMITH land in COUNTY OF TIOGA. Several roads are added in lower right portion of map.

Published Separately.

Reference Harvard University Library, *A Catalogue of the Maps and Charts,* p. 193.

Locations MH, MiU-C.

361 [1794]

Description Under ornament at left center: A / MAP / OF / MESSRS: GORHAM & PHELPS'S / PURCHASE; / NOW THE COUNTY OF / ONTARIO, / IN THE STATE OF / NEW YORK; / FROM ACTUAL SURVEY / BY A. PORTER. In loop below title: ENGRAVED BY A. DOOLITTLE N HAVEN. This map shows the survey of the Purchase into ranges and townships. Several of the Finger Lakes, rivers, and streams are shown as well as the roads, grist and saw mills, and settlements. A table explaining four conventional signs used appears at upper left. CANADARGUA settlement is shown thus on CANUNDARGUA L. Evans ascribes to it the date "1795"; Phillips gives "1794." The author is Augustus Porter.

Size 23¹¹⁄₁₆″ x 15″. *Scale* 1″ = 4 miles.

Published Separately.

References Evans 29341; Philip L. Phillips, *A List of Maps of America,* p. 640; Robert W. G. Vail, *Old Frontier,* no. 999.

Locations CtY, DLC, MiU-C, NCanHi, NHi.

362 1795 *State* I (II post-1799, see below, Description)

Description At lower left center: THE STATE OF / NEW YORK, / COMPILED FROM THE BEST AUTHORITIES, / BY SAMUEL LEWIS. / 1795. Beneath bottom neat line at right corner: HARRISON JUNR. SC. The western limit is shown after the 1786 land adjustment with Pennsylvania. TICONDERAGO, SARATOGHA, PECKS KILL, SCHENECTADA, are examples of spelling. The NIAGARA ROAD is shown across the entire state. The engraver is probably William Harrison, Jr. The same map was used in the 1800 edition of *Carey's General Atlas* with the numeral "31" added to the upper right corner.

Size 15¹⁵⁄₁₆" x 19⅞".   *Scale* 1" = 21 miles.

Published in Mathew Carey, *Carey's American Atlas*, no. 31; idem, *The General Atlas for Carey's Edition of Guthrie's Geography Improved*, no. 31.

363 [1795?]

Description In upper left corner: [A Map / of the Late / Cayuga / Reservation / Surveyed into Lots / Generally of / 250 Acres each / 1795]. This title is taken from a manuscript copy of the map at Harvard. Evans gives the following title and imprint: "Map of the Cayuga Reservation. Albany: 1796." A vertical scale is given along the lower left side of the manuscript copy.

Size Unknown.   *Scale* Unknown.

Published Separately.

Reference Evans 30735.

Location No copy located.

364 1795

Description In scroll over top: A MAP / OF THE LATE / ONONDAGA RESERVATION / LAID OUT INTO LOTS OF 250 ACRES EACH / 1795. A number of houses and roads are shown, also a settlement at the edge of the Salt Lake. The Indian town of Onondaga Castle is located. Some names are inscribed on lots along Onondaga Creek.

Size 15¹¹⁄₁₆" x 10⁹⁄₁₆".   *Scale* 1" = 1 mile.

Published Separately.

Location MH.

365 [c. 1795]

Description In oval cartouche in upper left corner: A MAP OF THE / MILITARY LANDS AND / 20 TOWNSHIPS IN THE / WESTERN PART OF THE / STATE OF NEW YORK. Shown here are the primary land purchases and grants, as well as the several counties, townships, and settlements as they existed at this date. Only the larger streams are indicated and many not by name. The Oswego is noted as the ONONDAGO RIVER and among the townships are the following: HANIBAL, VERGIL, and CINCINATUS.

Size 12⁵⁄₁₆" x 11½".   *Scale* 1" = 10 miles.

Published Separately.

Location NHi.

366 [1795]   *State* I (II post-1799, see below, Description)

Description At lower left: NEW YORK. Forts ERIE, SCHLOSSER, NIAGARA, OSWEGO, and SCHUYLER are located. Oneida County is shown south of Lake Oneida. MASSACUSETTS [sic] was first engraved with one "T"; the final "S" was then erased and another "TS" added. This map was re-issued in Scott's *The New and Universal Gazetteer*, 4. The second state was recut but the only geographical addition appears to be the extension of the line showing the road to New York. This line stops in State I where it touches the "E" of W. CHESTER; on the second state the line is continued down Manhattan Island.

Size 6" x 7¼".   *Scale* 1" = 50 miles.

Published in Joseph Scott, *An Atlas of the United States*; idem, *The United States Gazetteer*, opp. "New-York." Reproduced in Joseph Scott, *Atlas of the United States 1795–1800*, [no. 13].

367 [1796]   *State* I (II post-1799, see below, Description)

Description At lower left center: NEW YORK. Below bottom neat line at right: W. BARKER SCULP. PECKSKILL and HAVERSTRA appear thus. This map was reissued in the 1801 edition of *Carey's American Pocket Atlas*. No roads appear in the first state while they were added for the 1801 issue. A number of place names have been added in the second state, among them: "Plattsburg," "Peru," "Willsboro," and "Athens."

Size 5¾" x 7⅝".   *Scale* 1" = 60 miles.

Published in Mathew Carey, *Carey's American Pocket Atlas*, opp. p. 47.

368 [1796]

Description In oval at lower left: MAP / OF / THE STATE OF / NEW YORK / BY J DENISON. Beneath oval: A DOOLITTLE SC:. Above top neat line: PUBLISHED BY THOMAS & ANDREWS BOSTON. CALAUGHAQUE L appears for Chautauqua; THOUSAND IS. and MC: COMBS PURCHASE are given.

Size 7⁷⁄₁₆" x 9½".   *Scale* 1" = 43 miles.

Published in Jedidiah Morse, *The American Universal Geography*, 3d ed., *1*, opp. 476.

369 [1796?]

Description On ribbon at top center: A MAP / OF THE ONEIDA / RESERVATION / INCLUDING THE LANDS / LEASED TO PETER SMITH. Beneath ribbon: FAIRMAN SCT. ALBY. This map shows the surveys in the eastern and southern part of the reservation with the township of NEW-STOCKBRIDGE outlined. Names shown on the land in the eastern portion are the same as on Map 357 which was issued in 1792. A settlement marked CSZCNOVIS appears at lower end of CANASERAGA LAKE. Fort Schuyler is shown but not Fort Stanwix. The creeks are carefully noted, also a number of roads. The Harvard University copy is printed on the same kind of paper as Map 364. The map was engraved by Gideon Fairman.

Size 11¹³⁄₁₆″ x 15³⁄₁₆″.   *Scale* 1″ = 2 miles.

Published Separately. Reproduced in New York (State), *Proceedings of the Commissioners of Indian Affairs*, 1, opp. 241.

Reference See reproduction above, under Published.

Location MH.

370 1796

Description At upper left: A MAP / OF THE NORTH EAST PART OF THE / TOWN OF MEXICO / THE PROPERTY OF GEORGE SCRIBA SITUATED ON THE / LAKE ONTARIO / ABOUT *13* MILES EAST FROM OSWEGO & *20* FROM / ROTTERDAM, ONEIDA LAKE. / AS SURVEYED & LAID OUT BY / BENJAMIN WRIGHT. / A. D. *1796*. Below title: ENGRAVED BY P. R. MAVERICK. *65* LIBERTY STREET. This is a plan showing the streets and many of the blocks divided into individual lots. Street names are given and WASHINGTON / SQUARE is indicated. Explanatory REMARKS are given at the lower left.

Size 17⅝″ x 14″.   *Scale* 1″ = 6 chains.

Published Separately.

Reference American Antiquarian Society, *Proceedings*, 71 (1961), 259.

Location MWA.

371 1796 *State* I (see also Map 372)

Description In oval at lower center: THE STATE OF / NEW YORK, / COMPILED FROM THE MOST / AUTHENTIC IMFORMATION [sic]. / *1796*; beneath oval: MARTIN SCULPT; below bottom neat line: PUBLISH'D BY J. REID N. YORK. This map follows and is copied from Map 362. It shows the *3* TREES at the westernmost corner of Connecticut and copies Samuel Lewis' error of PECKS KILL. A new spelling for BUFFULOE C. is used. The eastern portion of the Genesee Country is shown divided into ranges and townships. PAINTED POST is shown graphically. The neat line is broken for the southwestern boundary line. The engraver was probably David Martin.

Size 15¼″ x 17¹⁵⁄₁₆″.   *Scale* 1″ = 21 miles.

Published in John Reid, *The American Atlas*, [1796?], no. 10; ibid., 1796, no. 10; William Winterbotham, [*Atlas*].

372 1796 *State* II (see also Map 371)

Description The title is now corrected: THE STATE OF / NEW YORK . . . INFORMATION. *1796*.

Published in William Winterbotham, [*Atlas*]. Reproduced in U.S. Bureau of the Census, *Heads of Families at the First Census New York*, front.

Location MdBP.

373 [1796]

Description Below bottom neat line at center: THE ENGAGEMENT ON THE WHITE PLAINS THE *28*TH. OF OCTOBER *1776*, / BETWEEN THE AMERICAN & BRITISH FORCES. Below bottom neat line at right corner: D. MARTIN SCT. Below bottom neat line at left corner: PUBLISHD BY C. SMITH. Above top neat line at right: PL. III. The disposition and movements of the British and American troops are shown. THE BRUNX RIVER, DEEP appears thus, and also, TERRY TOWN. The map was engraved by David Martin. This is a copy with about the same scale of a small section of the map entitled: "A Plan of the Operations of the King's Army under the Command of General Sr. William Howe, K.B. in New York and East New Jersey," in C. A. Stedman's *History of the Origin, Progress, and Termination of the American War*, 1, opp. 214.

Size 7³⁄₁₆″ x 8⁵⁄₁₆″.   *Scale* None (1″ = c. 1 mile).

Published in *The Monthly Military Repository*, 1, opp. 173; Charles Smith, *The American War*, opp. p. 37.

374 [1796]

Description At upper center and right: PLAN OF THE POSITION WHICH THE ARMY UNDER LT. GENL. BURGOINE TOOK AT SARATOGA / ON THE *10*TH. OF SEPTEMBER *1777* AND IN WHICH IT REMAINED TILL THE CONVENTION WAS SIGNED. Below neat line at bottom right corner: D. MARTIN SCT. Below bottom neat line at center: PUBLISHED BY C. SMITH. NEW YORK. At upper right corner: PL. IV. The individual British units under Gen. Burgoyne are identified by name. The map was engraved by David Martin.

Size 8¼″ x 13¹¹⁄₁₆″.   *Scale* 1″ = 315 yards.

Published in *The Monthly Military Repository*, 1, opp. 257; Charles Smith, *The American War*, opp. p. 47.

375 [1797]

Description [A Map of the Countrey [sic] of the Five Nations . . .] A map of this title was to have been included in a proposed reprinting of Colden's *History*. (See Maps 317 and 318.)

Size Unknown.   *Scale* Unknown.

Published in Cadwallader Colden, *History of the Six Indian Nations,* (Published?).

References Evans 31952; Robert W. G. Vail, *Old Frontier,* no. 1110.

Location No copy located.

376 [1798]

Description In oval on scroll at lower left: MAP / OF / ONTARIO / AND / STEUBEN / COUNTIES. Below scroll: HESLOP DEL. FAIRMAN SCULPT. This map of the Phelps and Gorham Purchase shows the ranges of townships, the towns, rivers, and lakes. Grist mills and sawmills are also indicated. The map was probably engraved by Gideon Fairman.

Size 15³⁄₁₆″ x 13¼″.   *Scale* 1″ = 6½ miles.

Published in [Charles Williamson], *Description of the Genesee Country,* foll. p. 37.

References Evans 35033; Robert W. G. Vail, *Old Frontier,* no. 1182.

377 [1799]

Description [An accurate Map of Castor Land, No. 4, McCombs purchase, Pennits Square, Black River, Oneida County, State of New York, agreeable to actual survey by C. Broadhead, and for sale by Brown and Stansbury No. 114 Water Street, opposite the old Coffee House slip.] The title is taken from an advertisement in the (New York) *Daily Advertiser,* May 3, 1799. The surveyor was Charles Broadhead.

Size Unknown.   *Scale* Unknown.

Published Separately.

Reference Rita S. Gottesman, *The Arts and Crafts in New York 1777–1799,* p. 162.

Location No copy located.

NEW YORK CITY

378 [1731] *State* I (see also Map 380)

Description Across top of map below neat line: A PLAN OF THE CITY OF NEW YORK FROM AN ACTUAL SURVEY / MADE BY IAMES LYNE. The following dedication is in a cartouche at the upper left: TO HIS EXCELLENCY / IOHN MONTGOMERIE ESQ. / CAPT GENL L-GOVR IN CHIEF / OF HIS MAJESTIS PROVINCES / OF NEW YORK, NEW IERSEY, / &C / THIS PLAN OF THE CITY OF / NEW YORK IS HUMBLY DEDICD. / BY YOUR EXCELLENCYS. OBET / & MOST HUMBLE SERVT. / WM BRADFORD. Just under this dedication is a table with ten lettered and eleven numbered references. At the upper right is a second cartouche with the seal of New York City and the name: COLL. ROBT. LURTING / MAYOR within the oval. The date of the map is known from an advertisement by William Bradford in the *New-York Gazette* for August 30–September 6, 1731. The engraver has not thus far been identified. William Bradford, the publisher, was the first printer in New York. This is probably the first plan of the City published in New York and one of the first examples of copper engraving made there. Shown here are the several New York wards as they were laid out by the Montgomery Charter of 1730–31. There have been many reproductions prepared of this map and a number of these vary in their faithfulness to the original. Variations include a difference in size from the original, the inclusion of the date, 1728, and a number of other points. The first of these was published by G. Hayward from an original impression which belonged to G. B. Smith, Street Commissioner, in 1834. Another example is that "Reprinted by John Slater," and another was reproduced by H. D. Taylor about 1903.

Size 17⅞" x 22⅜". *Scale* 1" = 260 feet.

Published Separately. Reproduced in William L. Andrews, *The Bradford Map*, opp. p. ix; idem, "James Lyne's Survey," pp. 460–61; Norres J. O'Conor, *A Servant of the Crown*, front end papers; Isaac N. P. Stokes, *Iconography of Manhattan Island*, 1, pl. 27; idem and Daniel C. Haskell, *American Historical Prints*, pl. 12.

References Gerald D. McDonald, "A Gift of *The New-York Gazette*," pp. 487–88; see also reproductions above, under Published.

Locations NN, NHi (one copy also recorded in Division of Design, Bureau of Engineering, Borough of Manhattan, but now missing).

379 [1735]

Description In plaque at upper left: A / NEW MAP / OF THE / HARBOUR / OF / NEW-YORK / BY A LATE SURVEY. This map was published by William Bradford in 1735 as evidenced by this advertisement in the *New-York Gazette* of March 24–31, 1735: "There is now Published a new Map of the Harbour of New-York, from a late survey, containing the Soundings and setting of the Tydes, and the bearings of the most remarkable Places, with the Proper Places for Anchoring [shown on the map by Roman numerals] To be Sold by the Printer hereof." This map is very similar to the inset on Henry Popple's "A Map of the British Empire in America," published in London in 1733. Local names have been added; YORK ISLAND COUNTY is noted on Manhattan Island. The copy in the Huntington Library is thought to be unique.

Size 12" x 9¾". *Scale* 1" = 3¾ miles.

Published Separately. Reproduced in Isaac N. P. Stokes, *Iconography of Manhattan Island*, 1, pl. 29.

References Elihu D. Church, *A Catalogue of Books*, no. 920; Willard O. Waters, "American Imprints, 1648–1797," p. 15.

Location CSmH.

380 [1755] *State* II (see also Map 378)

Description Across top of map: A PLAN OF THE CITY OF NEW YORK FROM AN ACTUAL SURVEY ANNO DOMINI – M, DDC, L V, / BY F. MAERSCHALCK CITY SURVEYR [sic] (the V, in date appears to be MSS). On lower roll of scroll at lower right corner: PRINTED, INGRAVED [sic] FOR AND SOLD BY. G. DUYCKINCK. An advertisement by Gerardus Duyckinck for the map appeared in the *New-York Gazette*, March 3, 1755. The old plate of Bradford and Lyne's 1731 map has been altered and lengthened but is readily identified. Pierre E. Du Simitière, writing in 1768, noted the use of the plate of the Bradford Map in this way. It was republished on a reduced scale by Mary Ann Roque in England in 1755 and 1763. The dedication by William Bradford with its decorative accompaniments and the tablet of references below it has been replaced in this second state with a new dedication to Lt. Gov. James DeLancey by the new publisher, Gerardus Duyckinck. The seal of New York at upper right has been redrawn and carries the name: EDW HOLLAND ESQ / MAYOR. At the lower right corner has been added a scroll carrying thirteen lettered and 31 numbered references. There is an engraved ornamental scroll on the bottom and left border of the Library of Congress copy.

Size 17⅝″ x 33⅛″. *Scale* 1″ = 280 feet.

Published Separately. Reproduced in Isaac N. P. Stokes, *Iconography of Manhattan Island*, *I*, pl. 34.

References Philip L. Phillips, *A List of Maps of America*, p. 521.

Locations DLC, NHi, Trinity Church, New York.

381 [1763]

Description [A plan of the streets, &c.] This map of New York City was proposed by Michael De Bruls (or Michaelson Godhart) in a series of advertisements in several New York newspapers in 1762–63. (See the *New-York Mercury*, October 11, 1762, and February 28, 1763, and the *New-York Gazette*, March 7, 1763.) The map was to accompany four engraved views of the city and all were to be issued in the year 1763. No copy of the views or the map has been located. Pierre E. Du Simitière, in a notebook now in the Du Simitière Collection at the Library Company of Philadelphia (Book 1412Y), states that the views were never completed. The title is taken from the advertisement.

Size Unknown. *Scale* Unknown.

Published Separately.

Reference David M. Stauffer, *American Engravers*, *I*, 32–33.

Location No copy located.

382 [1775]

Description Above top neat line: PLAN OF THE CITY OF NEW YORK. This map is similar to the Bernard Ratzer, "Plan of the City," but it is greatly reduced. No streets are named except the: ROAD TO BOSTON, and there are no references. It differentiates the built up sections and indicates some topographical features in outlying sections. It is finely engraved.

Size 5⁹⁄₁₆″ x 7¹³⁄₁₆″. *Scale* 1″ = ⅓ mile.

Published in [Hugh Gaine], *Gaine's Universal Register, 1776*, front; idem, *Gaine's Univer-*

sal Register for 1778 (in pocket of New York Public Library [rebound] copy).

383 [1776] *State I* (see also Map 384)

Description [The Present Seat of War at and near New York.] This is a woodcut map showing Newark, Manhattan Island, part of Staten Island, and the eastern end of Long Island. Some of the lettering appears to have been done with inserted type. There are twelve lettered references. Eight of these are explained in the cartouche at the upper left and the balance on page four. It is very similar to Maps 385 and 386. The title given here is taken from these maps.

Size 4⅝″ x 3⁷⁄₁₆″. *Scale* 1″ = 8 miles.

Published in Samuel Stearns, *The North America's Almanack 1777*, title page.

384 [1776] *State II* (see also Map 383)

Description The directions in the note at lower right corner of the decorated rectangle now read: SEE P. 2D.

Published in Isaac Warren, *The North American's Almanack 1777*.

385 [1776]

Description In decorated rectangle at upper left: A VIEW OF THE / PRESENT SEAT OF WAR. / AT AND NEAR NEW YORK. This is a woodcut, very similar to Maps 383 and 384, but with this title given in place of the references in the cartouche at the upper left. The nine lettered references are explained on the page following. Map 386 is another re-engraving with the same title.

Size 4½″ x 3⅜″. *Scale* 1″ = 8 miles.

Published in Nathan Daboll, *Freebetter's New-England Almanack 1777*, Hartford, [1776]; idem, *The New-England Almanack, 1777*, New London, [1776].

386 [1776]

Description In decorated rectangle at upper left: A VIEW OF THE / PRESENT SEAT OF WAR,/ AT AND NEAR NEW-YORK. The title is the same as Map 385 with a comma after . . . SEAT OF WAR . . . instead of a period. Nine references are listed under the map. This is another woodcut engraving very similar to Maps 383, 384, and 385.

Size 4¾″ x 3⁷⁄₁₆″. *Scale* 1″ = 8 miles.

Published in Nathaniel Low, *An Astronomical Diary: or Almanack 1777*. Reproduced in Justin Winsor, ed., *Narrative and Critical History* 6, 342.

387 1789

Description Above top neat line at center: PLAN OF THE CITY OF NEW YORK. Below bottom neat line at left corner: I. M. COMB JUNR. DELT. At right corner: C. TIEBOUT SCULPT. *1789*. There are 37 numbered references with an explanatory table in the upper right corner. The seven wards are bounded with pricked lines and are numbered and named in table at left center. The numbers appear in the wards on the map. One of the residences (at right center) is marked: MR. BYWANK and this is sometimes called the "Bywank map." The author's full name, James M'Comb Jr., is ascertained from the *Directory*. BYARDS LANE is noted at upper center and PART OF LONG OR NASSAU ISLAND at lower right.

Size 9⅛″ x 14½″.   *Scale* 1″ = 1000 feet.

Published in *The New-York Directory 1789;* opp. title page; separately. Reproduced in *The Month at Goodspeed's,* 20 (1948–49), 130. Christopher Colles, *A Survey of the Roads,* 1961, p. 47.

Reference David M. Stauffer, *American Engravers,* 2 no. 3221.

Location DLC (as separate).

388 [1791] *State* I (see also Maps 389 and 390)

Description Above top neat line at center: PLAN OF THE CITY OF NEW YORK. Below bottom neat line at right corner: TIEBOUT SCULPT. There are 38 numbered references in the upper left corner. The wards are outlined with pricked lines and named numerically on body of map. BYARDS L., the residence of MR. BYVANK [sic], and PART OF NASSAU OR LONG ID. are shown. CROWN POINT OR CORLARS HOOK is engraved in one straight line. State Street is not named. (See also Map 396.)

Size 9″ x 14 3/16″.   *Scale* 1″ = 1000 feet.

Published in William Duncan, *The New-York Directory 1791,* opp. title page. Reproduced in New York (City), *Manual of the Corporation of the City of New-York,* New York, 1851, opp. p. 321 (with date "1791" added following the title, and "G. Hayward" and "Valetine [sic]" imprints at lower left and right corners); ibid., 1857, opp. p. 372 (with "1791" omitted but imprint: "From the Original Copy published 1789" at bottom center, and Manual and Hayward imprint at right corner. This later reproduction shows two additional city blocks south of Division Street shaded).

389 [1792] *State* II (see also Maps 388 and 390)

Description BYARDS S and FISHERS ST are now continuous, as are NICHOLAS ST and PUMP ST.

Published in William Duncan, *The New-York Directory 1792;* ibid., 1792 [1793].

390 [1794] *State* III (see also Maps 388 and 389)

Description "Great George St." has been removed and replaced by a second BROAD WAY; PEARL ST now runs from the North River to CHATHAM ST.; and "Queen St." has been removed. BEAVER ST now extends to WILLIAM. STATE ST is noted at the BARRACKS. (See also Map 396.)

Published in William Duncan, *The New-York Directory 1794;* ibid., 1795.

391 [1796]

Description [Map of the City.] The title is taken from the title page of the *Almanack*. No copy is known with the map.

Size Unknown.   *Scale* Unknown.

Published in David Longworth, *The American Almanack, New-York Register, and City Directory embellished with an accurate Map of the City.*

392 1796

Description [A Plan of the City of New York, and Its Environs. Taken from actual Survey. Philadelphia, 1796.] Evans states: "133d Pennsylvania District Copyright, issued to Gouin Dufief, junior, as Proprietor, 29 April, 1796." No such printed map by Nicholas Gouin-Dufief, Jr. has thus far been discovered.

Size Unknown.   *Scale* Unknown.

Published Separately.

Reference Evans 30504.

Location No copy located.

393 1796

Description [Plan of the City and Part of Long Island.] The title of this map is taken from the title page of the *Directory*. A notice on the original paper cover of this volume (at the New-York Historical Society) states that no map was issued with it because new surveys had not been completed in time. A map was promised for the following year's issue. No such map or directory has thus far been discovered.

Size Unknown.   *Scale* Unknown.

Published in John Low, *The New-York Directory and Register 1796.*

394 1797

Description Across top above neat line: A NEW & ACCURATE PLAN OF THE CITY OF NEW YORK IN THE STATE OF NEW YORK IN NORTH AMERICA. PUBLISHED IN *1797;* at left under bottom neat line: B. TAYLOR DEL; at right under bottom neat line: J. ROBERTS SCULPT. This is an excellent topographical map showing the City as it appeared in 1796. Streets are named, the several wards are noted, and a number of residences and public buildings are indicated by small sketches. The author is Benjamin Taylor; the engraver, John Roberts.

Size $22\frac{5}{8}''$ x $36\frac{7}{8}''$.   *Scale* None ($1''$ = c. 400 feet).

Inset At lower right: A VIEW OF THE CITY FROM LONG ISLAND. Below this profile view is a short geographical description of New York. Size: $2\frac{3}{8}''$ x $6\frac{3}{4}''$. Scale: None.

Published Separately. Reproduced in *The Month at Goodspeed's, 14* (1942–43), 16–17; New York (City), *Manual of the Corporation of the City of New York,* New York, 1853, opp. p. 324; Isaac N. P. Stokes, *Iconography of Manhattan Island, 1,* pl. 64; idem and Daniel C. Haskell, *American Historical Prints,* pl. 36b.

References David M. Stauffer, *American Engravers, 2,* 446; see also reproductions above, under Published.

Locations CtY, NN (2 copies), NHi.

395 [1799]

Description [Plan of New-York.] Longworth refers to a "Plan" with this title on p. 138 but no copy of the *Almanack* has thus far been found which includes it.

Size Unknown.   *Scale* Unknown.

Published in David Longworth, *Longworth's American Almanack, New-York Register and City Directory,* 1799.

396 (after 1795]

Description In oval at upper corner: PLAN / OF THE CITY OF / NEW YORK. Beneath title in oval: TANNAR [sic] SC. This is a re-engraving of Cornelius Tiebout's map as used in the 1791–95 directories of William Duncan (see Maps 388–90). There are 41 numbered references tabulated below the title at left. No residences are named. No street names appear north of Vestry, Bleeker, and Stanton, or east of Norfolk and Montgomery. Referring to Map 390 the following additions have been made: Barley St. now appears continuous from Greenwich St., across Broadway and Chatham to Rose St. Beyond Barley now appear Thomas, Catharine, Leonard, Duane, Jay, Harrison, Provost, Moore, and Vestry Sts. North of Grand St., now appear Bullock, Delancey, Rivington, Stanton, Oliver, Prince, Clinton, Columbia, Bleeker, Crosby, Mary, and Catharine (which runs out of Mulberry St.). There are three separate Catharine streets, two Washington streets, and two Clinton streets. Other changes have also been made.

Size $8\frac{3}{4}''$ x $14\frac{3}{8}''$.   *Scale* $1''$ = 1050 feet.

Published Separately.

Location MH.

397 [1747]

Description In cartouche at lower right: MAP NO II. In cartouche below title: ENGRAV'D BY JAMES TURNER / NEAR THE TOWN HOUSE BOSTON NE / WHERE ALL SORTS OF ENGRAVING / ARE DONE AFTER THE BEST MANNER / AND AT THE MOST REASONABLE / RATES. This is a chorographical map showing old surveys of Province boundary lines, old main roads, Indian paths, and the bounds of old Indian grants. Many references are made to the map and its contents in the *Bill*. This map ". . . is copied from part of a Map made by *Cadwallader Colden*, Esq; Surveyor-General of the Province of *New York*, except the red, blue, green and yellow Colours, and the Notes which are added . . ." (p. 5 of the text). It was engraved by James Turner and may have been adapted for publication by Lewis Evans. (See also Maps 294 and 398.)

Size 16⅞″ x 13½″.   *Scale* 1″ = 5 miles.

Published in Board of General Proprietors of the Eastern Division of New Jersey, *A Bill in the Chancery of New Jersey*, foll. p. 124. Reproduced in George J. Miller, "The Printing of the Elizabethtown Bill," p. 11.

398 [1747]

Description In cartouche at lower right: MAP NO. III. In cartouche below title: ENGRAV'D & PRINTED / BY JAMES TURNER NEAR THE / TOWN HOUSE BOSTON / N ENGLAND. This map, prepared by Lewis Evans and engraved by James Turner, shows land surveys in the Newark-Elizabeth area which were made during the period 1676 to 1743, and are listed in "Schedule, Numb. III" on pp. 88–91 of the *Bill*. There is an explanation of the combined use of the map and tables on pp. 22–23 (see also Maps 294 and 397).

Size 11¼″ x 24⅜″.   *Scale* 1″ = 150 chains.

Published in Board of General Proprietors of the Eastern Division of New Jersey, *A Bill in the Chancery of New Jersey*, foll. p. 124. Reproduced in George J. Miller, "The Printing of the Elizabethtown Bill," pp. [18–19].

399 [1760]

Description [Survey of a tract between the Raritan and the Passaic Rivers.] This map shows the courses of the several rivers in the area in dispute as well as the outline of the tract in question. The division line between the allocated land and the nonallocated is also given. The MILLSTONE RIVER breaks through the double line border to the right.

Size 12¼″ x 6¾″.   *Scale* None (1″ = 4 miles).

Published in [New Jersey (Colony)], *The Bill of Complaint in the Chancery of New-Jersey, brought by Thomas Clarke*, opp. p. 20.

400 [1784]

Description Across face of map: THE STATE / OF / NEW JERSEY, [sic]. This is an outline map showing the New Jersey partition lines run in 1687, in 1743, and as claimed by the West Jersey proprietors. Partition lines between New Jersey and New York as intended by the original charter and as ordered in 1769 are also shown. The "3" of the various "30"s in the right and left marginal degree lines is always reversed. DELAWAR RIVER is given thus. The following note is given on the verso of the Errata page of the book:

"The editor begs leave to mention that when the title page was printed it was intended that a map of the state should be affixed; giving the lines of the different counties and townships and the names of all the places of note, but the expense and delay of such undertaking, were so great, as to occasion the design to be laid aside, and the present map was substituted, which contains all those matters that relate to the subject in controversy, and is accurately extracted from Mr. Ratzer's general map, which is compiled the most part from actual survey; the lines of division, and their descriptions, being added thereto. August 7th, 1784."

The first state of the Bernard Ratzer map, "The Province of New Jersey divided into East and West, commonly called The Jerseys," was published in London in 1777. The name of Evert Bancker, Jr. is given on p. 72 of the book as the author of the map used here.

Size 22⁹⁄₁₆″ x 10⁵⁄₁₆″.   *Scale* 1″ = 10 statute miles.

Published in Council of Proprietors of the Western Division of New Jersey, *The Petitions and Memorials*, at end; ibid., 1785 ed.

Reference John Carter Brown Library, *Report, 1956*, pp. 57–58.

401 [1789]

Description Above top neat line: FROM NEW-YORK (*40*) TO ELIZABETH TOWN. This map shows, in two vertical strips, the road from PAULUS (letter "a" reversed) HOOK opposite New York, past BERGEN, over the HACKINSACK and PASSAICK rivers to NEWARK (10 miles).

Size 7" x 4⅞". *Scale* None (1" = ⁴⁄₇ mile).

Published in Christopher Colles, *A Survey of the Roads*. Reproduced, ibid., 1961, p. 154.

402 [1789]

Description Above top neat line: FROM NEW YORK (*41*) TO BRUNSWICK. This map shows, in three vertical strips, the road from Newark through Elizabethtown, past the WHEAT SHEAF Tavern, over the RAWAY [sic] River to a point 22½ miles from Paulus Hook.

Size 7" x 4⅞". *Scale* None (1" = ⁴⁄₇ mile).

Published in Christopher Colles, *A Survey of the Roads*. Reproduced, ibid., 1961, p. 155.

403 [1789]

Description Above top neat line: FROM NEW YORK (*42*) TO BRUNSWICK. This map shows, in two strips, the road from 22½ miles from Paulus Hook, past the BLUEHORSE (letter "s" reversed) Tavern (24 miles), missing Perth Amboy by about three miles, through BONUM TOWN to the edge of Piscataway.

Size 7" x 8". *Scale* None (1" — ¼ mile).

Published in Christopher Colles, *A Survey of the Roads*. Reproduced, ibid., 1961, p. 156.

404 [1789]

Description Above top neat line: FROM NEW-YORK (*43*) TO KINGSTON. This map shows, in three vertical strips, the road from PIS CATAWAY across the RARITON RIVER to BRUNS WICK, then west and south west to a point 44 miles from Paulus Hook.

Size 7" x 4⅝". *Scale* None (1" = ⁴⁄₇ mile).

Published in Christopher Colles, *A Survey of the Roads*. Reproduced, ibid., 1961, p. 157.

405 [1789]

Description Above top neat line: FROM NEW-YORK (*44*) TO TRENTON. This map shows, in three vertical strips, the road from 44 miles south-west of Paulus Hook, through KINGSTON (at 48 miles and PRINCETON (at 51), to MAID EN HEAD (at 56½ miles).

Size 7" x 4¾". *Scale* None (1" = ⁴⁄₇ mile).

Published in Christopher Colles, *A Survey of the Roads*. Reproduced, ibid., 1961, p. 158.

406 [1789]

Description Above top neat line: FROM NEW-YORK (*45*) TO BRISTOL. This map shows, in three vertical strips, the road from Maidenhead, through TREN TON, across the DELAWARE RIVER, to just beyond MARTIN'S OR COOK'S RUN, four miles north-east of Bristol.

Size 7" x 4½". *Scale* None (1" = ⁴⁄₇ mile).

Published in Christopher Colles, *A Survey of the Roads*. Reproduced, ibid., 1961, p. 159.

407 [1789]

Description Above top neat line: FROM NEW-YORK (*45**) TO CRANBERRY. This map shows, in three vertical strips, the road FROM BRUNSWICK / AT E PLATE *43* (35 miles from Paulus Hook), 12½ miles south-west, to about 2½ miles from Cranbury.

Size 7" x 4½". *Scale* None (1" = ⁴⁄₇ mile).

Published in Christopher Colles, *A Survey of the Roads*. Reproduced, ibid., 1961, p. 160.

408 [1789]

Description Above top neat line: FROM NEW-YORK (*46**) TO ALLEN TOWN. This map shows, in three vertical strips, the road from about 2½ miles north-north-west of CRAN BERRY (47¼ miles south-west of Paulus Hook), through CRAN BERRY and HIGHTS TOWN, through CAT TAIL, to within half a mile of Allentown.

Size 7¼" x 4½". *Scale* None (1" = ⁴⁄₇ mile).

Published in Christopher Colles, *A Survey of the Roads*. Reproduced, ibid., 1961, p. 162.

409 [1789]

Description Above top neat line: FROM NEW-YORK (*47**) TO THE BLACKHORSE. This map shows, in two vertical strips, the road from half a mile north-west of ALLEN TOWN, through ALLEN TOWN

(60 miles from Paulus Hook), through CROSS WICKS, to about four miles south-west.

Size 7″ x 4½″. *Scale* None (1″ = 4/7 mile).

Published in Christopher Colles, *A Survey of the Roads.* Reproduced, ibid., 1961, p. 164.

410 [1789]

Description Above top neat line: FROM NEW-YORK (*48*) TO MOUNT HOLLY. This map shows, in two vertical strips, the road from four miles south-west of Crosswicks (68 miles from Paulus Hook), through RISING SUN, to within four miles of MOUNT HOLLY.

Size 7¼″ x 4½″. *Scale* None (1″ = 4/7 mile).

Published in Christopher Colles, *A Survey of the Roads.* Reproduced, ibid., 1961, p. 165.

411 [1789]

Description Above top neat line: FROM NEW-YORK (*49*) TO PHILADELPHIA. This map shows, in three vertical strips, the road from four miles north-west of Mount Holly (78 miles from Paulus Hook), through MOUNT HOL LY TOWN, to beyond MOORS TOWN.

Size 7⅛″ x 4½″. *Scale* None (1″ = 4/7 mile).

Published in Christopher Colles, *A Survey of the Roads.* Reproduced, ibid., 1961, p. 166.

412 [1789]

Description Above top neat line: FROM NEW-YORK (*50*) TO PHILADELPHIA. This map shows, in four strips, the road from half a mile past Moorestown (90 miles from Paulus Hook), past THE GEN. WASH INGTON Tavern on PENNSAW KIN CR., to COOPER'S FERRY and PHILADELPHIA.

Size 7¼″ x 4½″. *Scale* None (1″ = 4/7 mile).

Published in Christopher Colles, *A Survey of the Roads.* Reproduced, ibid., 1961, p. 167.

413 1791

Description In cartouche at upper right: A MAP OF THE GROUND & / DIFFERENT ROUTS FROM NEW- / -ARK TO PAULAS HOOK. SURVEYED / BY ORDER OF JOHN NEILSON, / SAMUEL TUTHILL, WIL-LIAM / MAXWELL, ROBERT KEMBLE, & / JOHN PINTARD, ESQRS. COMMISSION- / -ERS FOR ERECTING BRIDGES OVER HACK- / -INSACK & PASSAICK RIVERS. / BY CASIMIR TH. GOERCK. FEB. *1791.* Above top neat line at extreme left: NEW YORK MAG. Below bottom neat line at left: TAKEN FROM THE ORIGI-NAL DRAUGHT IN THE POSSESSION OF JOHN PINTARD

ESQR. BY J. ANDERSON. Below bottom neat line at right: TIEBOUT SCULPT. The map shows the re-gion between Paulus-Hook, in Bergen County, New Jersey, and the City of Newark. It de-scribes the proposed routes leading to different points on the North River, suitable for bridges over the Hackensack and Passaic Rivers. Data on the different routes are given in "Description of the Map," pp. 367–68 of the *Magazine.*

Size 6⅜″ x 15¾″. *Scale* 1″ = c. 40 chains.

Published in *New York Magazine,* 2 (1791), opp. 367.

Reference David M. Stauffer, *American En-gravers,* 2, no. 3220.

414 [1795] *State* I (II and III post-1799, see below, Description)

Description In oval at upper left corner: THE STATE OF / NEW JERSEY, / COMPILED FROM THE MOST / AUTHENTIC INFORMATION; beneath bottom neat line at left corner: COMPILED BY SAM-UEL LEWIS; At right corner: ENGRAVED BY W. BARKER; at center: ENGRAVED FOR CAREY'S AMER-ICAN EDITION OF GUTHRIES GEOGRAPHY IMPROVED. This is a topographical map showing also the counties, the division line of East from West Jersey, and many roads and towns. SHIPMANS TVN. is shown near Phillipsburg and a road is noted leading directly from HICCORY TVN. to BUNNELS TVN. Carey advertised a map of New Jersey for sale in the (Philadelphia) *Gazette of the United States,* May 8, 1794. No copy of this has thus far been located although it may have been a prior separate publication of this map. The second state appears in the September, 1800 edition of *Carey's General Atlas* with the number "32" added at the upper left corner. State III, in the 1814 edition of the *General Atlas,* has the number "13" at the upper left corner with the "2" of the old "32" erased; a "13" also appears at the lower right corner.

Size 18¼″ x 12⅟₁₆″. *Scale* 1″ = 9½ American miles.

Published in Mathew Carey, *Carey's Ameri-can Atlas,* no. 9; idem, *Carey's General Atlas,* no. 32; idem, *The General Atlas for Carey's Edition of Guthrie's Geography Improved,* no. 32.

415 [1795] *State* I (II post-1799, see below, Description)

Description At upper left: NEW JERSEY. Thirteen counties are shown, also the primary towns and roads. This map was used again with recutting in Scott, *The New and Universal Gaz-etteer,* 4. No new geographical addition is noted. State II may be identified by the two short straight lines which the retoucher has added to strengthen each of the small circles locating the following towns: Bergen, Newton, Easton, Trenton, Pittstown, Mount Holly, and Bordentown.

Size 7¼" x 6⅛".   *Scale* 1" = 16½ miles.

Published in Joseph Scott, *An Atlas of the United States*, no. 9; idem, *The United States Gazetteer*, opp. "Jersey." Reproduced in Joseph Scott, *Atlas of the United States 1795–1800* [no. 12].

416 [1796]   *State* I (II post-1799, see below, Description)

Description   At lower right: NEW JERSEY. Below scale: ENGRAVED BY A. DOOLITTLE NEWHAVEN. RARITION R and RAWAY appear thus. This map was republished in the 1801 edition of *Carey's American Pocket Atlas* with the addition of important roads. No roads are shown on the first state. Several place names appear on the State II which are not shown on the first state including: "M. Hamburg," "Allentown," "Taunton," "Tuckerton," and, "Easton" and "Bristol" in Pennsylvania. The title is not underlined in State I.

Size 7½" x 5¹¹⁄₁₆".   *Scale* 1" = 25 American miles.

Published in Mathew Carey, *Carey's American Pocket Atlas*, foll. p. 52.

417 [1796]

Description   At lower right: NEW JERSEY; beneath title and scale: HILL SC; above top neat line: PUBLISHED BY THOMAS & ANDREWS, BOSTON. Many topographical features are noted and settlement names but no political boundaries are drawn.

Size 7⅜" x 5⅝".   *Scale* 1" = 26 American miles.

Published in Jedidiah Morse, *The American Universal Geography*, 3d ed., *1*, opp. 515.

418 [1796]

Description   In oval at left center: THE STATE OF / NEW JERSEY, / COMPILED FROM THE MOST / ACCURATE SURVEYS; beneath oval: MARTIN SCULPT; below bottom neat line: PUBLISH'D BY JOHN REID. This map is copied from Map 414. It omits "Shipmans Tvn" near Phillipsburg, and HICCORY

TWN appears instead of "Tvn." as on Samuel Lewis' map (but without a spot to locate it). It also omits the road leading directly from it to "Bunnels Tvn." HUDSON R. is given without the "'s."

Size 17⁹⁄₁₆" x 14⅛".   *Scale* 1" = 9½ American miles.

Published in John Reid, *The American Atlas*, [1796?], no. 11; ibid., 1796, no. 11; William Winterbotham, [*Atlas*].

419 1797

Description   At upper right: A PLAN / OF THE / ISLAND OF BURLINGTON, / AND A VIEW OF THE / CITY FROM THE RIVER DELAWARE. / *1797*. In lower right corner: DESIGNED & PUBLISHED BY / W. BIRCH ENAMEL PAINTER / & SOLD AT M. CAREY'S / MARKET STREET / PHILADELPHIA. At the left of the view are seven numbered references to the map and at the right are several conventional sign references. Street names are given and a number of the town buildings are identified in the references. The author is William Birch.

Size 15" x 20".   *Scale* None (1" = c. 500 feet).

Inset   At bottom is the view mentioned in the title. Size: 2¼" x 16¹⁄₁₆".

Published   Separately.

Reference   Philip L. Phillips, *List of Maps of America*, p. 182.

Location   DLC.

420 [1799]

Description   At left center: STATE OF / NEW JERSEY. Below bottom neat line: ENGRAVED FOR PAYNE'S GEOGRAPHY PUBLISHED BY J LOW, NEW YORK. At right: W. BARKER, SCULP PHILADA. This is a topographical map giving also county names, boundaries, and many roads and settlements. It is a reduced copy, with many omissions, of Map 418. AN EXTENSIVE FOREST OF PINE TREES appears in the south central portion and the DIVISION LINE OF E. & W. JERSEY runs from Little Egg Harbor to the South Branch of the Raritan.

Size 10⅝" x 7⅜".   *Scale* None (1" = c. 16 miles).

Published in John Payne, *A New and Complete Universal Geography*, *4*, opp. 320.

PENNSYLVANIA

421 [1759]

Description [Sketch of Fort Du Quesne, now Pittsburgh, with the adjacent Country.] The course of the Ohio is shown to below Beaver Creek. Sixteen numbered references are indicated and identified. Seven Indian towns are located. This is a woodcut map and was copied from a map appearing in the *London Magazine, 28* (1759), 56. Two additional references have been added to the *Almanac* map: "15 Turtle Creek" and "16 Pine Creek." The title is taken from the "References" just below the map.

Size 4¹⁄₁₆" x 3⅛". *Scale* None (1" = c. 23 miles).

Published in Roger More [pseud.], *Poor Roger, 1760;* Abraham Weatherwise [pseud.], *Father Abraham's Almanac 1761.*

422 1759 *State* I (see also Map 423)

Description In cartouche at lower left corner: TO THE HONOURABLE / THOMAS PENN AND RICHARD PENN ESQRS. / TRUE & ABSOLUTE PRO-PRIETARIES & GOVERNOURS OF THE PROVINCE OF / PENNSYLVANIA & COUNTIES OF NEW-CASTLE KENT & SUSSEX ON DELAWARE / THIS MAP / OF THE IM-PROVED PART OF THE PROVINCE OF / PENNSYL-VANIA. / IS HUMBLY DEDICATED BY / NICHOLAS SCULL. At lower center below the Pennsylvania-Maryland boundary line: PHILADELPHIA. EN-GRAVED BY JAS. TURNER, AND PRINTED BY JOHN DAVIS, FOR THE AUTHOR. At lower right, above bottom neat line: PUBLISHED ACCORDING TO ACT OF PARLIAMENT JAN. IST 1759. & SOLD BY THE AUTHOR, NICHOLAS SCULL, IN SECOND-STREET PHILA-DELPHIA. In lower right corner appears this note: – THE AUTHOR CAN ASSURE THE PUBLICK, THAT IN LAYING DOWN THIS MAP . . . ALMOST ALL THE ROADS . . . HAVE BEEN ACTUALLY SURVEY'D & MEASUR'D, LATELY, / WITH GREAT EXACTNESS . . . THE WEST BRANCH OF THE SUSQUEHANNAH . . . WERE TAKEN BY MAJOR SHIPPEN . . . AND I . . . THANK . . . COL. ARMSTRONG, GEO. STEVENSON ESQR. / BENJ. LIGHTFOOT, JOHN WATSON AND ALL OTHERS WHO HAVE GIVEN ME ANY ASSISTANCE IN THIS / WORK. At lower right appears: THE CITY OF PHILADELPHIA LIES IN / *39°* = *58'½* NORTH LATITUDE – AND / *74* = *50.* WEST LONGITUDE FROM LONDON. At the extreme left the road thru ALLEGUIPPY'S GAP is shown meeting a BRANCH OF THE YOHIOGENI R at A and this note appears:

FORT DU QUESNE LIES IN *40°* = *26'* N. LAT. / AND BEARS FROM THE POINT A. W.N.W. ½W. / DISTANT ABOUT *70* MILES. In lower left appears: NB THE AUTHOR OF THIS MAP, IN PLACING OF / FORT CUMBERLAND, HAS FOLLOWED FRY & / JEFFERSON; BUT IS OF OPINION, THAT WHENEVER / THE LINE IS RUN BETWEEN PENNSYLVANIA, / AND MARYLAND, IT WILL PASS TO THE SOUTH- / WARD OF THAT FORT.

The northern limits of the map are the West and North East Branches of the Susquehanna River and Upper Smithfield on the Delaware. The most western points shown are FORT CUM-BERLAND and CHINGLECLAMOUCHE, where Loyas Skutchanning Creek enters the West Branch of the Susquehanna. Newcastle, Delaware is the southernmost point and no details are shown on the New Jersey side of the Delaware. This map is included in Thomas Jeffery's atlas of 1768, assembled and issued in London: *A General Topography of North America and the West Indies.* The title page states: "Engraved by Tho. Jefferys." He re-engraved Lewis Evans' map of 1755 for this atlas but an impression from the original Turner plate of this map is used and so described in the table of contents. In a French compiled, *Atlas des Colonies Angloises en Amerique,* in the Massachusetts Historical Society, which includes many maps from the Jefferys atlas of 1768, appears an impression from the original Turner plate with the follow-ing inscription, possibly in manuscript, added in lower right corner above the scale: A PARIS CHEZ JULIEN AL' HOTEL DE SOUBIZE.

Size 29¾" x 59⁵⁄₁₆". *Scale* 1" = 4 Brit-ish statute miles.

Published Separately.

References Evans 8489; Philip L. Phillips, *A List of Maps of America,* p. 673.

Locations BM, CtY, DLC, MiU-C, PHi, PP, RPJCB.

423 1759 *State* II (see also Map 422)

Description Four long lines of text have been added at right of the Narrows of the Sus-quehannah at Nelson's Ferry. A road now leads east from Carlisle direct to Pine Ford.

Published Separately.

Location Private coll. of Mr. Nicholas B.

Wainwright; another offered by the Old Print Shop, New York, January, 1944.

424 [1765]

Description On scroll at upper right: PLAN / OF THE / BATTLE NEAR BUSHY-RUN / GAINED BY HIS MAJESTY'S TROOPS, COMMANDED BY / COLONEL HENRY BOUQUET / OVER THE / DELAWARE, SHAWANESE, MINGOES, / WYANDOTS, MOHIKONS, MIAMIES & OTTAWAS, / ON THE 5TH AND 6TH: OF AUGUST, *1763*. / FROM AN ACTUAL SURVEY / BY THOS: HUTCHINS / ASSISTANT ENGINEER. Above top line at far left: PLATE III. Much topographic detail is shown as well as the disposition of the troops. A short set of REFERENCES are given at the upper left. The PLAN was made in April, 1765, at Col. Bouquet's orders.

Size 11⅜" x 12⅞". *Scale* 1" = 26 perches.

Published in [William Smith], *An Historical Account of the Expedition under the Command of Henry Bouquet*, opp. p. XII.

References Thomas Hutchins, *A Topographical Description*, 1904, pp. 14, 16.

[1768] see Map 497.

425 1770

Description In elaborate cartouche at upper center: TO THE HONORABLE / THOMAS PENN AND RICHARD PENN ESQUIRES / TRUE AND ABSOLUTE PROPRIETARIES AND GOVERNORS OF THE / PROVINCE OF PENNSYLVANIA AND THE TERRITORIES THEREUNTO BELONGING / AND TO THE / HONORABLE JOHN PENN ESQUIRE / LIEUTENANT-GOVERNOR OF THE SAME / THIS MAP / OF THE PROVINCE OF / PENNSYLVANIA. IS HUMBLY DEDICATED BY THEIR / MOST OBEDIENT HUMBLE SERVT: / W SCULL. Under scale at left of cartouche: HENRY DAWKINS. SCULPT. At bottom right, just above neat line: PHILADELPHIA, PRINTED BY JAMES NEVIL, FOR THE AUTHOR, APRIL *4*ST [SIC], *1770*. At the upper right is a note of acknowledgement to Joseph Shippen, John Lukens, and others. At the lower left appears the following: THE WHOLE LINE RUN BY MESSRS. / MASON & DIXON IS DELINEATED IN / THIS MAP; BUT, CONSIDERED AS A / BOUNDARY, THAT LINE SHOULD HAVE EXTENDED NO FARTHER WEST THAN / SOMEWHERE ABOUT THE LINE AB, OR THE TRUE MERIDIAN OF THE / *1*ST FOUNTAIN OF POTOMACK ∴ [SIC] WHICH IS THE WESTERN BOUNDARY OF / MARYLAND. PENNSYLVANIA BY THE ROYAL GRANT IS THEN ENTITLED / TO RUN DUE SOUTH BY THE LINE AB FOR ABOUT *50* MILES TO THE BEG- / INNING OF THE *40*TH. DEGREE, AND THEN WEST TO THE END OF *5*. / DEGREES, FROM DELAWARE. A large BUFFELOE / SWAMP appears north of the headwaters of the West Branch of Susquehannah

and a GREAT / SWAMP appears just east of modern Scranton extending from Mauche Chunk and POKONO / POINT to where Carbondale is now. THE CITY OF PHILADELPHIA LIES IN / LAT: *39°, 56'. 54"* LONG. *5*H. *0'. 35"* appears at lower right.

Size 21⅞" x 32 1/16". *Scale* 1" = 10 miles.

Published Separately. Reproduced in Emerson D. Fite and Archibald Freeman, *A Book of Old Maps*, p. 224; *Pennsylvania Archives*, 3d ser., Appendix.

References John Carter Brown Library, *Report, 1947*, pp. 20–22; Evans 11850; Philip L. Phillips, *A List of Maps of America*, 647; see also reproductions above, under Published.

Locations BM, DLC, MiU-C, NN, PHi, PP, RPJCB.

426 [1788]

Description In cartouche at upper center: TO THE PATRONS OF THE COLOMBIAN MAGAZINE / THIS MAP OF PENNSYLVANIA / IS DEDICATED BY THEIR OBLIGED AND OBEDT. SERVNTS. / THE PROPRIETORS. This is an excellent chorographical map showing a great amount of detail. Many mountain range sections are named. It was advertised in June, 1787, as being prepared for the September issue. After repeated apologies for the delay, it appeared in January, 1788. The boundaries recently ascertained by commissioners from this and adjoining states are shown. PART OF INDIANA appears below the southern boundary west of Maryland. ERIE DISTRICT is marked west of Presque Isle along the southern shore of Lake Erie. BUFFALOE LOW LANDS are shown as a large swampy area east of FENANGO F. GREAT SWAMP, covering a large area, is shown north east of WILKSBURG (Wilkesbarre). The CHENANGU RIVER extends past the upper neat line. A large scale indicator and longitude reference markings are explained in the lower right corner. (See also Map 431.)

Size 12¼" x 20 15/16". *Scale* 1" = 15½ miles.

Published in *Columbian Magazine*, 2 (1788), opp. 3; separate copies exist at Harvard and the Library of Congress.

427 [1789]

Description Above top neat line: FROM NEW-YORK (*46*) TO FRANKFORD. This map shows, in three vertical strips, the road from four miles north-east of BRISTOL (73 miles from Paulus Hook), through BRISTOL, to within six miles of FRANKFORD.

Size 7" x 4½". *Scale* None (1" = 4/7 mile).

Published in Christopher Colles, *A Survey of the Roads.* Reproduced, ibid., 1961, p. 161.

428 [1789]

Description Above top neat line: FROM NEW-YORK (*47*) TO PHILADELPHIA. This map shows, in three vertical strips, the road from six miles northeast-by-east of FRANKFORD, past HOLMES'S Tavern, through FRAN KFORD to PHILADELPHIA.

Size 7" x 4½". *Scale* None (1" = 4/7 mile).

Published in Christopher Colles, *A Survey of the Roads.* Reproduced, ibid., 1961, p. 163; Robert M. Lunny, *Early Maps of North America*, p. 44.

429 [1789]

Description Above top neat line: FROM PHIL-ADELPHIA (*51*) TO ANNAPOLIS MARYLAND. This map shows, in three vertical strips, the road from PHI LADELPHIA, west on MARKET ST. across the SCHUYLKILL R, then south-west through DAR BY, to about 2½ miles north-east of Chester.

Size 7" x 4½". *Scale* None (1" = 4/7 mile).

Published in Christopher Colles, *A Survey of the Roads.* Reproduced, ibid., 1961, p. 168.

430 [1789]

Description Above top neat line: FROM PHIL-ADELPHIA (*52*) TO ANNAPOLIS MARYLD. This map shows, in three vertical strips, the road from 2½ miles north-east of CHES TER (12½ miles from Philadelphia), through CHES TER, into Delaware, and to four miles north-east of Wilmington.

Size 7" x 4⅝". *Scale* None (1" = 4/7 mile).

Published in Christopher Colles, *A Survey of the Roads.* Reproduced, ibid., 1961, p. 169.

431 1790

Description [A Pocket Map of the State of Pennsylvania. Philadelphia: Printed by William Spotswood 1790.] This title and imprint are taken from Evans. Both the Library of Congress and Harvard have separate copies of Map 426 but these show no changes from the map included in the *Columbian Magazine*, 2 (1788), opp. 3.

Size Unknown. *Scale* Unknown.

Published Separately.

Reference Evans 22804.

Location No copy located.

432 [1791]

Description At lower right corner: A / MAP / EXHIBITING / A GENERAL VIEW / OF THE / ROADS AND INLAND NAVIGATION / OF / PENNSYLVANIA, / AND PART OF THE ADJACENT STATES. / RESPECT-FULLY INSCRIBED TO / THOMAS MIFFLIN, GOVERNOR, / AND THE / GENERAL ASSEMBLY OF THE COMMON-WEALTH / OF PENNSYLVANIA: / BY JOHN ADLUM, AND / JOHN WALLIS. Some topographical features are noted. Several proposed roads and canals are given as well as the already existing roads, trails, and canals. The Genesee appears as: CHENESEEO. BUFFALO SWAMP appears along the headwaters of the CONEWANGO RIVER. The Erie triangle is shown separately and marked: TERRITORY ANNEXED TO PENNSA. Evans 23104 states that the copyright was issued in February, 1791, and the title regis-tered contained the following statement: "Com-piled . . . at the particular request of the Society lately formed in Pennsylvania, for promoting the Improvements of Roads and Inland Naviga-tion."

Size 32¹³⁄₁₆" x 36¼". *Scale* 1" = 10 miles.

Insets [a] In lower left corner: FIG. *1* / PER-SPECTIVE VIEW OF PART OF A CANAL WITH LOCKS. This and the following inset figures contain numerous lettered references that are explained in three engraved script paragraphs, two above and one to the right of the insets. A re-engrav-ing of these same views is found in Thomas Dobson, *Encyclopedia*, 4, pl. CXIV; the explan-atory text is given on page 78. Size: 3¹⁄₁₆" x 5¼".

[b] At right of [a]: FIG. 2. / SECTION OF A LOCK. Size: 2⅛" x 6¼".

[c] Under [b]: FIG. 3. / SECTION OF A LOCK FULL OF WATER. Size: 2⅛" x 6¼".

[d] Under [c]: FIG. *4.* PLAN OF A / LOCK. Size: 2" x 6¼".

Published Separately. Reproduced in *Penn-sylvania Archives*, 3d ser., *1*, front.

Reference Evans 23104.

Locations CtY, DLC, MB, MiU-C, NHi, PPL.

433 1792 *State* I (see also Maps 434–36, 440–41 and 453; VIII post-1799, see Map 453, Description)

Description In plain oval cartouche at up-per right: A / MAP / OF THE / STATE / OF / PENNSYLVANIA, / BY / READING HOWELL, / MDCCXCII; below title at extreme right: TO / THOMAS MIFFLIN / GOVERNOR / THE / SENATE, AND HOUSE OF REPRESENTATIVES / OF THE / COM-MONWEALTH / OF / PENNSYLVANIA, / THIS MAP / IS RESPECTFULLY INSCRIBED BY THE / AUTHOR; at top center a copyright statement beginning:

DISTRICT OF PENNSYLVANIA TO WIT. BE IT REMEMBERED, THAT ON THE ELEVENTH DAY OF JANUARY IN THE FIFTEENTH YEAR OF THE INDEPENDENCE OF THE UNITED STATES OF AMERICA, CAME READING HOWELL, OF THE SAID DISTRICT, HATH DEPOSITED IN THIS OFFICE, THE TITLE OF A MAP, THE RIGHT WHEREOF HE CLAIMS AS AUTHOR IN THE / WORDS FOLLOWING, TO WIT. "A MAP OF THE STATE OF PENNSYLVANIA . . ." This is the best map of Pennsylvania to appear in the 18th century, and the first detailed map of the State to show its exact boundaries. Many topographical features are noted as well as settlements, donation lands, counties, and townships. The map was published from four plates and several different states of each plate were issued over a period of years. Shown in these are the changing county and township lines, the many new settlements, and, as more of the State was thoroughly surveyed, an increasingly accurate portrayal of its topographic features. Due to the fact that the several states of the plates of this map were distributed at varying times, and that the usual copy is composed of differing states, each will be listed and located to facilitate further research. The following is a list of complete reported holdings of this map in eleven selected map collections:

BM	(2)	OClWHi	(1)
CtY	(2)	P	(1)
DLC	(5)	PHi	(5)
MH	(2)	PPL	(2½)
MiU-C	(2)	RPJCB	(1)
NN	(1½)		

The four plates of this Howell map are identified in the diagram below. The locations and identification of the plates follow. Of this group of maps only the two Harvard University copies contain like states of the four plates. In a larger sample, more may perhaps be found.

b	a
d	c

Four plates of Howell 1792
map of Pennsylvania

BM	copy 1 State I: abc; State IV: d
	copy 2 State II: abc; State IV: d
CtY	copies 1&2 State II: abc; State III: d
DLC	copy 1 State I: abc; State III: d
	copies 2&3 State II: abc; State III: d
	copy 4 State II: bc; State V: a; State VI: d
	copy 5 All plates: 1800 or after
MH	copies 1&2 State II: abcd

MiU-C	copy 1 State I: abc; State III: d
	copy 2 State I: d; State II: abc
NN	copy 1 State II: abc; State IV: d
	copy 2 State V: a; plate c 1800 (two plates only)
OCl WHi	State II: abc; State VI: d
P	State II: abc; State V: d
PHi	copy 1 State I: ac; State II: b; State III: d
	copy 2 State I: abc; State III: d
	copy 3 State V: ad; plates bc 1800 or after
	copy 4 State II: abc; State III: d
	copy 5 State I: a; State II: bc; State III: d
PPL	copy 1 State I: ac; State II: b; State III: d
	copy 2 State V: ad; plates bc 1800 or after
	copy 3 All plates: 1800 or after (plates ac only)
RPJCB	State I: abc; State III: d

Size 36¾" x 62⅞". *Scale* 1" = 5 miles.

Published Separately. Reproduced in *Pennsylvania Archives*, 3d ser., Appendix I–X, no. 4; State I, ac, State II, bd.

References British Museum, *Catalogue of Printed Maps*, 2, 3233; Evans 23453 and 24411; Hazel S. Garrison, "Cartography of Pennsylvania before 1800," pp. 281–83.

Locations See above, Description.

434 1792 *State* II (see also Maps 433, 435, 436, 440, 441, and 453; VII post-1799, see Map 453, Description)

Description The cartouche at upper right has now been embellished with a design of flora and agricultural implements. R. R. LEVINGSTON now appears on the tributary of the eastern branch of the Delaware into which the BEAVER KILL empties. The dedication now has a flower garland border and below it a scene showing a ship bearing the name PENN at dockside. OR PEACH BOTTOM FERRY has been added following the upper COOPERS near where the Susquehanna crosses the southern border. At the upper left CONEWANGO is inscribed on the most northeasterly tributary of the Conewango Creek. No London imprint has yet appeared. The following names are given along the south half of the western boundary at the lower left: WELLS'S on Cross Creek, NORTH FORK on Buffaloe Creek, NORTH FORK and SOUTH FORK on Wheeling Creek, and RYERSON'S at the mouth of Warrior Fork. FORT MC INTOSH is also named at the mouth of the Beaver River. IRON is marked on Conquenesing Creek, east of the Beaver River. BUTLERS, STREETS RUN, BECKS, and

SAWMILL RUN, all appear on the south side of the Monongahela, west of Turtle Creek.

Published Separately.

Locations See Map 433, Description.

435 1792 *State* III (see also Maps 433, 434, 436, 440, 441, and 453; VIII post-1799, see Map 453, Description)

Description The following imprint now appears at the lower left corner: PUBLISHED *I* AUGUST *1792*, FOR THE AUTHOR; & SOLD BY JAMES PHILLIPS, GEORGE YARD, LOMBARD STREET, LONDON. The name TURKEY RUN is now inscribed across the western border line just north of NORTH FORK WHEELING CREEK.

Published Separately.

Locations See Map 433, Description.

436 1792 *State* IV (see also Maps 433–35, 440, 441, and 453; VIII post-1799, see Map 453, Description)

Description At the lower left GENTLE RUN now appears, flowing south into the Little Conemaugh between South Branch and the Forks.

Published Separately.

Locations See Map 433, Description.

437 [1792] *State* I (see also Maps 443 and 447)

Description In copyright notice lower right corner: DISTRICT OF PENNSYLVANIA, TO WIT: BE IT REMEMBERED, THAT ON THE THIRTEENTH DAY OF JUNE, IN THE FIFTEENTH YEAR OF THE INDEPENDENCE OF THE / UNITED STATES OF AMERICA, READING HOWELL . . . HATH DEPOSITED . . . "A MAP OF PENNSYLVANIA, & THE PARTS CONNECTED THEREWITH, RELATING TO THE ROADS AND INLAND / NAVIGATION, ESPECIALLY AS PROPOSED TO BE IMPROVED BY THE LATE PROCEEDINGS OF ASSEMBLY. (COPIED FROM HIS LARGER MAP) BY READING HOWELL" . . . At lower right corner in marginal degree line: J. TRENCHARD SCULP. This map gives some topographic details and shows the roads and trails between the towns and settlements of the State. As indicated in the title, the map is based upon Map 433. An EXPLANATION is given at the upper right corner ending with the word: PRACTICABLE. No counties are indicated. A canal is shown between Lebanon and Myerstown. The following dedication is given at the upper center: TO THE / LEGISLATURE AND THE GOVERNOR / OF PENNSYLVANIA / THIS MAP IS RESPECTFULLY INSCRIBED / BY READING HOWELL. The map was engraved by James Trenchard.

Size 18⅛″ x 26⅛″. *Scale* 1″ = 12 miles.

Published Separately.

Reference Evans 24412.

Locations DLC, PHi, PPL.

438 [1793]

Description In oval at lower left: A / MAP / OF / PENSYLVANIA, / WITH PART OF THE ADJA / CENT STATES, / FROM / THE LATEST SURVEYS / O. CARLETON, DEL. PENNSYLVANIA is inscribed correctly on the map. BUFFALO SWAMP is shown in Western New York State. NORTHEAST BRANCH OF SUSQUECHERRY VAL appears. The Erie Triangle is shown as part of New York. Oneida Lake is inscribed twice, once upside down. The map was drawn by Osgood Carleton.

Size 7⅛″ x 7¹³⁄₁₆″. *Scale* 1″ = 65 English miles.

Published in Jedidiah Morse, *The American Universal Geography,* I, opp. 469.

439 [1794?]

Description At upper right corner: A / MAP / OF THE / STATE / OF / PENNSYLVANIA / FROM / MR. HOWELL'S / LARGE / MAP / J.T. SCOTT SCULP; above neat line at center: ENGRAVED FOR CAREY'S AMERICAN EDITION OF GUTHRIE'S GEOGRAPHY IMPROVED. The Erie Triangle is not included. Some topographical detail is given and many roads are shown. ELLICOT'S ROAD runs from TYOGA POINT, at the juncture of the Tyoga River and the EAST SUSQUEHANNA RIVER, to Stockport. At the lower right corner is a table of REFERENCES. This is not the same map found in any of the early Carey atlases examined.

Size 11¹⁵⁄₁₆″ x 19⅞″. *Scale* 1″ = 16 miles.

Published Separately.

Location MH.

440 [1795] *State* V (see also Maps 433–36, 441, and 453; VIII post-1799, see Map 453, Description)

Description Lycoming COUNTY is shown but not named at the upper right. Both WAYNE and TYOGA counties are now indicated by name. At the lower left SOMERSET County has been added. Clearfield Creek has been extended to the northern edge of plate "d" of the map. The name "Beaver Dam Branch" has been removed from the main eastern tributary of Clearfield Creek. CHEST CREEK is now spelled out fully with the word CREEK engraved on the southern (separated) section of the stream which is not shown continuously. ALLEGENY M. is abbreviated thus.

93

Published Separately.

Locations See Map 433, Description.

441 [1795?] *State* VI (see also Maps 433–36, 440, and 453; VIII post-1799, see Map 453, Description)

Description At the lower left, "Husbands" on the northern road from PREATORS to CHERRYS has been changed to SOMERSET.

Published Separately.

Locations See Map 433, Description.

442 [1795]

Description In oval at upper center: THE STATE OF / PENNSYLVANIA. / REDUCED WITH PERMISSION FROM / READING HOWELLS MAP, / BY SAMUEL LEWIS; in oval below title: SMITHER SCULP; below bottom neat line at center: ENGRAVED FOR CAREY'S AMERICAN EDITION OF GUTHRIE'S GEOGRAPHY IMPROVED. This is a topographical map showing also county boundaries, roads, and towns. ALLEGANY COUNTY is given thus and also ALLEGENY RIVER. SCHUYLKILL has the modern spelling. LOCHARTSBURG is shown at the junction of the TYOGA R. (Chemung) and the EAST BRANCH (Susquehanna). The Erie Triangle is included in Pennsylvania. The map was engraved by James Smither.

Size 11⅜" x 18".   *Scale* 1" = 18 American miles.

Published in Mathew Carey, *Carey's American Atlas*, no. 10; idem, *Carey's General Atlas*, no. 33; idem, *The General Atlas for Carey's Edition of Guthrie's Geography Improved*, no. 33.

443 [1795?] *State* II (see also Maps 437 and 447)

Description NO. 1. 2. 3. &C. / ARE SURVEYORS / DISTRICTS. has been added in the EXPLANATION at the upper right corner. The counties of the State are now named and their boundaries indicated. A number of new place names, streams, and roads have been added. New canals are shown, one beginning at the mouth of CONEWAGO C. on the Susquehanna River, and the other beginning on the Delaware River just north of Philadelphia and going to NORRIS TOWN.

Published in Schuylkill and Susquehanna Navigation, *An Historical Account of the Rise, Progress and Present State of the Canal Navigation*, front. Reproduced in U.S. Congress, *American State Papers*, Class X, Misc. *1*, opp. 830 (copied, not a facsimile).

Locations MiD-B, PPL (as separates).

444 [1795] *State* I (II post-1799, see below, Description)

Description At upper center: PENNSYLVANIA. The Erie triangle is included as part of Pennsylvania. The ALLEGANY River, Mountain, and County are all spelled alike. The counties are named but their boundaries are not shown. LYCOMING and SOMERSET counties, established in April, 1795, are shown. Mountain ranges and streams are shown but not roads. This map was reissued in Scott's *The New and Universal Gazetteer, 4*. This later state has been recut; Green County, organized in 1796, is now shown (at lower left), but Wayne County, also organized in 1796, does not appear.

Size 6⅟₁₆" x 8⁷⁄₁₆".   *Scale* 1" = 45 miles.

Published in Joseph Scott, *An Atlas of the United States*, no. 10; idem, *The United States Gazetteer*, opp. "Pennsylvania." Reproduced in Joseph Scott, *Atlas of the United States 1795–1800*, [no. 15].

445 [1796] *State* I (II post-1799, see below, Description)

Description At upper center: PENNSYLVANIA. Below bottom neat line: W. BARKER SCULP. LOCKHARTSBURG is shown at the junction of the TYOGA R and the EAST BRA: of the Susquehanna. This map was reissued in the 1801 edition of *Carey's American Pocket Atlas* with the addition of important roads; no roads are shown on the first state. The following place names do not appear on the first state: "Legionville," "Hanover," "Somerset," "Columbia," and "Downing." None of the figures for latitude and longitude are emphasized in the first state, but in the 1801 edition lines are drawn between marginal degree line and neat line for each fifth degree.

Size 5¾" x 7⅝".   *Scale* 1" = 50 miles.

Published in Mathew Carey, *Carey's American Pocket Atlas*, opp. p. 58.

446 [1796]

Description Left of center: PENNSYLVANIA / DRAWN FROM THE BEST AUTHORITIES / BY / CYRUS HARRIS; below title: ENGRAVED BY A DOOLITTLE; above neat line: PUBLISHED BY THOMAS & ANDREWS. The Erie Triangle is shown as part of New York. Many roads and county boundaries are shown, together with the main streams and portages. A few orographical features appear.

Size 7⁹⁄₁₆" x 13³⁄₁₆".   *Scale* 1" = 24½ miles.

Published in Jedidiah Morse, *The American Universal Geography*, 3d ed., *1*, opp. 533.

447 1796 *State* III (see also Maps 437 and 443)

Description A new title appears in rectangle at upper center replacing dedication: A MAP OF THE STATE / OF / PENNSYLVANIA, / BY / READING HOWELL, / M. DCCXCVI. The copyright notice at lower left has been removed, as has "J. Trenchard Sculp." in marginal degree line. The following has been added at lower left: PENNSYLVANIA, COPIED FROM THE LARGE MAP. / THE MARYLAND PART FROM GRIFFITH'S. The EXPLANATION at the upper right has been altered: the statement beginning: "Roads to be opened . . ." has been omitted and the several divisions of the map are noted as: SURVEYORS / DISTRICTS I. II. &C. Many place names and streams have been added and "Cedar Falls," at the upper right, has been removed. The LARGE MAP referred to is, of course, Map 433; the Maryland map is the Dennis Griffith's "A Map of the State of Maryland" (see Map 511).

Published Separately.

Location MH.

448 [c. 1796]

Description [Map of Pennsylvania, reduced from Reading Howell's map by Samuel Lewis.] The title is taken from Stauffer and he states that the map was engraved by John Scoles.

Size 18″ x 11½″. *Scale* Unknown.

Published Separately.

Reference David M. Stauffer, *American Engravers*, 2, no. 2841.

Location No copy located.

449 [1796]

Description At upper center: PLAN / OF THE TOWN OF / ERIE / ON LAKE ERIE; at lower left: F MOLINEUX DEL; at bottom center: PUBLISHED AS THE ACT DIRECTS; at lower right: F SHALLUS SCULPT. The written copyright statement accompanying the Library of Congress copy states: "Deposited 16 Sept. 96 by Frederic Molineux-as Author- ." Two REFERENCES are given at the lower right. All of the streets have been named and the lots numbered. The ROAD TO THE FORT is indicated at the upper right. The NOTE at the lower left indicates the size of the lots. Francis Shallus is the engraver.

Size 11½″ x 21½″. *Scale* None (1″ = c. 410 feet).

Published Separately.

Location DLC.

450 [1796] *State* I (see also Map 451)

Description In oval at upper center: THE STATE OF / PENNSYLVANIA. / FROM THE LATEST SURVEYS; below bottom neat line at left: D. MARTIN SCT; at center: PUBLISH'D BY J. REID NEW YORK. This map is evidently reduced from Reading Howell's map. It shows ALLEGANY for both County and River. TYOGA POINT is shown at the junction of the Tyoga River (Chemung) and the EAST SUSQUEHANNA. The West Branch of the Schuylkill, Little Schuylkill, and Potomac rivers are shown. The new New York-Pennsylvania boundary has been used at the upper left and the old one erased from the plate.

Size 12¹¹⁄₁₆″ x 17¾″. *Scale* 1″ = 18 American miles.

Published in John Reid, *The American Atlas*, [1796?], no. 12; ibid., 1796, no. 12; William Winterbotham, [*Atlas*].

451 1796 *State* II (see also Map 450)

Description The date: *1796.* has been added below: FROM THE LATEST SURVEYS., in the title at upper center. No original copy of this map with this date added has thus far been discovered. It may have been added at the time of the facsimile noted below.

Published Separately (?). Reproduced in U.S. Bureau of the Census, *Heads of Families at the First Census Pennsylvania*, front.

452 [c. 1797]

Description In scroll at top center: PLAN OF / BEULA / PENNSYLVANIA. At bottom right of town plan: W. BARKER SCULP. A short description of the newly founded town is given below the bottom neat line. The streets are named but not the five town squares.

Size 13¼″ x 10⅝″. *Scale* 1″ = 1280 feet.

Published Separately.

Location MiU-C.

453 [1798] *State* VII (see also Maps 433–36, 440, 441; VIII post-1799, see below, Description)

Description BEULA now appears at the lower left on a tributary of Black Lick Creek on a new road from Frankstown west to that creek, and another new road appears from Somerset, up the valley to BEULA. A number of changes appear in the next state of the map, appearing after 1800, probably after March, 1804. Wayne, Tyoga, and Adams counties are named in the eastern portion of the State; in the western portion, the following: Crawford, Erie, Mercer,

Venango, Warren, Potter, McKean, "Clerfield" [i.e. Clearfield], Green, Adams, Butler, Beaver, Center, Indiana, and Cambria. The interior of the state east of the Allegheny at the upper left has been completely erased from the plate and reengraved with many small drainage details filling previously blank spaces. One copy of the map at the Library of Congress Map Division bears the following, printed at the upper right corner: "Registered and Copy right secured agreeable to Act of Congress, August 11th. 1806. D. Caldwell, Clerk of the District of Pennsylvania." On the verso is a printed statement, pasted on: "The Map of Pennsylvania Improved," and dated January 13, 1809.

Published Separately.

Location See Description, Map 433.

454 [1752] *State* I (see also Map 455)

Description In cartouche across top: A MAP OF PHILADELPHIA, AND PARTS ADJACENT. / WITH A PERSPECTIVE VIEW OF THE STATE-HOUSE. BY N. SCULL AND G. HEAP. At bottom right under neat line: LHEBERT SCULPT. This plan of Philadelphia by Nicholas Scull and George Heap has proven, at least in the manner of time, to be the most popular ever issued. Many reproductions have been published of it during the years since it was first issued, both in America and in Europe. The FAMOUS VIEW, or modifications of it, has also been repeated on many of the reproductions. At the lower right is given: A TABLE OF DISTANCES OF / PARTICULAR PLACES WITHIN / THIS MAP . . . A short summary of the public and private buildings of the City is given at the upper right. The streets of the City are shown in their familiar pattern but are not named. A detailed view of the surrounding countryside is given to an extent of six to eight miles. On this first state the LUTHERAN CHURCH 7 (MILS) and 7 (FUR.) is given on the TABLE OF DISTANCES but this was substituted on State II by the name of William Allen. The date of this map has been established as 1752, not 1750 as heretofore believed (see the article by Mr. Wainwright noted below). An advertisement in the (Philadelphia) *Pennsylvania Gazette* for June 4, 1752, states that the map has been "Just published."

Size 20½" x 11⅞".   *Scale* 1" = 1 mile.

Inset At top under the title is the: PERSPECTIVE VIEW OF THE STATE-HOUSE. This is the earliest known printed view of the building known today as Independence Hall. A short description of it is given at the upper left. Size: 5⁹⁄₁₆" x 11⅝". Scale: 1" = 25 feet.

Published Separately. Reproduced in John Carter Brown Library, *In Retrospect*, pl. II; Nicholas B. Wainwright, "Scull and Heap's Map of Philadelphia," opp. p. 70. Included in this article (pp. 69–75) is a discussion of the various important facsimile editions, American and foreign, of this map. No later reprintings were apparently made of this first state, however. All seem to have been prepared from State II.

References John Carter Brown Library, *Report, 1947*, pp. 16–19; John T. Scharf and

Thompson Westcott, *History of Philadelphia*, *1*, 14; see also reproductions above, under Published.

Location RPJCB.

455 [1752] *State* II (see also Map 454)

Description The home of Chief Justice William Allen, Scull's personal friend, is shown below the top margin on the road north of Germantown. The "Lutheran Church" has been deleted from the: TABLE OF DISTANCES and, W. ALLEN *8* (MILS) and *6* (FUR.) has been substituted.

Published Separately. Reproduced in John T. Scharf and Thompson Westcott, *History of Philadelphia*, *1*, opp. 14. Most of the known reproductions of this map were based upon this second state. These begin with the reproduction of the State House in the *Gentlemen's Magazine* for September, 1752 (*22*, opp. 396), and the map itself in the August, 1753, issue (*23*, opp. 373). Later foreign reproductions include those by Faden and by Lotter. American reproductions include those by David Lobach in 1850 and by Benjamin R. Boggs in 1893.

Location CtY.

456 1762

Description In decorative cartouche at lower left corner: TO THE / MAYOR / RECORDER ALDERMEN / COMMON COUNCIL / AND FREEMEN OF / PHILADELPHIA / THIS PLAN / OF THE IMPROVED PART OF THE CITY SURVEYED AND LAID / DOWN BY THE LATE NICHOLAS SCULL ESQR. SURVEYOR / GENERAL OF THE PROVINCE OF PENNSYLVANIA IS HUMBLY / INSCRIB'D BY / THE EDITORS. Just above bottom neat line: PUBLISHED ACCORDING TO ACT OF PARLIAMENT, NOVR. 1ST 1762, AND SOLD BY THE EDITOR'S MATTHEW CLARKSON, AND MARY BIDDLE IN PHILADELPHIA. This is the most important engraved plan of Philadelphia since the Thomas Holme plan of 1682. It is not signed by an engraver. Stauffer attributes it to James Turner from the character of the work, but Turner died in late 1759. Henry Dawkins seems the probable engraver. REFERENCES, A to Z are given at the upper right corner.

Size 21" x 27".   *Scale* 1" = 400 feet.

Insets [a] At upper left are two inset plans

of the City. The titles are taken from the REFER-ENCES. A THE PLAN OF THE CITY, WITH THE FIVE PUBLICK SQUARES / AS PUBLISH'D BY THOS. HOLMES. SURVEYOR GENERAL. Size: 6¾" x 2¾". Scale: None (1" = 3000 feet).

[b] B A SUBSEQUENT PLAN DRAWN BY BENJN: EASTBURN / SURVEYOR GENERAL. Size: 6¾" x 4¾". Scale: None (1" = 3200 feet).

Published Separately. Reproduced separately by Joseph H. Bonsall and Samuel L. Smedley in 1858 with title: "Philadelphia 100 years ago" at the top; ibid., [1875]; by Miller and Moss in Philadelphia, 1876. Reproduced in Ellis P. Oberholtzer, *Philadelphia, 1*, opp. 216.

References Edward L. Burchard and Edward B. Matthews, "Manuscripts and publications relating to the Mason and Dixon Line," p. 339; Evans 9267; Philip L. Phillips, *A Descriptive List of Maps and Views*, nos. 152–54; idem, *A List of Maps of America*, p. 698; David M. Stauffer, *American Engravers*, no. 3333; Issac N. P. Stokes and Daniel C. Haskell, *American Historical Prints*, p. 35.

Locations NN, PHi, PPL.

457 [1774] *State* I (see also Map 458)

Description In elaborate cartouche at upper center: TO THE HONOURABLE HOUSE OF REPRESENTATIVES / OF THE FREEMEN OF PENNSYLVANIA / THIS MAP OF THE CITY AND LIBERTIES OF PHILADELPHIA / WITH THE CATALOGUE OF PURCHASERS IS HUMBLY / DEDICATED BY THEIR MOST OBEDIENT / HUMBLE SERVANT / IOHN REED. Beneath cartouche to left: JAMES SMITHER SCULP. To right: PRINTED BY THO: MAN. The streets and squares are shown on the main map as originally laid out by Thomas Holme and advertised by William Penn when he printed the Holme map before the changes later authorized. Lists of: NAMES OF THE FIRST / PURCHASERS, and NAMES OF THE PERSONS WHO TOOK UP THE L [iberty] LAND are given, beginning at the upper left, with references to the numbered lots assigned them on the inset Holme plan, under the heading: AN ACCOMPT [sic] OF THE LANDS IN PENNSYLVANIA GRANTED BY WILLIAM PENN ESQR. SOLE PROPRIETARIE AND GOVERNOR / OF THAT PROVINCE TO THE SEVERAL PURCHASERS AS FOLLOWS. VIZ- . The names are listed in three groups or CATALOGUES. The following note appears at the right: NB. THE DOUBLE=OR YELLOW LINES / IS LAND SOLD BY THE PROPRIETORS, / THE BLACK—OR RED LINES IS LAND HELD UNDER / THE SWEEDS. THE DOTED [sic] . . . OR BLUE LINES IS WHAT / WAS SOLD TO THE DUTCH. FOR FURTHER EXPLANATION / REFER TO THE BOOK.

Size 30" x 60". *Scale* 1" = 100 perches.

Insets [a] At lower right corner: A GROUND PLAN OF THE CITY OF PHILADELPHIA. This inset map is also really the Holme plan but the revised street arrangement is indicated. The new position of the Schuylkill Front Street is shown with dotted lines and the revised positions of the numbered streets between the original Penn Square and the Schuylkill is indicated in the upper margin of the inset. The lot numbers on the inset map do not follow the Holme numbering accurately. Size: 9½" x 19⅝". Scale: None (1" = c. 35 perches).

[b] At right center: STATE HOUSE. Size: 5¼" x 9¼".

[c] At bottom left: THE HOUSE OF EMPLOYMENT & ALMS HOUSE. Size: 4" x 6¾".

[d] At lower left of cartouche: PENNSYLVANIA HOSPITAL. Size: 3" x 4¾".

Published with John Reed, *An Explanation of the Map of the City*. Reproduced separately by Lloyd Smith in 1846; by Charles L. Warner, Philadelphia, 1870; in *Pennsylvania Archives* 3d ser., *4*, at end.

References Evans 13564; Historical Society of Pennsylvania, *Pennsylvania Magazine of History and Biography*, 19 (1895), 423; Philip L. Phillips, *A Descriptive List of Maps and Views*, nos. 157–60; idem, *A List of Maps of America*, p. 699.

Locations CtY, DLC, MiU-C, PHi, PP, PPL.

458 [1774] *State* II (see also Map 457)

Description The words under the cartouche: "Printed by Tho: Man" have been crudely erased from the plate.

Published with John Reed, *An Explanation of the Map of the City*.

Location PP.

459 [1777]

Description In upper left corner: A PLAN OF / THE CITY OF / PHILADELPHIA. The more important streets are shown by name and some of the others are identified by letter and number on a list of REFERENCES at the upper right. BAR / RACKS are noted on THIRD STREET north of CALLOWHILL STREET. Evans states that the title page of the *Almanack* was engraved by John Norman.

Size 6⅞" x 6⅝". *Scale* None (1" = c. 1500 feet).

Published in *The Philadelphia Almanack For 1778*, front.

Reference Evans 15553.

[1778] see Map 304.

460 [1792]

Description [Plan of thirty-six lots between Locust and Spruce streets on Twelfth.] The lots were advertised to be sold by auction on the 29th. of March.

Size 4⅞" x 2¾". *Scale* 1" = 85 feet.

Published in *Dunlap's American Daily Advertiser,* March 10, 1792; reprinted in issues of March 12, 14, 15, 21, 23, 27, 29.

461 [1794]

Description [Map of the Wards of Philadelphia.] This is a diagrammatic map with the exact dimensions of the various wards, blocks, and streets of the City being stated in feet.

Size 4⅞" x 6⅞". *Scale* None.

Published in Benjamin Davies, *Some Account of the City of Philadelphia,* opp. p. 1.

462 1794

Description In cartouche at upper right: TO / THOMAS MIFFLIN / GOVERNOR AND COMMANDER IN CHIEF OF / THE STATE OF PENNSYLVANIA / THIS PLAN / OF THE CITY AND SUBURBS OF / PHILADELPHIA / IS RESPECTFULLY / INSCRIBED BY / THE EDITOR / *1794.* Below bottom neat line at left corner: A. P. FOLIE DEL.; at right corner: R. SCOT & S. ALLARDICE SCULPSIT. This is a detailed plan of the City. Sixty-four numbered REFERENCES are given at the upper left. Above the cartouche is a shield and crest supported by two figures. The engravers are Robert Scot and Samuel Allardice.

Size 25" x 25¼". *Scale* 1" = 568 feet.

Inset Under cartouche at right profile view of: CITY HALL, STATE HOUSE, and CONGRESS HALL. There is no tower on the STATE HOUSE. Size: 1¾" x 6⅜".

Published in Benjamin Davies, *Some Account of the City of Philadelphia,* foll. p. 93. Reproduced in Isaac N. P. Stokes and Daniel C. Haskell, *American Historical Prints,* pl. 29; U.S. Bureau of the Census, *A Century of Population Growth,* opp. p. 14.

References Carl W. Drepperd, *Early American Prints,* p. 60; David M. Stauffer, *American Engravers,* no. 2865; see also reproductions above, under Published.

463 [1794] *State* I (see also Map 467)

Description At upper left center: PLAN / OF THE CITY OF / PHILADELPHIA. The shading lines in the letters of PLAN are diagonal. A list of REFERENCES are given at the far left. PETTY'S ISLAND is identified at upper right.

Size 9⅝" x 14⁷⁄₁₆". *Scale* 1" = 90 perches. (legend states 100 to an inch)

Published in James Hardie, *Philadelphia Directory and Register,* 2d ed., opp. p. 1; idem, *A Short Account of the City of Philadelphia,* front.

464 [1794]

Description [A map of the County of Philadelphia in Pennsylvania shewing the rivers Delaware and Schuylkill and the other waters hills townships lines canals roads water works . . . Exhibiting also the ground plan of the City of Philadelphia Southwark and the Liberties &c. houses of worship &c. By Reading Howell. Philadelphia. March 5th 1794.] The title is taken from Evans who cites a 57th Pennsylvania District copyright issued on the above date.

Size Unknown. *Scale* Unknown.

Published Separately.

Reference Evans 27141.

Location No copy located.

465 [c. 1794] *State* I (II post-1799, see below, Description)

Description In tablet cartouche at upper left: TO THE / CITIZENS OF / PHILADELPHIA / THIS / PLAN OF THE CITY AND ITS / ENVIRONS / IS RESPECTFULLY DEDICATED / BY THE / EDITOR; below bottom neat line at left: P.C. VARLÈ GEOGRAPHER & ENGINR. DEL.; at right: R SCOTT SCULP. PHILADA. There are twenty-four lettered and twenty-seven arabic numbered references in a column alongside the left neat line. The names of many residents in the environs are given beside the house locations. Some detail is given across both rivers from the city, as well as to 600 perches north of Callowhill St. and 300 perches south of South Street (Cedar). The city is shown as of about the date depicted by the Folie map of 1794, and earlier than the John Hills map of 1796. There is a state of the map carrying the date 1802 in the New York Public Library with fourteen Roman numbered references added and an additional Arabic numbered reference. The author is probably Peter Varle.

Size 17¾" x 24¼". *Scale* 1" = 75 perches.

Insets [a] At lower left corner: CITY HALL, STATE HOUSE, CONGRESS HALL. Size: 1½" x 3⅝".
[b] At lower left: LIBRARY. Size: 1" x 1¾".
[c] At lower center: U.S. BANK. Size: 1⅛" x 1⅞".

Published Separately. Reproduced separately by The Colonial Trust Co., Philadelphia, 1926.

Reference Isaac N. P. Stokes and Daniel C. Haskell, *American Historical Prints,* p. 83 (State II).

Locations CtY, ICHi, PPL.

99

466 1796

Description [A Plan of the City of Philadelphia, and its Environs. Taken from Actual Survey.] Evans cites a 134th Pennsylvania District copyright issued to Nicholas Gouin-Dufief, Jr., April 29, 1796.

Size Unknown.　　*Scale* Unknown.

Published Separately.

Reference Evans 30505.

Location No copy located.

467 [1796]　*State* II (see also Map 463)

Description The name: STEPHENS has been added above the title. The title itself is now in a floral design. (See also Map 470.)

Published in Thomas Stephens, *Stephen's Philadelphia Directory, for 1796*, front.

References Philip L. Philips, *A Descriptive List of Maps and Views of Philadelphia*, no. 174; idem, *A List of Maps of America*, p. 702.

468 1797　*State* I (see also Map 471)

Description At upper left beside seal of the city: THIS PLAN OF THE CITY OF PHILADELPHIA / AND ITS ENVIRONS, (SHEWING THE IMPROVED PARTS,) IS DEDICATED / TO THE MAYOR, ALDERMEN AND CITIZENS THEREOF, / BY THEIR MOST OBEDIENT SERVANT, / JOHN HILLS, / SURVEYOR AND DRAUGHTSMAN. / MAY 30TH 1796. Above bottom neat line at lower left: PHILADELPHIA. PUBLISHED. AND SOLD. BY JOHN HILLS. SURVEYOR. & DRAUGHSMAN. [sic] 1797. In narrow rectangle at lower right corner: ENGRAVED BY JOHN COOKE, OF- / HENDON, MIDDLESEX, (NEAR LONDON [sic]. This is a fine detailed, topographical map. There are 48 numbered references in Philadelphia proper, three in the part of the Northern Liberties shown, and three in Southwark. The REFERENCE section is given at left center. The different wharves in use are identified together with their new boundaries. At upper left, below the seal, is an appreciation from the Corporation for the map from Matthew Clarkson, Mayor, dated Philadelphia, September 5, 1796.

Size 27⅝" x 37¼".　　*Scale* 1" = 600 feet.

Published Separately.

Reference Evans 32253.

Locations DLC, MH, NHi, PP.

469 [1797]

Description [Plan for the North East Public Square.] This is a plan showing land allegedly encroached upon by the German Calvinist Society and bounded by Sixth, Vine, and Sassafras Streets, and the German Lutheran Burying Ground.

Size 3¾" x 4".　　*Scale* 1" = 160 feet.

Published in Philadelphia (City), *The Committee Appointed to Examine into the Title*.

470 [1797]

Description At upper left in floral design: PLAN / OF THE CITY OF / PHILADELPHIA; below scale: J. BOWES SC. This is a re-engraving of Map 467. The shading lines in the letters of PLAN are now horizontal. "Petty's Island" is no longer identified by name at the upper right. M. NEW BANK U.S. has been added to the REFERENCES at the lower left. The name "Stephens" has been omitted above the title.

Size 9½" x 14".　　*Scale* 1" = 90 perches.

Published in Cornelius W. Stafford, *The Philadelphia Directory for 1797*, front.

471 1798　*State* II (see also Map 468)

Description This plate was reissued shortly with the following imprint below the bottom neat line at center: PUBLISHED. 1ST. JANUARY. 1798. BY MSSRS. JOHN & JOSIAH BOYDELL AT THE SHAKESPEARE GALLERY. & AT NO. 90. CHEAPSIDE. This may have been published in England.

Published Separately. Reproduced by Samuel L. Smedley, Chief Engineer and Surveyor, Philadelphia, May 30, 1881, carrying the following additional imprint: "Photo-lith. 1881 by Thomas Hunter 716 Filbert St. Phila."

Reference Evans 32253.

Locations BM, DLC, NN, PPL.

472 [1798]

Description At upper center below elevation of building: PLAN & ELEVATION OF THE JAIL AT PHILADELPHIA; above bottom neat lines at center: PHILADELPHIA PUBLISHED FOR THOS. CONDIE BOOKSELLER; below elevation of building at upper right: J. BOWES DELR. SCULPR. Explanations for the references on the Plan are given in the accompanying article (pp. 97–101). The article notes the lot being four hundred by two hundred feet. The map was engraved by Joseph Bowes.

Size 13¼" x 7½".　　*Scale* 1" = 35 feet.

Inset At top above PLAN: ELEVATION OF THE JAIL. Size: 2⅝" x 5⅝".

Published in *The Philadelphia Monthly Magazine, I* (1798), opp. 100.

473 1799

Description [A map of Philadelphia, taken from actual survey, and engraved in the neatest manner, on a plate twenty-six inches square. Exhibiting a correct view of all the streets, lanes and alleys in the city; the Northern Liberties, and South-wark, and showing the present extent of building in each. Philadelphia, 1799. Published by Benjamin Davies.]

Size 26″ x 26″.   *Scale* Unknown.

Published Separately.

Reference Evans 35385.

Location No copy located.

DELAWARE

474 [1733]

Description [Map of Delaware, Maryland, and parts of Pennsylvania and Virginia.] This is a woodcut map showing the shore lines, rivers, and streams for the area from just above Philadelphia to the entrance of Chesapeake Bay. The map has no border and inserted type is used for the lettering of the province and district names. It was copied from the map drawn in England by John Senex under Lord Baltimore's directions and engraved there by Thomas Hutchinson. This English map has a double line border. There is some probability that Benjamin Franklin himself cut the wood block of the American map. A "Receipted Bill to the Proprietors" endorsed by his wife for Franklin in June, 1733, includes the following: ". . . 4. For cutting the Mapp in Wood £ 2— . . ." (see *Papers* in References, below). It is the earliest known map to be printed in the English Colonies south of New York. This map may have been reprinted in an advertised ([Philadelphia] *Pennsylvania Gazette*, January 27–February 3, 1736/37) republication of the *Articles*.

Size 13¾" x 9½". *Scale* None (1" = c. 28 miles).

Published in Baltimore, Charles Calvert, 6th baron, *Articles of Agreement between Maryland, and Pensilvania*, opp. p. 3. Reproduced in Baltimore Museum of Art, *The World Encompassed*, pl. LIV; Alexander O. Vietor, "Printed Maps," pl. 278 (A).

References John Carter Brown Library, *In Retrospect, 1923–1949*, p. 24; idem, *Report, 1947*, pp. 14–15; Benjamin Franklin, *The Papers of*, Leonard W. Labaree, ed., *1*, 324; John T. Scharf, *History of Maryland*, *1*, 395; Nicholas B. Wainwright, "Tale of a Runaway Cape," pp. 260–62, 270, 272.

475 1756

Description In elaborate cartouche at lower right corner: TO THE / MERCHANTS & INSURERS / OF THE CITY OF PHILADELPHIA / THIS CHART OF / DELAWARE BAY / FROM THE SEA-COAST TO REEDY-ISLAND. / CONTAINING A FULL AND EXACT DESCRIPTION OF THE SHORES, / CREEKS, HARBOURS, SOUNDINGS, SHOALS, SANDS, AND BEARINGS / OF THE MOST CONSIDERABLE LAND-MARKS; WITH A TIDE-TABLE / FROM THE CAPES TO PHILADELPHIA, AND THE SET OF THE TIDE / ON THE SEVERAL QUARTERS OF THE FLOOD AND EBB / IS DEDICATED / BY A FRIEND TO TRADE AND NAVIGATION / JOSHUA FISHER. Above neat line at lower left corner under list of SUBSCRIBERS: PUBLISHED ACCORDING TO ACT OF PARLIAMENT, BY JOSHUA FISHER, FEB: *28. 1756*. Above bottom neat line near center: ENGRAVED BY JAS. TURNER, AND PRINTED BY JOHN DAVIS, FOR, AND SOLD BY THE AUTHOR IN FRONT-STREET PHILADELPHIA. This CHART shows the various channels of Delaware Bay, with soundings, shoals, oyster beds, and range lines from Cape James, as surveyed by Joshua Fisher. CAPE JAMES is shown for the modern Cape Henlopen and CAPE HENLOPEN is applied at Fenwick's Island. Proper application of the name Cape Hinlopen, or Henlopen, was controversial. It was originally the southern limit of the three counties of Pennsylvania. Note that on this map a dotted line extends west from this name, marked: PENN'S SOUTH BOUNDS. This chart was suppressed by Governor Robert Hunter Morris after only a few copies were distributed for fear it would aid the French. Fisher had it re-engraved later (see Map 476), on a smaller scale, covering the river up just past Philadelphia. The smaller chart was then extensively copied at the start of the Revolutionary War. In a cartouche at the lower left corner is a table beginning: WE THE SUBSCRIBERS HAVING PERUSED . . . , with the names of 22 pilots and 20 masters of vessels listed. In a third cartouche at bottom center is: A / TIDE-TABLE.

Size 23¾" x 45¹⁵⁄₁₆". *Scale* 1" = 2 English miles.

Published Separately. Reproduced in John Carter Brown Library, *The French and Indian War*, pl. 15; Lawrence C. Wroth, "Some American Contributions," opp. p. 22; ibid., in Massachusetts Historical Society, *Proceedings*, (3d ser.) *68* (1944–47), opp. 93.

References Baltimore Museum of Art, *The World Encompassed*, no. 246; John Carter Brown Library, *Report, 1949*, pp. 26–29; Evans 7657; Charles H. B. Turner, comp., *Some Records of Sussex County, Delaware*, p. 319; John F. Watson, *Annals of Philadelphia*, *2*, 474; Lawrence C. Wroth, "Joshua Fisher's 'Chart of Delaware Bay and River,'" pp. 90–109; see also reproductions above, under Published.

Locations MdHi, RPJCB.

[1768] see Map 497.

476 [1776?]

Description In cartouche at lower right: TO THE / MERCHANTS & INSURERS / OF THE CITY OF PHILADELPHIA / THIS CHART OF / DELAWARE BAY AND RIVER, / CONTAINING A FULL AND EXACT DESCRIPTION OF / THE SHORES, CREEKS, HARBOURS, SOUNDINGS, SHOALS / SANDS, AND BEARINGS OF THE MOST CONSIDERABLE / LAND-MARKS WITH A TIDE TABLE / FROM THE CAPES TO PHILADELPHIA AND THE / SET OF THE TIDE ON THE SEVERAL QUARTERS / OF THE FLOOD AND EBB / IS DEDICATED / BY A FRIEND TO TRADE AND NAVIGATION / JOSHUA FISHER. This is a smaller, reoriented, re-engraving of Map 475 with the river extended on past PHILADELPHIA to PENNIPACK CR. C JAMES appears again as the modern Cape Henlopen and CHINLOPEN at Fenwick's Island. This chart records again the survey made by Joshua Fisher of the shoals and channels in the Bay, which had not yet been made generally available to the public because of the suppression of the first chart. This CHART was quickly copied, and in 1776 four full sheet re-engravings appeared in London: in March by William Faden; in July by Sayer and Bennett; in November by Andrew Drury; and also in that year by Mount and Page. Two similar French maps appeared in the next couple of years and others in Europe and America until well into the 19th century (see also Map 478).

The list of subscribers for the 1756 chart appears again at upper left. Two additional masters of vessels, JOHN BOLITHO and DANIEL DINGEE, have been added to the list. The engraving appears to be the work of Henry Dawkins who was active in Philadelphia from 1757 to 1774, when he moved to New York. The date may be set after the 1759 death of James Turner, who engraved the first chart, and before March, 1776, when the first English copy appeared. The only contemporary date for it appears on the re-engraving in the *Gentleman's Magazine, 49* (1779), opp. 369, entitled "A Chart of Delaware Bay / and River, / from the Original / by Mr. Fisher of / Philadelphia / 1776." However, the re-use of the list of subscribers for the 1756 chart, as well as the out of date naming of the Delaware Capes, seems to indicate a much earlier completion. Ten of the subscribers flourished before 1750 and none of the pilots listed were appointed Chevaux de Frise pilots in 1775–77. A study of the watermarks in the paper used in the known copies of the two charts did not help to differentiate their dating.

Size 18⅞" x 27½". *Scale* 1" = 4⅜ miles.

Published Separately. Reproduced in Historical Society of Pennsylvania, *Pennsylvania Magazine of History and Biography, 63* (1939), 93 (evidently prepared from a Historical Society copy with MSS date, February 28, 1756); in 1904 by Julius E. Sachse, bearing the date "February 28, 1756" (added in MSS to a Historical Society of Pennsylvania original); prepared to be the Complainant's Exhibit No. 144 in State of New Jersey *vs.* State of Delaware, January 1904 (per note on example at Historical Society); see also above, Description.

References Lawrence C. Wroth, "Joshua Fisher's 'Chart of Delaware Bay and River,'" pp. 104–07; idem, *Some American Contributions*, p. 23; ibid., in Massachusetts Historical Society, *Proceedings*, (3d Ser.) *68* (1944–47), 94.

Locations Atwater Kent Museum, BM, MiU-C, PHi.

477 [1778?] *State* I (see also Map 479)

Description In cartouche at lower right: TO THE AMERICAN / PHILOSOPHICAL SOCIETY / THIS MAP OF THE PENINSULA / BETWEEN DELAWARE & / CHESOPEAK [sic] BAYS / WITH THE SAID BAYS / AND SHORES ADJACENT / DRAWN FROM THE MOST / ACCURATE SURVEYS IS / INSCRIBED BY / JOHN CHURCHMAN. This map shows the principal roads, streams, and rivers of the Delmarva Peninsula and the contour of the shores adjacent to the other sides of the two bays. A note at left center reads: THE PROPOSED CANALS ARE DESCRIBED BY DOTTED LINES. Five such proposed routes are shown. The Susquehanna River barely extends beyond the Maryland border, the highest tributary shown being the CANAWANGO. The top border line is not broken. George Johnston, in his *History of Cecil County, Maryland*, states that this map was "executed" in 1778. An advertisement on the cover of the *American Museum* for June and July, 1789 (5, no. 6; 6, no. 1), gives thanks to those who "furnished him, during the late war, with materials and other encouragement relating to his map of the peninsula between Chesapeak and Delaware." The map is referred to in the *Early Proceedings* of the American Philosophical Society on July 23, and August 20, 1779. Phillips indicates that this map was printed in Baltimore. Stauffer attributes the engraving to Henry Dawkins.

Size 22½" x 17". *Scale* 1" = 10 British statute miles.

Published Separately.

References American Philosophical Society, *Early Proceedings 1744–1838*, pp. 103–04; John S. Futhey and Gilbert Cope, *History of Chester County, Pennsylvania*, pp. 497–98; George Johnston, *History of Cecil County, Maryland*, p. 526; Philip L. Phillips, *List of Maps of America*, p. 263; idem, *Virginia Cartography*, pp. 58–59; David M. Stauffer, *American Engravers*, 2, no. 465.

Locations BM, DLC, MiU-C, NHi, NN, PHi, PPAmP, PPL.

478 [1783?]

Description At upper left: A CHART OF / DELAWARE BAY AND RIVER / CORRECTED FROM THE BEST SURVEYS. Map 476 has been copied here with many detail changes and additions especially as to roads, islands, and creeks close to the river. The tide table and the set of the tides is the same as on the original Fisher map. The copy at Harvard is marked in contemporary MSS: "Engraved at Philadelphia 1783."

Size 18¹⁄₁₆″ x 25¹¹⁄₁₆″.   *Scale* 1″ = 3¾ miles.

Published Separately.

Locations MH, PHi (2).

479 [1786] *State* II (see also Map 477)

Description The word: HUMBLY / has been inserted before: INSCRIBED in the dedication. The Susquehanna River has been extended well beyond the Maryland border, breaking thru the upper marginal degree line at MIDLE T. Seven named tributaries have been added above the CANAWANGO. There is still a blank space in the cartouche above the dedication which is the only title. On the Harvard College Library copy this has been filled with the following contemporary MSS title: "The State of Delaware with the Eastern Shore of Maryland." Ebeling refers to a "New Emission, improved, Baltimore, 1788." Evans evidently copies an advertisement or the copyright notice describing the second state as "Philadelphia: Printed and sold by Eleazer Oswald, 1787." The map was advertised for sale by William Spotswood in the (Philadelphia) *Herald and General Advertiser* on July 12, 1786, and in several issues following. It was also advertised in *The Carlisle Gazette* on August 23, 1786, as: "This day published and sold by Thomas Dobson, at the new Book and Stationery Store, in Second Street, two doors above Chesnut [sic] street, Philadelphia . . ."

Published Separately. Reproduced in the series reproduced by the U.S. Geological Survey for the U.S. Constitution Sesquicentennial Commission, Washington, 1937.

References Christoph D. Ebeling, *Erdbeschreibung und Geschichte von Amerika*, 5, 2; Evans 20272; U.S. Library of Congress, *Report 1907*, p. 44.

Locations BM, DLC, MH.

480 [1789]

Description Above top neat line: FROM PHILA (53) TO ANNAPOLIS MARYLD. This map shows, in three vertical strips, the road from four miles north-east of WIL MINGTON (24 miles from Philadelphia), through WIL MINGTON and NEW PORT, within two miles of Christiana Bridge.

Size 7⅜″ x 4¾″.   *Scale* None (1″ = 4/7 mile).

Published in Christopher Colles, *A Survey of the Roads*. Reproduced, ibid., 1961, p. 170.

481 [1789]

Description Above top neat line: FROM PHILADELPHIA (54) TO ANNAPOLIS MARYLAND. This map shows, in three vertical strips, the road from from two miles north-northeast of CHRISTA BR (35½ miles from Philadelphia), past the Bridge (not taking it, however), over COUCHES BR., across CHRISTA CR., passing the south side of IRON HILL, into MARYLAND three miles from Head of Elk.

Size 6⅞″ x 4¾″.   *Scale* None (1″ = 4/7 mile).

Published in Christopher Colles, *A Survey of the Roads*. Reproduced, ibid., 1961, p. 171.

482 [1793]

Description [Map of the Bay and River Delaware. By Andrew Snape Hammond, Philadelphia, sold by Eleazer Oswald. September, 1793.] This may refer to a copy of "A Chart of Delaware Bay . . . by Capt. Sir Andrew Snape Hammond of the Navy and others . . . London, 1779," used by Joseph F. W. DesBarres in *The Atlantic Neptune*.

Size Unknown.   *Scale* Unknown.

Published Separately.

Reference Evans 25581.

Location No copy located.

483 [1795] *State* I (II and III post-1799, see below, Description)

Description In oval at upper right: DELAWARE, / FROM THE BEST / AUTHORITIES; beneath title in oval: W. BARKER, SCULP. PHILA; beneath oval: ENGRAVED FOR CAREY'S AMERICAN EDITION OF GUTHRIE'S GEOGRAPHY IMPROVED. This map shows the rivers and streams, principal roads and towns, and the boundaries of the three counties. Carey advertised a map of Delaware for sale in the (Philadelphia) *Gazette of the United States* for May 8, 1794, and this may be an earlier publication of this map. State II appears in the 1800 edition of *Carey's General Atlas* with the number "34" added at upper right corner. Later (in State III), extensive changes have been made to the plate: many place names are added including the township names; Dover has been recut in heavier type; the state line has been reinforced with an added dot and dash line; and the county lines have been given added emphasis with a dotted line. Roads have also been added and extended, and creeks named.

Size 15¹⁵⁄₁₆" x 8¹⁵⁄₁₆". *Scale* 1" = 7 miles.

Published in Mathew Carey, *Carey's American Atlas*, no. 11; idem, *Carey's General Atlas*, no. 34; idem, *The General Atlas for Carey's Edition of Guthrie's Geography Improved*, no. 34.

484 [1795]

Description At upper right: DELAWARE. The counties are given as well as primary towns and main roads. LEWIS appears for Lewes.

Size 7¼" x 5¹⁵⁄₁₆". *Scale* 1" = 16 miles.

Published in Joseph Scott, *An Atlas of the United States*, no. 11; idem, *The New and Universal Gazetteer*, 2; idem, *The United States Gazetteer*, opp. "Delaware." Reproduced in

Joseph Scott, *Atlas of the United States 1795–1800*, no. 5.

485 [1796] *State* I (II post-1799, see below, Description)

Description At upper right above scale: DELAWARE; below scale: ENGRAVED BY A. DOOLITTLE NEWHAVEN. This map was reissued in the 1801 edition of *Carey's American Pocket Atlas* with the addition of two lines underneath the title and the road extended from Marcus Hook thru Chester to Philadelphia, and indicated running south from Georgetown to join other roads. "F. Mifflin on Mud Island" is not inscribed south of Philadelphia on the first state, nor is "Reedy I" in the Delaware.

Size 7⁹⁄₁₆" x 5¹¹⁄₁₆". *Scale* 1" = 15 miles.

Published in Mathew Carey, *Carey's American Pocket Atlas*, foll. p. 82.

[1796] see Map 514.

[1796] see Map 515.

[1796] see Map 516.

486 [1799]

[Map of the State of Delaware and Eastern Shore of Maryland, with the soundings of the Bay of Delaware. Philadelphia (1799).]

Size Unknown. *Scale* Unknown.

Published Separately.

Reference Evans 35768.

Location PPL (copy missing).

1799 see Map 518.

487 [¹775]

Description [Map of the Country of the Savage Nations.] In an advertisement at the end of Bernard Romans, *A Concise Natural History of East and West Florida,* the author makes the following statement: "The map of the country of the savage nations, intended to be put facing page 72, was engraved by a Gentlemen who resides in the country 60 or 70 miles from New-York, to whom the plate was sent; but when it was sent back, it miscarried, through the carelessness of the waggoner." The map was promised for a future second volume but no copy is known of either book or map.

Size Unknown.   *Scale* Unknown.

Published See above, Description.

Location No copy located.

488 [¹775]

Description Below bottom neat line at center: MOBILE BAR; above top neat line at left: PAGE LXXXV OF THE APPENDIX. Soundings and outlines of the shoals are given.

Size 3½" x 5¹⁵⁄₁₆".   *Scale* 1" = 2 miles.

Published in Bernard Romans, *A Concise Natural History of East and West Florida.* Reproduced in ibid., 1962.

489 [¹776]

Description In a cartouche at lower center: A NEW MAP OF / NORTH & SOUTH / CAROLINA, / & GEORGIA. Below title inside cartouche: FOR THE PENNSYLA. / MAGAZINE. Between marginal degree line and bottom neat line at right corner: AITKEN SCULP. The map shows many Indian towns in the interior and indicates the boundaries of the three colonies, although the eastern end of the division line between the Carolinas is not clear. Some topographical details are noted.

Size 6⅝" x 8¹³⁄₁₆".   *Scale* 1" = 110 miles.

Published in *Pennsylvania Magazine,* 2 (1776), opp. 268.

490 [¹781]

Description [A map of the coast of West-Florida, including its bays and lakes, with the course of the Mississippi, from the junction of the Akansa River, to it's entrance into the Gulf of Mexico . . . By Thomas Hutchins.] This map was announced in Hutchins' broadside: *Proposals for publishing by subscription, a map . . . Philadelphia, October 15th, 1781.* Thomas Hutchins' *An Historical Narrative and Topographical Description of Louisiana, and West-Florida,* was apparently designed to explain this map. An indication that such a map was published is noted by Mr. Robert W. G. Vail in citing several references found in the Belknap Papers (see below, *References*).

Size Unknown.   *Scale* Unknown.

Published Separately.

References Massachusetts Historical Society, *Collections,* 5th ser., 3 (1877), pt. 2, pp. 53, 57; Robert W. G. Vail, *Old Frontier,* no. 706.

Location No copy located.

491 1788   *State* I (see also Map 494)

Description In oval cartouche at lower right: A / MAP / OF THE STATES OF / VIRGINIA NORTH CAROLINA / SOUTH CAROLINA AND GEORGIA / COMPREHENDING THE SPANISH PROVINCES OF / EAST AND WEST FLORIDA / EXHIBITING THE BOUNDARIES AS FIXED BY THE LATE / TREATY OF PEACE BETWEEN THE UNITED STATES AND / THE SPANISH DOMINIONS / COMPILED FROM LATE SURVEYS AND / OBSERVATION. BY / JOSEPH PURCELL. Below bottom neat line at center: ENGRAV'D FOR MORSES GEOGRAPHY BY AMOS DOOLITTLE AT NEW HAVEN 1788. This map shows much detail, including boundaries claimed by various Indian Nations at this time. Trading paths are shown through the West. The neat line has been broken at top center for the 7 RANGES and ALEGANY [SIC] R, with the erasure of the old neat line visible. EKANFANOKA appears for Okefenokee Swamp; POST VINCIENT for Vincennes; and INDI / ANA is shown as a small tract south of the Seven Ranges. The NEW STATE OF FRANKLIN appears between modern Tennessee and North Carolina, and the lower part of the Tennessee River is shown as CHEROKEE R. MUSCLE SHOALS, shown first on an American map by Abel Buell, appears here also. CHUCAMAGA T. appears in the northern part of modern Alabama.

In the Preface (pp. VI–VII) Morse states: ". . .

The Map of the southern states, was compiled from original and authentic documents, by Mr. Joseph Purcell, of Charleston, South Carolina, a Gentleman fully equal to the undertaking, and is the most accurate yet published respecting that country, on so small a scale . . ." This map was re-engraved and used in various other editions of Morse's geographies in London and Dublin. It was copied by Cornelius Tiebout (see Maps 492 and 495) and used in books published by Samuel Campbell in New York.

Size 12⅞" x 14⅝".   *Scale* 1" = 95 miles.

Published in Jedidiah Morse, *The American Geography*, opp. p. 1; in some copies of *American Magazine* (August, 1788).

References Evans 21412; Benjamin M. Lewis, *A Guide to Engravings in American Magazines 1741–1810*, p. 1; Woodbury Lowery, *The Lowery Collection, A Descriptive List of Maps*, no. 678 (note by Philip L. Phillips).

492   1789   *State* I (see also Map 495)

Description   In ornate cartouche at lower right: NEW MAP OF THE STATES / OF GEORGIA SOUTH AND NORTH / CAROLINA VIRGINIA AND MARYLAND / INCLUDING THE SPANISH PROVINCES OF / WEST AND EAST FLORIDA / FROM THE LATEST SURVEYS; above top neat line: ENGRAVED FOR GORDON'S HISTORY OF THE AMERICAN WAR; below bottom neat line at right: CORNELIUS TIEBOUT SCULP N. YORK. *1789.* This map is a re-engraving of Map 491. The "New State of Franklin," and the "Seven Ranges" are not shown on this Tiebout version. LUNINBURG C. and WILNINGTON, North Carolina, appear on this map instead of "Lunenburg C." and "Wilmington" as on the map engraved by Doolittle. Similarly JEFERSON County, Kentucky, and NEILSON County instead of "Jefferson" and "Nelson." MADDISON appears thus on both.

Size 12¹⁄₁₆" x 14⁹⁄₁₆".   *Scale* 1" = 98 miles.

Published in William Gordon, *History of the Rise of the United States*, 1, front.

493   1790

Description   [Map of the Southern Division of the United States of America. By William Tatham.] The proposed future publication of this map was announced in the following: *Proposals for publishing a large and comprehensive Map of the southern division of the United States of America. By subscription only. By William Tatham. Richmond in Virginia*, September 30, 1790.

Size Unknown.   *Scale* Unknown.

Published   Separately.

Reference   Evans 22924.

Location   No copy located.

494   [1793]   *State* II (see also Map 491)

Description   The title has been changed in part and now reads: . . . EXHIBITING THE BOUNDARIES BETWEEN THE UNITED STATES / AND SPANISH DOMINIONS AS FIXED BY THE / TREATY OF PEACE IN *1783* . . . OBSERVATIONS . . . ; above top neat line has been added: PUBLISHED BY THOMAS & ANDREWS BOSTON. The "New State of Franklin" has been changed to: COUNTRY OF FRANKLAND. FRENCH has been added before BROAD R. The Cumberland Mountains have been extended southwest and GREAT LAUREL RIDGE OR added before CUMBERLAND. WHIRL OR SUCK has been added where the Tennessee River crosses this range. OR PELISON R. has been added after CLINCHES R.

Published in Jedidiah Morse, *The American Universal Geography*, opp. p. 532.

495   [1793]   *State* II (see also Map 492)

Description   The inscription above the top neat line of this: NEW MAP OF THE STATES . . . has been removed. The date following engravers imprint below bottom neat line at right has been erased.

Published in William Gordon, *History of the Rise of the United States*, 2d ed., 1, front.; Gilbert Imlay, *A Topographical Description*, 1, front.

496   [1797]

Description   At lower right: MAP / OF THE / SOUTHERN PARTS / OF THE / UNITED STATES / OF / AMERICA / BY / ABRAHAM BRADLEY JUNR; below bottom neat line at right: S HILL SC.; at center: DRAWN, & ENGRAVED FOR MORSE'S AMERICAN GAZETTEER. A dot-dash line is shown inscribed: ALL WEST OF THIS LINE IS CLAIMED BY THE UNITED STATES & ALSO BY GEORGIA. The number of men in the Creek Nations and in some of the Indian villages is given. The bottom neat line is broken through at the mouth of the Mississippi River and at the eastern and western Florida peninsula coastline.

Size 7¾" x 15³⁄₁₆".   *Scale* 1" = 68 miles.

Published in Jedidiah Morse, *The American Gazetteer*, opp. "Southern States." Reproduced in U.S. Bureau of the Census, *A Century of Population Growth*, opp. p. 20.

MARYLAND

[1733]   see Map 474.

1756   see Map 475.

497   [1768]

Description   In cartouche at center: A PLAN / OF THE / BOUNDARY LINES / BETWEEN THE / PROVINCE OF MARYLAND / AND THE / THREE LOWER COUNTIES ON DELAWARE / WITH PART OF / THE PARALLEL OF LATITUDE WHICH IS THE / BOUNDARY BETWEEN THE PROVINCES OF / MARYLAND AND PENNSYLVANIA. This is one part of the famous Mason and Dixon survey that was published by Robert Kennedy in Philadelphia in 1768. For the second part, published at the same time, see Map 498. The plan was engraved by Henry Dawkins and James Smither. Recorded in these maps is the final solution to a long and costly boundary dispute between the provinces of Pennsylvania and Maryland. Both Charles Mason and Jeremiah Dixon were well known English astronomers, and their calculations, considering their instruments and the level of scientific knowledge of the time, have stood up remarkably well to later and more advanced surveys. This is definitely one of the landmarks of American 18th Century mapping. This particular part of the survey was also the scene of Mason and Dixon's measurement of a degree of latitude which was later reported in the *Philosophical Transactions* of the Royal Society of London.

Size   14¹¹⁄₁₆″ x 26½″.   *Scale*   1″ = 4 miles.

Published   Separately. Reproduced with Pennsylvania Department of Internal Affairs, *Report of the Secretary of Internal Affairs containing reports of surveys and re-surveys* (in accompanying portfolio); *Report on the Resurvey of the Maryland-Pennsylvania Boundary* in *Maryland Geological Survey*, 7 (on pocket at end of volume); Thomas W. Streeter, "Princeton's Mason and Dixon map," in *Princeton University Library Chronicle*, 16 (1954–55), foll. 96; Nicholas B. Wainwright, "Tale of a Runaway Cape," pp. [289–290].

References   Baltimore Museum of Art, *The World Encompassed*, no. 254; Great Britain, Colonial Office, *Catalogue of the Maps, Plans, and Charts*, North American Colonies section, p. 21; Charles Mason and Jeremiah Dixon,

"Observations for determining the Length of a degree of Latitude," pp. 274–325; Thomas W. Streeter, *Americana-Beginnings*, no. 24; see also reproductions above, under Published.

Locations   DLC, MdHi, NjP, NN, PHi, PPAmP, private coll. of Thomas W. Streeter (both latter copies in original form—PPAmP copy is slightly damaged), PRO, State of Maryland-Land Commissioners Office.

498   [1768]

Description   In ornamental cartouche at right end of top strip: A PLAN / OF THE / WEST LINE / OR / PARALLEL OF LATITUDE. WHICH IS / THE BOUNDARY BETWEEN THE PROVINCES / OF MARYLAND AND PENSYLVANIA [sic]; under cartouche at right: J. SMITHER SCULPS. T. This portion of the famous Mason and Dixon survey was originally published in three separate strips on one sheet. Only two known copies exist of the map in its original form. Usually it has been cut up and assembled with the three sections forming one long strip measuring 5′ ⅝″ x 6′ 5³⁄₁₆″. It was engraved by Henry Dawkins and James Smither, and published by Robert Kennedy in Philadelphia in 1768. The boundary as shown here is a continuation of the Mason and Dixon survey shown on Map 497 and constitutes what has come to be known as the famous Mason and Dixon Line.

Size   19¾″ x 25¼″.   *Scale*   1″ = 4 miles.

Published   Separately. Reproduced (see Map 497).

References   see Map 497.

Locations   see Map 497.

[1778?]   see Map 477.

499   [1789]

Description   Above top neat line: FROM PHILADELPHIA (55) TO ANNAPOLIS MARYLD. This map shows, in three vertical strips, the road from three miles east of HEAD OF ELK (47 miles from Philadelphia), over BIG and LITTLE ELK creeks, over NORTH EAST RIVER, to just beyond CHARLES / TOWN.

Size   7″ x 4⅞″.   *Scale*   None (1″ = ⁴⁄₇ mile).

Published in Christopher Colles, *A Survey of the Roads*. Reproduced, ibid., 1961, p. 172.

500 [1789]

Description Above top neat line: FROM PHILADELPHIA (*56*) TO ANNAPOLIS MD. This map shows, in three vertical strips, the road from a half-mile north-west of Charlestown (58½ miles from Philadelphia), across the SUS QUE / HAN NAH LOWER FERRY (at present Havre-de-Grace), to about 6½ miles from Harford.

Size 7″ x 4¾″. *Scale* None (1″ = 4/7 mile).

Published in Christopher Colles, *A Survey of the Roads*. Reproduced, ibid., 1961, p. 173.

501 [1789]

Description Above top neat line: FROM PHILADELPHIA (*57*) TO ANNAPOLIS MD. This map shows, in three vertical strips, the road from 6½ miles east of Harford (71½ miles from Philadelphia), through HARTFORD [sic] OR / BUSHTOWN and NEWTON, passing one mile north of JOPPA.

Size 7″ x 4⅝″. *Scale* None (1″ = 4/7 mile).

Published in Christopher Colles, *A Survey of the Roads*. Reproduced, ibid., 1961, p. 174.

502 [1789]

Description Above top neat line: FROM PHILADELPHIA (*58*) TO ANNAPOLIS MD. This map shows, in three strips, the road from one half mile north of Joppa and one half mile east of LITTLE GUNPOWDER (83½ miles from Philadelphia), across the two Gunpowders, to about six miles from Baltimore.

Size 7″ x 4½″. *Scale* None (1″ = 4/7 mile).

Published in Christopher Colles, *A Survey of the Roads*. Reproduced, ibid., 1961, p. 175.

503 [1789]

Description Above top neat line: FROM PHILADELPHIA (*59*) TO ANNAPOLIS MD. This map shows, in three vertical strips, the road from about six miles east of Baltimore (95 miles from Philadelphia), across BACK RIVER, through BALTIMORE, to about 2½ miles from Elk Ridge Landing.

Size 7″ x 4½″. *Scale* None (1″ = 4/7 mile).

Published in Christopher Colles, *A Survey of the Roads*. Reproduced, ibid., 1961, p. 176.

504 [1789]

Description Above top neat line: FROM PHILADELPHIA (*60*) TO ANNAPOLIS MD. This map shows, in three vertical strips, the road from 2½ miles north-east of ELK R IDGE LANDING (107½ miles from Philadelphia), across the PATAPSCO RR. at ELK R IDGE LANDING, and then past BOYAN's Tavern.

Size 7⅛″ x 4⅝″. *Scale* None (1″ = 4/7 mile).

Published in Christopher Colles, *A Survey of the Roads*. Reproduced, ibid., 1961, p. 177.

505 [1789]

Description Above top neat line: FROM PHILADELPHIA (*61*) TO ANNAPOLIS MD. This map shows, in three vertical strips, the road from ten miles south-east of Elk Ridge Landing (120 miles from Philadelphia), across the SEVERN RIVER, to within one and one half miles of Annapolis.

Size 7″ x 4¾″. *Scale* None (1″ = 4/7 mile).

Published in Christopher Colles, *A Survey of the Roads*. Reproduced, ibid., 1961, p. 178.

506 [1789]

Description Above top neat line: FROM ANNAPOLIS (*62*) TO BLADENSBURG. This map shows, in two vertical strips, the road from one and one half miles west of ANNA POLIS into the Town. Then, FROM G PLATE *61* (near the 131 mile point from Philadelphia or three miles from the center of Annapolis) easterly past WETHERINGTON's Mill, across HOG-NECK and NORTH Run, to 7½ miles from ANNA POLIS.

Size 7″ x 4¾″. *Scale* None (1″ = 4/7 mile).

Published in Christopher Colles, *A Survey of the Roads*. Reproduced, ibid., 1961, p. 179.

507 [1789]

Description Above top neat line: FROM ANNAPOLIS (*63*) TO BLADENSBURG. This map shows, in three vertical strips, the road from 7½ miles west of Annapolis, past GRAY's Mill, over the GOVERNOR's BR. across the PATUXEN RIVER, to BALDWIN's Tavern, 21 miles from Annapolis.

Size 7⅛″ x 5¼″. *Scale* None (1″ = 4/7 mile).

Published in Christopher Colles, *A Survey of the Roads*. Reproduced, ibid., 1961, p. 180.

508 [1789]

Description Above top neat line: FROM AN-NAPOLIS *(64)* TO ALEXANDRIA. This map shows, in three vertical strips, the road from 21 miles west of Annapolis, through BLADENS BURGH, to within four miles of Georgetown.

Size 7⅛" x 4½". *Scale* None (1" = ⁴⁄₇ mile).

Published in Christopher Colles, *A Survey of the Roads*. Reproduced, ibid., 1961, p. 181.

509 [1789]

Description Above top neat line: FROM AN-NAPOLIS *(65)* TO ALEXANDRIA. This map shows, in three vertical strips, the road from four miles east of GEORGE TOWN (34 miles from Annapolis), across the POTOWMACK [sic] RR. at GEORGE TOWN, to ALEX ANDRIA.

Size 7½" x 4". *Scale* None (1" = ⁴⁄₇ mile).

Published in Christopher Colles, *A Survey of the Roads*. Reproduced, ibid., 1961, p. 182.

510 [1795] *State* I (II post-1799, see below, Description)

Description In rectangle at lower left: THE STATE OF / MARYLAND, / FROM THE BEST AUTHOR-ITIES. / BY SAMUEL LEWIS; in rectangle below title: W. BARKER SCULP; above top neat line GEOGRAPHY IMPROVED. Some topographical features are noted as well as names of counties, though no boundaries are included, and many roads and towns. The western boundary line is shown extending north from the source of the POTOWMAC, which is indicated as SPRING HEAD on the inset map. Evitts Creek, near Ft. Cumberland, is shown as EVETS CR.; YOHIOGANY R., for the Youghiogheny. The same map appears in the September, 1800 edition of *Carey's General Atlas* with the number "35" added at upper left corner.

Size 11⅛" x 16⁵⁄₁₆". *Scale* 1" = 12 American miles (69½ to a degree).

Inset At left center: CONTINUATION OF THE / POTOWMAC [sic] RIVER, / FROM / FORT CUMBER-LAND. Size: 3¹³⁄₁₆" x 3¹⁵⁄₁₆". Scale: None (same as main map).

Published in Mathew Carey, *Carey's American Atlas*, no. 12; idem, *Carey's General Atlas*, no. 35; idem, *The General Atlas for Carey's Edition of Guthrie's Geography Improved*, no. 35.

511 1795 *State* I (II post-1799, see below, Description)

Description In lower left corner: MAP / OF THE STATE OF / MARYLAND / LAID DOWN FROM AN ACTUAL SURVEY OF ALL THE / PRINCIPAL WATERS, PUBLIC ROADS, / AND DIVISIONS OF THE COUNTIES THEREIN; / DESCRIBING / THE SITUATION OF THE CITIES, TOWNS, VILLAGES, / HOUSES OF WORSHIP AND OTHER PUBLIC BUILDINGS / FURNACES, FORGES, MILLS, AND OTHER REMARKABLE PLACES; / AND OF THE / FEDERAL TERRITORY; / AS ALSO / A SKETCH OF THE STATE OF DELAWARE; / SHEWING / THE PROBABLE CONNEXION OF THE CHESAPEAKE AND DELAWARE BAYS; / BY / DENNIS GRIFFITH / JUNE 20TH *1794*. Under line below title: ENGRAVED BY J. THACKARA & J. VALLANCE. / PHILADA. PUBLISHED JUNE 6TH, *1795*, BY J. VALLANCE ENGRAVER NO. *145* SPRUCE STREET. This is a detailed, topographical map, the best of Maryland to this time. Roads, political boundaries, and many other features are noted. To the right of the title is given: REGIS-TERED AND COPY RIGHT SECURED / AGREEABLE TO ACT OF CONGRESS JUNE 20TH. *1794*. / PHILIP MOORE CLK: OF THE DISTRICT OF MARYLAND; at lower center: TO THE / GOVERNOR / THE / SENATE AND HOUSE OF REPRESENTATIVES / OF THE / STATE OF MARYLAND / THIS MAP / IS RESPECTFULLY INSCRIBED BY THE / AUTHOR. An EXPLANATION of symbols is given at the right of the dedication. State II was published by John Melish in Phila-delphia in 1813. It was also published in re-duced form with the title: "Maryland und Delaware vor D. F. Sotzman," in the atlas accom-panying Christoph D. Ebeling, *Erdbeschreibung und Geschichte von Amerika.*

Size 29½" x 51⅜". *Scale* 1" = 5 miles.

Inset At left: PLAN / OF THE CITY OF WASH-INGTON / AND / TERRITORY OF COLUMBIA. Size: 22⁹⁄₁₆" x 22⅝". Scale: 1" = 200 poles.

Published Separately. Reproduced in Ed-ward B. Mathews, "The Maps and Map-Makers of Maryland," p. 399; see also above, Descrip-tion.

References Evans 27070 & 28772.

Locations BM, DLC, ICU, M, MdBP, MdHi, MII, MiU-C.

512 [1795] *State* I (II post-1799, see below, Description)

Description At lower left: MARYLAND. The POTOMAC RIVER is consistently so spelled. BELLE AIR, HAVRE DE GRACE, LEONARD T., PALUXENT R., and WIGHCOMICO all appear. The YOUGHIOGINI R. is so spelled. State II appeared in Scott's *The New and Universal Gazetteer, 3.* Some lines have been recut but no geographical changes or addi-tions seem to have been made. It may be recog-nized by the recut shore line of Chesapeake Bay. The shading in the Bay has not been recut so the islands and land are sharply outlined against the worn shading of the water.

Size 6¼" x 7⅜". *Scale* 1" = 28 miles.

Inset [Western Maryland.] Size: 1⁹⁄₁₆″ x 1½″. Scale: None (same as above).

Published in Joseph Scott, *An Atlas of the United States;* idem, *The United States Gazetteer,* opp. "Maryland." Reproduced in Joseph Scott, *Atlas of the United States 1795–1800,* [no. 9].

513 [1796] *State* I (II post-1799, see below, Description)

Description At lower left: MARYLAND; below bottom neat line at right: W BARKER SCULP. Some topographical features are noted. No roads are given. In the second state, appearing in *Carey's American Pocket Atlas* issued in 1801, the District of Columbia is outlined, roads are shown, and a number of place names have been added.

Size 5¹¹⁄₁₆″ x 7⅝″. *Scale* 1″ = 26 miles.

Inset At left: MARYLAND / WEST OF / FORT CUMBERLAND. Size: 1⅝″ x 1¹³⁄₁₆″. Scale: None (same as main map).

Published in Mathew Carey, *Carey's American Pocket Atlas,* foll. p. 90.

514 [1796]

Description In oval at lower left: MAP / OF / THE STATES OF / MARYLAND / AND / DELAWARE / BY J. DENISON; beneath oval: A. DOOLITTLE SCULP; above top neat line: PUBLISHED BY THOMAS & ANDREWS BOSTON. Many roads appear on the main map as well as county boundaries, names of settlements, and a few indications of orographical features. (See also Map 515.)

Size 7⅝″ x 9⅝″. *Scale* 1″ = 20 miles.

Inset At left: THE WESTERN PART OF MARYLAND. This shows names of the mountain ridges. Size: 1⅝″ x 2⅝″. Scale: None (1″ = c. 15 miles).

Published in Jedidiah Morse, *The American Universal Geography,* 3d ed., *1,* opp. 566.

515 [1796]

Description [Map of the States of Maryland and Delaware. Engraved by Amos Doolittle. Boston, 1796.] This entry is taken from Evans. This may be Map 514 by J. Denison but with the addition of the date.

Size Unknown. *Scale* Unknown.

Published Separately.

Reference Evans 30334.

Location No copy located.

516 [1796] *State* I (see also Map 517)

Description In oval at lower left: THE / STATES / OF / MARYLAND / AND / DELAWARE, /

FROM THE LATEST SURVEYS. / *1795;* beneath oval: D. MARTIN SCULPT. N. YORK; below bottom neat line: PUBLISHED BY WAYLAND, REID, & SMITH. Some topographical details are noted. POTOMAC RIVER appears near the mouth and POTOWMAC RIVER further upstream. Evitts Creek near Ft. Cumberland is shown as EVETS CR., and YOHIOGONY RIVER is given for the Youghiogheny.

Size 14⅛″ x 17⅛″. *Scale* 1″ = 13 American miles.

Inset At left: CONTINUATION OF THE / POTOWMAC RIVER / FROM / FORT CUMBERLAND. This is similar to the inset in Map 510, but has no western boundary line. Size: 3¾″ x 3¹⁵⁄₁₆″. Scale: None (same as main map).

Published in William Winterbotham, [*Atlas*]; some copies of John Reid, *The American Atlas,* no. 13. Reproduced in U.S. Bureau of the Census, *Heads of Families at the first census Maryland,* front.

517 [1796] *State* II (see also Map 516)

Description Imprint changed to: PUBLISHED BY JOHN REID, NEW YORK.

Published in John Reid, *The American Atlas,* [1796?], no. 13; ibid., 1796, no. 13.

518 1799 *State* I (see also Map 519)

Description In oval at lower left: THE / STATES OF / MARYLAND / AND / DELAWARE / FROM THE LATEST SURVEYS. / *1799;* below oval: ANDERSON DEL. SCOLES. SC.; below bottom neat line: ENGRAVED FOR PAYNES GEOGRAPHY. PUBLISH'D BY I LOW NEW YORK. This is a topographical map with much detail, showing roads, county names, and the larger settlements. Lewes appears as LEWISTOWN. CLEMENTS BAY is shown on the Potomac River in St. Marys County. Potomac appears three times with a "w" and once without. It is a reduced copy of Map 516.

Size 7⁵⁄₁₆″ x 9⁵⁄₁₆″. *Scale* 1″ = 22½ miles.

Inset At left center: CONTINUATION OF THE / POTOWMAC RIVER / FROM / FORT CUMBERLAND. Size: 2⅛″ x 2³⁄₁₆″. Scale: None (same as main map).

Published in John Payne, *A New and Complete Universal Geography,* 4, opp. 345.

519 1799 *State* II (see also Map 518)

Description Statement below bottom neat line now reads: ENGRAVED FOR NEW ENCYCLOPAEDIA, PUBLISH'D BY I LOW NEW YORK.

Published Separately.

Locations DLC, PHi.

520 1799

Description At upper center: A MAP / OF THE HEAD OF CHESAPEAKE BAY AND / SUSQUE-HANNA RIVER / SHEWING THE NAVIGATION OF THE SAME WITH A TOPOGRAPHICAL DESCRIPTION OF THE / SURROUNDING COUNTRY FROM AN ACTUAL SURVEY BY C. P. HAUDUCOEUR ENGINEER. / *1799.* Below bottom neat line at left corner: HAUDUCOEUR DEL., and at right corner: ALLARDICE SC. This is a very detailed topographical map of the area at the mouth of the Susquehanna River and several miles inland. Property lines and the names of owners are indicated as well as roads, settlements, and many other features. Wooded and cultivated fields are differentiated. Soundings are given. At the upper left is a description of the flow of the River and of a change in the channel at its mouth. The map was advertised in the (Philadelphia) *Porcupine's Gazette* on July 16, 1799, as published and sold by Thomas Dobson and William Cobbett.

Size 22″ x 29½″.   *Scale* 1″ = c. 230 poles.

Inset In lower right corner: PLAN / OF THE TOWN OF / HAVRE DE GRACE / WITH ITS ADDITIONS / SURVEYED AND LAID OUT / BY THE AUTHOR. There are ten lettered references to the inset map in the EXPLANATION at the lower left corner. The streets are named and blocks numbered. Size: 9³⁄₁₆″ x 10″. Scale: 1″ = 1000 feet.

Published Separately.

References U.S. Library of Congress, *Report 1915,* p. 87; idem, *Report 1916,* p. 69.

Locations BM, CtY, DLC, MdHi, MH, MHi, PHi, PPL.

BALTIMORE

521 [1792] *State* I (see also Maps 522 and 523)

Description In ornate cartouche at lower left corner: PLAN / OF THE TOWN / OF / BALTIMORE / AND IT'S ENVIRONS / DEDICATED TO THE CITIZENS OF BALTIMORE / TAKEN UPON THE SPOT BY THEIR MOST HUMBLE SERVANT / A. P. FOLIE / FRENCH GEOGRAPHER. Below cartouche: JAMES POAPARD [sic] SCULPSIT PHILADELPHIA. This is a topographical plan showing the TOWN and BASIN. A list of twenty-six REFERENCES are given at the upper right. Projected as well as actual streets are shown. The engraver is James Poupard.

Size 21⅝″ x 24″.   *Scale* 1″ = 40 perches.

Published Separately. Reproduced in Isaac N. P. Stokes and Daniel C. Haskell, *American Historical Prints*, pl. 29a.

References Evans 24323; see also reproductions above, under Published.

Locations CtY, NN.

522 1792 *State* II (see also Maps 521 and 523)

Description The date *1792.* has been added at the bottom of the cartouche.

Published Separately.

Locations DLC, MdBP, MH, MHi, NN, RPJCB.

523 1794 *State* III? (see also Maps 521 and 522)

Description [Plan of the Town of Baltimore and its environs. Taken upon the spot, by . . . A. P. Folie. Baltimore: Published by Ghequiere & Holmes. 1794.] The entry is taken from Evans and this may be a third state of the original A. P. Folie map with some changes in title and imprint. Any changes in the map itself are not noted.

Published Separately.

Reference Evans 26984.

Location No copy located.

524 [1797]

Description [Plan of Baltimore.] The "Plan" was advertised in the (Baltimore) *Telegraphe and Daily Advertiser* for December 9, 1797, as "This day is published," and, "with the names of all the streets, lanes and alleys, public buildings, wharfs, &c. elegantly engraved by Galland, from actual survey." John Galland was a Philadelphia engraver, established there from 1796 to 1817. The map was published by George Keatinge.

Size Unknown.   *Scale* Unknown.

Published Separately.

References Amanda Rachel Minick, *A History of Printing in Maryland, 1791–1800*, no. 364; John T. Scharf, *Chronicles of Baltimore*, p. 283.

Location No copy located.

525 [1799]

Description [Plan of Baltimore.] The two reference sources given below list a map for this volume.

Size Unknown.   *Scale* Unknown.

Published in John Mullin, *The Baltimore Directory 1799*.

References Sabin 2998 (note); Dorothea N. Spear, *Bibliography of American Directories*, p. 34.

Location No copy of *Directory* located with map.

526 1799 *State* I (II post-1799, see below, Description)

Description In lower left corner: A PLAN / OF THE CITY AND ENVIRONS OF / BALTIMORE, / RESPECTFULLY DEDICATED TO THE MAYOR, CITY COUNCIL, / & CITIZENS THEREOF BY THE AUTHOR *1799*; below neat line at lower right corner: ENGRAVED BY FRANCIS SHALLUS, PHILADELPHIA. This is a topographical plan of the City and the surrounding area. A list of REFERENCES is given at the right. Many outlying residences are identified by the names of the owners. At the right also is a: NOTE. / THE RED COLOUR DESIGNATES THE / BUILT PART OF THE CITY, & THE / YELLOW THE PART UNBUILT. The PLAN is ascribed to

BIBLIOGRAPHY OF MAPS AND CHARTS

Charles Varlé by Col. John T. Scharf. State II appeared in 1801 under the names of William Warner and Andrew Hanna, with the title now beginning "Warner and Hanna's / Plan . . . ," and the title and dedication now signed: ". . . by the Proprietors, 1801." Two residences, those of SMITH and STEWART, have been removed to provide space for the new title heading. Several place names have been changed or added.

Size 19⅛" x 28⅜". *Scale* 1" = 40 perches.

Insets [a] At upper right corner: NEW ASSEMBLY ROOM. Shown is the façade of the building. Size: 2½" x 3¾".
[b] At lower right corner: VIEW OF THE MARKET SPACE CANAL. Size: 2½" x 4⅞".

Published Separately.

References John T. Scharf, *Chronicles of Baltimore*, p. 283; George H. Williams, "Maps of the Territory included within the State of Maryland," p. 43.

Location MdHi.

527 [1792]

Description In oval vignette at upper right: PLAN / OF THE CITY OF / WASHINGTON; below title outside vignette: THACKARA & VALLANCE FC. This is the first known publication of the Andrew Ellicott survey of Washington, based upon the original design drawn by Pierre Charles L'Enfant. At lower left appears: LAT: CAPITOL *38: 53*, N. / LONG: *0:0*. GEORGE TOWN is indicated in outline at the upper left. James Thackara and John Vallance also engraved the folio "Official plan" of Washington (Map 531).

Size 8½" x 10¼".   *Scale* None (1" = c. 2400 feet).

Published in *The Universal Asylum and Columbian Magazine*, March, 1792, opp. p. 155; some copies of [Tobias Lear], *Observations on the River Potomack;* ibid., 2d ed.

Reference Frederick R. Goff, "The Federal City in 1793," pp. 5–7.

528 1792

Description In oval vignette at upper right: PLAN / OF THE CITY OF / WASHINGTON; below title outside vignette: S. HILL, BOSTON; at upper left: MASSA. MAG. *1792*. This is an almost exact copy of Map 527. The engraver of this map, Samuel Hill, also engraved the earliest folio version of the Andrew Ellicott survey (Map 530).

Size 8" x 10".   *Scale* None (1" = c. 2400 feet).

Published in *Massachusetts Magazine, 4* (1792), opp. [284].

529 [1792]

Description In oval vignette at upper right: PLAN / OF THE CITY OF / WASHINGTON; below vignette: TIEBOUT; at upper left corner: N. YORK MAG. This is nother copy of the Andrew Ellicott survey. The engraving is by Cornelius Tiebout. An article describing the projected capital city appeared in the *New-York Magazine,* 2 (1791), 656–58. It is very much like Maps 527 and 528.

Size 9⅝" x 10¹/₁₆".   *Scale* None (1" = c. 2400 feet).

Published in the *New-York Magazine; or, Literary Repository, 3* (1792), no. VI, front.

530 [1792]

Description At upper left corner: PLAN / OF THE CITY OF WASHINGTON / IN THE TERRITORY OF COLUMBIA. / CEDED BY THE STATES OF / VIRGINIA AND MARYLAND / TO THE UNITED STATES OF AMERICA. / AND BY THEM ESTABLISHED AS THE / SEAT OF THEIR GOVERNMENT, / AFTER THE YEAR / M D C C C; below title: ENGRAV'D BY SAML. HILL. BOSTON. This is the earliest folio engraved plan of the new capital. Both this and Map 531, taken from the survey made by Andrew Ellicott, are based in turn upon the original design prepared by Pierre Charles L'Enfant. The soundings given in the Thackara and Vallance engraving are lacking here. OBSERVATIONS / EXPLANATORY OF THE PLAN are given at the lower left. The blocks are numbered and some of the streets named. The BREADTH OF THE STREETS is explained at the lower right.

Size 16¼" x 19⅝".   *Scale* 1" = 100 poles.

Published Separately. Reproduced in Philip L. Phillips, *The Beginnings of Washington*, p. [16]; separately by U.S. Coast & Geodetic Survey, Chart No. 3043; U.S. Senate, *Maps of the District of Columbia* (with engraver's name omitted under title).

References Philip L. Phillips, *List of Maps and Views of Washington*, p. 20; see also reproductions above, under Published.

Locations DLC, MH, MHi, MiU-C, NHi, NN.

531 1792

Description Under decorative device at upper right: PLAN / OF THE CITY OF / WASHINGTON / IN THE TERRITORY OF COLUMBIA, / CEDED BY THE STATES OF / VIRGINIA AND MARYLAND / TO THE / UNITED STATES OF AMERICA, / AND BY THEM ESTABLISHED AS THE / SEAT OF THEIR GOVERNMENT, / AFTER THE YEAR, M D C C C; beneath short line under title: ENGRAV'D BY THACKARA & VALLANCE PHILADA. *1792*. This publication of the Andrew Ellicott survey is usually referred to as the "official" plan of Washington. It was printed in November of 1792. It has been reproduced many times. This map is larger than the Hill engraving (see Map 530) and contains the soundings which are lacking there. Channels are indicated in the POTOMAK RIVER, and streets are shown in GEORGE TOWN. Andrew Ellicott based his plan upon the original design prepared by Pierre Charles L'Enfant.

Size 20¼" x 27".   *Scale* 1" = 100 poles.

Published Separately. Reproduced in Isaac N. P. Stokes and Daniel C. Haskell, *American Historical Prints*, pl. 30b; separately by U.S. Coast & Geodetic Survey, Chart no. 3035.

References Nelson R. Burr, "The Federal City Depicted, 1612–1801," pp. 69–70; Evans 24296; Philip L. Phillips, *The Beginnings of Washington*, pp. 37–38; David M. Stauffer, *American Engravers*, 2, no. 3153; Thomas W. Streeter, *Americana-Beginnings*, pp. 35–36.

Locations BM, CtY, DLC, MiU-C, MWA, RPJCB, Private coll. of Mr. T. W. Streeter.

532 [1792?]

Description At upper left: PLAN / OF THE CITY OF WASHINGTON / IN THE TERRITORY OF COLUMBIA. / CEDED BY THE STATES OF / VIRGINIA AND MARYLAND / TO THE UNITED STATES OF AMERICA / AND BY THEM ESTABLISHED AS THE / SEAT OF THEIR GOVERNMENT / AFTER THE YEAR / M D C C C. This is a "handkerchief map," printed in red ink on cloth and based upon Map 530. It has an elaborate border design with corner illustrations of allegorical figures at the upper left, a seated Indian at lower right, a ship at upper right, and a design of various agricultural products at lower left. All the explanatory notes appearing on the 1792 map appear here, but in different arrangement, the BREADTH OF THE STREETS appearing at the top left.

Size 24" x 25".   *Scale* 1" = 100 poles.

Published Separately. Reproduced in Nelson R. Burr, "The Federal City Depicted, 1612–1801," foll. p. 72; Federal Writers' Project, *Washington City and Capital*, as end papers; U. S. Library of Congress, *District of Columbia Sesquicentennial*, foll. p. 10.

References Philip L. Phillips, *The Beginnings of Washington*, p. 40; see also reproductions above, under Published.

Locations Private coll. of Mr. Philip W. Bonsal, DLC, Fairbanks Museum of Natural Science, St. Johnsbury, Vermont.

533 [1792?]

Description Under heraldic device at upper right: PLAN / OF THE CITY OF / WASHINGTON / IN THE TERRITORY OF COLUMBIA, CEDED BY THE STATES OF / VIRGINIA AND MARYLAND / TO THE / UNITED STATES OF AMERICA, / AND BY THEM ESTABLISHED AS THE / SEAT OF THEIR GOVERNMENT /

AFTER THE YEAR / M D C C C; immediately under device: J W SCULPSIT. The full name of the engraver is not decipherable in the Library of Congress copy. This "handkerchief map" is evidently a copy of Map 531. It is printed in brown on heavy cotton cloth, has a border of stars, an oval portrait of GEORGE WASHINGTON / PRESIDENT / OF THE UNITED STATES OF / AMERICA in the upper left corner, and an adaptation of Washington's coat of arms at the upper right.

Size 21½" x 24".   *Scale* 1" = 100 poles.

Published Separately. Reproduced in Philip L. Phillips, *The Beginnings of Washington*, p. [31].

Reference U.S. Library of Congress, *District of Columbia Sesquicentennial*, no. 68; see also reproduction above, under Published.

Locations DLC, 2 copies; MSaE, 7 copies at one time in possession of Dr. Ephraim Hackett, Kennebunk, Maine.

534 1792

Description [Plan of the City intended for the permanent seat of government of the United States, projected agreeable to the direction of the President of the United States, in pursuance of an Act of Congress, passed on the 16th of July, 1790 "establishing the permanent seat on the banks of the Potowmack." By Peter Charles L'Enfant. Philadelphia: Printed by John Dunlap, 1792.] The entry is taken from Evans. A manuscript map with almost the same title is listed in Phillips, *List of Maps and Views of Washington*. The same title is given in the (Philadelphia) *Gazette of the United States*, January 4, 1792, in an article describing the map forwarded by President Washington to the Congress. The "Observations explanatory of the plan" and the "Breadth of the streets" sections of the article are very similar to the same sections appearing on Maps 530 and 531. No mention is made of its being a printed map or being printed by John Dunlap, however.

Size Unknown.   *Scale* Unknown.

Published Separately.

References Evans 24471; Philip L. Phillips, *The Beginnings of Washington*, p. 17; idem, *List of Maps and Views of Washington*, p. 16.

Location No copy located.

535 [1794]

Description In double lined angle at upper left corner: TERRITORY OF COLUMBIA. In lower left corner: DRAWN BY ANDW. ELLICOTT. This is a topographical map showing the ten-mile square District which was prepared by Andrew Ellicott, who submitted his report to the Commissioners on January 1, 1793. Miles are indicated by roman numerals at each of forty boundary stones, and scale is deduced from this. GEORGE TOWN and ALEXANDRIA are both noted, as are the primary roads of the area. This first map of the District was probably engraved by James Thackara and John Vallance in 1793–94 and printed by Joseph T. Scott.

Size 21¾" x 21¾". *Scale* None (1" = ½ mile).

Published Separately. Reproduced separately by U.S. Coast & Geodetic Survey, Chart no. 3059; in U.S. Senate, *Maps of the District of Columbia* (with Author's name omitted).

References Nelson B. Burr, "The Federal City Depicted, 1612–1801," p. 71; Philip L. Phillips, *List of Maps and Views of Washington*, p. 21; idem, *A List of Maps of America*, p. 265; U.S. Library of Congress, *District of Columbia Sesquicentennial*, no. 39.

Locations DLC, NHi, NN.

536 [1796]

Description [A Plan of the City of Washington. By Thomas Freeman, surveyor of the Territory of Columbia and City of Washington.] This is taken from Evans who also states: "Proposals for publishing the above were made in June, 1796."

Size Unknown. *Scale* Unknown.

Published Separately.

References Evans 30452; Philip L. Phillips, *The Beginnings of Washington*, pp. 64–65.

Location No copy located.

537 [1796] *State I (see also Map 538)*

Description At lower left: PLAN / OF THE CITY OF / WASHINGTON / IN THE TERRITORY OF COLUMBIA / CEDED BY THE STATES OF / VIRGINIA AND MARYLAND / TO THE / UNITED STATES OF AMERICA / AND BY THEM ESTABLISHED AS THE / SEAT OF THEIR GOVERNMENT, / AFTER THE YEAR / *1800;* in scroll below title: ROLLINSON SCULPT. N.YORK; beneath scroll: PUBLISH'D BY I. REID L. WAYLAND AND C. SMITH *1795.* This plan is evidently a copy of Map 531. The title is given at the lower left instead of the upper right and the "Breadth of the Streets" and "Observations . . ." notes are wanting here. Several other notes

given on the other map are now grouped at the upper right under REMARKS. Soundings are also given here. The map was engraved by William Rollinson.

Size 15¹¹⁄₁₆" x 20½". *Scale* 1" = 100 poles.

Published in John Reid, *The American Atlas*, [1796?], foll. no. 20; some copies, idem, *The American Atlas*, 1796, foll. no. 20; William Winterbotham, [*Atlas*]; some copies of idem, *An Historical, Geographical View of the United States, 2.*

Reference Carl W. Drepperd, *Early American Prints*, pp. 56–57.

538 [1796] *State II (see also Map 537)*

Description The imprint beneath the scroll has been changed to read: PUBLISHED BY J. REID N. YORK.

Published in some copies of John Reid, *The American Atlas*, 1796, foll. no. 20.

539 1798

Description In upper right corner: PLAN. / OF THE TOWN OF / ALEXANDRIA. / IN THE DISTRICT OF COLUMBIA / *1798;* at bottom center: ALEXANDRIA; on same line: PUBLISHED BY I. V. THOMAS. / ENGRAV'D BY T. CLARKE NEW YORK. Some topographical details are noted and street names are given. Under the heading: REMARKS, in the upper left corner, are nine engraved lines of script followed by an explanation of the ten numbered references on the map. John V. Thomas advertised the publication of the map on December 4, 1799, in the (Alexandria) *Times and District of Columbia Daily Advertiser* as follows: ". . . A plan of the town of Alexandria drawn by Col. Gilpin, and hansomely engraved." P. L. Phillips states in his *List of Maps of America* that the plan was drawn by Col. George Gilpin. Thomas Clarke is the engraver.

Size 23⅝" x 18⅝". *Scale* 1" = 800 feet.

Published Separately. Reproduced separately by Mr. and Mrs. Mangum Weeks, June 26, 1944; the restrike is on Whatman paper with a 1942 watermark.

Reference Philip L. Phillips, *List of Maps of America*, p. 97.

Locations DLC, MB.

VIRGINIA

540 [1776]

Description In double lined oval at lower right: MAP / OF THE MARITIME PARTS OF / VIRGINIA / EXHIBITING THE SEAT OF WAR. AND OF / LD. DUNMORE'S DEPREDATIONS. / IN THAT COLONY; below title between lines of double oval at left: P. E. D. DELINT.; at right: R. A. SCULP.; below bottom neat line at right: FOR THE PENNSA. MAG. P. *184*. Most of Tidewater Virginia and the eastern and ocean shores are shown, with many names and a few primary roads. Forts are shown at YORK and GLOUCESTER. The map was drawn by Pierre Eugène Du Simitière and engraved by Robert Aitken. It was derived from Peter Jefferson and Joshua Fry's "A Map of the most inhabited part of Virginia, London, 1755."

Size 9¹¹⁄₁₆″ x 10¾″.   *Scale* 1″ = 11 miles.

Published in *Pennsylvania Magazine*, 2 (1776), opp. 184. Reproduced in Coolie Verner, "The Aitken Map of Virginia," opp. p. 153.

Reference See reproduction above, under Published.

541 1782

Description On scroll at upper right corner: TO HIS EXCELLENCY GENL WASHINGTON. / COMMANDER IN CHIEF OF THE ARMIES OF THE / UNITED STATES OF AMERICA. / THIS PLAN OF THE INVESTMENT / OF YORK AND GLOUCESTER HAS BEEN SUR- / VEYED AND LAID DOWN, AND IS / MOST HUMBLY DEDICATED BY HIS EXCELLENCY'S / OBEDIENT AND VERY HUMBLE SERVANT, / SEBASTN. BAUMAN. MAJOR / OF THE NEW YORK OR 2ND REGT / OF ARTILLERY. At lower right corner above bottom neat line: R. SCOT SCULP. PHILAD. *1782*. This is a topographical plan of the battlefield. At the lower center is a large, ornate cartouche containing a detailed EXPLANATION above which, within the cartouche, is this statement: THIS PLAN WAS TAKEN BETWEEN THE 22ND & 28TH OF OCTOBER, *1781*. It was prepared during the week following Lord Cornwallis' surrender. In the lower left corner is the following: NOTE. THE LAND WITHIN THE DOTED[sic] LINES HAS BEEN LAID DOWN BY SURVEY. There are twenty-two references to the British Lines explained on a scroll at the upper left corner. The plan was published in Philadelphia by subscription and an advertisement appeared in the (Chatham) *New-Jersey Journal*, January 30, 1782. It was engraved by Robert Scot. Many reduced copies have been published. This map was later redrawn by J. F. Renault and presented to the Marquis de Lafayette in 1824 on his visit to this country. This redrawing was then engraved by Benjamin Tanner and published the following year.

Size 25⅛″ x 17⅜″.   *Scale* 1″ = 400 yards.

Published Separately. Reproduced in *Magazine of American History*, 6 (1881), opp. [54]; Massachusetts Historical Society, *Prints, Maps and Drawings 1677–1822*, no. 21; Alexander O. Vietor, "The Bauman Map of the Siege of Yorktown," opp. p. [15].

References Carl W. Drepperd, *Early American Prints*, p. 60; Edmund D. Fite and Archibald Freeman, *A Book of Old Maps*, pp. 287–88; David M. Stauffer, *American Engravers*, no. 2870; Isaac N. P. Stokes and Daniel Haskell, *American Historical Prints*, pp. 57–58; see also reproductions above, under Published.

Locations CtY, DLC, French War Office, MHi, MiU-C, NHi, NN, PPL, RPJCB.

542 1782 *State* I (see also Maps 543 and 544)

Description Type set below map: A PLAN OF THE INVESTMENT OF / YORK- TOWN AND GLOUCESTER. This is a woodcut map showing the battle field area probably with some type inset. On the verso is an explanation of the map, referring to twenty lettered references on the map (P is referred to twice, once in place of N). The same woodcut and the same type inserts, except the title, are used without changes from the other states. These states are numbered in the order given by Bates, below, for the three editions of the *Almanack*.

Size 5″ x 3¼″.   *Scale* None (1″ = c. 1 mile).

Published in Andrew Beers, *The United States Almanack, 1783*, on cover leaf.

Reference Albert C. Bates, "Check List of Connecticut Almanacs," p. 134.

543 [1782] *State* II (see also Maps 542 and 544)

Description Type set below map now reads: A PLAN OF THE INVESTMENT OF YORK-TOWN AND / GLOCESTER. Several brief poems are inserted below the "Explanation" on verso of cover leaf. "Gen. Clinton's quart." is correctly referred to here as "N."

Size 4¾" x 3¼". *Scale* None (1" = c. 1 mile).

Published in Andrew Beers, *The United States Almanack, 1783*, on cover leaf.

Reference Albert C. Bates, "Check List of Connecticut Almanacs," p. 134.

544 [1782] *State* III (see also Maps 542 and 543)

Description Type set below map now reads: A PLAN OF THE INVESTMENT OF / YORK-TOWN AND GLOCESTER. This is probably Evans No. 17467. The same type forms were used, with only a few minor changes, as for the *Almanack* containing our State I. On the verso is the same explanation used for State I.

Published in Andrew Beers, *The United-States Almanack, 1783*, on cover leaf.

Reference Albert C. Bates, "Check List of Connecticut Almanacs," p. 135; Evans 17467.

545 [1785]

Description On scroll at upper right: PLAN / OF / THE INVESTMENT OF / YORK & GLOUCESTER, / BY THE ALLIED ARMIES: / IN SEPTR. & OCTR. *1781*. At the upper right corner is a table of twenty-two numbered references to the British Lines. The American lines show reference letters A–R, but no explanatory table is provided for them. Some topographical details are noted. French and American units are identified by name.

Size 8⁷⁄₁₆" x 7⅝". *Scale* 1" = 800 yards.

Published in David Ramsay, *The History of the Revolution of South-Carolina*, 2, opp. 326.

546 [1789]

Description Above top neat line: FROM ANNAPOLIS (*66*) TO DUMFRIES. This map shows, in three vertical strips, the road from the edge of Alexandria (45½ miles from Annapolis), past GEN. WASHINGTON'S / LAND near Mt. Vernon, across ACCOHICK CR. to within three miles of Colchester.

Size 7⅛" x 4½". *Scale* None (1" = 4⁄₇ mile).

Published in Christopher Colles, *A Survey of the Roads*. Reproduced, ibid., 1961, p. 183.

547 [1789]

Description Above top neat line: FROM ANNAPOLIS (*67*) TO FREDERICKSBURG VA. This map shows, in three vertical strips, the road from within three miles of COLCHES TER (58¼ miles from Annapolis), across the OCCAQUAN Creek at COLCHES TER, to DUM FRIES where QUANTOCCO [sic] CR. is crossed.

Size 7⅛" x 4½". *Scale* None (1" = 4⁄₇ mile).

Published in Christopher Colles, *A Survey of the Roads*. Reproduced, ibid., 1961, p. 184.

548 [1789]

Description Above top neat line: FROM ANNAPOLIS (*68*) TO FREDERICKSBURG. This map shows, in three vertical strips, the road from Dumfries (71 miles from Annapolis), to one mile past STAFFORD C H.

Size 7⅛" x 4½". *Scale* None (1" = 4⁄₇ mile).

Published in Christopher Colles, *A Survey of the Roads*. Reproduced, ibid., 1961, p. 185.

549 [1789]

Description Above top neat line: FROM ANNAPOLIS (*69*) TO TODD'S ORDINARY. This map shows, in three vertical strips, the road from one mile past Stafford Court House (84 miles from Annapolis), across the RAPAHANNOCK [sic] at FALMOUTH, to about two miles beyond FREDRICKSBURGH [sic].

Size 7" x 4½". *Scale* None (1" = 4⁄₇ mile).

Published in Christopher Colles, *A Survey of the Roads*. Reproduced, ibid., 1961, p. 186.

550 [1789]

Description Above top neat line: FROM ANNAPOLIS (*70*) TO BOWLING-GREEN ORDY, [sic]. This map shows, in three vertical strips, the road from two miles south of Fredericksburg (97 miles from Annapolis), across MASSAHONICK Creek, past TODDS Tavern (at 105 miles), to a point seven miles from Bowling Green.

Size 7" x 4¾". *Scale* None (1" = 4⁄₇ mile).

Published in Christopher Colles, *A Survey of the Roads*. Reproduced, ibid., 1961, p. 187.

551 [1789]

Description Above top neat line: FROM ANNAPOLIS (*71*) TO HEAD LYNCHS ORDY. This map shows, in three vertical strips, the road from seven miles north-west of Bowling Green (110 miles from Annapolis), past the BOWLING / GREEN ORDY, to a point six miles further south.

Size 7" x 4⅝". *Scale* None (1" = 4/7 mile).

Published in Christopher Colles, *A Survey of the Roads*. Reproduced, ibid., 1961, p. 188.

552 [1789]

Description Above top neat line: FROM AN-NAPOLIS (72) TO HANOVER COURT-HOUSE. This map shows, in two vertical strips, the road from six miles south of Bowling Green (123 miles from Annapolis), across the MATTAPONYE [sic] River, to a point one mile beyond the HEAD LYNCH Tavern.

Size 7" x 4¾". *Scale* None (1" = 4/7 mile).

Published in Christopher Colles, *A Survey of the Roads*. Reproduced, ibid., 1961, p. 189.

553 [1789]

Description Above top neat line: FROM AN-NAPOLIS (73) TO HANOVER & NEWCASTLE. This map shows, in three vertical strips, the road from one mile south of the Head Lynch Tavern (132½ miles from Annapolis), across the PAMUN-KEY River two miles north of HANOVER C H, to about four miles past the Court House.

Size 7" x 4⅝". *Scale* None (1" = 4/7 mile).

Published in Christopher Colles, *A Survey of the Roads*. Reproduced, ibid., 1961, p. 190.

554 [1789]

Description Above top neat line: FROM AN-NAPOLIS (74) TO NEW KENT COURT-HOUSE. This map shows, in three vertical strips, the road from four miles south-east of Hanover Court House (145 miles by this road from Annapolis), across TOTOPOTOMOY Creek, to about four miles south east of NEW CASTLE.

Size 7" x 4½". *Scale* None (1" = 4/7 mile).

Published in Christopher Colles, *A Survey of the Roads*. Reproduced, ibid., 1961, p. 191.

555 [1789]

Description Above top neat line: FROM AN-NAPOLIS (75) TO NEW KENT, COURT-HOUSE. This map shows, in three vertical strips, the road from four miles south-east of Newcastle (158 miles from Annapolis by this route), past JOHN-SONS TUB MILL, about 13 miles to about two miles west of New Kent Court House.

Size 7" x 4¾". *Scale* None (1" = 4/7 mile).

Published in Christopher Colles, *A Survey of the Roads*. Reproduced, ibid., 1961, p. 192.

556 [1789]

Description Above top neat line: FROM AN-NAPOLIS (76) TO WILLIAMSBURGH. This map shows, in three vertical strips, the road from about two miles west of NEW KENT / COURT-HOUSE (171½ miles from Annapolis by this road), past RAWSON's Tavern (at 176 miles), to half-a-mile from the Duncastle or Birds Ordinary. At the bottom of the center strip is a note beginning: TO G. PLATE *80*. & TO WEST-POINT. . . .

Size 7" x 4½". *Scale* None (1" = 4/7 mile).

Published in Christopher Colles, *A Survey of the Roads*. Reproduced, ibid., 1961, p. 193.

557 [1789]

Description Above top neat line: FROM AN-NAPOLIS (77) TO WILLIAMSBURGH. This map shows, in three vertical strips, the road from a half mile north-west of DUNCASTLE OR BIRDS ORDY. (185½ miles from Annapolis by this route), past ALLENS Tavern, to two miles north-west of Williams-burg.

Size 7" x 4½". *Scale* None (1" = 4/7 mile).

Published in Christopher Colles, *A Survey of the Roads*. Reproduced, ibid., 1961, p. 194.

558 [1789]

Description Above top neat line: FROM AN-NAPOLIS (78) TO YORK. This map shows, in two vertical strips, the road from two miles north-west of WILLIAMS / BURGH (198 miles from Annapolis by this highway), through the town, to about six miles from YORK.

Size 7" x 4½". *Scale* None (1" = 4/7 mile).

Published in Christopher Colles, *A Survey of the Roads*. Reproduced, ibid., 1961, p. 195.

559 [1789]

Description Above top neat line: FROM AN-NAPOLIS (79) TO YORK. This map shows, in two vertical strips, the road from six miles west of YORK into that town, 213 miles from Annapolis by the road shown.

Size 7" x 4½". *Scale* None (1" = 4/7 mile).

Published in Christopher Colles, *A Survey of the Roads*. Reproduced, ibid., 1961, p. 196.

560 [1789]

Description Above top neat line: FROM WIL-

LIAMSBURGH (*80*) TO AYLETTS WAREHOUSE. This map shows, in three vertical strips, the road: FROM F. PLATE *76*, seventeen miles from Williamsburg (184 miles from Annapolis by the route measured), past FRANKS Tavern, across the PAMUNKY River at RUFFINS FERRY and one mile north. In a rectangle at the lower left corner: FROM THE CAPITOL OF WILLIAMS / BURGH PLATE *78* TURN BACK TO F / PLATE *76*.

Size 7″ x 4¾″. *Scale* None (1″ = 4/7 mile).

Published in Christopher Colles, *A Survey of the Roads*. Reproduced, ibid., 1961, p. 197.

561 [1789]

Description Above top neat line: FROM WILLIAMSBURG (*81*) TO AYLETT'S WARE-HOUSES. This map shows, in three vertical strips, the road from one mile north of Ruffin's Ferry over the Pamunky (29 miles from Williamsburg), through KING WM. COURT-HOUSE and about one mile west.

Size 7″ x 4½″. *Scale* None (1″ = 4/7 mile).

Published in Christopher Colles, *A Survey of the Roads*. Reproduced, ibid., 1961, p. 198.

562 [1789]

Description Above top neat line: FROM WILLIAMSBURG (*82*) TO SNEED'S ORDINARY. This map shows, in three vertical strips, the road from a mile west of King Williams Court House (41½ miles from Williamsburg), past AYLETT'S WARE-HOUSES on the MATTAPONYE [sic] River, over this River at TODDS BRIDGE and on about a mile and a half.

Size 7″ x 4½″. *Scale* None (1″ = 4/7 mile).

Published in Christopher Colles, *A Survey of the Roads*. Reproduced, ibid., 1961, p. 199.

563 [1789]

Description Above top neat line: FROM WILLIAMSBURG (*83*) TO PORT-ROYAL. This map shows, in three vertical strips, the road from about 1½ miles north-west of Todd's Bridge over the MATTAPONYE [sic] (54½ miles from Williamsburg), to about six miles south-east of Sneed's Ordinary or Tavern.

Size 7″ x 4½″. *Scale* None (1″ = 4/7 mile).

Published in Christopher Colles, *A Survey of the Roads*. Reproduced, ibid., 1961, p. 200.

564 [1789]

Description Above top neat line: FROM WILLIAMSBURG (*84*) TO PORT-ROYAL. This map shows,

in two vertical strips, the road from six miles south-east of SNEEDS Tavern (67 miles from Williamsburg), past SNEEDS Tavern, to about nine miles south of Port Royal.

Size 7″ x 4½″. *Scale* None (1″ = 4/7 mile).

Published in Christopher Colles, *A Survey of the Roads*. Reproduced, ibid., 1961, p. 201.

565 [1789]

Description Above top neat line: FROM WILLIAMSBURG (*85*) TO HOOE'S FERRY. This map shows, in three vertical strips, the road from nine miles south of PORT ROYAL (77 miles from Williamsburg), past TOMBS's Tavern, across the RAPAHANNOCK [sic] / RIVER at PORT ROYAL, to about four miles north-west of PORT ROYAL.

Size 7″ x 4½″. *Scale* None (1″ = 4/7 mile).

Published in Christopher Colles, *A Survey of the Roads*. Reproduced, ibid., 1961, p. 202.

566 [1789]

Description Above top neat line: FROM WILLIAMSBURG (*86*) TO HOOE'S FERRY. This map shows, in three vertical strips, the road from four miles north-west of Port Royal (90 miles from Williamsburg), past Hooe's mill on the LITTLE MACHOTICK [Upper Machodoc] 12½ miles, to about two miles west of Hooe's Ferry across the Potomac.

Size 7″ x 4½″. *Scale* None (1″ = 4/7 mile).

Published in Christopher Colles, *A Survey of the Roads*. Reproduced, ibid., 1961, p. 203.

567 [1790]

Description In oval at lower right: CHART / OF THE / COAST OF AMERICA / FROM / CAPE HENRY / TO / ALBERMARLE [sic] SOUND; in oval below title: BOSTON PUBLISHED & SOLD BY MATTHEW CLARK; in lower left corner: NO. *11*. Many soundings are given in Chesapeake Bay. A number of towns are indicated and under Norfolk is noted: BURNT JAN *1 1776*. The chart bears an engraved inscription, which was signed by Osgood Carleton when sold singly, stating that it was examined and compared with the best charts and found accurate. In the Library of Congress copy of the [*Chart*] this and Map 576 are pasted together.

Size 16⅜″ x 24¾″. *Scale* None (1″ = c. 5 miles).

Published in Matthew Clark, [*A Complete Chart*], no. 11.

BIBLIOGRAPHY OF MAPS AND CHARTS

Reference Philip L. Phillips, comp., *A List of Geographical Atlases, 3,* 492.

568 1794 *State* I (II post-1799, see below, Description)

Description At upper left: THE STATE OF / VIRGINIA / FROM THE BEST AUTHORITIES, / BY SAMUEL LEWIS. / *1794;* beneath scale: SMITHER SCULPT.; below bottom neat line: ENGRAVED FOR CAREY'S AMERICAN EDITION OF GUTHRIES GEOGRAPHY IMPROVED. This is a topographical map showing much detail. Many towns and court houses are indicated; county names are given but no boundaries; and a number of roads are shown. The western boundary follows the west fork instead of the east fork of the GR: SANDY R. [i.e. Big Sandy River] to the Cumberland Divide. The northwest corner of North Carolina is shown on the Blue Ridge Divide instead of on Stone Mountain. The second state appears in the 1800 edition of *Carey's General Atlas* with the number "36" added at the upper right corner.

Size 13⁹⁄₁₆″ x 19¾″. *Scale* 1″ = 15 American miles (69½ to a degree).

Published in Mathew Carey, *Carey's American Atlas,* no. 13; idem, *Carey's General Atlas,* no. 36; idem, *The General Atlas for Carey's Edition of Guthrie's Geography Improved,* no. 36; Thomas Jefferson, *Notes on the States of Virginia,* 2d Am. ed.;

References Earl G. Swem, "Maps relating to Virginia," no. 354; Coolie Verner, "The Maps and Plates," p. 28; idem, "Some observations," p. 204.

569 [1795] *State* I (II post-1799, see below, Description)

Description At upper left: VIRGINIA. This is a topographical map indicating settlements but not counties. As in Map 568 the western boundary follows the west fork instead of the east fork of the Big Sandy River. The northwest corner of North Carolina is again shown on the Blue Ridge divide instead of on Stone Mountain. The HOLSTEIN R. appears for the Holston. TENNASEE is noted thus at the lower left. This map was reissued in Scott's *The New and Universal Gazetteer, 4.* No geographical additions are noted but some recutting was done to the plate. This state may be identified by the two short straight lines which the retoucher has added to strengthen each of the small circles locating all the towns except Richmond.

Size 6″ x 7⁵⁄₁₆″. *Scale* 1″ = 68 miles.

Published in Joseph Scott, *An Atlas of the United States;* idem, *The United States Gazetteer,* opp. "Virginia." Reproduced in Joseph Scott, *Atlas of the United States 1795–1800,* [no. 20].

570 [1796] *State* I (II post-1799, see below, Description)

Description At upper left: VIRGINIA; below bottom neat line at right: W. BARKER, SCULP:. This is a topographic map very similar to Map 569. The western boundary is again shown incorrectly. More streams are identified than in the previous map. Tennessee is not indicated by name. ONANCOOK appears for Onancock. This map was reissued in the 1801 edition of *Carey's American Pocket Atlas* with the addition of important roads. The following place names are among those not appearing on State I: "W. Liberty," "Wheeling," and, "Fishing C." The outlines of the District of Columbia are not shown. No lines appear at the degree figures between neat lines and marginal degree lines.

Size 5¹³⁄₁₆″ x 7⅝″. *Scale* 1″ = 65 miles.

Published in Mathew Carey, *Carey's American Pocket Atlas,* opp. p. 95.

571 [1796]

Description At upper left: VIRGINIA; below bottom neat line at center: HILL SC:; above top neat line: PUBLISHED BY THOMAS & ANDREWS, BOSTON. This is a topographical map, almost exactly the same as Map 570. ONAUCOOK appears for Onancock.

Size 5¹¹⁄₁₆″ x 7⅝″. *Scale* 1″ = 67 miles.

Published in Jedidiah Morse, *The American Universal Geography,* 3d ed., *1,* opp. 602.

572 1796

Description In oval at upper left: THE STATE OF / VIRGINIA / FROM THE BEST AUTHORITIES, / *1796;* beneath oval: PUBLISHED BY JOHN REID N. YORK; beneath scale: B. TANNER, SCULPT. This map was apparently copied from Map 568 but is slightly shorter east and west. Fairfax County is shown as FAIRFEX. A symbol is explained at the upper left as indicating COURT HOUSES.

Size 13⅜″ x 18¼″. *Scale* 1″ = 26 American miles.

Published in John Reid, *The American Atlas,* [1796?], no. 14; ibid., 1796, no. 14; William Winterbotham, [*Atlas*]. Reproduced in Earl G. Swem, "Maps relating to Virginia," no. 358; U.S. Bureau of the Census, *Heads of Families at First Census, Virginia,* front.

573 [1797]

Description At upper left corner: A PLAN OF / THE INVESTMENT OF / YORK AND GLOUCESTER, / VIRGINIA; below title: TANNER, SCU. / PUBLISHED

BY C. SMITH N. YORK. Some topographical details are shown and the several French and American military units identified; British units are noted by symbol but are not identified. Three REFERENCES are given at the lower left. At the lower center is: THE FIELD / WHERE THE BRITISH LAID DOWN THEIR ARMS.

Size 17⅛″ x 15⅜″.   *Scale* 1″ = 400 yards.

Published in *The Monthly Military Repository*, 2, opp. 127; Charles Smith, *The American War*, opp. p. 167.

574 1799

Description In oval at upper right: THE STATE OF / VIRGINIA / FROM THE BEST AUTHORITIES. / *1799;* below bottom neat line at center: ENGRAVED FOR PAYNE'S NEW GEOGRAPHY, PUBLISHED BY I. LOW, NEW-YORK; at right: A. ANDERSON. This is a topographical map with many place names indicated. It was copied from Map 572 with some omissions.

Size 7½″ x 9⅞″.   *Scale* 1″ = 48 American miles.

Published in John Payne, *A New and Complete Universal Geography, 4,* opp. 385.

575 [1761?] *State* I(?) (see also Maps 578, 580, and 589; V(?) post-1799, see Map 589, Description)

Description [Chart of the coast of America from Cape Hateras (sic) to Cape Roman (sic) from the actual surveys of Dl. Dunbibin esqr.] Evidence for the publication of this earlier state of the Dunbibin chart of the Carolina Coast is given in the following advertisement which appeared in the *Boston Gazette*, September 14, 1761:

"The Navigation on the Coast of *North* and *South Carolina* being very dangerous on account of the many Bars, Shoals, Sandbanks, Rocks, etc. The late Daniel Dunbibin, Esq: of *North Carolina*, has, at a very great Expence and Labour, draughted the Sea Coast of both the Provinces in a large whole Sheet Chart of 33 Inches by 23; together with all the Rivers, Bays, Inlets, Islands, Brooks, Bars, Shoals, Rocks, Soundings, Currents, &c. with necessary Directions to render the Navigation both easy and safe, and are much esteemed by the most expert Pilots:—A few of the Draughts may be had of the Subscriber if apply'd for directly. EDMUND QUINCY, jun, Broker."

Although the advertisement does not definitely state this is a published copy, it can probably be assumed that it is. The same plates were probably then used later by John Norman in his 1791 and subsequent publications of the chart. The title is taken from Map 578.

Size Unknown.   *Scale* Unknown.

Published Separately.

References William P. Cumming, *The Southeast in Early Maps*, p. 52; ibid., 2d ed., pp. 52, 282; George F. Dow, *The Arts & Crafts in New England*, p. 31; Gary S. Dunbar, *Historical Geography of the North Carolina Outer Banks*, p. 21; App. B, no. 13.

Location No copy located.

576 [1790]

Description At lower right in oval: CHART / OF THE / COAST OF AMERICA / FROM / ALBERMARLE [sic] SOUND / TO / CAPE LOOKOUT. In oval below title: BOSTON PUBLISHED & SOLD BY MAT-

THEW CLARK. The modern Pamlico is given as PAMTICO R. and PANTICOE / SOUND. PORTSMOUTH is indicated on OCCACOKE (modern Ocracoke) INLET. The chart bears an engraved inscription, signed by Osgood Carleton when sold singly, stating that it had been examined and compared with the best charts and found accurate. In the Library of Congress copy of the [*Chart*] this and Map 567 are pasted together.

Size 23″ x 17⅛″.   *Scale* None (1″ = c. 5 miles).

Published in Matthew Clark, [*A Complete Chart*], no. 12.

Reference Philip L. Phillips, comp., *A List of Geographical Atlases, 3,* 492.

577 [1790]

Description At lower left: CHART OF THE COAST / OF AMERICA FROM CAPE / FEAR TO CAPE LOOK OUT / FROM THE LATEST SURVEYS; continuing after title: BOSTON PUBLISHED / AND SOLD BY M CLARK; in lower left corner: NO. *13*. THE COAST OF NORTH CAROLINA is noted in large letters. In the Library of Congress copy of the [*Chart*], this and Map 598 are pasted together.

Size 24¼″ x 16½″.   *Scale* None (1″ = c. 5 miles).

Inset At lower right: A PLAN OF THE HARBOUR / AND ENTRANCE / OF CAPE FEAR AND THE / SHOALS. Size: 14¼″ x 8½″. Scale: None (1″ = c. ¾ mile).

Published in Matthew Clark, [*A Complete Chart*], no. 13.

Reference Philip L. Phillips, comp., *A List of Geographical Atlases, 3,* 492.

[1790] see Map 567.

578 [1791] *State* II(?) (see also Maps 575, 580, and 589; V(?) post-1799, see Map 589, Description)

Description In oval at upper left: CHART / OF THE / COAST OF AMERICA / FROM / CAPE HATERAS [sic] / TO / CAPE ROMAN [sic] / FROM THE ACTUAL SURVEYS / OF / DL. DUNBIBIN ESQR. The neat line is broken at the lower left corner for an extension of the coast line below CHARLES

Johnston, A Chart of Canada River, 1746 (No. 76)

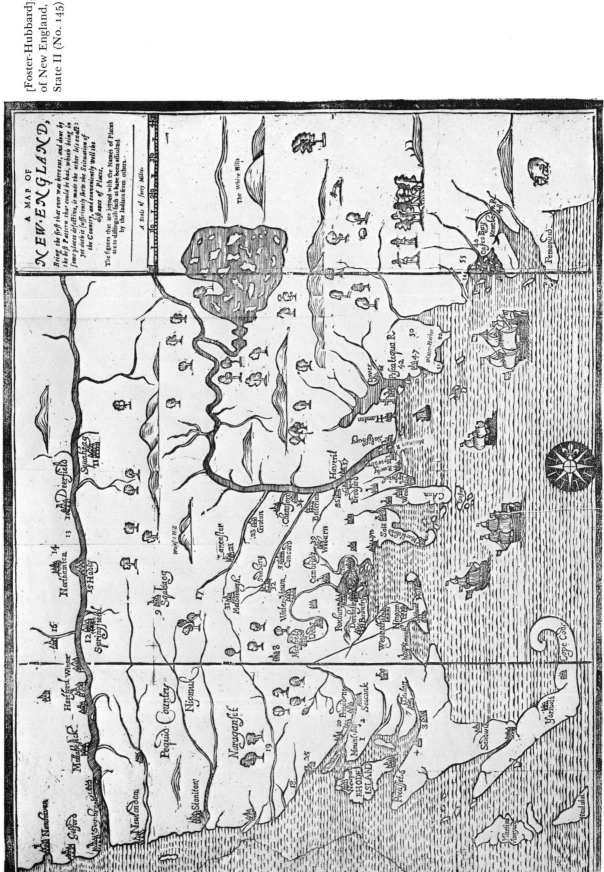

A MAP OF

NEW ENGLAND,

Being the first that ever was here cut, and done by
the best Pattern that could be had, which being in
some places defective, it made the other less exact:
Yet doth it sufficiently shew the Scituation of
the Country, and conveniently well the
distances of Places.

The figures that are joyned with the Names of Places
are to distinguish such as have been assaulted
by the Indians from others.

A Scale of forty Miles.

Romans, Map of the Seat of Civil War in America, 1775 (No. 203)

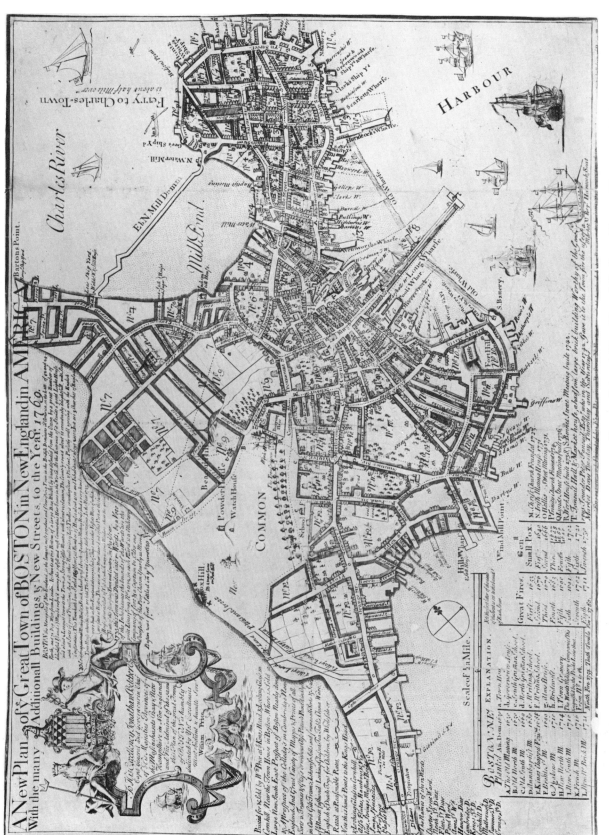

Bonner-Price, A New Plan of Ye Great Town of Boston, 1769, State IX (No. 234)

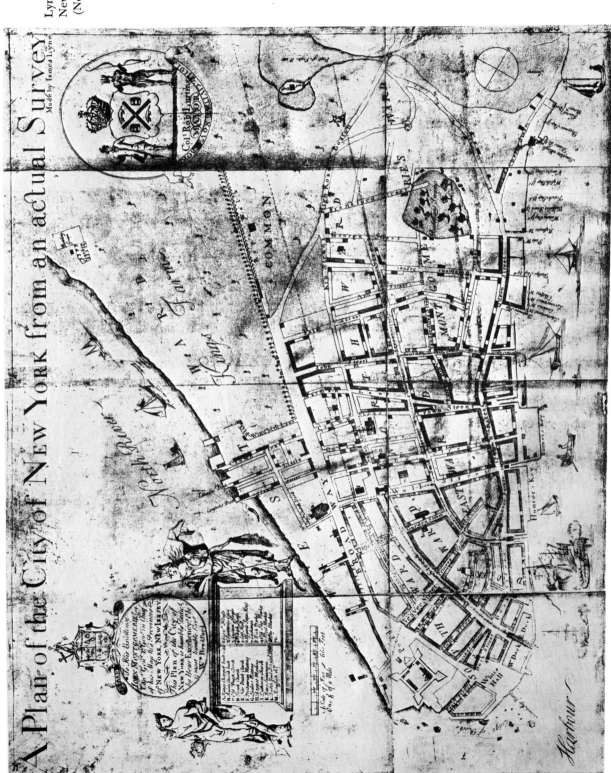

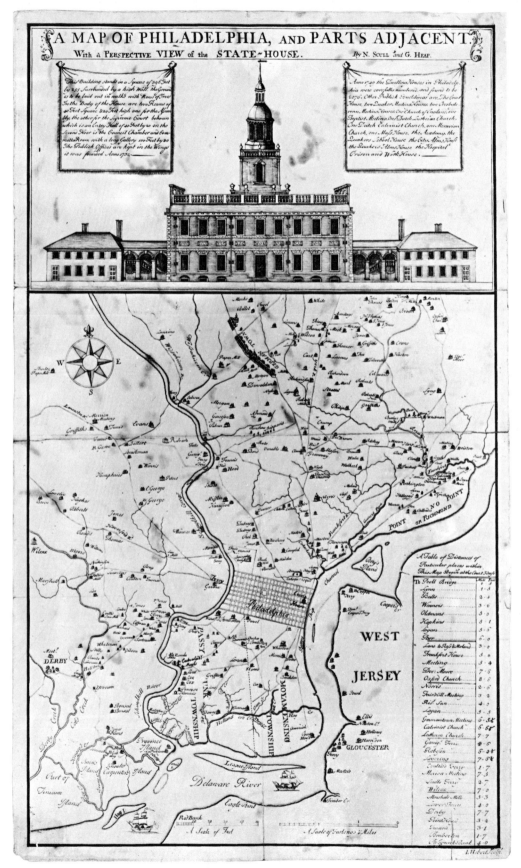

Scull, A Map of Philadelphia [1752], State I (No. 454)

Fisher, This Chart of Delaware Bay and River [1776?] (No. 476)

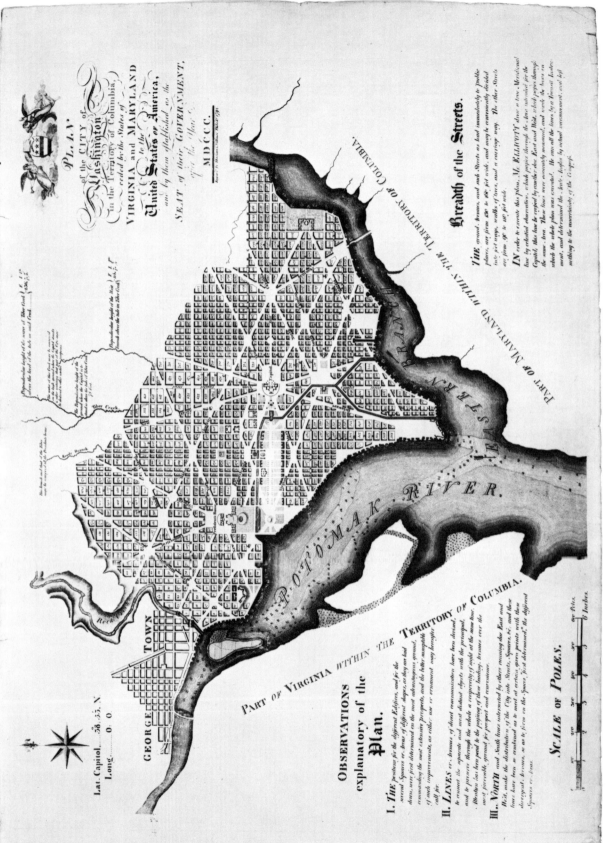

Bauman, Plan of the Investment of York and Gloucester, 1782 (No. 541)

Filson, This Map of Kentucke, 1784, State V (No. 635)

Hutchins, A Topographical Plan of that part of the Indian Country [1765] (No. 658)

Norman, J., A New General Chart of the West Indies [1790] (No. 683)

PLAN OF THE BLOCKADE OF CADIZ

BY THE

ENGLISH FLEET

Under the Command of the Earl of St. Vincent,

As taken on the spot by a British Officer, on the 18th of May, 1797.

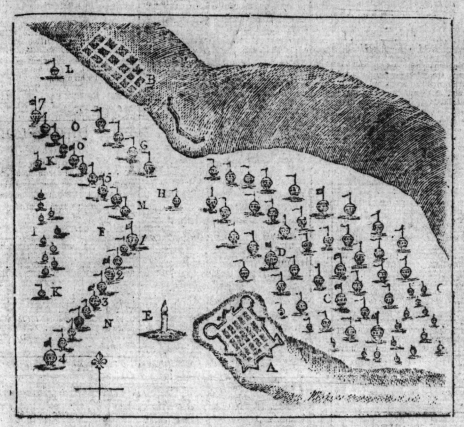

REFERENCES.

A. Cadiz.
B. Rota.
C. Cadiz Bay.
D. Spanish Admiral in Chief.
E. Light House.
F. British Fleet.
G. Four British Line of Battle Ships moored in Shore.
H. British Guard Frigate.
I. English Transports.
K. English Frigates.
L. English Guard Frigate, off Rota.
M. Centre Division of the British Fleet, consisting of Seven Ships of the Line.
N. Starboard Division of Seven ditto.

O. Larboard Division of Seven ditto.
FIG. 1. Ville de Paris, Admiral Earl St. Vincent.
2. Prince George.
3. Victory.
4. Namur.
5. Britannia.
6. Blenheim.
7. Barfleur.

There are 36 sail of the Spanish Line, 10 Frigates, and 8 other vessels, in Cadiz Bay.—The British Fleet consists of 25 sail of the Line, 4 Frigates, and 10 Transports.

The British are moored at 2 1-2 Cable's length asunder.

The advanced Spanish ships are very close to the British in-shore ships.

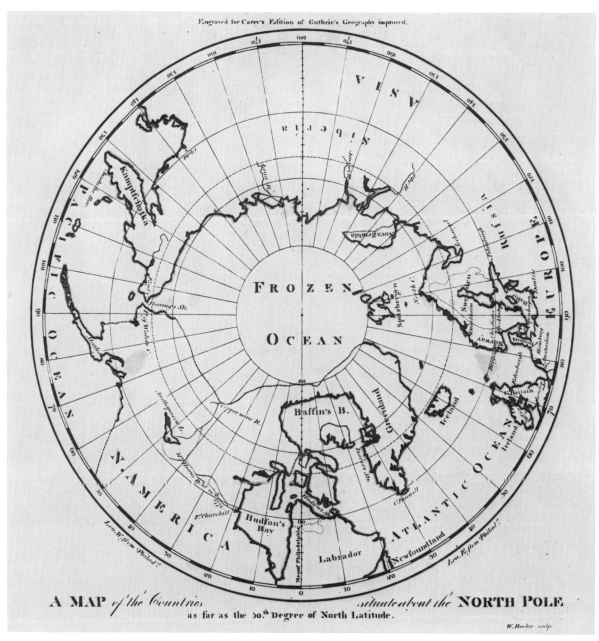

Carey, A Map of the Countries situate about the North Pole [1796] (No. 915)

T. Two plates are used. GOV HOUSE is shown near Brunswick. For a possible earlier state of this chart by Daniel Dunbibin see Map 575.

Size 20½" x 32". *Scale* 1" = 4⅓ English leagues.

Published in John Norman, *The American Pilot*, 1791, no. 4; ibid., 1792, no. 5.

References William P. Cumming, *The Southeast in Early Maps*, p. 52; Evans 19211.

579 [1793]

Description Across top margin above dotted neat line: PLAN OF THE CITY OF RALEIGH; / (THE SEAT OF GOVERNMENT OF THE STATE OF NORTH-CAROLINA.). The PLAN was advertised as being on sale in the (NEW BERN) *North-Carolina Gazette*, January 4, 1794. This is a type set map showing the five public squares and the twenty-three streets of the original plan. The marginal neat line consists of a row of dots. 276 lots of one acre each are shown with owners' names on 234 of them.

Size 16" x 12¾". *Scale* None (1" = 114 feet).

Published in North Carolina (State), *The Acts of the General Assembly*, opp. p. 48; separately.

580 [1794] *State* III(?) (see also Maps 575, 578, and 589; V(?) post-1799, see Map 589, Description)

Description Identical to Map 578 except that the following has been added just north of Cape Fear: NEW INLET.

Published in John Norman, *The American Pilot*, 1794, no. 5; William Norman, *The American Pilot*, 1794, no. 5.

581 [1795] *State* I (II post-1799, see below, Description)

Description In lower corner: THE STATE OF / NORTH CAROLINA / FROM THE BEST AUTHORITIES, &C. / BY SAMUEL LEWIS. Beneath title: ENGRAVED BY VALLANCE. This is a topographical map showing also roads and towns, and giving county names but not the boundaries. The longitude of the state line corner at Richmond County is drawn as about 79° 12' W. instead of about 79° 40' W. THE SWASH WAY is noted in South Carolina. The engraver is John Vallance. The map appears in the 1800 edition of *Carey's General Atlas* with the number "37" added at the upper right corner.

Size 11" x 18½". *Scale* 1" = 21 American miles.

Published in Mathew Carey, *Carey's American Atlas*, no. 14; idem, *Carey's General Atlas*, no. 37; idem, *The General Atlas for Carey's Edition of Guthrie's Geography Improved*, no. 37.

582 1795

Description At upper right corner: OCCACOCK / FROM / ACTUAL SURVEY. / BY I PRICE / 1795. Above neat line at lower right: W. JOHNSTON SC. This is a chart of what is known today as Ocracoke Inlet, showing WALACE'S CHANNEL and SHIP CHANNEL through the several shoals and islands of the harbor. The "s" in PORTSMOUTH Island is reversed. The map was drawn by Jonathan Price.

Size 10¾" x 10⅜". *Scale* 1" = 1 mile.

Published in [Jonathan Price], *A Description of Occacock Inlet*. Reproduced in *North Carolina Review, 3* (1926), 633.

References Evans 29351; Douglas C. McMurtrie, *Eighteenth Century North Carolina Imprints*, no. 214.

583 [1795] *State* I (II post-1799, see below, Description)

Description At lower right: NORTH-CAROLINA. Some topographical details are shown and the more important towns indicated. The State is shortened east and west, and the northwest boundary (with Virginia and the S. W. TERRITORY) is located a little less than 6° west of Philadelphia instead of about 6½°. The boundary is shown along the crest of the Blue Ridge Mountains instead of the Stone and Smoky Mountains. HOLSTEIN appears for the Holston River. This map was reissued in Scott's, *The New and Universal Gazetteer, 4*. There was some recutting on the plate for this second state but no geographical additions are noted. It may be identified by the two short straight lines which the retoucher has added, to strengthen each of the small circles marking all the towns except "Tarborough," Raleigh, and Brunswick.

Size 6⅛" x 7½". *Scale* 1" = 62 miles.

Published in Joseph Scott, *An Atlas of the United States*, no. 14; idem, *The United States Gazetteer*, opp. "North-Carolina." Reproduced in Joseph Scott, *Atlas of the United States 1795-1800*, [no. 14].

584 [1796] *State* I (II post-1799, see below, Description)

Description At lower left: NORTH CAROLINA. Below bottom neat line at right: W BARKER SCULP. Some topographical details are given. The southwest corner is not shown. No roads appear. This map was republished in the 1801 edition of *Carey's American Pocket Atlas* with an added double underlining beneath title. Roads have been added as well as a number of place names.

Size 5¾" x 7⅝".   *Scale* 1" = 50 miles.

Published in Mathew Carey, *Carey's American Pocket Atlas,* foll. p. 102.

585 [1796]

Description In oval at lower right: MAP / OF / NORTH AND SOUTH / CAROLINA / BY J. DENISON. In oval below title: DOOLITTLE SCULP:; above top neat line: ENGRAVED FOR MORSE'S UNIVERSAL GEOGRAPHY. PUBLISHED BY THOMAS & ANDREWS. There is an EXPLANATION of various markings in the lower left corner. Many roads are indicated. County names are given but not the boundaries.

Size 7⁷⁄₁₆" x 9³⁄₁₆".   *Scale* 1" = 54 miles.

Published in Jedidiah Morse, *The American Universal Geography,* 3d ed., *1,* opp. 640.

586 1796

Description [A map of the State of North-Carolina, agreeable to its present boundaries. By Jonathan Price, and John Strother. New-bern: Printed by Francois-X. Martin. 1796.] A North Carolina District copyright was issued to Jonathan Price and John Strother as authors on March 7, 1796. An advertisement concerning this was published on April 1, 1796, in the (New Bern) *North-Carolina Gazette.* The title is taken from Evans.

Size Unknown.   *Scale* Unknown.

Published Separately.

Reference Evans 31047; Douglas C. Mc-Murtrie, *Eighteenth Century North Carolina Imprints,* no. D 35.

Location No copy located.

587 [1796]   *State* I (see also Map 588)

Description In oval at lower left: THE STATE OF / NORTH CAROLINA / FROM THE BEST AUTHORITIES; beneath title in oval: TANNER, SCULPT.; below bottom neat line: PUBLISHED BY JOHN REID N. YORK. This is a topographical map showing also roads, towns, and giving county names but not the boundaries. Mecklenburg County is spelled MACKLENBURG. This map was copied from Map 581.

Size 10¹⁵⁄₁₆" x 18½".   *Scale* 1" = 21 American miles.

Published in John Reid, *The American Atlas,* [1796?], no. 16; ibid., 1796, no. 16; William Winterbotham, [*Atlas*].

588 1796   *State* II (see also Map 587)

Description The date: *1796,* has been added below: FROM THE BEST AUTHORITIES in oval at lower left. No original copy of this map with this date has thus far been discovered. It could have been added at the time of the preparation of the facsimile noted below.

Published Separately(?). Reproduced in U.S. Bureau of the Census, *Heads of Families at the First Census . . . North Carolina,* front.

Location No copy located.

589 [1798]   *State* IV(?) (see also Maps 575, 578, and 580; V(?) post-1799, see below, Description)

Description This is identical to Map 578 except that many of the lines on the plate have been strengthened by recutting, and the *3* LOOK-OUT SHOALS below Cape Lookout are now definitely outlined, each with a single line of uniform dots. The plate was used again in William Norman's *American Pilot* of 1803 with further recutting. The lettering in DL. DUNBIBIN in the title is now fully shaded as is also COAST OF AMERICA.

Published in William Norman, *The American Pilot,* 1798. no. 4.

590 1798

Description In rectangular frame in lower left corner: TO NAVIGATORS / THIS CHART, / BEING AN ACTUAL SURVEY OF THE SEA COAST AND INLAND NAVIGATION / FROM CAPE HENRY TO CAPE ROMAN IS MOST RESPECTFULLY INSCRIBED BY / PRICE & STROTHER. In rectangle below title: PUBLISHED AGREEABLE TO ACT OF CONGRESS / ENGRAVED BY W JOHNSTON NEW-BERN NORTH CAROLINA *1798.* This is a chart showing the immediate coastline and giving some details concerning the navigation of ALBEMARLE SOUND and the lower reaches of the rivers in the area. Wilmington, New Bern, Washington, and Edenton are shown. The Virginia and South Carolina lines are indicated. The North Carolina District copyright for this chart was issued on March 7, 1796. Later that same year, beginning on August 6, Jonathan Price and John Strother advertised in the (New Bern) *North-Carolina Gazette* that the "Chart of the sea coast" was ready for the engraver, but that heavy costs were forcing them to request subscriptions. It was probably engraved by William Johnston.

Size 14½" x 38½".   *Scale* 1" = 2⅕ leagues.

Published Separately.

References Gary S. Dunbar, *Historical Geog-*

raphy of the North Carolina Outer Banks, p. 26, App. B., no. 16; Evans 31046; Harvard University, Library, *A Catalogue of the Maps and Charts,* p. 198; Douglas C. McMurtrie, *Eighteenth Century North Carolina Imprints,* pp. 185–86, no. D34.

Locations DLC, MH, PPAmP.

591 [before 1800?]

Description In oval under eagle and shield at upper left: A MAP / OF / CAPE FEAR RIVER AND ITS VICINITY / FROM THE / FRYING PAN SHOALS TO WILMINGTON / BY ACTUAL SURVEY / ADDRESSED TO THE COMMISSIONERS OF NAVIGATION / OF / PORT WILMINGTON / BY PRICE & STROTHER. Below oval:

W. BARKER, SCULP. PHILADA. In bottom neat line at center: COPYRIGHT SECURED ACCORDING TO LAW. This is a detailed chart, by Jonathan Price and John Strother, of the river approach to Wilmington, with soundings up the river. Bearings are given to enter the river at its mouth and at the NEW INLET. This INLET appeared in a recutting on a chart in John Norman's *American Pilot,* Boston, 1794. Roads and settlements are shown, and also the soundings near Frying Pan Shoals.

Size 18⅞″ x 14″.   *Scale* 1″ = 2½ miles.

Reference Harvard University Library, *A Catalogue of the Maps and Charts,* p. 198.

Location MH.

SOUTH CAROLINA

[1761?]   see Map 575.

592 [1777]

Description   In rectangle at upper right corner: A PLAN / OF THE / ATTACK / OF / FORT SULIVAN / THE KEY OF / CHARLES TOWN / IN / SOUTH CAROLINA / ON THE 28TH OF JUNE 1776 / BY / HIS MAJESTY'S SQUADRON / COMMANDED BY SIR PETER PARKER / BY AN OFFICER ON THE SPOT. Below letterpress at bottom center: PHILADELPHIA: PRINTED FOR DANIEL HUMPHREYS, BY STYNER AND CIST, IN SECOND-STREET, SIX DOORS ABOVE ARCH-STREET. [PRICE ONE DOLLAR.] Advertisements in the (Philadelphia) *Pennsylvania Gazette* for June 11, 1777, and the (Philadelphia) *Pennsylvania Journal,* July 9, 1777, refer to the American map as "Just printed," and "Engraved from the original printed in London." Below the map proper, which is enclosed by a neat line, is an account of the battle entitled: THE FOLLOWING DESCRIPTION OF THE ATTACK OF FORT SULIVAN, WAS RECEIVED IN A LETTER FROM SIR PETER PARKER TO MR. STEPHENS, SECRETARY OF THE ADMIRALTY. This letter press section measures 6¼" x 14" including the title and bottom type ornaments but not the bottom imprint. The map is copied from one with the same title bearing the following imprint below the bottom neat line: "London. Printed for Robt. Sayer & Jno. Bennett, Map & Sea Chartsellers, No. 53 Fleet Street as the Act directs. 7th. Septr. 1776." The Daniel Humphreys map is copied from the Sayer and Bennett engraving with apparently no additional information. "Hetheral Pt." (along the shore of Christ Church Parish) on the English map becomes HETHERALS PT. on the American copy. The note at the northeastern tip of Sulivan's Island reads: 1500 PROVINCIALS / INTRENCH'D on the American map while on the English the word Provincials is abbreviated and the "a" elided.

Size   12⅜" x 15¹¹⁄₁₆".   *Scale*   1" = ⅓ mile.

Published   Separately.

Reference   Randolph G. Adams, "The Cartography of the British Attack," p. 43.

Locations   CSmH, DLC, MiU-C.

593 [1785]

Description   Across bottom below neat line:

A SKETCH OF CHARLESTON HARBOUR SHOWING THE DISPOSITION OF THE BRITISH FLEET UNDER THE COMMAND OF / VICE ADML. MARIOT ARBUTHNOT UPON THE ATTACK ON FORT MOULTRIE ON SULIVAN ISLAND IN 1780. Below neat line at right corner: ABERNETHIE SCULPT CHARLESTON. The various defense works of the CHARLESTOWN HARBOUR area are shown, as well as many topographical features. No soundings are given but the shoals and islands are outlined. The engraver is Thomas Abernethie.

Size   6⅞" x 11⅝".   *Scale*   1" = ⅔ nautical mile.

Published in David Ramsay, *The History of the Revolution,* 2, opp. 59.

594 [1785]   *State* I (see also Map 595)

Description   In decorated oval at lower center: A SKETCH / OF THE OPERATIONS BEFORE / CHARLESTON / THE CAPITAL OF / SOUTH CAROLINA / 1780. In lower right corner: ABERNETHIE SCULPT. CHARLESTON. This is a plan of the Town, its defences, and the British lines during the attack. A table of references is given at the lower left. Among the points identified are the: REDOUBTS APPROATCHES [SIC] & BATTERIES OF THE / BRITISH ARMY . . .

Size   14⅛" x 11¼".   *Scale*   1" = c. ⅕ statute miles.

Published in David Ramsay, *The History of the Revolution,* 2, opp. 52.

595 [1785?]   *State* II (see also Map 594)

Description   A correction has been made in the table of lettered references at the lower left: APPROACHES now appears instead of "approatches," with signs of the erasure.

Published in David Ramsay, *The History of the Revolution,* 2, opp. 42 (MWA copy); separately.

Location   MWA (2 cop. as separates).

596 [1785]

Description   In decorated oval at right: A SKETCH / OF THE SITUATION, & STATIONS / OF THE BRITISH VESSELS, UNDER / THE COMMAND OF, / SIR PETER PARKER / ON THE ATTACK UPON / FORT MOULTRIE / ON SULIVAN ISLAND / JUNE 28TH.

1776. Below bottom neat line at right: ABER-
NETHIE SCULPT. CHARLESTON. Shallow areas are
indicated by contour lines. Each British war-
ship is indicated by name.

Size 6⁷⁄₁₆″ x 11⁵⁄₁₆″.   *Scale* None (1″ =
c. ⅓ mile).

Published in David Ramsay, *The History of
the Revolution, 1,* opp. 144.

Reference Randolph G. Adams, "The Cartography of the British Attack," p. 43.

597 [1785]

Description At lower left: SOUTH-CAROLINA /
AND / PARTS ADJACENT; / SHEWING / THE MOVE-
MENTS OF THE / AMERICAN / AND / BRITISH /
ARMIES. The more important rivers and streams
are indicated but few other topographical features. The sites of all the more important military actions are noted as well as the related
towns and settlements. The TUGOOLO R. is shown
thus. Longitude is indicated from the meridian
of Charleston. The various advances, routes, and
retreats are noted by means of dotted lines.
This is probably the map referred to in Evans
19847. The Evans Microprint entry states:
"From an advertisement probably for separates
of the map in [Evans] 19211 [i. e. David Ramsay,
The History of the Revolution]."

Size 19⅜″ x 22¹¹⁄₁₆″.   *Scale* 1″ = 16
common miles.

Published in David Ramsay, *The History of
the Revolution, 2,* opp. [1].

598 [1790]

Description At upper left: CHART / OF / THE
COAST OF AMERICA / FROM / CAPE FEAR TO
HELENS / SOUND. Below title: BOSTON PUBLISHED
AND SOLD BY M CLARK. The degree and minute
marks outside the left marginal degree line are
upside down. The chart bears an engraved inscription, signed by Osgood Carleton when sold
singly, stating that it was examined and compared with the best charts and found accurate.
In the Library of Congress copy of the [Chart],
this and Map 577 are pasted together.

Size 23¹¹⁄₁₆″ x 15″.   *Scale* None (1″ =
c. 5 miles).

Published in Matthew Clark, [*A Complete
Chart*], no. 14.

599 [1790]

Description At lower center: PLAN OF THE
CITY OF CHARLESTON, SOUTH CAROLINA. / FROM A
SURVEY TAKEN BY E. PETRIE *1788.* In lower right
corner: ABERNETHIE SCUT. This is a reduced
copy of the Edmund Petrie's "Ichnography of

Charleston, South-Carolina, At the Request of
Adam Tunno, Esq. for the use of the Phoenix
Fire-Company of London, taken from actual survey, 2d August 1788 by Edmund Petrie. [Lon-
don] 1790." The list of 77 references to streets
in Charleston given on the London printed
map has now been reduced to 62 and these are
included on the list of "References" given on
the page opposite. HARLESTON appears thus at
the upper right as in the other map as does also
the FAEDERAL GREEN at the lower right. The
north end of Church Street is now shown extended on filled-in ground and "O," the "New
Market," has been added between Church and
Meeting streets.

Size 7⅝″ x 9⅞″.   *Scale* None (1″ = c.
700 feet).

Published in Jacob Milligan, *The Charleston
Directory,* front.

References Charleston Library Society, *Catalogue of the Books,* no. 4507; Helen G. McCormack, "A Catalogue of Maps of Charleston,"
no. 27.

[1790] see Map 609.

600 [1791] *State* I (see also Map 607; III
post-1799, see Map 607, Description)

Description At upper left: A CHART / OF /
SOUTH CAROLINA / AND / GEORGIA. The coastal
area is shown from JAMES / ISLD to ST JOHNS R.
There is a marginal degree line on two sides
and bottom only.

Size 20⅜″ x 16½″.   *Scale* None (1″ =
c. 10 miles).

Inset At lower right: A CHART / OF THE /
BAR AND HARBOUR / OF / CHARLES TOWN. SHULES
[sic] / FOLLY is given. Size: 10″ x 11⅝″. Scale:
None (1″ = c. 3½ miles).

Published in John Norman, *The American
Pilot,* 1791, no. 3; ibid., 1792, no. 4; William
Norman, *The American Pilot,* 1794, no. 4.

601 1795 *State* I (II and III post-1799, see
below, Description)

Description At lower left: THE STATE OF /
SOUTH CAROLINA: / FROM THE BEST AUTHORITIES,
/ BY / SAMUEL LEWIS. *1795.* Beneath title: W.
BARKER SCULP.; beneath lower neat line: EN-
GRAVED FOR CAREY'S AMERICAN EDITION OF
GUTHRIE'S GEOGRAPHY IMPROVED. This is a topographical map of the State showing also the
eight precincts, their names and boundaries, and
the principal towns and roads. The latitude
measurements are laid down to a scale about 15
percent larger than the longitude, thus elon-
gating the map north and south. The longitude

of the state boundary corner near the Peedee River is shown about 79° 20' W., instead of about 79° 40' W. The northwest Georgia boundary is confused and out of shape as the north branch of the Tugaloo (modern Chattooga River) is swung over where the South Branch (modern Tallulah River) runs. This changes the northwest corner of the state, carrying the extreme westernmost point ½° further west. Washington Precinct is outlined but not named. Pinkney is not shown. The map appears in the 1800 edition of *Carey's General Atlas* with the number "38" added at upper right corner. It appears again in *Carey's General Atlas*, 1814, with the inscription below bottom neat line removed and number "19" now given at upper right.

Size 17⅜" x 15¼". *Scale* 1" = 15½ American miles (69½ to a degree).

Published in Mathew Carey, *Carey's American Atlas*, no. 15; idem, *Carey's General Atlas*, no. 38; idem, *The General Atlas for Carey's Edition of Guthrie's Geography Improved*, no. 38.

602 [1795] *State* I (II post-1799, see below, Description)

Description At lower left: SOUTH CAROLINA. The state is divided into nine districts. The Ninety-six and Cheraw districts are outlined but not named. Some counties are shown. TUGELO is given for the Tugaloo River. This map was re-issued in Scott's *The New and Universal Gazetteer, 4*. No geographical additions are noted. This second state may be identified by the two short straight lines which the retoucher has added to strengthen each of the small circles locating the following towns: "Pinkneyville," "Chatham," "Greenville," "Granby," and "George T."

Size 6⅛" x 7¼". *Scale* 1" = 40 miles.

Published in Joseph Scott, *An Atlas of the United States*, no. 15; idem, *The United States Gazetteer*, opp. "South-Carolina." Reproduced in Joseph Scott, *Atlas of the United States 1795–1800*, [no. 17].

603 [1796] *State* I (II post-1799, see below, Description)

Description At lower left: SOUTH CAROLINA. Beneath scale: ENGRAVED BY DOOLITTLE NEW-HAVEN. Some topographical features are shown, especially rivers and streams. Although only one scale is shown, the map is actually drawn to a larger north and south scale than for east and west distances. This gives a peculiar shape to the State. This map was republished in 1801 edition of *Carey's American Pocket Atlas* with

the addition of important roads. No roads are shown on the first state, nor do the following place names appear: "Lancaster," "Greenville" above Black Creek, "Greenville" below Reedy River, "Washington," "Union," "Chester," "Pinckneyville," and "York.'

Size 5¹¹⁄₁₆" x 7½". *Scale* 1" = 45 American miles.

Published in Mathew Carey, *Carey's American Pocket Atlas*, foll. p. 110.

604 [1796]

Description [Plan of the City.] The only known copy of the *Directory* is lacking the map. The engraver may be W. Ralph of Philadelphia. The title is taken from the title page of the *Directory*.

Size Unknown. *Scale* Unknown.

Published in *Clarke's Charleston Directory with Large and Elegant Plan of the City Engraved by Ralph*.

Reference Dorothea N. Spear, *Bibliography of American Directories*, p. 81.

605 1796

Description In oval at lower left: THE STATE OF / SOUTH CAROLINA. / FROM THE BEST AUTHORITIES. / *1796*; in oval below title: TANNER SC.; beneath bottom neat line: PUBLISHED BY JOHN REID NEW YORK. This map is almost exactly the same as Map 601. The courses of the boundary rivers in the northwest corner are again shown incorrectly. The misnamed north branch of the TUGELOO [sic] (modern Chatooga River) is shown about where the south branch (modern Tallulah River) should be, thus changing the contour of the northwest corner of the state and extending the state line about ½° further west than it should be.

Size 15⅛" x 17". *Scale* 1" = 16 American miles.

Published in John Reid, *The American Atlas*, [1796?], no. 17; ibid., 1796, no. 17; William Winterbotham, [*Atlas*]. Reproduced in U.S. Bureau of the Census, *Heads of Families at the first Census South Carolina*, front.

606 [1796]

Description At lower right: PLAN / OF THE SIEGE OF / CHARLESTOWN / IN / SOUTH CAROLINA; beneath title: TANNER, SC.; below neat line at center: PUBLISHED BY C. SMITH, NEW YORK. This is a topographical plan of the Charleston area. Military fortifications are indicated including the three parallels used by the British forces in their successful attack of 1780. This is a copy of the map in Charles Stedman's *The History of the Origin, Progress, and Termination of the American War.*

Size 9⅞" x 11½". *Scale* 1" = 5 furlongs.

Published in *The Monthly Military Repository, 1,* foll. 300; Charles Smith, *The American War,* opp. p. 92.

[1796]   see Map 585.

607 [1798]   *State* II (see also Map 600; III post-1799, see below, Description)

Description   The worn plate has been recut in many places. "Shules Folly" in the inset has been corrected to SHUTES. This chart was republished in William Norman's *American Pilot* of 1803. In this third state more recutting has been done to the plate and five islands in "Altamaha In" are fully shaded.

Published in William Norman, *The American Pilot,* 1798, no. 3.

608   1799

Description   In oval at lower left: THE STATE OF / SOUTH CAROLINA / FROM THE BEST AUTHORITIES / *1799*. Below bottom neat line at center: ENGRAVED FOR PAYNE'S GEOGRAPHY PUBLISH'D BY I LOW NEW YORK. At right SCOLES SC. This is copied from either Map 601 or Map 605. TUGELLOO R. appears thus.

Size 7¼" x 8⁵⁄₁₆". *Scale* 1" = 35 miles.

Published in John Payne, *A New and Complete Universal Geography, 4,* opp. 429.

GEORGIA

609 [1790]

Description In oval at lower right: CHART / OF THE / COAST OF AMERICA / FROM / ST HELLENS SOUND / ST JOHNS RIVER; in oval beneath title: BOSTON PUBLISHED & SOLD BY MATTHEW CLARK; at upper left corner: NO. *16*. No soundings are given. The spelling ST. HELENA SOUND is used on the CHART itself differing from the title. It has an engraved inscription, which was signed by Osgood Carleton when sold singly, stating that it was examined and compared with the best charts and found accurate. In the Library of Congress copy of the [*Chart*] it is pasted to Map 625 and is placed fifteenth in order despite its NO. *16* at the upper left.

Size 24⅞" x 16".   *Scale* None (1" = c. 5 miles).

Published in Matthew Clark, [*A Complete Chart*], no. 15 (marked "16").

[1791] see Map 600.

610 [c. 1795]

Description [Charts of the coast of Georgia and South Carolina.] Parker, Hopkinson, and Meers, surveyors, began surveys of the coasts of Georgia and South Carolina but were stopped by the loss of their sloop and boats together with their instruments. A subscription list was begun to provide funds to finish the project and one sheet of this list carrying the signatures of George Washington and Alexander Hamilton is now in the John Carter Brown Library at Brown University. Thus far no other information concerning any further surveys or any resulting printed maps has been discovered.

Size Unknown.   *Scale* Unknown.

Published Separately(?).

Location No copy located.

611 [1795] *State* I (II post-1799, see below, Description)

Description In oval at upper right: GEORGIA, / FROM THE LATEST / AUTHORITIES. In oval beneath title: W. BARKER. SCULP. Beneath oval: ENGRAVED FOR CAREY'S AMERICAN EDITION OF GUTHRIE'S GEOGRAPHY. This map, covering an area extending from the Atlantic Seaboard to the Mississippi River, shows some topographical features, particularly in the eastern section. Counties are named and their boundaries given. A number of Creek and Cherokee towns are noted. Several trading paths to the interior are indicated. Mathew Carey advertised a map of Georgia for sale in the (Philadelphia) *Gazette of the United States,* May 8, 1794, and this may be an earlier publication of the same map. State II appears in the 1800 edition *Carey's General Atlas* with the number "39" added at the upper left corner.

Size 8⅞" x 15½".   *Scale* 1" = c. 50 miles.

Published in Mathew Carey, *Carey's American Atlas,* no. 16; idem, *Carey's General Atlas,* no. 39; idem, *The General Atlas for Carey's Edition of Guthrie's Geography Improved,* no. 39. Reproduced in Kenneth Coleman, *The American Revolution in Georgia,* p. [182].

612 [1795]

Description At upper right: GEORGIA. A few topographical features are noted. Major settlements are given as well as a number of Indian towns. ALABAMA and BRUNSWIC towns are shown thus.

Size 6¼" x 7½".   *Scale* 1" = 115 miles.

Published in Joseph Scott, *An Atlas of the United States,* no. 16; idem, *The New and Universal Gazetteer,* 2; idem, *The United States Gazetteer,* opp. "Georgia." Reproduced in Joseph Scott, *Atlas of the United States 1795–1800,* [no. 6].

613 [1796] *State* I (II post-1799, see below, Description)

Description At upper right: GEORGIA. Below bottom neat line at right: W. BARKER SC. Some topographical features are noted, many mountains being indicated in the north and west. No roads are shown. OKENFONOKO SWAMP appears thus. This map was republished in the 1801 edition of *Carey's American Pocket Atlas* with the addition of important roads and a number of place names, including: "Elberton," north of the Broad River, and the "Iberville R."

Size 5⅞" x 7⅝".   *Scale* 1" = 95 miles.

Published in Mathew Carey, *Carey's American Pocket Atlas,* foll. p. 114.

614 [1796]

Description At upper right: A MAP OF / GEORGIA, / ALSO THE TWO / FLORIDAS, / FROM THE BEST / AUTHORITIES; below title: DOOLITTLE SCULP:; above top neat line: ENGRAVED FOR MORSE'S UNIVERSAL GEOGRAPHY. PUBLISHED BY THOMAS & ANDREWS. BOSTON. TIEGOLOO R and EOKENFONOOKA SWAMP appear thus, LA BALIGE is given for Balise, PASCACOLA R for Pascagoula, ST. JOHOHNS RIVER for St. John's in Florida, and NICKAJAAK, a Cherokee village. Some topographical features are noted. Main trading paths are indicated in the west. The counties are named and their boundaries drawn. Mobile, Pensacola, and New Orleans are located.

Size 7⅝" x 12⅛".   *Scale* 1" = 65 miles.

Published in Jedidiah Morse, *The American Universal Geography,* 3d ed., *1,* opp. 693.

615 [1796]   *State* I (see also Map 616)

Description In oval at upper right: GEORGIA, / FROM THE LATEST / AUTHORITIES; in oval below title: B. TANNER, SCULPT. N. Y.; beneath bottom neat line: PUBLISHED BY J. REID L. WAYLAND & C. SMITH. This map is copied from Map 611. The Tugaloo River is again given as the TONGALOO and the Okefenokee Swamp as AKENFONOGO.

Size 8¾" x 15¼".   *Scale* 1" = c. 50 miles.

Published in William Winterbotham, [*Atlas*].

616 [1796]   *State* II (see also Map 615)

Description The imprint is now changed to: PUBLISHED BY J. REID NEW YORK.

Published in John Reid, *The American Atlas,* [1796?], no. 18; ibid., 1796, no. 18.

617 [1796]

Description At lower left: PLAN / OF THE SIEGE OF / SAVANNAH; below bottom neat line at right: ST. MEMIN SCULP.; at upper right corner: PL. V; below bottom neat line at center: PUBLISHED BY C. SMITH NEW YORK. The town plan

and outlying fortifications are shown as well as the American and French positions. It was engraved by Charles B. J. F. de Saint-Mémin. This is a reduced copy of the similar map in Charles Stedman's, *The History of the Origin, Progress, and Termination of the American War.*

Size 8½" x 9⅛".   *Scale* 1" = 200 yards.

Published in *The Monthly Military Repository,* opp, p. 289; Charles Smith, *The American War,* opp. p. 83.

618 [1797]

Description At lower right: A CORRECT MAP OF THE / GEORGIA / WESTERN TERRITORY; below bottom neat line at right: CALLENDER SC.; at center: ENGRAVED FOR MORSE'S AMERICAN GAZETTEER. A few topographical features are indicated. Land holdings are shown including those of the Tennessee and Georgia companies. Mobile Bay is shown extending north of 31° latitude. On the verso of the title page of the *Gazetteer* is the following note: "The Map of the GEORGIA WESTERN TERRITORY, not being received in season to accompany some of the copies first delivered; those who may receive the Work without it, may have a copy of the Map, after the first of July next, by calling on Mr. EBENEZER LARKIN, Cornhill, Boston." The engraver is probably Benjamin Callender.

Size 7¼" x 6⅟₁₆".   *Scale* 1" = 70 miles.

Published in Jedidiah Morse, *The American Gazetteer,* opp. "Georgia Western Territory"; idem, *Description of the Georgia Western Territory,* front.

619 1799

Description In oval at upper right: GEORGIA / FROM THE LATEST / AUTHORITIES / *1799;* in oval below title: I SCOLES, SC.; below bottom neat line: ENGRAVED FOR PAYNE'S GEOGRAPHY PUBLISH'D BY I LOW, NEW YORK. This is a re-engraving of Maps 611 and 615. TONGALOO still appears for the Tugaloo River.

Size 8" x 15⅛".   *Scale* 1" = c. 50 miles.

Published in John Payne, *A New and Complete Universal Geography, 4,* opp. 438.

FLORIDA

620 [1742]

Description In rectangle across right end: A PLAN OF THE HARBOUR OF ST AUGUSTINE AND THE / ADJACENT PARTS IN FLORIDA REPRESENTING THE FIELD OF / ACTION WITH THE DISPOSITION OF THE FORCES BEFORE THAT / CASTLE IN THE EXPEDITION UNDER GENERAL OGLETHORPE IN *1740.* In lower left corner: P HARRISON DELT.; in lower right corner of lower map rectangle: M SARRAZIN SCULP.; in lower right corner of title rectangle: P *98.* Two separate maps are given under one title which reads perpendicularly to the rest of the map. The upper map is a rectangle measuring 3¾" x 7¾", showing a 70 mile strip of the coast of Florida and the St. Johns River from east of St. Augustine to its mouth. This is drawn to the scale of nine miles to an inch. The lower map, 2⅞" x 7¾", shows the close environs of the City and harbor and the disposition of General Oglethorpe's forces. Seventeen numbered references to the units of the forces appear on the lower map with a table in the upper left corner of the upper map explaining them. A further description of the map is given on p. 98 of the *Report.*

Size 6⅝" x 9⅜". *Scales* 1" = 9 miles, and 1" = 3¾ miles.

Published in South Carolina, *The Report of the Committee, of both Houses of Assembly.*

621 [1774]

Description At right center: PART OF THE PROVINCE OF EAST FLORIDA. Beneath dedication cartouche: B ROMANS INV. DELIN: & IN AERE INCIDIT. This is one of the "two whole sheet maps" which were listed on the title page of the Bernard Romans' *A Concise Natural History,* and which compose his famous chart of the East and West Florida coast. Each of the two "maps" is enclosed in separate neat lines. In this, the upper section, the Atlantic coast is shown from the RIVER ST MARY south to MUSKETO INLET, and the Gulf coast, within the same range of latitude, is shown west, past the mouth of the Mississippi River, to BAY COS. Many soundings are given and a very detailed study of the coastline and the immediate interior is presented. A river, probably representing the Sabine, extends over the neat line to the left. This detail

134

is inaccurate and was taken by Romans from French manuscript sources. A dedication: TO THE / MARINE SOCIETY / OF THE CITY OF NEW YORK IN THE / PROVINCE OF NEW. YORK IN NORTH AMERICA / THIS CHART IS HUMBLY INSCRIBED BY THEIR MOST OBEDT / SERVANT B ROMANS, is given in an elaborate cartouche at the lower left. Although his name appears under this cartouche as B ROMANS INV. DELIN: & IN AERE INCIDIT, and under one of the dedications on Map 622 (the lower section of the chart) as "sculpt," in all probability he engraved only the cartouches, and even this is not absolutely proven. The engraving of the "map" plates themselves was done by Paul Revere and Abel Buell with perhaps the aid of other, so far unknown, engravers. The printing was probably done by James Rivington of New York.

Bernard Romans issued the following broadside advertisement prior to publication of the "maps": *Philadelphia, August 5, 1773. Proposals for printing by subscription, Three Very Elegant and Large Maps of the Navigation, to, and in, the new ceded Countries.* For further details concerning the engraving and printing of the "map" see the studies of Clarence S. Brigham and Lawrence C. Wroth cited below, under *References.*

Size 24½" x 87". *Scale* 1" = 7 British statute miles.

Insets [a] At upper right: VIEW OF FORT ST MARKS, AT APALACHE SEEN FROM THE SOUTHWARD. A SQUALL RISING OVER THE LAND. Size: 4⅜" x 11".

[b] At upper right corner: VIEW OF THE ENTRANCE OF ST MARY'S RIVER. Size: 2½" x 12½".

Published with Bernard Romans, *A Concise Natural History of East and West Florida.* Reproduced by Philip L. Phillips, *Notes on the Life and Works of Bernard Romans,* in accompanying folder.

References Clarence S. Brigham, *Paul Revere's Engravings,* pp. [91]–101; Evans 14441; Lawrence C. Wroth, *Abel Buell of Connecticut,* pp. 55–56; idem, *Abel Buell,* rev. ed., pp. 66–71; idem, "Source Materials of Florida History," pp. 40–41; see also reproduced above, under *Published.*

Locations DLC, MiU-C (⅔ section), PHi.

622 1774

Description At upper center: PART OF THE PROVINCE OF EAST FLORIDA. Beneath ornate center dedication cartouche: B. ROMANS INVT ET SCULPT *1774*. This is the second of the "two whole sheet maps" listed on the title page of Bernard Romans' *A Concise Natural History*, and which compose his famous chart of the East and West Florida coast. As on the upper portion (See Map 621), the coastline is shown in much detail and with many soundings. The area included comprises the Florida peninsula from the R AMAXURA north of SPIRITO SANTO / OR / TAMPE BAY on the west coast, and MOUNT TUCKER just north of CAPE CANAVERAL on the east, the Bahamas, and part of the ISLAND OF CUBA. A number of profiles of the coastline of Cuba are given on the interior of the Island. The neat line is broken at the lower left by the smaller dedication and at the left bottom by part of the Cuban south shore.

Two dedications appear on this portion of the larger chart. At the upper center in an ornate cartouche: TO ALL COMMANDERS OF VESSELS ROUND THE GLOBE, / THIS CHART IS RESPECTFULLY DEDICATED; BY THEIR / VERY HUMBLE SERVANT B ROMANS. Under this appears: B. ROMANS INVT ET SCULPT *1774*. As noted in the Description of Map 621 this is usually taken to signify that Romans probably engraved only the dedications themselves. The charts themselves were engraved by Paul Revere and Abel Buell with the aid of other, so far unknown, engravers. They were probably printed by James Rivington of New York. For information concerning the engraving and printing of the chart see the studies of Clarence S. Brigham and Lawrence C. Wroth cited in References, Map 621. A second dedication is given at the lower left: TO THE HONBLE. / THE PLANTERS / IN JAMAICA / AND ALL MARCHANTS CONCERNED IN THE / TRADE OF THAT ISLAND BEING THE / TWO SOCIETIES CHIEFLY INTERESTED / IN THE NAVIGATION HEREIN EXPLAINED / THIS CHART IS MOST RESPECTFULLY / DEDICATED BY THEIR VERY HBLE SERVT. / B ROMANS.

Size 57¾" x 66½". *Scale* 1" = 8 British statute miles.

Published with Bernard Romans, *A Concise Natural History of East and West Florida*. Reproduced in Philip L. Phillips, *Notes on the Life and Works of Bernard Romans*, in accompanying folder.

References see Map 621.

Locations DLC, PHi.

623 [1775]

Description Below bottom neat line at center: ENTRANCES OF TAMPA BAY. Above top neat line at left: PAGE LXXVIIII OF THE APPENDIX.

Soundings and outlines of shoals are noted. FISHERMANS PT: is shown at the upper left.

Size 3⅝" x 6¹⁄₁₆". *Scale* 1" = 3⅓ "geometric" miles.

Published in Bernard Romans, *A Concise Natural History of East and West Florida*. Reproduced, ibid., 1962.

624 [1775]

Description Below bottom neat line: PENSACOLA BAR. Above top neat line at left: PAGE LXXXIV OF THE APPENDIX. The outlines of the islands and lagoons extend beyond the neat lines in several cases. Soundings and outlines of the shoals are given.

Size 4" x 5⅞". *Scale* 1" = 2 geometric miles.

Published in Bernard Romans, *A Concise Natural History of East and West Florida*. Reproduced, ibid., 1962.

625 [1790]

Description In oval at lower left: CHART / OF THE / COAST OF AMERICA / FROM THE / ND OF ST AUGUSTIN / TO / AYES INLET. In oval below title: BOSTON PUBLISHED & SOLD BY MATTHEW CLARK. It bears an engraved inscription, signed by Osgood Carleton when sold singly, stating that it was examined and compared with the best charts and found accurate. AYS INLET is given on the chart differing from the spelling in the title. In the Library of Congress copy of the [*Chart*] it is pasted to Map 609 and placed sixteenth in order.

Size 23⅞" x 17⅞". *Scale* None (1" = c. 6 miles).

Published in Matthew Clark, [*A Complete Chart*], [no. 16].

626 [1790]

Description In oval at left: CHART / OF THE / COAST OF AMERICA / THRO' THE / GULPH / OF / FLORIDA. In oval below title: BOSTON PUBLISHED & SOLD BY MATTHEW CLARK. In upper left hand corner: NO. *17*. It bears an engraved inscription, signed by Osgood Carleton when sold singly, stating that it was examined and compared with the best charts and found accurate. The coast is shown from LEACH SHOAL to LLOYDS LAKE.

Size 23⅛" x 16¼". *Scale* None (1" = c. 8 miles).

Published in Matthew Clark, [*A Complete Chart*], no. 17.

627 [1790]

Description In oval at left: CHART / OF THE

/ COAST OF AMERICA / THROUGH THE / GULPH OF FLORIDA / TO THE ENTRANCE OF THE / GULPH OF MEXICO. In oval below title: BOSTON PUBLISHED & SOLD BY MATTHEW CLARK. In upper right hand corner: NO *18*. The Florida Keys are shown to 82° West Longitude and also the section of the coast of Cuba opposite. There is no engraved certification on this chart.

Size 16¼" x 24¼". *Scale* None (1" = c. 8 miles).

Published in Matthew Clark, [*A Complete Chart*], no. 18.

628 [1791]

Description In ornate cartouche at lower left corner: A MAP / OF THE COAST / OF / EAST FLORIDA / FROM THE RIVER ST. / JOHN SOUTHWARD / NEAR TO CAPE / CANAVERAL. No soundings are given but shoals are indicated. The CITY OF / ST AUGUSTINE is noted but no exact site is marked. This map was copied and used in the London, 1792, edition of the *Travels*. There are several changes in this map. One is that the title has been modified slightly to read: ". . . Southward, to near Cape Canaveral."; another is that the "Town of / St. Augustine" has been located by a miniature town plan.

Size 9¾" x 5¾". *Scale* None (1" = c. 10 miles).

Published in William Bartram, *Travels through North & South Carolina, Georgia, East & West Florida*, opp. p. 1. Reproduced in idem, *The Travels of William Bartram: Naturalist's Edition*, Francis Harper, ed., opp. p. 1.

629 1795

Description Above top neat line: THE PENINSULA AND GULF OF FLORIDA OR NEW BAHAMA CHANNEL WITH THE BAHAMA ISLANDS BY THOS. JEFFERYS GEOGRAPHER TO HIS MAJESTY. Below bottom neat line: LONDON PUBLISHED BY LAURIE & WHITTIE MAY *12*TH *1794* BOSTON REPUBLISHED BY W. NORMAN SEPR. *1795* AND SOLD AT HIS SHOP N. *75*. NEWBURY STREET. Many soundings are given along the Florida coast and among the Bahamas. Some topographical details are noted on the Florida Peninsula. Several roads and trails are shown leading to ST AUGUSTINE. There is a printed certification by Osgood Carleton at the upper right.

Size 18⅜" x 24⅜". *Scale* None (1" = c. 10 miles).

Published in [William Norman, *A Pilot for the West Indies*], no. 2.

[1796] see Map 614.

LOUISIANA

630 [c. 1763]

Description In cartouche at upper right corner: A GENERAL CHART / OF ALL THE COAST OF THE / PROVINCE OF / LOUISIANA. / THE BAYS OF ASCENSION & MOBILLE [SiC] / PENSACOLA AND ST. JOSEPH; / WITH THE RIVERS / MISSISIPI AND APALACHY, / IN THE GULPH OF / MEXICO. In lower left corner: PHILADELPHIA PUBLISHED BY MATHEW [sic] CLARKSON. Below dedication cartouche at left: HENRY DAWKINS SCULPT. This chart of the Gulf Coast was advertised by Matthew Clarkson in the (Philadelphia) *Pennsylvania Gazette*, July 7, 1763, as: ". . . Published from a Draught taken by Order of the French King." Some soundings are given. The Mississippi River is shown as far north as ST. CATHARINE and NATCHEZ FORT. The following dedication is given in an ornate cartouche at the left: TO / HENRY BOUQUET ESQR / COLONEL IN HIS MAJESTY'S SERVICE / AND LIEUT. COLONEL / OF THE ROYAL AMERICAN REGIMENT / THIS CHART IS HUMBLY INSCRIB'D BY / HIS MOST OBEDT, HUMBLE SERVT, / THE EDITOR.

Size 14" x 40".   *Scale* 1" = 4 leagues.

Inset At upper center: THE EAST MOUTH / OF THE / MISSISIPI. FORT LA BALISE is shown. Size: 4⅞" x 6¼". Scale: 1" = 2½ British miles.

Published Separately.

Reference Mantle Fielding, *American Engravers*, no. 330.

Locations MiU-C, PHi.

631 [1784] *State* I (see also Maps 632–39)

Description In ornate cartouche at upper left: THIS MAP / OF / KENTUCKE, / DRAWN FROM ACTUAL OBSERVATIONS, / IS INSCRIBED WITH THE MOST PERFECT RESPECT, / TO THE HONORABLE THE CONGRESS OF THE / UNITED STATES OF AMERICA; AND / TO HIS EXCELLCY. GEORGE WASHINGTON / LATE COMMANDER IN CHIEF OF THEIR / ARMY. BY THEIR / HUMBLE SERVANT, / JOHN FILSON. Below bottom neat line at center: PHILADA. ENGRAV'D BY HENRY D. PURSELL & PRINTED BY T. ROOK FOR THE AUTHOR. This, one of the best known of early American printed maps, was apparently published to accompany John Filson's *Kentucke*. Some copies also were sold separately. There were numerous changes made during its printing, at least nine separate states have been thus far identified. Only this first state lacks the date, 1784. The eastern and western portions of the map are badly distorted but the center section is considered very accurate for the time. Three counties are shown: Fayette, Jefferson, and Lincoln. Some mountains are indicated and a portrayal is also given of Kentucky's intricate network of creeks and rivers; but many of these are shown in a wavy sketch form. Towns, forts, roads, trails, and salt springs are among the other features noted. An EXPLANATION identifying the symbols used is given at the right of the cartouche. The following appears at the top right: WHILE THIS WORK SHALL LIVE, / LET THIS INSCRIPTION REMAIN A MONUMENT OF / THE GRATITUDE OF THE AUTHOR, TO COLLS. DANL. BOON, / LEVI TODD, & JAS. HARROD, CAPTS. CHRISTR, GREENHOOP / INO. COWAN, & WM. KENNEDY ESQRS. OF KENTUCKE: FOR / THE DISTINGUISH'D ASSISTANCE, WITH WHICH THEY HAVE / HONOR'D HIM, IN ITS COMPOSITION: & A TESTIMONY, / THAT IT HAS RECIEVED [sic] THE APROBATION OF THOSE, / WHOM HE JUSTLY ESTEEMS, THE BEST QUALIFIED TO / JUDGE OF ITS MERIT. The map was published by Tenoor Rook. Notice of publication of the book and map was given in the (Philadelphia) *Pennsylvania Packet, and Daily Advertiser*, October 22, 1784. Both were republished with some modifications in France in 1785 and in England in 1793. These were only the beginning of many reproductions and reprintings down to the present day.

Size 19¾" x 17¹³⁄₁₆". *Scale* 1" = 10 miles.

Published with John Filson, *Kentucke*; separately. Reproduced in Charles F. Heartman, *Americana*, opp. p. 40; Willard R. Jillson, "Early Kentucky Maps (1673–1823)," opp. p. 32; idem, *Filson's Kentucke*; John Walton, *John Filson of Kentucky*, at end.

References Reuben T. Durrett, *John Filson*; Evans 18467; Lawrence Martin, "The Association of Filson's Map"; Philip L. Phillips, *The First Map of Kentucky*; Martin F. Schmidt, "Existing Copies of the 1784 Filson Map," pp. 55–57; Rogers C. B. Thruston, "Filson's History and Map of Kentucky," pp. 1–38; Robert W. G. Vail, *Old Frontier*, No. 694. See also reproductions above, under Published.

Location ICN.

632 1784 *State* II (see also Maps 631 and 633–39)

Description The date *1784* has been added to the imprint below the neat line.

Published with John Filson, *Kentucke*; separately. Reproduced in Philip L. Phillips, *The First Map of Kentucky*, opp. p. 22.

Location DLC.

633 c. 1784 *State* III (see also Maps 631, 632, and 634–39)

Description Thirteen houses are shown at LOUISVILLE, eleven at CLARKVILLE. Otherwise it is the same as State II.

Published with John Filson, *Kentucke*; separately.

Location ICN.

634 c. 1784 *State* IV (see also Maps 631–33 and 635–39)

Description The TOWN FORK of the ELKHORN has been extended through LEXINGTON. Four other minor stream additions or extensions have been made. The inscription in the lower left corner refers to the Carolina Line in 36° North Latitude instead of 36½° as in previous states.

Published with John Filson, *Kentucke*; separately.

Locations BM, PPRF.

635 c. 1784 *State* V (see also Maps 631–34 and 636–39)

Description The figures for latitude have been altered so the bottom of the map now starts at 36° 15′ North Latitude instead of 36°, and the Ohio River now meets the left border at 37° North Latitude. The William L. Clements Library copy is on paper watermarked "Pieter de Vries."

Published with John Filson, *Kentucke;* separately. Reproduced in John Filson, *Kentucke,* New York, [1962], foll. p. IX.

Locations Archivo Historico Nacional, Biblioteca Nacional, Madrid, CSmH, MiU-C, PHi, PRO, Private coll. of Martin F. Schmidt, Louisville, Kentucky.

636 c. 1784 *State* VI (see also Maps 631–35 and 637–39)

Description A small creek has been added on the Green River between Nolin and Sinking Creeks with CRAGG's Station located near its headwaters.

Published with John Filson, *Kentucke;* separately. Reproduced in Rogers C. B. Thruston, "Filson's History and Map of Kentucky," p. 21.

Locations KyLoF (The Pendleton copy), PP.

637 c. 1784 *State* VII (see also Maps 631–36, 638, and 639)

Description This shows the Sciota River extended but does not add Johnson's Fork. Little Barren Creek has not been extended.

Published with John Filson, *Kentucke;* separately.

Location OCHP.

638 c. 1784 *State* VIII (see also Maps 631–37 and 639)

Description The SCIOTHA [sic] R has been extended through the top marginal degree line and several branches added. JOHNSTON's FORK has been added to the MAIN LICKING branch of the Licking River.

Published with John Filson, *Kentucke;* separately. Reproduced in *The Month at Goodspeed's, 14* (1942–43), 212–13.

Reference See reproduction above, under Published.

Location ViU.

639 c. 1784 *State* IX (see also Maps 631–38)

Description An Indian trail has been added running south from the mouth of the SCIOTHA [sic] to the WARRIOR's PATH.

Published with John Filson, *Kentucke;* separately. Reproduced in Willard R. Jillson, *The Kentuckie Country,* at end; Reuben T. Durett, *John Filson,* opp. p. 28 (with some differences).

Locations KyLoF (The Hooe copy), MH, NHi, RPJCB.

640 1793

Description At upper left: A MAP OF / THE STATE OF / KENTUCKY, / DRAWN FROM THE / BEST AUTHORITIES. / *1793.* Above top neat line: ENGRAV'D FOR S. CAMPBELL'S EDITION OF IMLAY'S DESCRIPTION OF KENTUCKY. This map was based upon John Filson's (Map 631) and is mentioned on page 111 of this second volume of Imlay's *A Topographical Description,* actually a reprinting of Filson's *Kentucke* with a new title page. Substantially the same area is shown as in Filson's map but the original three counties have now grown to nine: Mason, Bourbon, Woodford, Jefferson, Nelson, Mercer, Lincoln, Fayette, and MADDISON [sic]. CINCINNATI appears and four forts along a road north from that point. A number of roads are shown leading to and from Lexington, one of them being a NEW & SHORT ROAD TO VIRGINIA.

Size 6¹⁄₁₆″ x 7⁵⁄₁₆″. *Scale* 1″ = 42½ British statute miles.

Published in Gilbert Imlay, *A Topographical Description, 2,* front.

Reference Willard R. Jillson, "Early Kentucky Maps," pp. 33–34.

641 [1794]

Description At upper right: A / MAP / OF / KENTUCKY / FROM / ACTUAL SURVEY / BY / ELIHU BARKER. At left center: ENTERED AS THE ACT DIRECTS. Below bottom neat line at far left: ENGRAVED FOR & SOLD BY MATHEW CAREY PHILADA. This is a detailed topographical map showing Kentucky and part of the NORTH WESTERN TERRITORY. Roads and trails are indicated and many interesting notes appear. The eastern Kentucky boundary is shown following the west fork of the Big Sandy River instead of the east fork. The neat line is broken for the Mississippi, Red, Ohio, and Miami rivers. The original manuscript copy of this map, drawn by Elihu Barker, together with the copyright, was advertised for sale by Oliver Barker on January 8, 1793, in the (Philadelphia) *Dunlap's American Daily Advertiser,* after the author's death. The map was advertised in the (Philadelphia) *Gazette of the United States,* April 29, 1794, as being just published. A reduced re-engraving was published by

Mathew Carey in 1795 (see Map 642). It was republished in London in 1797, appearing in Gilbert Imlay's *A Topographical Description,* 3d ed.

Size 17⅜" x 38¾". *Scale* 1" = 11 American miles.

Published Separately. Reproduced in Willard B. Jillson, "Early Kentucky Maps," opp. p. 36.

References Evans 26616; Willard R. Jillson, "Early Kentucky Maps," p. 35; idem, "Elihu Barker Map of Kentucky," pp. 322–23.

Locations DLC, MH, MiU-C.

642 [1795] *State* I (II post-1799, see below, Description)

Description In oval at upper right: KENTUCKY, / REDUCED FROM / ELIHU BARKER'S / LARGE MAP. In oval below title: W. BARKER SCULP. Under bottom neat line: ENGRAVED FOR CAREY'S AMERICAN EDITION OF GUTHRIE'S GEOGRAPHY IMPROVED. This map, taken from Map 641, has some topographical details, roads, and trails, and shows the names of counties and settlements. The eastern boundary here also follows the west fork of the Big Sandy River. The map appears in the 1800 edition of *Carey's General Atlas* with the number "40" added at the upper right corner.

Size 9⁵⁄₁₆" x 20". *Scale* 1" = 22 American miles.

Published in Mathew Carey, *Carey's American Atlas,* no. 17; idem, *Carey's General Atlas,* no. 40; idem, *The General Atlas for Carey's Edition of Guthrie's Geography Improved,* no. 40.

Reference Willard R. Jillson, "Early Kentucky Maps," p. 36.

643 [1795] *State* I (II post-1799, see below, Description)

Description At upper left: KENTUCKY. Some topographical features are noted, and settlement and county names are given. The northern half of the Virginia border follows the incorrect locations of Elihu Barker's map. Lincoln County is spelled LINOCLN. The plate was used again with many changes and additions in Scott's *The New and Universal Gazetteer, 3.* The S.W. TERRITORY below Kentucky has been changed to "Tennassee." Some names have been added, among them: "Ft. / Jefferson," "Trade / Water," "Big Blue Lick," "Cumberland Mts.," "Danville," Louisville," and "Boonsboro."

Size 6⅛" x 7⅜". *Scale* 1" = c. 57 miles.

Published in Joseph Scott, *An Atlas of the United States; idem, The United States Gazetteer,* opp. "Kentucky." Reproduced in Joseph Scott, *Atlas of the United States 1795–1800,* [no. 7].

Reference Willard R. Jillson, "Early Kentucky Maps," p. 37.

644 [1796] *State* I (II post-1799, see below, Description)

Description At upper left: KENTUCKEY [sic]. Below bottom neat line at right: W. BARKER SCULP. Some topographical features are noted. No roads or trails are shown. FORT WASHINGTON is indicated but not Cincinnati. The eastern boundary is incorrectly drawn along the west fork of the Big Sandy. The map was reissued in the 1801 edition of *Carey's American Pocket Atlas* with the addition of roads, trails, and a few place names, including: "Franklin" and "Shelbyville."

Size 5¾" x 7⅝". *Scale* 1" = c. 57 miles.

Published in Mathew Carey, *Carey's American Pocket Atlas,* opp. p. 99.

Reference Willard R. Jillson, "Early Kentucky Maps," p. 39.

645 [1796]

Description In oval at lower right: A / MAP / OF THE STATE OF / KENTUCKY / AND THE / TENNESSEE / GOVERNMENT / COMPILED FROM THE / BEST AUTHORITIES / BY / CYRUS HARRIS. In oval below title: ENGRAVED BY A DOOLITTLE. Above top neat line: PUBLISHED BY THOMAS & ANDREWS BOSTON. Some topographical features are shown and also a few roads, including a NEW & SHORT ROAD TO VIRGINIA. FORT JEFFERSON is indicated and inscribed above the top neat line. The SCIOTHA RIVER appears thus.

Size 7¾" x 11⅜". *Scale* 1" = c. 47 miles.

Published in Jedidiah Morse, *The American Universal Geography,* 3d ed., 1, opp. 633.

Reference Willard R. Jillson, "Early Kentucky Maps," pp. 39–40.

646 [1796] *State* I (see also Map 647)

Description In oval at lower left: MAP / OF THE STATE OF / KENTUCKY; / WITH THE / ADJOINING TERRITORIES. / 1795. In oval below title: A. ANDERSON SCULP. Beneath bottom neat line: PUBLISHED BY SMITH, REID AND WAYLAND. This is copied from John Russell's map of the same name, published in England in 1794. It is the best map produced of the area so far. Seven subdivisions of the original three counties are indicated. The pioneer roads or traces through the wilderness are shown. The mouth of the Ohio is shown about 36° 38′ N. by 89° 45′ W. instead of about 37° N. by 89° 12′ W. The eastern border of Kentucky is given as a straight north and south line from 38° 30′ N. to Great Sandy Creek along about an 82° 42′ West Longitude line.

Size 14⅞″ x 17⅜″.   *Scale* None (1″ = c. 20 miles).

Published in William Winterbotham, [*Atlas*]; some copies of John Reid, *The American Atlas*, 1796, no. 15.

647 [1796]   *State* II (see also Map 646)

Description Imprint now changed to: PUBLISHED BY JOHN REID, NEW-YORK.

Published in John Reid, *The American Atlas*, [1796?], no. 15; ibid, 1796, no. 15.

Reference Willard R. Jillson, "Early Kentucky Maps," p. 37.

648 [1796]

Description At upper left corner: PLAN OF / FRANKLINVILLE, / IN MASON COUNTY, / KENTUCKY. Below bottom neat line at right corner: TANNER, SC. This is a plan of the proposed town that was to be built at the junction of the NORTH BRANCH and the MIDDLE BRANCH of the Kentucky River. Each street has been given two names.

Size 6⅜″ x 4⁹⁄₁₆″.   *Scale* 1″ = 3200 feet.

Published in William Winterbotham, *An Historical View of the United States, 3,* opp. 145.

649 [1796]

Description Across upper center: PLAN OF LYSTRA, / IN NELSON-COUNTY; KENTUCKY. Below bottom neat line: TANNER, SC. This is a plan of the proposed town located on THE SOUTH CREEK OF THE ROLLING FORK of the Salt River. A short list of REMARKS or references is given at the lower left. The streets all have two names.

Size 6⅜″ x 4½″.   *Scale* 1″ = c. 800 feet.

Published in William Winterbotham, *An Historical View of the United States, 3,* opp. 144.

TENNESSEE

650 [1794] *State* I (see also Map 653; III post-1799, see Map 653, Description)

Description In rectangle at lower right: A / MAP OF THE / TENNASSEE [sic] GOVERNMENT / FORMERLY PART OF / NORTH CAROLINA / TAKEN CHIEFLY FROM SURVEYS BY / GENL, D. SMITH. & OTHERS. Below title in rectangle: J. T. SCOTT SCULP. Above top neat line: ENGRAVED FOR CAREYS AMERICAN EDITION OF GUTHRIES GEOGRAPHY IMPROVED. This is a topographical map that also shows settlements, trails, and roads. Indian boundaries are noted, and also Indian towns. A short table of REFERENCES is given at the lower left. Mathew Carey advertised as "just published" a "Map of the Tenesee [sic] government, north-west of the river Ohio, with a description of it in a pamphlet, [price] ⅞." in the (Philadelphia) *Independent Gazetteer*, January 29, 1794. He had published Daniel Smith's *A Short Description of the Tennassee* [sic] *Government to accompany and explain a Map of that Country* in 1793 but it was apparently sold without a map until this map was published and inserted. Evans collates Smith's pamphlet with a map but states that it had been inserted at a later time.

Size 9¾" x 20⅜".   *Scale* 1" = 22 miles.

Published in Mathew Carey, *Carey's American Atlas*, no. 18; idem, *The General Atlas for Carey's Edition of Guthrie's Geography Improved*, no. 41; separately. Reproduced by the U.S. Geological Survey in 1938 and issued by the U.S. Constitution Sesquicentennial Commission.

References Evans 26168; Willard R. Jillson, "Early Kentucky Maps," pp. 37–38; Robert W. G. Vail, *Old Frontier*, no. 955.

651 [1795] *State* I (II post-1799, see below, Description)

Description At upper center: S.W. TERRITORY. Some topographical features are shown, and also the MERO district, divided into three counties. NASKVILLE is given for Nashville. In the second state, published in Scott's *The New and Universal Gazetteer*, 4, the title has been changed to "Tennassee" [sic] but no geographical additions are noted.

Size 6⅛" x 7⅜".   *Scale* 1" = 66 miles.

Published in Joseph Scott, *An Atlas of the United States*; idem, *The United States Gazet-teer*, opp. "Territory South of the Ohio." Reproduced in Joseph Scott, *Atlas of the United States 1795–1800*, no. 3.

652 [1796] *State* I (II post-1799, see below, Description)

Description At upper center: TENNASSEE [sic]: / LATELY THE / S.WN: TERRITORY. Below bottom neat line at right: W. BARKER SCULP. Some topographical features are noted. The northeastern corner of Tennessee has been placed too far east. At the lower left the YASZOO R. and the TOMBIGBEE R. are given thus. State II was published in *Carey's American Pocket Atlas*, 1801, with the addition of important roads and lines at the degree figures between the margin lines.

Size 5⅞" x 7⅝".   *Scale* 1" = c. 70 miles.

Published in Mathew Carey, *Carey's American Pocket Atlas*, foll. p. 106.

653 [1796] *State* II (see also Map 650; III post-1799, see below, Description)

Description The title has been changed to read: A / MAP OF THE / TENNASSEE [sic] STATE / FORMERLY PART OF / NORTH CAROLINA . . . The names and boundaries of eight counties have been added. In 1796 Mathew Carey published Daniel Smith's *A Short Description of the State of the Tennassee* [sic] *to accompany and explain a Map of that Country*. Evans collates no map with this work though it apparently refers to this map. The American Antiquarian Society copy of this pamphlet contains a copy of State I. This map appears again in the 1800 edition of *Carey's General Atlas* with the numeral "41" added in the upper right corner.

Published in Mathew Carey, *Carey's General Atlas*, no. 41.

References Evans 31199; Willard R. Jillson, "Early Kentucky Maps," pp. 38–39.

654 [1796] *State* I (see also Map 655)

Description In oval at lower right: A MAP OF THE / TENNASSEE [sic] GOVERNMENT / FORMERLY PART OF / NORTH CAROLINA / FROM THE / LATEST SURVEYS. / *1795*. In oval below title: B. TANNER DELT. & SCULPT. Below bottom neat line: PUB-

142

LISHED BY J. REID, L. WAYLAND, & C. SMITH. This map is reduced from Map 650. WEDTH OF RIVERS IN YARDS appears in the REFERENCES at the lower left. The outer neat line is broken through at the lower left.

Size 7⅜" x 15⅜".   *Scale* 1" = 40 miles.

Published in William Winterbotham, [*Atlas*].

655 [1796] *State* II (see also Map 654)

Description The imprint has been changed to: PUBLISHED BY J. REID N. YORK.

Published in John Reid, *The American Atlas*, [1796?], no. 20; ibid., 1796, no. 20.

[1796] see Map 645.

[1796] see Map 646.

656 1798

Description [A map and description of the State of Tennessee. By John Rivington Parring-ton. Knoxville: Printed by George Roulstone and John R. Parrington. 1798.] A notice of the proposed publication of this map and a descrip-tion of it was given in the *Knoxville Register*, August 14, 1798.

Size Unknown.   *Scale* Unknown.

Published Separately (?)

Reference Evans 34310.

Location No copy located.

657 1799

Description In oval at lower right: A MAP OF THE / TENNASSEE [sic] GOVERNMENT / FROM THE / LATEST SURVEYS / 1799. Above top neat line at the center: ENGRAVED FOR PAYNE'S GEOGRAPHY. This has been copied from Map 654 or 655. WEDTH OF RIVERS IN YARDS appears again here in the REFERENCES.

Size 7 3/16" x 15⅛".   *Scale* 1" = 30 miles.

Published in John Payne, *A New and Com-plete Universal Geography*, 4, opp. 422.

658 [1765]

Description In cartouche at lower left: A TOPOGRAPHICAL / PLAN / OF THAT PART OF THE / INDIAN-COUNTRY / THROUGH WHICH THE ARMY / UNDER THE COMMAND OF / COLONEL BOUQUET / MARCHED IN THE YEAR *1764*. / BY THOS: HUTCHINS. ASST: ENGINEER. Above top neat line at right: TO FACE THE TITLE. This is a fine topographical map of the route from Fort Pitt to the Old Wyandotte Town at the forks of the Muskingum near the present Dennison, Ohio. Many Indian towns are located as well as main rivers and trails. Notes are given concerning the country. The inset map is undoubtedly the work of Thomas Hutchins. Among the Gage Papers in the William L. Clements Library is a similar MSS map signed "Guy Johnson fecit," and inscribed: "Taken from a Draft made on a Tour Thro' yt. Country in 1762," with later MSS additions in a good 18th. Century hand: "By Mr. Hutchins then in the Indian Department." The topographical map of the route may be by Lieut. Bernard Ratzer. Among the Gage Papers also is a large MSS map showing the same details and carrying the inscription: "Copy'd from yt. original by Lt. Ratzer." Lawrence C. Wroth in the catalog noted below suggests that Henry Dawkins may be the engraver of this map.

Size 14¾" x 19". *Scale* 1" = 6 miles.

Inset In cartouche at upper center: A GENERAL MAP / OF THE COUNTRY ON THE / OHIO AND MUSKINGHAM / SHEWING THE SITUATION OF THE / INDIAN-TOWNS / WITH RESPECT TO THE ARMY / UNDER THE COMMAND OF / COLONEL BOUQUET / BY THOS: HUTCHINS ASST: ENGINEER. Size: 12⅝" x 15⅛". Scale: 1" = 30 miles.

Published in [William Smith], *An Historical Account of the Expedition*, front.

References Thomas Hutchins, *A Topographical Description of Virginia*, 1787, pp. 15, 16, 40, and 59; Michigan, University of, William L. Clements Library, *Guide to the Manuscript Maps in the William L. Clements Library*, Christian Brun, comp., nos. 698, 717; Lawrence C. Wroth and Marion W. Adams, *American Woodcuts and Engravings*, no. 22.

659 [1775]

Description [A Plan of an old Fort and Intrenchment in the Shawanese country, / taken on horseback, by computation only. October 17, 1772.] This is a type set map made up entirely by the printer with two paragraphs of description and more descriptive matter on the verso including explanations for six lettered references on the map. The ancient works are described as being located "toward the head waters of the river Sciota, which empties into the Ohio on the N. w." This notation and the title are taken from the printed text on the verso of the map.

Size 7¾" x 4⅝". *Scale* None (1" = c. 13 perches).

Published in *The Royal American Magazine*, 2 (1775), 30.

660 [1785]

Description In oval at upper right: A MAP / OF THE NORTH WEST PARTS OF / THE UNITED STATES / OF AMERICA. Below bottom neat line: ENGRAVED & PRINTED BY THE AUTHOR. This is a map by John Fitch showing the Great Lakes area south to the NORTH CAROLINA LINE, which extends here to the MISSISSIPPI, and east from the Mississippi to include part of Lake Ontario. Some topographical details are given and geographical legends appear on various parts of the map giving interesting descriptions of the country. Lake Superior is shown to contain the fictitious Charlevoix-Bellin islands and is poorly drawn. The ten Jeffersonian states are indicated by broken line boundaries but without names; a note at the left of the cartouche refers to this. The map was probably based, in part at least, upon William McMurray's "The United States According to the Definitive Treaty of Peace" (see Map 111), and Thomas Hutchins' "A New Map of the Western Parts of Virginia, Pennsylvania, Maryland and North Carolina, London, 1778." An acknowledgement to McMurray and Hutchins is given below the title. An advertisement concerning the map was published in the (Philadelphia) *Pennsylvania Packet, and Daily Advertiser*, July 30, 1785. It is the only American map of the period known to be made, engraved, and printed by the same person. Only one state of the plate is known; the variant indicated by Evans was based upon the advertisement of a dealer and not from an examination of a map. A dedication: TO THOS. HUTCHINS ESQR. / GEOGRAPHER TO THE UNITED STATES . . . is given at right center. Fitch is thought to have done some of the work upon the map while a prisoner of war at Detroit.

Size 27½" x 20¼". *Scale* 1" = 40 miles.

Published Separately. Reproduced in Louis C. Karpinski, *Bibliography of the Printed Maps of Michigan,* pp. 176–77; Philip L. Phillips, *The Rare Map of the Northwest 1785 by John Fitch,* foll. p. 43.

References Evans 19648; Justin Winsor, ed., *Narrative and Critical History,* 7, 529–30; idem, [Remarks on John Fitch Map], pp. 364–66; see also reproductions above, under Published.

Locations CtY, DLC, MH, PHi, RPJCB.

661 [1785]

Description [Map of an area of land between Lake Erie and the Ohio River.] Below lower neat line at left: BIRCH SCULP N. YORK. The map covers approximately the region now included in the present state of Ohio and shows the bounds of the land petitioned for by Nathaniel Sackett and his associates in the accompanying *Memorial.* A triangular arrangement of 22 townships is shown adjoining Sandusky Bay. SANDUSKY FT. and COCHRAN'S are the only place names given. The engraver may be either "Birch" or "B. Birch," cited in the New-York Historical Society's *Dictionary of Artists.*

Size 7¾" x 5⅝". *Scale* 1" = c. 57 British miles.

Published in Nathaniel Sackett, *A Memorial &c.* (opp. p. 3 in William L. Clements Library copy; front. in Library of Congress copy).

662 [1787]

Description In cartouche at lower right: A MAP / OF THE FEDERAL TERRITORY FROM THE WESTERN / BOUNDARY OF PENNSYLVANIA TO THE SCIOTO / RIVER LAID DOWN FROM THE LATEST INFORMATIONS / AND DIVIDED INTO TOWNSHIPS AND FRACTIONAL PARTS / OF TOWNSHIPS AGREEABLY TO THE ORDINANCE OF THE / HONLE. CONGRESS PASSED IN MAY 1785. This has been identified by Philip L. Phillips as Manasseh Cutler's map accompanying his *Explanation of the Map.* The engraving resembles the work of John Norman who advertised the map as being for sale at his shop. It is the first map showing the famous Seven Ranges of Townships. OMIE RIVER appears for the Maumee and COYABOGA for Cuyahoga. Much of the land shown is divided into townships. THE TRACT OF LAND PURCHACED BY THE OHIO COMPANY appears prominently on the lower townships of the next ten ranges after the first Seven Ranges. In the cartouche below the title appears this note: NB. THE SMALL BLANK SQUARES IN EACH TOWNSHIP / SHEW THE LOTS RESERVED BY THE UNITED STATES FOR AFTER / SALES THOSE WHICH ARE SHADED CONGRESS HAVE BEEN / PLEASED TO GIVE FOR SCHOOLS AND RELIGIOUS / PURPOSES. The Pennsylvania western line is marked: A TRUE MERIDIAN LINE — THE WESTERN BOUNDARY OF PENNSYLVANIA WHICH RUNS INTO LAKE ERIE ABOUT 1½ MILE.

The "Geographer's Line" of the Act of May, 1785, forming the northern boundary of the Seven Ranges of Townships, is marked: A CONTINUATION OF THE EAST AND WEST LINE COMMENCING AT THE LITTLE BEAVER WHERE IS A 1° 15' EASTERLY VARIATION. The Western Reserve tract is marked: CONNECTICUT LANDS, EXTENDING FROM / THE 41°. TO THE 42° OF LATITUDE, AND BOUNDED /ON THE EAST, BY THE WESTERN BOUNDARY / OF PENNSYLVANIA. The land west of the Western Reserve is marked with a long note as allotted to the Wyandot and Delaware nations and specifies small reservations as trading posts. GREAT PLAINS OF THE SCIOTO appears west of the Scioto River. THE INDIANA TRACT appears northeast of the LITTLE KANHAWA on the Virginia side of the Ohio. The following contemporary advertisements have been found. In the *Salem* [*Mass.*] *Mercury* for November 27, 1787, the *Explanation* was advertised alone. In the December 4 and 11 issues, the pamphlet and map were both listed: "Subscriptions for a new map of the territory described in this pamphlet are taken in by the printers hereof; who expect to receive a small number, in about two weeks." In *Weatherwise's Federal Almanack for 1788,* underneath the map of the ruins of an Indian city on the second page of folio C, appears: "NB A pamphlet containing a geographical description of the western country, (Price two shillings) may be had of J. Norman near the Boston — Stone; also a large map of said country, for twelve shillings." An advertisement in the May 27, 1788, issue of the *Salem Mercury* identifies this map as the one accompanying the *Explanation* and gives its full title. The map was advertised alone, with no mention of the *Explanation,* in the *Norwich* [Conn.] *Packet* during June and July, 1788. A French map based upon it, "Plan / des achats des / Compagnies de / L'Ohio et du Scioto," [Paris, 1789?], is reproduced in Archer B. Hulbert, ed., *Ohio in the Time of Confederation,* opp. p. 100. The inset is omitted here (see Vail, no. 793).

Size 26⅜" x 19⁹⁄₁₆". *Scale* 1" = 10 miles.

Inset At the lower left: A PLAN / OF THE CITY TO / BE BUILT ON THE / MUSKINGUM / RIVER. Size: 2¾" x 4". Scale: 1" = 5000 feet.

Published with Manasseh Cutler, *An Explanation of the Map,* 1787 and 1788; separately. Reproduced in Philip L. Phillips, *The First Map and Description of Ohio,* at end; U.S. Library of Congress, *Ohio,* foll. p. 12.

Reference Robert W. G. Vail, *Old Frontier,* nos. 753 and 793. See also reproductions above, under Published.

Locations DLC, MHi, MiU-C, MWA, PHi, PPAmP.

663 [1787]

Description Below bottom neat line: PLAN OF THE REMAINS OF SOME ANCIENT WORKS ON THE MUSKINGUM; below title at right: BY JONA. HEART CAPTN. 1ST. AMERN. REGT.; above top neat line at right: COLUMB. MAG. The archaeological ruins shown on this plan were located on the east bank of the Muskingum River, one half mile from the Ohio River, at Marietta. A short reference table of symbols is given at the upper right. An "Explanation of the Plate" is given on page 427 of the accompanying: "Account of some Remains of Ancient Works, on the Muskingum, with a Plan of these Works. By J[onathan] Heart, Capt. in the first American regiment. (See also Maps 666 and 671.)

Size 8" x 85⁄8".   *Scale* 1" = 10 chains.

Published in *Columbian Magazine, 1* (1787), opp. 425.

664 [1787]

Description At upper right: A PLAN OF THE / RAPIDS / IN THE RIVER OHIO. / BY / THOS. HUTCHINS. This is a topographical map with several references given at left center. On page five of the accompanying *Description* (note) Hutchins states: "See the annexed Plan. It is a *correct* Description of these Rapids, made by the Editor, on the spot in the year 1766." This plan was re-engraved from the copy appearing in the English edition of 1778, probably by John Norman, the publisher. The engraver's name, "I. Cheevers," appears below the bottom neat line at right on the English map.

Size 51⁄2" x 73⁄16".   *Scale* 1" = 80 yards.

Published in Thomas Hutchins, *A Topographical Description of Virginia,* opp. p. 8.

665 [1787]

Description At right center: A PLAN / OF THE SEVERAL VILLAGES IN THE / ILLINOIS COUNTRY, / WITH PART OF THE / RIVER MISSISSIPPI & C. / BY / THOS. HUTCHINS. This is a topographical map of the Mississippi River and the country along its eastern bank from St. Louis down to the mouth of the Kaskaskia River. It shows many features: forts, settlements, Indian villages, streams, and also the road from Cahokia to Kaskaskias. It is re-engraved from the map in the English edition of 1778. The English map may be identified by an arrow indicating the current in the Mississippi which was engraved on that map in the river below the mouth of the "Kaskaskias." This American version was probably engraved by John Norman, who also published it.

Size 7" x 5".   *Scale* 1" = 10 miles.

Published in Thomas Hutchins, *A Topographical Description of Virginia,* front.

666 [1787]

Description [Plan of the Ruins of an Indian City.] The ruins shown on this woodcut are at the site of the present city of Marietta, Ohio. A short list of references is given below the map. The title is taken from the verso of the map. (See also Maps 663 and 671.)

Size 31⁄4" x 23⁄4".   *Scale* None.

Published in Abraham Weatherwise, [pseud.], *Weatherwise's Federal Almanack for 1788.*

667 [1788?]

Description [Map of the Kentucky Country or, Map of the Western Territory.] The June, 1788, issue of the (New York) *American Magazine* promised a forthcoming: "Map of the Kentucky Country," and the July issue of the same year stated: "An excellent map of the Western Territory is preparing for the next number." As far as can be determined this map was never actually published as part of the periodical.

Size Unknown.   *Scale* Unknown.

Published in *American Magazine* (?).

668 [1788]

Description At center: A PLAN / OF CAMPUS MARTIUS, AT THE CITY / OF MARIETTA, / TERRITORY OF THE UNITED STATES, N.W. / OF THE RIVER OHIO. At upper right: COLUMB. MAG. This plan shows the arrangement of the block houses and dwellings into a protective unit about the central town square. Four EXPLANATIONS are given at the lower right within the PLAN.

Size 61⁄2" x 55⁄8".   *Scale* 1" = 40 feet.

Inset Above the PLAN: ELEVATION OF CAMPUS MARTIUS / AT A.B. Size: 11⁄4" x 55⁄8".

Published in *Columbian Magazine, 2* (1788), opp. 646.

669 [1789]

Description At bottom: INDIAN WORKS, ON HURON RIVER OR BALD EAGLE CREEK. At upper right: COLUMB. MAG. This is a drawing showing two plans of old Indian fortifications. FIG. I, at the left, gives a series of Indian mounds on the east side of the Huron River about 20 miles east of Sandusky. FIG. II, at the right, shows a larger group located two miles north of the other. The references are explained in the accompanying "Account of some Old Indian Works, on Huron River, with a Plan of them, taken the 28th of May, 1789, by Abraham G. Steiner," pp. 543–44.

Size 3⅞" x 6⅜". *Scale* None (1" = c. 200 feet).

Published in *Columbian Magazine, 3* (1789), opp. 543.

670 [1789]

Description In cartouche at upper right: PLAN / OF THE / CITY / MARIETTA / LAID OUT AT THE CONFLUENCE / OF THE RIVERS / OHIO / AND / MUSKINGUM. In lower left corner: E. RUGGLES JUNR SCULPT. This is a plan of Marietta showing the blocks divided into numbered lots. Several squares are indicated and also the CAMPUS MARTIUS. FT. HARMER [sic] is located across the Muskingum. Evans states that the plan was printed in 1789, probably by Timothy Green in New London. However, Edward Ruggles, Jr., was printing, at least from his own engravings, in Pomfret, Connecticut, about that time. A note at the lower left contains eight lines of descriptive matter.

Size 16¼" x 20". *Scale* 1" = ⅒ mile.

Published Separately.

Reference Evans 22121.

Location MWA.

671 [1791]

Description Across bottom below neat line: VIEW OF THE CELEBRATED INDIAN FORTIFICATIONS NEAR THE JUNCTION OF / THE OHIO & MUSKINGUM RIVERS. Above top neat line at right corner: N. YORK MAGAZINE; below bottom neat line at left corner: H. LIVINGSTON DEL.; at right corner: TIEBOUT SCT. This is another plan of the ruins at Marietta shown on Maps 663 and 666. An "Explanation of the Plate" is given on the page opposite.

Size 4⁹⁄₁₆" x 6½". *Scale* 1" = 20 chains.

Published in *New-York Magazine or Literary Repository, 2* (1791), front.

672 [1793]

Description In square at upper right: A PLAN OF / THE RAPIDS / OF THE / OHIO. Above top neat line: ENGRAV'D FOR S. CAMPBELL'S EDITION OF IMLAYS DESCRIPTION OF KENTUCKY. This is a topographical map of the Rapids. LOUISVILLE is shown, also FORT / FENNY, on the opposite bank, and CLARKVILLE. Two references are given at the left. A similar map, engraved by Thomas Conder, appears in the 1797, English edition of the book.

Size 6⅛" x 7". *Scale* 1" = 800 yards.

Published in Gilbert Imlay, *A Topographical Description, 1,* opp. 109.

673 [1794]

Description At bottom: SKETCH OF THE GROUND AT THE RAPIDS OF THE MIAMI OF THE LAKE, SHEWING THE POSITION / OF GEN: WAYNE'S ARMY PREVIOUS TO AND AFTER THE ACTION OF 20TH. AUGT. 1794. Below title at right: ANDERSON s. This is a detailed, topographic map of the Battle of Fallen Timbers. A list of REFERENCES is given at right center.

Size 12⅝" x 7¾". *Scale* 1" = ½ mile.

Published in *New-York Magazine, or Literary Repository, 5* (1794), opp. 643.

674 [1795] *State* I (II post-1799, see below, Description)

Description At lower left: N.W. TERRITORY. Many rivers, streams, and a few settlements and forts are indicated. LIT. FORT appears at mouth of the Chicago River and OLD FT. ORLEANS appears on MISOURI [sic] R. The southern end of Lake Michigan is placed almost a full degree further north than the southern shore of Lake Erie, while Scott's map of the United States in the same Gazetteer (see Map 125) shows a reversal of these positions. The fictitious Charlevoix-Bellin islands appear in Lake Superior. The second state appears in Scott's *The New and Universal Gazetteer, 4.* No geographical additions are noted. It may be identified by the two short straight lines which the engraver has added to strengthen each of the small circles locating: Detroit, Sandusky, Marietta, and a number of other places.

Size 7⅛" x 6". *Scale* 1" = 140 miles.

Published in Joseph Scott, *An Atlas of the United States,* no. 19; idem, *The United States Gazetteer,* opp. "Territory North-West of the Ohio." Reproduced in Louis C. Karpinski, *Bibliography of the Printed Maps of Michigan,* p. 189; Joseph Scott, *Atlas of the United States 1795–1800,* no. 2; Justin Winsor, ed., *Narrative and Critical History, 7,* 542.

References See reproductions (Karpinski and Winsor) above, under Published.

675 [1796] *State* I (II post-1799, see below, Description)

Description At lower right: N.W. TERRITORY. Below bottom neat line at right: W. BARKER SCULP. Many rivers and streams are shown as well as forts and settlements. R. ROSINE is given for the Raison. Several large fictitious islands are shown in Lake Superior. The northern United States boundary line stops at the Grand Portage. The second state of this map appeared in *Carey's American Pocket Atlas*, 1801. "An extensive high Plain" in Michigan, the "7 Ranges," and "Indiana / Territory" are among the additions to the plate. The northern border is now completed to the left inner neat line.

Size 7⁹⁄₁₆" x 5¹³⁄₁₆". *Scale* 1" = 130 miles.

Published in Mathew Carey, *Carey's American Pocket Atlas*, foll. p. 84.

676 [1796] *State* I (see also Map 677; III post-1799, see Map 677, Description)

Description At lower right: PLAT / OF / THE SEVEN RANGES OF TOWNSHIPS / BEING PART OF THE / TERRITORY OF THE UNITED STATES N. W. OF THE / RIVER OHIO / WHICH BY A LATE ACT OF CONGRESS ARE DIRECTED TO BE SOLD. Below title and following note: W. BARKER SCULP. This map depicts the famous survey, made in accordance with the Ordinance of 1785, dividing public lands into ranges and townships for the first time. This system has been widely adopted in the United States and in other countries. Thomas Hutchins, at that time Geographer of the United States, personally conducted the surveys of the first four and part of the fifth of the Seven Ranges. The neat line is broken at the lower left to show MARIETTA and the Muskingum. The first surveying expedition in 1785 had to be abandoned because of hostility of the Indians but a military escort protected them the following year. Evans gives September 30, 1796, as the copyright date issued to Mathew Carey.

Size 24" x 13¼". *Scale* 1" = 4 miles.

Published Separately. Reproduced in Elroy M. Avery, *History of the United States, 6, 406.*

References Evans 30918; Thomas Hutchins, *Topographical Description*, 1904, pp. 34–48; Ohio, Cooperative Topographical Survey, *Final Report, 3, 38–50;* Robert W. G. Vail, *Old Frontier,* no. 1081.

Locations OClWHi, PHi.

677 [1796] *State* II (see also Map 676; III post-1799, see below, Description)

Description Below bottom neat line has been added: PUBLISHED BY MATTHEW [sic] CAREY NO. *118* MARKET STREET PHILADA. COPY RIGHT SECURED. This is the usual state encountered and is usually seen on paper watermarked "1794." This state is found in Mathew Carey atlases dated from 1796 to 1809. In a later state of the map Barker's name and the Carey imprint has been erased.

Published Separately.

Locations DLC, ICN, MH, MiU-C, MWA.

678 1796

Description In lower left corner: A MAP / OF PART OF THE / N:W: TERRITORY / OF THE / UNITED STATES: / COMPILED / FROM ACTUAL SURVEYS, AND THE BEST INFORMATION, / BY SAMUEL LEWIS *1796*. Below title: W. BARKER SCULP. This is a map of the Northwest showing the lower portion of Lake Michigan, most of Lake Erie, and the area south to the Ohio River. Especially noted are the existing land divisions of the area including the Fire Lands and the Seven Ranges. The Indian boundary determined by the Treaty of Greenville and the various lands ceded by the Indians are designated. This map is also found in copies of Mathew Carey's atlases of 1796, 1802, and 1814. The map was published by Carey in Philadelphia, and Evans gives January 17, 1797 as the date of the copyright issued to him.

Size 19⅛" x 25½". *Scale* 1" = 17 miles.

Published Separately.

Reference Evans 30691.

Locations DLC, MiU-C, NNA.

679 [1796]

Description At lower left: A MAP / OF THE / NORTH WESTERN / TERRITORY. In lower left corner: S. HILL SC. Above top neat line: PUBLISHED BY THOMAS & ANDREWS, BOSTON. Some topographical details are noted. A HIGH EXTENSIVE PLAIN is shown on the lower Michigan peninsula. The fictitious Bellin-Charlevoix islands appear in Lake Superior. The INDIAN LINE and other land divisions are shown, including the Ohio Company lands and the Seven Ranges.

Size 7½" x 9½". *Scale* 1" = 140 American miles.

Published in Jedidiah Morse, *The American Universal Geography*, 3d ed., *1*, opp. 573.

680 1798 *State* I (II and III post-1799, see below, Description)

Description At upper left on western section: A MAP OF THE / CONNECTICUT / WESTERN RESERVE, / FROM ACTUAL SURVEY, / BY / SETH PEASE. Below bottom neat line at right on eastern section: ENGRAVED & PRINTED FOR THE AUTHOR BY AMOS DOOLITTLE NEWHAVEN 1798. This is a map with some topographical features and showing the surveys east of the Cuyahoga River. West of the Cuyahoga, extending to the VERMILLION River, is a section carrying the notation: UNSURVEYED LAND / AND / SUBJECT TO INDIAN CLAIMS. West of that again is shown the FIRE LAND, its eastern boundary being indicated by a broken line. Thirty-two townships are named in the eastern section. Longitude is given west from London at the top and from Philadelphia at the bottom. The words: NORTH WEST TERRITORY appear within the inner neat lines at the bottom and left side of the western section of the map. All of the three known states of this map were published in two sections: the eastern section having neat lines on all four sides; the western on three sides, the right side being open. On some copies of the eastern section, the left side has been trimmed and the two open sides joined together. The map was republished in 1807 with 67 townships shown on the eastern section as well as other changes. The date, *1798*, below the neat line was retained, however. The map was again republished in 1808 with the river systems redrawn and townships added on the western section. Abraham Tappen is given as co-author on the second state.

Size   Eastern section: 19″ x 16⅝″.
Western section: 19″ x 16¼″.

Scale   1″ = c. 3¾ miles.

Published   Separately. Reproduced in Russell Anderson, "The Pease Map of the Connecticut Western Reserve," opp. p. 276.

References   John Carter Brown Library, *Report, 1947*, pp. 22–26; Evans 34317; see also reproduction above, under Published.

Locations   CtY, DLC, OClWHi, RPJCB.

681   [c. 1798]

Description   At upper left: PLAT OF THAT TRACT OF COUNTRY IN THE TERRITORY NORTHWEST OF THE OHIO APPROPRIATED / FOR MILITARY SERVICES; AND DESCRIBED IN THE ACT OF CONGRESS, INTITULED [sic] "AN ACT REGULATING / THE GRANTS OF LAND APPROPRIATED FOR MILITARY SERVICES, AND FOR THE SOCIETY OF UNITED / BRETHREN FOR PROPAGATING THE GOSPEL AMONG THE HEATHEN" SURVEY'D UNDER THE DIRECTION / OF RUFUS PUTNAM SURVEYOR GENERAL TO THE UNITED STATES.

Below neat line at lower right corner: WESTON SC. PHILADA. This is a detailed plan of the United States Military District. There are twenty ranges of five mile townships, numbered from east to west; the townships themselves are numbered from south to north. The width of the rivers and streams is indicated in many cases and their direction as well. The Moravian Indian towns of Schoenbrunn, Gnadenhutten, and Salem are identified through the references at the upper left. The "Act" referred to in the title is that of June 1, 1796. Money was not appropriated until March, 1797, and the surveying was begun immediately thereafter. The long straight portion of the Greenville Treaty line, part of which forms most of the northern boundary of this District, was run by the end of August, 1797, by Israel Ludlow. The boundaries of the three Moravian tracts were surveyed by William Rufus Putnam, son of the Surveyor General, in the same year. The northeast corner of the Treaty line appears accurately on this map for the first time with its proper relationship to the "geographer's" line, i.e. the northern boundary line of the Seven Ranges adjacent to this plat. The inaccuracy of the surveys is not allowing for convergence of the meridian, and errors resulting from not running the section lines interior to the townships, necessitated the passage of the Land Act of March 1, 1800. The engraver is probably Henry W. Weston. The map was later re-engraved on a smaller scale by Thomas Wightman and appeared in Thaddeus M. Harris' *The Journal of a Tour, 1803*.

Size   13⅜″ x 25⁵⁄₁₆″.   *Scale*   1″ = 400 surveyor's chains.

Published   Separately.

Reference   Ohio-Co-operative Topographical Survey, *Final Report, 3*, 89–106.

Locations   MH, MiU-C, NHi, PHi.

682   [1799]

Description   [North-Western Territory.] This map was not found in any of the copies examined although it appears in all the "Directions to Binders" as being placed opposite page 349. The title is taken from the "Directions" on p. 17 of the accompanying "Supplement to Volume IV of the Universal Geography."

Size   Unknown.   *Scale*   Unknown.

Published in John Payne, *A New and Complete Universal Geography, 4*.

683 [1790]   *State* I (see also Map 688)

Description In oval at upper right: A NEW / GENERAL CHART / OF THE / WEST INDIES / FROM THE LATEST MARINE JOURNALS AND SURVEYS / REGULATED AND ASCERTAINED BY ASTRONOMICAL OBSERVATIONS. In oval below title: PRINTED & SOLD BY J. NORMAN NO. 75 NEWBURY STR. On the marginal degree lines are indicated the longitude from London, Kingston, and the Isle of Ferro. As part of the title appears a certification by Osgood Carleton, dated: DECR. 28 1789, that it is a true and accurate copy of a London publication. Four plates are used. Evans evidently saw a 1790 newspaper advertisement offering this chart for sale at John Norman's shop. Many soundings are given off East Florida and the Yucatan Peninsula.

Size 27¼" x 39¼".   *Scale* 1" = 19¼ nautical leagues (20 to a degree).

Published in John Norman, *The American Pilot,* 1791, no. 2; ibid., 1792, no. 3; ibid., 1794, no. 3.

Reference Evans 22698.

684 [1793]

Description In scroll at upper right: WEST / INDIES; below title: S. ALLARDICE SC.; in upper right border: PLATE CCLV. This map includes an area from Charleston, South Carolina, to Surinam and west to Mexico City. VIRGIN INLANS appears thus; also, JUCATAN.

Size 6¾" x 11".   *Scale* 1" = 240 miles (60 to a degree).

Published in Thomas Dobson, *Encyclopaedia,* 9, foll. 218.

685 [1793]

Description [Plan of Cape-Françoise.] This plan of Cap-Français, Haiti, was advertised as "this day published" in the (New York) *Columbian Gazetteer,* September 12, 1793, by James Harrison.

Size Unknown.   *Scale* Unknown.

Published Separately.

Reference Rita S. Gottesman, *The Arts and Crafts in New York 1777–1799,* pp. 57–58.

Location No copy located.

686 [1793]

Description In decorative oval at upper right: WEST INDIES / ACCORDING TO THE BEST / AUTHORITIES. Below bottom neat line: ENGRAVED FOR MORSES AMERICAN GEOGRAPHY BY A. DOOLITTLE N. HAVEN. Above top neat line: PUBLISHED BY THOMAS & ANDREWS BOSTON. Relatively few place names are given. CARIBEAN, PORTO BELLOO, and BAY OF HUNDURAS appear thus. This is the first Morse map of the West Indies.

Size 8⅛" x 12¼".   *Scale* None (1" = c. 225 miles).

Published in Jedidiah Morse, *The American Universal Geography,* 1, opp. 666.

687 [1794]

Description In oval at upper right: A CHART / OF THE / WEST INDIES, FROM THE LATEST MARINE / JOURNALS AND SURVEYS. In oval beneath title: W. BARKER SCULP. PHILADA. Below oval: ENGRAVED FOR CAREY'S AMERICAN EDITION OF GUTHRIE'S GEOGRAPHY IMPROVED. Many place names appear. Cat Island is marked: THE FIRST LAND / DISCOVERED BY COLUMBUS / IN 1492. San Salvador Island is shown as WATLANDS I., and Martinique is shown as MARTINICO. No soundings are given.

Size 11⅛" x 15¾".   *Scale* 1" = 53 nautical leagues (20 to a degree).

Published in Mathew Carey, *Carey's American Atlas,* no. 21; idem, *Carey's General Atlas,* no. 43; ibid., 1800 (New York Historical Society copy); idem, *The General Atlas for Carey's Edition of Guthrie's Geography Improved;* idem, *A General Atlas for the Present War,* no. 7.

688 [1794]   *State* II (see also Map 683)

Description "J." NORMAN has been changed to W. NORMAN. The worn plate has been recut in many places. The letters in CARIBEAN [sic] SEA and TERRA FIRMA are now shaded instead of open capitals.

Published in William Norman, *The American Pilot,* 1794, no. 3; ibid., 1798, no. 2; ibid., 1803; idem, *The New East-India Pilot,* 1804; idem, *The New West-India Pilot,* 1803; [idem, *A Pilot for the West-Indies*], 1795, no. 1.

689 [1795]

Description Above neat line across top: THE WINDWARD PASSAGE WITH THE SEVERAL PASSAGES FROM THE EAST END OF CUBA & FROM THE NORTH PART OF ST. DOMINGO BY THOS. JEFFERYS GEOGRAPHER TO HIS MAJESTY. The chart covers the area from GUANAHANI (Columbus' St. Salvador) at the upper left, including the east tip of Cuba, all Hispaniola, to the extreme west tip of Puerto Rico. Some topographical detail is noted and a number of passages are shown. Some soundings are given. The following certification appears at upper right: I HAVE EXAMINED AND FIND THIS TO BE AN / EXACT COPY OF A CHART LATELY PUBLISHED / IN LONDON BY LAURIE AND WHITTLE SUCCESSORS / TO THE LATE ROBERT SAYER / OSGOOD CARLETON / TEACHER OF MATHEMATICS / BOSTON.

Size 24½″ x 23¾″.   *Scale* None (1″ = c. 20 miles).

Published in [William Norman, *A Pilot for the West Indies*], no. 4.

690 1795

Description In circle at upper right: A / NEW AND IMPROVED CHART / OF THE / WEST INDIA / OR / CARRIBBEE ISLANDS / DRAWN / FROM THE BEST AUTHORITIES / BY / WILLIAM HEATHER. *1795*. Within circle at bottom: LONDON PUBLISHED BOSTON REPUBLISHED BY W NORMAN AT HIS BOOKSTORE NO 75 NEWBURY STREET. SOMBRERO islet is shown above neat line north and west of ST. MARTIN Island. A certificate by Osgood Carleton is just below the cartouche.

Size 24″ x 19⅝″.   *Scale* None (1″ = c. 10 miles).

Published in [William Norman, *A Pilot for the West Indies*], no. 5.

691 1795

Description Across top above neat line: THE ISLAND OF CUBA WITH PART OF THE BAHAMA BANKS AND THE MARTYRS BY THOS JEFFRYS [sic] GEOGRAPHER TO HIS MAJESTY. At bottom under neat line: LONDON PUBLISHED BY LAURIE & WHITTLE MAY *1794* BOSTON REPUBLISHED BY W NORMAN SEPR *1795* AND SOLD AT HIS SHOP NO 75 NEWBURY STREET. This is a topographical map of the major portion of Cuba, Jamaica, and the surrounding islands. Some soundings are given. A certification of the contents by Osgood Carleton is given in the center of the map.

Size 24″ x 23⅞″.   *Scale* None (1″ = c. 20 miles).

Published in [William Norman, *A Pilot for the West Indies*], no. 3.

1795   see Map 629.

692 [1796?]

Description At upper left: CARTE DE LA PARTIE FRANÇOISE / DE ST. DOMINGO / FAITE PAR BELLIN INGR. DE LA MARINE / ET DEPUIS AUGMENTÉE PAR P. C. VARLÉ ET AUTRES INGRS. / A / MAP / OF THE / FRENCH PART / OF / ST. DOMINGO. Below title and NOTE at left center: J. T SCOTT SCULP. PHILADA. This is a political map of the western end of Hispaniola with the border between the Spanish and French parts of the Island labeled: LINE OF DEMARCATION BETWIXT THE FRENCH AND SPANIARDS AS FIXED IN *1776*. Notes appearing on the map are in both French and English. This was taken from a map by Jacques Nicolas Bellin.

Size 14⅝″ x 18⅞″.   *Scale* 1″ = 5 French leagues.

Published in Mathew Carey, *Carey's General Atlas* (inserted in William L. Clements Library copy); ibid., later editions; Nicolas Ponce, *Recueil de Vues des lieux Principaux de la Colonie Française de Saint-Domingue*.

References John Carter Brown Library, *Report, 1958*, p. 46; Philip L. Phillips, comp., *A List of Geographical Atlases, 1*, no. 2717.

693 1796   *State* I (see also Map 694)

Description In ornamental cartouche at upper right: CARTE / DE / L'ISLE ST. DOMINGUE / DRESSÉE POUR L'OUVRAGE DE / M. L. E. MOREAU DE ST. MÉRY. In cartouche below title: DESSINÉE PAR I. SONIS *1796* / GRAVÉE PAR VALLANCE. This is a fine topographic map of the Island showing also the major towns and roads. Moreau de St. Méry was forced to flee France before completing the several projected parts of his ambitious study of Santo Domingo. This map, engraved in Philadelphia, was a substitute for one of two maps which had been originally intended for the Nicolas Ponce's *Recueil de Vues des lieux Principaux de la Colonie Française de Saint-Domingue*, but which were inserted after 1791 when the atlas was first published. The second state of the map is the one usually found in the Atlas.

Size 14⁵⁄₁₆″ x 24⁵⁄₁₆″.   *Scale* 1″ = 9 lieues of 2000 toises each.

Published in Médéric L. É. Moreau de St. Méry, *Description Topographique et Politique de la Partie Espagnole de L'Isle Saint-Domingue*, opp. p. 1; idem, *Description Topographique, Physique, Civile, Politique et Historique de la Partie Française de l'Isle Saint-Domingue, 2*, opp. 1; idem, *A Topographical and Political*

Description, 1796 and 1798 eds. (some copies); separately.

References John Carter Brown Library, *Report, 1958*, pp. 44–46; Médéric L. É. Moreau de St. Méry, *Moreau de Méry's American Journey*, p. 213; Philip L. Phillips, comp., *A List of Geographical Atlases, 1*, no. 2717.

694 1796 *State* II (see also Map 693)

Description PARTIE ESPAGNOLE has now been lettered across eastern section of the island. The French section is divided into three provinces with the following designations: PARTIE DU NORD, PARTIE DE L'OUEST, PARTIE DU SUD.

Published in Médéric L. É. Moreau de St. Méry, *Description Topographique, Physique, Civile, Politique et Historique de la Partie Française de L'Isle Saint-Domingue, 2,* opp. 1; Nicolas Ponce, *Recueil de Vues des lieux Principaux de la Colonie Française de Saint-Domingue.* Reproduced in Médéric L. É. Moreau de St. Méry, *Description Topographique, Physique, 1,* opp. 14 (partial reproduction tipped into Library of Congress copy with following title: "Carte de St. Dominque / Dresse pour l'ouvrage de / Mr. L. É. Moreau de St. Méry / Dessinée par I. Sonis 1796." "Plate No. 3" appears above neat line at upper right and "Bowen & Co Lith Phila," at lower right. After 1859–60); C. Fitzhugh Talman, "Climatology of Haiti in the Eighteenth Century," p. 65 (only French part of island is reproduced).

Reference John Carter Brown, *Report, 1958*, pp. 45–46.

695 [1796]

Description In oval at lower left: WEST / INDIES / FROM THE BEST AUTHORITIES. In oval below title: DOOLITTLE SCULP: Above top neat line: PUBLISHED BY THOMAS & ANDREWS BOSTON. Many place names are shown. THE / LEEWARD / ISLANDS is applied to those lying between Martinique and the VIRCIN [sic] ISLANDS, and LEEWARD ISLES to the islands lying off the South American mainland. An EXPLANATION appears at the upper right corner. This is the second Morse map of the West Indies.

Size 7⅜″ x 12¼″.   *Scale* 1″ = 230 miles.

Published in Jedidiah Morse, *The American Universal Geography*, 3d ed., *1,* opp. 760.

696 [1796]

Description In decorated oval at lower left: PLAN / OF THE / PLANTATION / OF M. SAMOUAL / SITUATED IN THE DISTRICT / OF THE RIVER BARE / AT PORT ST. LOUIS OF / THE NORTH. SURVEYED / BY

US THE *17*TH. OCTR. *1785* / NAZE / KINGS SURVEYOR. This topographical map was included in a pamphlet advertising for sale a plantation owned by Jean Baptiste and Louis Samoual at Petit St. Louis near Port-de-Paix, Haiti.

Size 9⅞″ x 7⅝″.   *Scale* 1″ = 200 feet.

Published in Jean B. Samoual and Louis Samoual, *Description of a Plantation*, front.

697 1796

Description In oval at upper right: AN / ACCURATE MAP / OF THE / WEST INDIES / WITH THE / ADJACENT COAST / OF / AMERICA. / *1796.* Beneath oval: D. MARTIN SCULPT. Below bottom neat line: PUBLISH'D BY J. REID NEW YORK. Some topographical detail is shown. LEEWARD ISLANDS is applied to those lying off South America, and THE / LEEWARD / ISLES to those south of the Virgin Islands. MOUTHS OF THE / ORONOKO breaks through the outer neat line at the lower right.

Size 14″ x 17⅝″.   *Scale* None (1″ = c. 100 miles).

Published in John Reid, *The American Atlas*, [1796?], no. 20; ibid., 1796, no. 20; William Winterbotham, [*Atlas*], no. 20.

698 [1797]

Description In oval at upper right: A / CORRECT CHART / OF THE / WEST INDIA ISLANDS / ENGRAVED FOR / MALHAM'S NAVAL GAZETEER [sic]. Beneath oval: S. H. SC. Below bottom neat line at center: PUBLISHED BY SPOTSWOOD & NANCREDE, BOSTON. This is a small chart on Mercator's projection, engraved by Samuel Hill. TEXAS appears both as a town name and the name of a district.

Size 6¾″ x 9⁹⁄₁₆″.   *Scale* None (1″ = c. 400 miles).

Published in John Malham, *The Naval Gazetteer, 1,* opp. 515.

699 [1797]

Description In oval at lower left: WEST / INDIES / FROM THE BEST / AUTHORITIES; below bottom neat line at right: HILL SC.; above top neat line: ENGRAVED FOR MORSE'S AMERICAN GAZETTEER. This is a re-engraving by Samuel Hill of Map 695. Additional names have been added in the Bahama Islands and in Cuba. JAMAICAE still appears thus, but VIRGIN ISLANDS and CARTHAGENA appear correctly. Two sets of islands are inscribed LEEWARD as before.

Size 7½″ x 12½″.   *Scale* 1″ = 225 British statute miles.

Published in Jedidiah Morse, *The American Gazetteer*, opp. "West Indies."

700 [1799]

Description In oval at upper right: WEST INDIES. Above top neat line: ENGRAVED FOR PAYNES GEOGRAPHY, PUBLISHED BY JOHN LOW N. YORK. This is very similar to Map 699. The EXPLANATION is given at the lower left.

Size 7½" x 12¼".   *Scale* None (1" = c. 225 miles).

Published in John Payne, *A New and Complete Universal Geography, 4*, opp. 486.

701 [1790]

Description In oval at lower left: SOUTH / AMERICA / FROM THE BEST / AUTHORITIES. In lower right corner: SCOT PHILADA. In border at top right: PLATE XV. Many place names are noted but few topographical details. The LITTLE AN- TILLES are given in the Caribbean. Political divisions are shown by dotted lines.

Size 6⅞" x 8¾". *Scale* None (1" = c. 800 miles).

Published in Thomas Dobson, *Encyclopaedia,* 1, foll. 538; Jedidiah Morse, *The History of America,* foll. p. 112; ibid., 2d ed.; ibid., 3d ed.

702 [1790]

Description In oval scroll at lower right: SOUTH / AMERICA; below neat line at lower right: DOOLITTLE SC. N HAVEN; above neat line at upper left: NO. V. PATAGOINA appears thus near Cape Horn. TUCUMAN and MAGELLANICA appear in modern Argentina. Few place names are given. This is the first Morse map of South America.

Size 4⅛" x 2¾". *Scale* None (1" = 20° latitude).

Published in Jedidiah Morse, *Geography Made Easy,* 2d ed., opp. p. 250.

703 [1790]

Description In vignette at lower right: SOUTH / AMERICA. This map is almost exactly the same as Map 702. The ANDES are noted here.

Size 4" x 2⅝". *Scale* None (1" = c. 22° latitude).

Published in Benjamin Workman, *Elements of Geography,* 2d ed., opp. p. 89; ibid., 4th, 5th, 6th, and 7th eds.

704 [1791]

Description At upper right: A NEW CHART / OF THE / SEA COAST / FROM THE / ISLAND OF CYENNE [sic] TO THE / RIVER POUMARON / COM- PREHENDING / SURINAM BERBICC DEMERARY & ES- SEQUEBO / TAKEN FROM THE LATEST SURVEYS AND OBSERVATIONS / OF THE DUTCH AND ENGLISH / BY OSGOOD CARLETON / TEACHER OF THE MATHE- MATICS BOSTON. Some soundings are given. The neat line is broken at upper left to show the

154

Poumaron River. A scale is laid out inside the left marginal degree line. Three profiles are shown on the lower part of the chart: APPEAR- ANCE OF LAND ABOUT CYENNE; THE 5 SMALL IS- LANDS / NEAR CYENNE; THE ENTRANCE OF THE RIVER DEMERARY S BY W DISTANT ABOUT 4 LEAGUES.

Size 16" x 20⅜". *Scale* 1" = 6½ nau- tical leagues (20 to a degree).

Published in John Norman, *The American Pilot,* [1791], no. 1; ibid., 1792, no. 2; ibid., 1794, no. 2.

705 [1791]

Description At top between marginal degree line and neat lines: SOUTH AMERICA. VENE ZUELA appears thus. LITTLE ANTILLIS is applied to Curaçao and neighboring coastal islands. This is the second Morse map of South America.

Size 5¹⁵⁄₁₆" x 3³⁄₁₆". *Scale* None (1" = c. 17° latitude).

Published in Jedidiah Morse, *Geography Made Easy,* 3d ed., opp. p. 250.

706 [1793]

Description In cartouche at lower left: SOUTH / AMERICA. Above top neat line at center: PUBLISHED BY THOMAS & ANDREWS, BOSTON. Below bottom neat line: ENGRAVED FOR MORSES AMERI- CAN GEOGRAPHY BY A. DOOLITTLE N.H. A few topo- graphic features are noted. CURASSOW appears for Curaçao. This is the third Morse map of South America.

Size 6⅝" x 8⅛". *Scale* None (1" = c. 1000 miles).

Published in Jedidiah Morse, *The American Universal Geography,* 1, opp. 642.

707 [1794] *State* I (see also Map 709)

Description [A Chart of the coast of Guyana from River Berbice to River Amanibo.] This is apparently an early state of one of the three sheets comprising Map 709. This part of the chart at least has been engraved on an old plate and many traces of the earlier use are evident, especially in the lower portion. The inset ap- pearing on the second state, "Surinam River from the Entrance to Paramarabo," does not ap- pear here.

Size 21¼" x 32¼". *Scale* 1" = c. 1½ sea leagues.

Published in William Norman, *American Pilot*, 1794, no. 2.

708 [1795] *State* I (II post-1799, see below, Description)

Description In oval at lower left: A / MAP / OF / SOUTH AMERICA / ACCORDING TO THE BEST / AUTHORITIES. Above top neat line: ENGRAVED FOR CAREY'S AMERICAN EDITION OF GUTHRIE'S GEOGRAPHY IMPROVED. Some topographical detail appears and many place names are shown. SANDWICH / LAND is located at the lower right. In the second state, appearing in the 1800 edition of *Carey's General Atlas*, "42" appears in upper left corner.

Size 13⅜" x 13¾". *Scale* 1" = 420 British statute miles (69 to a degree).

Published in Mathew Carey, *Carey's American Atlas*, no. 19; idem, *Carey's General Atlas*, no. 42; idem, *The General Atlas for Carey's Edition of Guthrie's Geography Improved*, no. 42.

709 [1795] *State* II (see also Map 707)

Description At lower left corner: A NEW CHART / OF THE / COAST OF GUAYANA / FROM / RIVER BERBICE TO RIVER MARROWINY / TAKEN FROM THE LATEST SURVEYS & OBSERVATIONS OF THE DUTCH & ENGLISH BY / OSGOOD CARLETON / TEACHER OF MATHEMATICS BOSTON. Below title: BOSTON PUBLISHED & SOLD BY W. NORMAN NO. 75 NEWBURY STREET. This chart was published in three separate sheets, the easternmost being irregular and measuring 14⅜" x 16¾". Much detail is given along the Berbice River and some soundings and indications of mud and sand bars are given along the coast. The peninsula on which N AMSTERDAM is located at the mouth of the SURINAM RIVER has been reshaped and a large sand bar is now indicated on the northwest side. The lower neat line is broken through just south of CAYENNE.

Size 21¼" x 50". *Scale* 1" = c. 1½ sea leagues.

Inset At lower center: SURINAM RIVER / FROM THE ENTRANCE TO / PARAMARABO. Many soundare given and sand bars indicated. Size: 8" x 9". Scale: 1" = 1 sea league.

Published in [William Norman, *A Pilot for the West Indies*], no. 7.

710 [1795]

Description At left center: A NEW CHART / OF THE COAST OF GUAYANA / FROM RIO ORINOCO TO RIVER DEMERARY / CONTAINING THE DUTCH

COLONIES OF / POUMARON / ISSEQUIBO AND DEMERARY / ALSO THE ISLANDS OF TABAGO AND TRINIDAD. Below title: LONDON PUBLISH'D BY LAUPIE [sic] & WHITTLE *1794*. BOSTON REPUBLISHED BY W. NORMAN / NO 75 NEWBURY STREET. An Osgood Carleton certificate appears at lower right. The following is given at the upper right: NOTE. THE SOUNDINGS IN THIS CHART / ARE ALL FEET. Much detail is shown at the mouth of the ISSQUEBO [sic] and DEMERARY rivers.

Size 33⅛" x 20½". *Scale* None (1" = c. 10 miles).

Inset At lower left: [Chart of Trinidad and Tabago]. Some soundings are given. Size: 15¾" x 12¼". Scale: None (1" = c. 5 miles).

Published in [William Norman, *A Pilot for the West Indies*], no. 6.

711 [1795]

Description In rectangle at lower right: SOUTH / AMERICA. This is very similar to Map 702. "Panama" and "Quito" are not given here.

Size 3¾" x 2⅜". *Scale* None (1" = c. 20° latitude).

Published in Charles Smith, *Universal Geography Made Easy*, opp. p. 172.

712 1796

Description In oval at lower left: A / GENERAL MAP / OF / SOUTH AMERICA / FROM THE BEST / SURVEYS, / *1796*. In oval below title: B. TANNER. SCULPT. Below bottom neat line: NEW-YORK. PUBLISHED BY JOHN REID. This is topographical map with many place names. L. PARIMA appears in GUIANA.

Size 14⅜" x 17½". *Scale* None (1" = c. 400 miles).

Published in John Reid, *The American Atlas*, [1796?], no. 2; ibid., 1796, no. 2; William Winterbotham, [*Atlas*], no. 2.

713 [1797]

Description In oval at upper center: A / CORRECT CHART / OF THE COASTS OF / SOUTH AMERICA / FROM THE EQUATOR TO CAPE HORN / ENGRAVED FOR / MALHAMS NAVAL GAZETTEER. In oval below title: ROLLINSON SCULT. Below bottom neat line at center: PUBLISH'D BY SPOTSWOOD & NANCREDE BOSTON. POYAS is given here, north of Patagonia, instead of "Poyus" as on the British, 1795, copy.

Size 9¼" x 7¼". *Scale* 1" = 125 leagues.

Published in John Malham, *The Naval Gazetteer*, *1*, foll. 30.

714 1797

Description At lower right: A MAP OF / SOUTH AMERICA / AND THE / ADJACENT ISLANDS / *1797*. Below bottom neat line at right: CALLENDER SCP. At center: ENGRAVED FOR MORSE'S AMERICAN GAZETTEER. CAPE VERD IS. are shown beyond the right neat line, as is the name: FERNANDO / NORONHO. The engraver is probably Joseph Callender, Jr. This is the fourth Morse map of South America.

Size 6¾" x 5". *Scale* None (1" = c. 1000 miles).

Published in Jedidiah Morse, *The American Gazetteer*, opp. "America."

715 [1798]

Description At lower right: BRASIL [sic]. Beneath title: J. ROCHE SCT. Above top neat line: *39*.

Size 3⅝" x 2½". *Scale* 1" = 700 miles (60 to a degree).

Published in John Gibson, *Atlas Minimus*, no. 39.

716 [1798]

Description At lower left: PARAGUAY / AND / TUCUMAN. Below title: J. ROCHE SCT. Outside right hand neat line: *40*.

Size 2⁷⁄₁₆" x 3⅝". *Scale* 1" = 600 miles (60 to a degree).

Published in John Gibson, *Atlas Minimus*, no. 40.

717 [1798]

Description At lower left: PERU. Below title: J. ROCHE SCT. Above top neat line: *41*.

Size 3⁹⁄₁₆" x 2½". *Scale* 1" = 665 miles (60 to a degree).

Published in John Gibson, *Atlas Minimus*, no. 41.

718 [1798]

Description Between scrolls at lower right: SOUTH / AMERICA. Beneath scroll under title: J. ROCHE SCT. Above top neat line at center: *6*. The River Amazon flows past Lima, Peru, as in the London, 1792, copy.

Size 4⅝" x 2⁷⁄₁₆". *Scale* None (1" = c. 20° latitude).

Published in John Gibson, *Atlas Minimus*, no. 6.

719 1799

Description In oval at lower left: SOUTH AMERICA / FROM THE BEST / SURVEYS / *1799*. Below bottom neat line at center: ENGRAVED FOR PAYNES GEOGRAPHY PUBLISHD BY I LOW NEW YORK. In border at lower left: SCOLES. SC. GALLIPACOS / ISLES appears thus. The map was engraved by John Scoles.

Size 7⅜" x 8¾". *Scale* None (1" = c. 800 miles).

Published in John Payne, *A New and Complete Universal Geography*, 4, opp. 461.

720 [1799]

Description In oval at lower left: A NEW MAP / OF / SOUTH AMERICA / FROM THE LATEST / DISCOVERIES. Some topographical details and many place names are shown. SANDWICH / LAND is given in the South Atlantic.

Size 8" x 9¼". *Scale* None (1" = c. 600 miles).

Published in Joseph Scott, *The New and Universal Gazetteer*, *1*, at leaf Q¹.

721 [1786]

Description In cartouche at lower right: A / CHART / OF THE / GULF STREAM. Below cartouche: JAMES POUPARD, SCULPT.; above top neat line at right: PLATE. 5; below bottom neat line at center: FACING PAGE 315. This well known chart, showing the course of the Gulf Stream off the eastern coast of North America, follows a draft obtained from Captain Timothy Folger, a Nantucket sea captain of Benjamin Franklin's acquaintance. The path of the current was engraved first upon an old chart in London and was later republished in France. This chart was made with a copy of the French edition before the engraver. On the same sheet, at the left, is printed Benjamin Franklin's "Remarks upon the Navigation from Newfoundland to New-York."

Size 7⅝" x 8¹⁄₁₆".   *Scale* None (1" = c. 4° latitude).

Inset At upper left: [Annual Passage of the Herrings]. The reference "B" appears at the upper left. PENNSIL is given thus. The inset is explained in John Gilpin's "Observations on the Annual Passage of Herrings," pp. 236–39. Size: 3½" x 4½". Scale: None (1" = c. 18° latitude).

Published in Benjamin Franklin, "A Letter from Dr. Benjamin Franklin"; idem, *Maritime Observations,* at end. Reproduced in John Elliot Pillsbury, "The Gulf Stream," opp. p. 488 (inset lacking).

References Lloyd A. Brown, "The River in the Ocean," pp. 69–84; Philip L. Phillips, *A List of Maps of America,* p. 592; Lawrence C. Wroth, *Some American Contributions,* Providence, 1947, p. 30.

722 [1786]

Description Below bottom neat line: ANNUAL PASSAGE OF THE HERRINGS. Above top neat line of plate at right: COLUMB. MAG. This map illustrates the supposed progress of the great school of herrings in the Atlantic Ocean, each month's location being noted by a separate roman numeral. It is taken from the inset on Map 721. Above the map here and within the same outside neat lines is a "Plan of Mr.

Fitch's Steam Boat." A "Table" explaining the roman numerals on the map is given on page 157.

Size 3⁹⁄₁₆" x 4" (plate 6¾" x 4⅛").   *Scale* None (1" = c. 18° latitude).

Published in John Gilpin, "Observations on the Annual Passage of Herrings," opp. p. 155.

723 [1789]

Description In rectangle at upper left: CHART / OF THE / GULF STREAM. This is a copy of Map 721. A new plate has been engraved of Benjamin Franklin's chart showing the same course of the Gulf Stream, but it has been superimposed upon a better chart of the North American coast. All states except Vermont are noted. The northern border of New Hampshire is south of part of Maine. The inset, given at the upper left on the earlier chart, is lacking here.

Size 7⅜" x 8¹⁄₁₆".   *Scale* None (1" = c. 4¼° latitude).

Published in Benjamin Franklin, "Remarks upon the Navigation," opp. p. 213.

724 [1792]   *State* I (see also Map 725)

Description [Chart of the North Atlantic Ocean.] Above top neat line at center: TO FACE PAGE 84. VOL. 3D. This is a chart on Mercator's projection of the North Atlantic Ocean showing the courses of several vessels that recorded water temperatures. The Gulf Stream is shown. A list of references is given at top center. A re-engraving of this chart appears in Jonathan Williams, Jr., *Memoria sobre el uso del Termómetro,* foll. p. 21.

Size 8¹⁄₁₆" x 16⅜".   *Scale* None (1" = c. 4° latitude).

Published in Jonathan Williams, Jr., *Memoir,* opp. p. 90; idem, "Memoir," opp. p. 84.

Reference Lloyd A. Brown, "The River in the Ocean," pp. 82–83; Lawrence C. Wroth, *Some American Contributions,* Providence, 1947, p. 31.

725 [1799]   *State* II (see also Map 724)

Description The inscription above the top

neat line has been erased and in the lower right corner has been added: ENGRAVED FOR WILLIAMS'S THERMOMETRICAL NAVIGATION. The shading for the Gulf Stream has been strengthened and carried past the center of the chart. Many arrows showing current directions have been added, only two having appeared on the original chart. The note above the neat line at center, "To face page 84. Vol. 3d," has been erased from the plate.

Published in [Jonathan Williams], *Thermometrical Navigation,* at end. Reproduced in John Elliot Pillsbury, "The Gulf Stream," opp. p. 492 (portion only).

EUROPE

726 [¹734]

Description At top: ORDER OF BATTLE OF THE FRENCH ARMY IN THE LINES BEFORE PHILIPSBURG, IN CASE OF AN ATTACK BY THE GERMANS. / TRANSMITTED TO US BY AN OFFICER OF CONSIDERATION IN THE SAID ARMY. The position of the troops is noted by the name of the unit and the commanding officer. Straight lines are used to separate the units and a half circle is used at the bottom to indicate PHILIPSBURG. Following the title there appears: N. B. THIS, IF THE PRINT WOULD HAVE PERMITTED, SHOULD HAVE BEEN DONE CIRCULARLY, LIKE A HALF-MOON.

Size 6¼" x 9⅛". *Scale* None.

Published in (Philadelphia) *American Weekly Mercury*, October 10 to October 17, 1734, p. 3.

Reference Clarence S. Brigham, *Journals and Journeymen*, p. 42.

727 [¹746]

Description Across top of sheet: THE ORDER OF BATTLE, FOUGHT ON STRAGHALLAN-MOOR, NEAR CULLODEN-HOUSE, ON / WEDNESDAY THE 16TH OF APRIL, 1746. This plan is not an engraving, but instead the printer, William Parks, has used type ornaments, straight lines, parentheses marks, small (degree) circles, and regular type to show the scene of the Battle. No geographical features are noted. A very similar plan appeared a week later in the August 7, 1746, issue of the *Boston Weekly News-Letter* (see Map 728). Both of these plans are accompanied by a verbatim reprinting of: "An accurate Account of the Battle . . . ," published in *The Gentleman's Magazine*, 16 (1746), 241–42. In the *Virginia Gazette* this is given on the page preceding the plan. In *The Gentleman's Magazine*, it is accompanied (on p. 240) by a "Plan of the Battle near Culloden House, April 16, 1746," which may have served as a model for the two American plans. THE ORDER OF MARCH on the lower part of the plan is given on p. 239 of the *Magazine*.

Size 10⅝" x 14½". *Scale* None.

Published in (Williamsburg) *Virginia Gazette*, July 24–31, 1746, pp. [2–3].

728 [¹746]

Description At left outside neat line: THE ORDER OF BATTLE: FOUGHT ON STRAGHALLEN-MOOR, NEAR COLLODDEN-HOUSE, APRIL 16. 1746. This plan is almost the same as Map 727, straight lines being used here instead of type ornaments to designate some of the units. The plan here occupies the upper two-thirds of pp. [2–3] and is oriented from the left. The "Account of the Battle," taken from *The Gentleman's Magazine*, is given in one column along the left edge of the map.

Size 8¼" x 15½". *Scale* None.

Published in *Boston Weekly News-Letter*, August 7, 1746, pp. [2–3].

729 [¹772]

Description In rectangular cartouche at bottom center: DIE MEER = ENGE DER DARDANLLEN. This is a pictorial map of the Straits of the Dardenelles. The woodcut was prepared by Justus Fox.

Size 6½" x 7⅝". *Scale* None.

Published in Christoph Saur, *Der Hoch-Deutsch-Americanische Calender 1773*. Reproduced in Sinclair Hamilton, *Early American Book Illustrators*, no. 24.

Reference See reproduction above, under Published.

730 [¹775]

Description [The environs of Soest, in Westphalia.] Above neat line at left: P. 90; above neat line at right: PLATE VIII; below neat line at left: AITKEN SCULP (very faintly and crudely cut). Soest appears in the center of this map in a circle enclosing all of the surrounding area within 2½ leagues of the town. The map illustrates the reconnoitering technique which is described beginning on page 85. This map was copied from the similar one appearing opposite page 98 in the anonymously published London, 1770, edition of this same book.

Size 5¾" x 7¼". *Scale* None (1" = 1 league).

Published in Roger Stevenson, *Military Instructions*, opp. p. 90.

731 [1776]

Description In rectangle at upper left corner: BATTLE / OF / FONTENOY. Above top neat line at center: EXAMPLE. At right: PL. *24*. Below bottom neat line at left: R A. SCULP. This is a map showing the position of the engaged troops at one point in the Battle which occurred on May 11, 1745. The engraving is by Robert Aitken.

Size 6⅝" x 9⅜". *Scale* 1" = 300 fathoms.

Published in Louis A. de La M. de Clairac, *L'Ingenieur de Campagne,* opp. p. 130.

732 [1776]

Description Above top neat line at center: *I*. INTRENCHED CAMP. At right: PL. *13*. This is a proposed plan for intrenching the camp at Russenheim near Philipsburg, Baden, May, 1734.

Size 6½" x 9⁹⁄₁₆". *Scale* 1" = c. 80 fathoms.

Published in Louis A. de La M. de Clairac, *L'Ingenieur de Campagne,* opp. p. 76.

733 [1776]

Description In rectangle at lower right corner: CAMP OF NORDHEIM / *1745*. Above top neat line at center: EXAMPLE. At right: PL. *30*. This is a plan showing the arrangement of the camp near Worms where the French army under the Prince de Conti recrossed the Rhine in 1745.

Size 6½" x 9⁹⁄₁₆". *Scale* 1" = 100 fathoms.

Published in Louis A. de La M. de Clairac, *L'Ingenieur de Campagne,* opp. p. 170.

734 [1776]

Description In rectangle at upper right corner: THE CASTLE OF O / IN BAVARIA. Above top neat line at center: COUNTRY HOUSE. At right: P. *10*. Below bottom neat line at right: R A. This is a plan of a large, fortified country house between Deckendorf and Ratisbon in Bavaria, which repelled a strong attacking force in 1742. The engraver is Robert Aitken.

Size 6¾" x 9½". *Scale* 1" = 30 fathoms.

Published in Louis A. de La M. de Clairac, *L'Ingenieur de Campagne,* opp. p. 42.

735 [1776]

Description At lower right within irregular wall and moat representing the main part of the town: DECKENDORF. Above top neat line at center: COMMUNICATIONS. At right: PL. *12*. This is a plan showing defenses erected at the end of 1742.

Size 6⁹⁄₁₆" x 9¼". *Scale* 1" = 100 fathoms.

Published in Louis A. de La M. de Clairac, *L'Ingenieur de Campagne,* opp. p. 66.

736 [1776]

Description Above top neat line at center: HEAD OF A BRIDGE. At right: PLATE *7*. Below bottom neat at left: R. A. SCULP. This plan shows a redoubt planned at Donaustauf, Bavaria, in 1742, and illustrates the defenses of the bridge approaches. The engraver is Robert Aitken.

Size 6¾" x 9⅜". *Scale* 1" = 28 [fathoms?].

Published in Louis A. de La M. de Clairac, *L'Ingenieur de Campagne,* foll. p. 24.

737 [1776]

Description Above top neat line at center: HEADS OF BRIDGES. At right: P. *8*. Below bottom neat line at right: R. A. This engraving shows a plan of a redoubt for the bridge at Fort Louis, Alsace, near Strasburg. The engraver is Robert Aitken.

Size 6⅝" x 9⅜". *Scale* 1" = 22 ½ fathoms.

Insets [a] At upper right center: FIG. *1*. The explanation for figures 1, 2, 3, and 4 appears on pp. 24–26. Size: 2⅜" x 3⅛". Scale: Same as above.

[b] At lower right center: FIG. 2. Size: 2⅝" x 3⅛". Scale: Some as above.

[c] At upper right: FIG. *3*. Size: 2¼" x 2¾". Scale: None.

[d] At lower right: FIG. *4*. Size: 1½" x 3¼". Scale: None.

Published in Louis A. de La M. de Clairac, *L'Ingenieur de Campagne,* opp. p. 26.

738 [1776]

Description Above top neat line at center: II. INTRENCHED CAMP. At right: PL. *14*. This is a modification of a plan for intrenchments at Russenheim near Philipsburg, Baden, as proposed in 1734.

Size 6⅝" x 9¼". *Scale* 1" = 80 fathoms.

Published in Louis A. de La M. de Clairac, *L'Ingenieur de Campagne,* opp. p. 78.

739 [1776]

Description Above top neat line at center:

III. CAMP INTRENCHED. At right: PL: *15*. This is the second modification of a plan for intrenchments at Russenheim, near Philipsburg, Baden, as proposed in 1734.

Size 6½″ x 9⅜″. *Scale* 1″ = 80 fathoms.

Published in Louis A. de La M. de Clairac, *L'Ingenieur de Campagne,* opp. p. 82.

740 [1776]

Description In rectangle at upper right corner: NATERBERGH, / CASTLE NEAR DECKENDORF. Above top neat line at center: AN OLD CASTLE. At right: PL. *9*. Below bottom neat line at right: R.A. This shows the plan of an old castle and the adjacent village near Deckendorf, Bavaria. The engraver is Robert Aitken.

Size 6½″ x 9¼″. *Scale* 1″ = 30 fathoms.

Published in Louis A. de La M. de Clairac, *L'Ingenieur de Campagne,* opp. p. 36.

741 [1776]

Description In rectangle at upper left corner: PILSTING / IN BAVARIA. Above top neat line at center: A TOWN TO BE FORTIFIED. At right: PL. *11*. This is a plan showing fortifications erected in 1742.

Size 6½″ x 8⁹⁄₁₆″. *Scale* 1″ = c. 48 fathoms.

Published in Louis A. de La M. de Clairac, *L'Ingenieur de Campagne,* opp. p. 56.

742 [1776]

Description In rectangle at upper right corner: SPIRE. Above top neat line at center: IV. INTRENCHED CAMP. At right: PL. *16*. Between bottom neat lines at left corner: R. A. SCULP. This is a plan for intrenchments at Speyer, Bavaria, made in 1735. The engraver is Robert Aitken.

Size 6½″ x 9⅜″. *Scale* 1″ = 150 fathoms.

Published in Louis A. de La M. de Clairac, *L'Ingenieur de Campagne,* opp. p. 84.

743 [1784]

Description [Action between the Bonhomme Richard, the Serapis, and the Alliance, September, 1779.] This is a series of fourteen small engraved plans showing the various phases of the naval engagement off Flamborough Head in September, 1779. The sketches have been printed separately and pasted above the appropriate paragraphs relating to the phase of the action described. The first plan, on page 37, shows FLAMBOROUGH HEAD and the positions of the Bonhomme Richard, Alliance, Serapis, and the other ships involved in the engagement. The ships are identified in a table at the left. The series continues on pages 38–43.

Size 3½″ x 4⅝″ to ½″ x 1″. *Scale* None (various).

Published in Pierre Landais, *Memorial,* pp. 37–43.

744 [1790]

Description In oval at lower left: EUROPE. Below bottom neat line: ENGRAV'D FOR MORSES GEOGRAPHY BY DOOLITTLE N. HAVEN. Above top neat line at left: NO. VI. Spitzbergen is marked GREENLAND. The ARTIC [sic] CIRCLE is noted. This is the first Morse map of Europe.

Size 4⅛″ x 2⅝″. *Scale* None (1″ = c. 20° latitude).

Published in Jedidiah Morse, *Geography Made Easy,* 2d ed., p. 262.

745 [1790]

Description In vignette at lower left: EUROPE. This is very similar to Map 744. GREENLAND is inscribed on Spitzbergen. The "Arctic Circle" is noted correctly here.

Size 3⅞″ x 2⅝″. *Scale* None (1″ = c. 20° latitude).

Published in Benjamin Workman, *Elements of Geography,* 3d ed., opp. p. 93; ibid., eds. of 1793, 1795, 1796, and 1799.

746 [1791]

Description In rectangle inside neat line at top: EUROPE. Spitzbergen is marked GREENLAND. Three Scilly Islands are indicated almost blocking the entrance to St. George's Channel. This is the second Morse map of Europe.

Size 5⅝″ x 3¼″. *Scale* (1″ = c. 18° latitude).

Published in Jedidiah Morse, *Geography Made Easy,* 3d ed., opp. p. 262.

747 [1792]

Description In scroll at upper right: DENMARK, / NORWAY, / SWEDEN, / AND / FINLAND. Below bottom neat line at right: J. SMITHER SCULPT. Above top neat line at right: PLATE CLVII. This is a map with some topographical detail. SAVANGER appears for Stavanger in Southern Norway, and KOXHOLM appears north of Ladoga Lake in Finland. Political divisions are noted.

Size 7⅛″ x 8⅜″. *Scale* 1″ = 160 British miles.

Inset At upper left: [Northern tip of Norway and EAST GREENLAND (i.e. Spitzbergen)]. Size: 2⅛″ x 2″. Scale: None (1″ = c. 400 miles).

Published in Thomas Dobson, *Encyclopaedia,* 5, opp. 752.

748 [1792]

Description In scroll at upper right: ENGLAND. Below bottom neat line at right: SCOT PHILADA. Above top neat line at right: PLATE CLXXXI. Both England and Wales are shown. Counties are named and boundaries indicated. EDISTON, off Plymouth, and PEEL C, off the Isle of Man, are indicated thus.

Size 6⅞″ x 7½″. *Scale* 1″ = 75 miles.

Published in Thomas Dobson, *Encyclopaedia,* 6, opp. 582.

749 [1792]

Description In scroll at upper left: EUROPE. Below bottom neat line at right: CREED SCULP. Above top neat line at right: PLATE CLXXXVIII. Much detail is shown, including political boundaries and some topographical features. The Adriatic is marked GULF OF VENICE. JOPPA is placed on an imaginary east-west coast south of Cyprus. BARBARY appears inscribed thus in northern Africa. The engraver is probably William Creed.

Size 6⅛″ x 7¾″. *Scale* None (1″ = c. 7° latitude).

Published in Thomas Dobson, *Encyclopaedia,* 7, opp. 40.

750 [1792]

Description At top of plate containing three illustrations: FORTIFICATION. At lower right of central plan: HUNNINGEN. At upper right: PLATE CXCIX. At top of plan: FIG. 3. This is a plan showing the fortress of Hunningen designed by Vaubon to protect the bridge crossing the Rhine at this point. Two other drawings are given at left and top.

Size 4⅜″ x 3″. *Scale* 1″ = 160 toises.

Published in Thomas Dobson, *Encyclopaedia,* 7, opp. 368.

751 [1792]

Description In scroll at lower left: FRANCE. Above top neat line at right: PLATE CCII. The ancient provinces are shown with some larger divisions. The MEREDIAN OF LONDON is inscribed thus.

Size 6¾″ x 8″. *Scale* 1″ = 95 miles (60 to a degree).

Published in Thomas Dobson, *Encyclopaedia,* 7, opp. 446.

752 [1792]

Description In lower right corner: GERMANY. Below title: W. BARKER SCULP. Above top neat line at upper right: PLATE CCXIX. Political divisions are indicated. COME L. appears for Lake Como.

Size 6⅞″ x 8⅜″. *Scale* 1″ = 110 miles.

Published in Thomas Dobson, *Encyclopaedia,* 7, opp. 696.

753 [1793]

Description [A sheet map of the French, Austrian, and Dutch Netherlands, in which the Progress of the Present War may be traced.] This is probably an earlier publication or state of Map 759. It was offered by Mathew Carey in the (Philadelphia) *General Advertiser,* September 2, 1793. The title is taken from the advertisement.

Size Unknown. *Scale* Unknown.

Published Separately.

Reference Evans 25258.

Location No copy located.

754 [1793]

Description [A Map of the Three Northern Districts of France, divided into Departments.] This is probably an earlier publication or state of Map 770. It was offered by Mathew Carey in the (Philadelphia) *General Advertiser,* September 2, 1793. The title is taken from the advertisement.

Size Unknown. *Scale* Unknown.

Published Separately.

Reference Evans 25259.

Location No copy located.

755 [1793]

Description In scroll at upper left corner: IRELAND. Below title in scrolls: S. ALLARDICE SC. Above top neat line at right corner: PLATE CCLVI. This map shows political divisions and a few topographical features. BALLAMORE appears for Baltimore.

Size 6¾″ x 6⁹⁄₁₆″. *Scale* 1″ = 50 miles.

Published in Thomas Dobson, *Encyclopaedia,* 9, opp. 344.

756 [1793]

Description In scrolls at upper right corner: ITALY. Below title in scrolls: S. ALLARDICE SC. Above top neat line at right corner: PLATE CCLVII. The Dalmatian coast is shown as Italian. A few topographical features are noted.

Size 6⅞″ x 8³⁄₁₆″.   *Scale* 1″ = 102 miles.

Published in Thomas Dobson, *Encyclopaedia, 9,* opp. 390.

757 [1793]

Description [The Royal Exchange, London.] This is a plan showing the Exchange, its several "walks," and identifying the surrounding streets. It is very rudimentary, the printer using only straight lines and regular type.

Size 3⅜″ x 4⅛″.   *Scale* 1″ = c. 60 feet.

Published in Thomas Dobson, *Encyclopaedia, 10,* 253.

758 [1793]

Description In decorative oval at upper left: EUROPE. Below bottom neat line, at center: ENGRAVED FOR MORSES AMERICAN GEOGRAPHY. At right: J. ALLEN SCT. Above top neat line: PUBLISH'D BY THOMAS & ANDREWS BOSTON. FRANCFORT and CONSTANTINOPL appear thus; WHALE FISHERY is noted in the Arctic. The engraver is John Allen.

Size 6¾″ x 8¼″.   *Scale* None (1″ = c. 7° latitude).

Published in Jedidiah Morse, *The American Universal Geography,* 3d ed., 2, front.

759 [1794] *State* I (see also Map 782; III post-1799, see Map 782, Description)

Description In oval at upper left: THE / AUSTRIAN / FRENCH AND DUTCH / NETHERLANDS, / FROM THE BEST / AUTHORITIES. In oval below title: JOSEPH T. SCOTT SCULP. Above top neat line: ENGRAVED FOR CAREY'S AMERICAN EDITION OF GUTHRIES GEOGRAPHY IMPROVED. Some topographical features are noted. Map 753 may be an earlier publication or state of this map.

Size 11½″ x 13¾″.   *Scale* None (1″ = c. 17½ miles).

Published in Mathew Carey *The General Atlas for Carey's Edition of Guthrie's Geography Improved,* no. 10; idem, *A General Atlas for the Present War,* no. 2.

760 [1794] *State* I (II post-1799, see below, Description)

Description In oval at upper left: THE EMPIRE OF / GERMANY / WITH THE *13* CANTONS OF /

SWITZERLAND / FROM THE BEST / AUTHORITIES. In oval beneath title: J. T. SCOTT SCULP. Above top neat line: ENGRAVED FOR CAREY'S AMERICAN EDITION OF GUTHRIE'S GEOGRAPHY IMPROVED. Many place names are shown in Germany. The second state of this map appeared in the September 9, 1800, edition of *Carey's General Atlas* with the figure "11" added at the upper left corner.

Size 16⅞″ x 16³⁄₁₆″.   *Scale* None (1″ = c. 41½ miles).

Published in Mathew Carey, *Carey's General Atlas,* no. 11; idem, *A General Atlas for the Present War,* no. 5; idem, *The General Atlas for Carey's Edition of Guthrie's Geography Improved,* no. 11.

761 [1794] *State* I (see also Map 808; III post-1799, see Map 808, Description)

Description In oval at lower left: FRANCE / DIVIDED INTO / CIRCLES / AND / DEPARTMENTS. The NAMES OF THE / METROPOLITAN CIRCLES are listed at the left with references by number to the boundaries shown on the map. Principal places in each department, capitals of the circles and departments, seats of the Bishops, and towns having a Tribunal of Justice are noted. The title page of Carey's *A General Atlas* indicates that this map was engraved by William Barker.

Size 12⅝″ x 14¹⁄₁₆″.   *Scale* 1″ = 55 British statute miles.

Published in Mathew Carey, *Carey's General Atlas,* no. 12; idem, *The General Atlas for Carey's Edition of Guthrie's Geography Improved,* no. 12; idem, *A General Atlas for the Present War,* no. 3.

762 [1794] *State* I (see also Map 780; III post-1799, see Map 780, Description)

Description In oval at upper right: ITALY, / AND, / SARDINIA, / FROM THE BEST / AUTHORITIES. Beneath oval: TIEBOUT NEW YORK. Above top neat line: ENGRAVED FOR CAREY'S AMERICAN EDITION OF GUTHRIE'S GEOGRAPHY IMPROVED. Political divisions are indicated and many place names given.

Size 13⅜″ x 14⅜″.   *Scale* 1″ = 65 Italian miles (75 to a degree).

Published in Mathew Carey, *The General Atlas for Carey's Edition of Guthrie's Geography Improved,* no. 16; idem, *A General Atlas for the Present War,* no. 6.

763 [1794] *State* I (II post-1799, see below, Description)

Description In oval at upper left: THE / SEVEN / UNITED PROVINCES / OF / HOLLAND /

163

FRIESLAND / GRONINGEN / OVERYSSEL / GELDERS / UTRECHT / AND / ZEALAND / FROM THE BEST AUTHORITIES. Beneath oval: C TIEBOUT SCULPT N YORK. Above top neat line: ENGRAVED FOR CAREY'S AMERICAN EDITION OF GUTHRIE'S GEOGRAPHY IMPROVED. The names of the first six provinces in the title are arranged in three double columns. Political divisions, place names, and some topographical features are noted. No. XV of the serial issue of William Guthrie's *Geography* was offered in the (Philadelphia) *General Advertiser*, September 2, 1793, as: "Embellished with a Map of the Seven United Provinces." No copy of this serial issue has been located. It may have included an earlier publication of the map described here.

Size 115⁄8″ x 135⁄8″. *Scale* 1″ = 38 English miles (691⁄2 to a degree).

Published in Mathew Carey, *Carey's General Atlas*, no. 9; idem, *The General Atlas for Carey's Edition of Guthrie's Geography Improved*, no. 9; idem, *A General Atlas for the Present War*, no. 1.

764 [1794] *State* I (II post-1799, see below, Description)

Description In oval at lower right corner: SPAIN / AND / PORTUGAL, / FROM THE BEST / AUTHORITIES. Above top neat line: ENGRAVED FOR CAREYS AMERICAN EDITION OF GUTHRIES GEOGRAPHY IMPROVED. Political divisions, place names, and some topographical features are noted. The title page of Mathew Carey's *A General Atlas* states that this map was engraved by Cornelius Tiebout. The second state of the map appeared in the September 9, 1800, edition of Carey's *The General Atlas* with the figure "15" added at the upper left corner.

Size 133⁄8″ x 141⁄2″. *Scale* 1″ = 55 British statute miles.

Published in Mathew Carey, *Carey's General Atlas*, no. 15; idem, *The General Atlas for Carey's Edition of Guthrie's Geography Improved*, no. 15; idem, *A General Atlas for the Present War*, no. 4.

765 [1794]

Description Between extended top neat line and marginal degree line: A MAP OF GENERAL DUMOURIER'S CAMPAIGN ON THE MEUSE, / IN *1792*. Below bottom neat line at center: ENGRAVED FOR BERRY. ROGER'S & BERRYS. EDITION. At far right: RALPH SCT. N-YORK. This is a map showing the victory of the French troops under General Charles François Dumouriez at Valmy over the forces of the Duke of Brunswick. Principal towns, roads, and some topographical features

are noted, as well as the routes of march of the armies. The engraver may be W. Ralph.

Size 101⁄8″ x 12″. *Scale* None (1″ = 9 miles).

Published in John D. Moore, *A Journal during a Residence in France, 2*, at end; ibid., 2, Chambersburg, Penna., 1797, at end.

766 [1794] *State* I (see also Map 790)

Description In rectangle inside neat line at top: EUROPE. At lower right corner: DOOLITTLE. GREENLAND appears again east of Spitzbergen. The SCILLY I are indicated at southern tip of Ireland. The last "o" in Constantinople is omitted. This is similar to Map 746 which, however, spells Constantinople correctly and does not name the meridian of London. This is the fourth Morse map of Europe.

Size 53⁄4″ x 31⁄4″. *Scale* None (1″ = c. 18° latitude).

Published in Jedidiah Morse, *Geography Made Easy*, 4th ed., opp. p. 312.

[1794] see Map 876.

767 [1795] *State* I (II post-1799, see below, Description)

Description In oval at upper right: AN / ACCURATE MAP / OF / ENGLAND AND WALES / WITH / THE PRINCIPAL ROADS FROM THE BEST / AUTHORITIES. Beneath oval: DOOLITTLE SC. NEWHAVEN. Above top neat line: ENGRAVED FOR CAREY'S AMERICAN EDITION OF GUTHRIE'S GEOGRAPHY IMPROVED. The county boundaries are noted and numbers on the map refer to an alphabetical list of REFERENCES TO THE COUNTIES in the upper left corner. Many roads are shown. The second state appears in the September 9, 1800, edition of *Carey's General Atlas* with the figure "7" added at the upper right corner.

Size 135⁄8″ x 123⁄4″. *Scale* 1″ = 30 British statute miles.

Published in Mathew Carey, *Carey's General Atlas*, no. 7; idem, *The General Atlas for Carey's Edition of Guthrie's Geography Improved*, no. 7.

768 [1795] *State* I (see also Map 778; III post-1799, see Map 778, Description)

Description In oval at upper left: AN / ACCURATE MAP OF / EUROPE / FROM / THE BEST AUTHORITIES. Below bottom neat line at right corner: ENGRAV'D BY S. HILL, BOSTON. Above top neat line at center: ENGRAVED FOR CAREY'S AMERICAN EDITION OF GUTHRIE'S GEOGRAPHY IMPROVED. Political divisions are shown and some topographical detail. The major banks or shallows of the North Sea are indicated.

Size 13⅜″ x 14¹⁵⁄₁₆″. *Scale* None (1″ = c. 3° latitude).

Published in Mathew Carey, *Carey's General Atlas*, no. 7; idem, *The General Atlas for Carey's Edition of Guthrie's Geography Improved*, no. 3.

769 [1795] *State* I (see also Map 779; III post-1799, see Map 779, Description)

Description In oval near lower center: A / MAP OF / IRELAND / ACCORDING TO THE BEST / AUTHORITIES. In oval beneath title: J. T. SCOTT. SCULP. Above top neat line: ENGRAVED FOR CAREY'S AMERICAN EDITION OF GUTHRIE'S GEOGRAPHY IMPROVED. County boundaries are shown and numbers keyed to the LIST OF THE COUNTIES at upper left. No number appears on County Mayo to correspond with the list in upper left corner.

Size 14⅝″ x 13¼″. *Scale* 1″ = 18 Irish miles (54½ & 34 poles to a degree).

Published in Mathew Carey, *The General Atlas for Carey's Edition of Guthrie's Geography Improved*, no. 8.

770 [1795] *State* I (II post-1799, see below, Description)

Description In oval at upper right: A MAP OF / THE SEAT OF WAR IN / FRANCE, / WITH THE COUNTRY DIVIDED INTO ITS / SEVERAL DEPARTMENTS. In oval under title: WM. BARKER SCULP. Beneath oval: ENGRAVED FOR CAREY'S AMERICAN EDITION OF GUTHRIE'S GEOGRAPHY IMPROVED. An explanation for the roman numerals appearing on the map is given above the upper neat line; several notes and the scale are given below the lower neat line. Map 754 may be an earlier publication or state of this map. The second known state appears in the September 9, 1800, edition of *Carey's General Atlas* with the figure "13" at the upper left corner.

Size 7¼″ x 10″. *Scale* 1″ = 15 leagues of 2280 toises.

Published in Mathew Carey, *Carey's General Atlas*, no. 13; idem, *The General Atlas for Carey's Edition of Guthrie's Geography Improved*, no. 13.

771 [1795] *State* I (II post-1799, see below, Description)

Description In a rectangle at lower left: POLAND, SHEWING THE CLAIMS OF / RUSSIA, PRUSSIA & AUSTRIA, UNTIL THE LATE / DEPREDATIONS, / THE EXTENT OF WHICH CANNOT AS YET / BE AS-CERTAINED. Below rectangle and marginal degree line: W. BARKER SCULP. Below bottom neat line: ENGRAVED FOR CAREY'S AMERICAN EDITION OF GUTHRIES GEOGRAPHY IMPROVED. Political divisions and place names are given, and the REMARKS at the lower left give the key to the claims of Russia, Prussia, and Austria in Poland. Some topographical features are noted. The second state of this map appears in the September 9, 1800, edition of *Carey's General Atlas* with the figure "18" added at the upper left corner.

Size 12⁵⁄₁₆″ x 14⅜″. *Scale* 1″ = 60 British statute miles.

Published in Mathew Carey, *Carey's General Atlas*, no. 18; idem, *The General Atlas for Carey's Edition of Guthrie's Geography Improved*, no. 18.

772 [1795] *State* I (II and III post-1799, see below, Description)

Description In oval at lower left: THE / RUSSIAN EMPIRE, / IN / EUROPE AND ASIA. In oval below title: W. BARKER SCULP. Beneath oval: ENGRAVED FOR CAREY'S AMERICAN EDITION OF GUTHRIE'S GEOGRAPHY IMPROVED. Political divisions, many place names, and some topographical details are given. The second state of the map was used in the September 9, 1800, edition of *Carey's General Atlas* with the figure "5" added at the upper left corner. The third state appeared in the 1814 edition of *Carey's General Atlas* with the inscription under the title oval removed and the number "39" added at the upper right.

Size 11⅜″ x 15⅞″. *Scale* 1″ = 300 British statute miles (69 to a degree).

Published in Mathew Carey, *Carey's General Atlas*, no. 5; idem, *The General Atlas for Carey's Edition of Guthrie's Geography Improved*, no. 5.

773 [1795] *State* I (II and III post-1799, see below, Description)

Description In oval at upper left: SCOTLAND / WITH THE / PRINCIPAL ROADS / FROM THE BEST / AUTHORITIES. Above top neat line: ENGRAVED FOR M. CAREY'S EDITION OF GUTHRIE'S GEOGRAPHY IMPROVED. Universities, presbyteries, and boroughs are especially indicated as well as roads and county boundaries. Some topographical features are noted. The second state appears in the September 9, 1800, edition of *Carey's General Atlas* with the figure "6" added at the upper right corner. Another state is given in the 1814 *Carey's General Atlas* with the inscription above the neat line removed and the number "49" now appearing at the upper right.

Size 14⅞″ x 11″.   *Scale* 1″ = 21 common Scotch miles.

Inset At upper right: [Shetland Isles]. Size: 3⅝″ x 2⅝″. Scale: same as above.

Published in Mathew Carey, *Carey's General Atlas,* no. 6; idem, *The General Atlas for Carey's Edition of Guthrie's Geography Improved,* no. 6.

774 [1795]   *State* I (II and III post-1799, see below, Description)

Description In oval at lower right: SWEDEN, / DENMARK, NORWAY / AND FINLAND. / FROM THE BEST / AUTHORITIES. Beneath oval to left: EN-GRAV'D BY S. HILL BOSTON. Above top neat line: ENGRAVED FOR CAREY'S AMERICAN EDITION OF GUTHRIE'S GEOGRAPHY IMPROVED. Political divisions and some place names are noted. The second state appears in the September 9, 1800, edition of *Carey's General Atlas* with the figure "4" added at the upper left corner. It appears again in the 1814 *Carey's General Atlas* with the inscription above the top neat line removed and the number "38" now given at the upper right.

Size 13⅛″ x 14⁷⁄₁₆″.   *Scale* 1″ = 100 British statute miles.

Inset At upper left: [Map of Iceland and part of Greenland.] The east Greenland coast is marked WEST / GREENLAND. Size: 3¹⁄₁₆″ x 4⁷⁄₁₆″. Scale: None (1″ = c. 35 miles).

Published in Mathew Carey, *Carey's General Atlas,* no. 4; idem, *The General Atlas for Carey's Edition of Guthrie's Geography Improved,* no. 4.

775 [1795]   *State* I (see also Map 781; III post-1799, see Map 781, Description)

Description In oval at upper left: SWITZER-LAND / ACCORDING TO THE BEST / AUTHORITIES. In oval below title: JOSEPH T. SCOTT SCULPT. Above top neat line: ENGRAVED FOR CAREY'S AMERICAN EDITION OF GUTHRIE'S GEOGRAPHY IMPROVED. Political divisions are noted and some topographical detail.

Size 8⅛″ x 11″.   *Scale* 1″ = 20 miles (60 to a degree).

Published in Mathew Carey, *The General Atlas for Carey's Edition of Guthrie's Geography Improved,* no. 17.

776 [1795]   *State* I (see also Map 783; III post-1799, see Map 783, Description)

Description In oval at lower right: TURKEY, / IN EUROPE AND / HUNGARY; / FROM THE BEST / AUTHORITIES. In oval below title: W. BARKER SCULP. Above top neat line: ENGRAVED FOR

CAREY'S AMERICAN EDITION OF GUTHRIE'S GEOGRAPHY IMPROVED. Political divisions are shown.

Size 13⅛″ x 14″.   *Scale* 1″ = 100 British statute miles.

Published in Mathew Carey, *The General Atlas for Carey's Edition of Guthrie's Geography Improved,* no. 14.

777 [1795]

Description In rectangle at lower left: EUROPE. This map appears to be copied from Map 745. GREENLAND is still inscribed at Spitzbergen.

Size 3¾″ x 2⅜″.   *Scale* None (1″ = c. 20° latitude).

Published in Charles Smith, *Universal Geography Made Easy,* opp. p. 21.

778 [1796]   *State* II (see Map 768; III post-1799, see below, Description)

Description The shading along the shore lines has been strengthened throughout, as has the stippling of the banks in the North Sea. The north east coast line of the Athos Peninsula has been shaded (under the "M" of MT. ATHOS). This map appears in the September 9, 1800, edition of *Carey's General Atlas* with the figure "3" added at the upper left corner.

Published in Mathew Carey, *Carey's General Atlas,* no. 3.

779 [1796]   *State* II (see Map 769; III post-1799, see below, Description)

Description Many of the lines, especially those indicating roads have been strengthened. The number: *21* has been added on the map in County Mayo as the reference to the list of names. This map appears again in the September 9, 1800, edition of *Carey's General Atlas* with the figure "8" added at the upper right corner.

Published in Mathew Carey, *Carey's General Atlas,* no. 8.

780 [1796]   *State* II (see also Map 762; III post-1799, see below, Description)

Description Some of the lines have been strengthened, especially the coast shading lines. These lines have been erased from between the "N" and "I" of the Gulf of ORISTAGNI in Sardinia. This map appears in the September 9, 1800, edition of *Carey's General Atlas* with the figure "16" added at the upper left corner.

Published in Mathew Carey, *Carey's General Atlas,* no. 16.

781 [1796] *State* II (see also Map 775; III post-1799, see below, Description)

Description The shading along the shores of the lakes has been strengthened. This map appears in the September 9, 1800, edition of *Carey's General Atlas* with the figure "17" added at the upper left corner.

Published in Mathew Carey, *Carey's General Atlas,* no. 17.

782 [1796] *State* II (see also Map 759; III post-1799, see below, Description)

Description Some of the lines have been strengthened, including the coastal shading, the imprint above the neat line, the neat line, and the marginal degree line. This map appears in the September 9, 1800, edition of *Carey's General Atlas* with the figure "10" added at the upper left corner.

Published in Mathew Carey, *Carey's General Atlas,* no. 10.

783 [1796] *State* II (see also Map 776; III post-1799, see below, Description)

Description Many lines have been strengthened, especially the coast line shading. This shading is evenly heavy, with lines extending from island to island from Zara to Sebenico, in Venetian Dalmatia. This map appears in the September 9, 1800, edition of *Carey's General Atlas* with the figure "10" added at the upper left corner.

Published in Mathew Carey, *Carey's General Atlas,* no. 14.

784 [1796]

Description At top center of page with two views and map: ISLAND OF PONZA. At bottom above map: FIG. *1.* At bottom right: THACKARA SC. At upper right: PLATE CCCCXII. This is an outline map of Ponza, one of the Pontine or Ponza Islands in the Tyrrhenian Sea off the Italian Coast. No place names or topographical details are given. It was copied from a map drawn and engraved by Andrew Bell in the 3d ed. of the *Encyclopaedia Britannica.* This in turn was taken from a plate appearing in the Royal Society of London, *Philosophical Transactions,* 76 (1785), opp. 380 (Tab. X).

Size 2" x 5¾" (on plate: 9¾" x 6¾"). *Scale* 1" = 1¼ miles.

Published in Thomas Dobson, *Encyclopaedia, 15,* opp. 372.

785 [1796]

Description In oval at upper right: POLAND / LITHUANIA / AND / PRUSSIA. Below title outside oval: VALLANCE SC. Above top neat line at right: PLATE CCCCX. Political divisions are shown.

Size 6¾" x 8". *Scale* 1" = 130 miles.

Published in Thomas Dobson, *Encyclopaedia, 15,* opp. 272.

786 [1796]

Description In oval at upper center: RUSSIA / OR / MOSCOVY. In oval below title: SCOT & ALLARDICE. Above top neat line at right corner: PLATE CCCCXLIII. Place names and political divisions are shown. The STRAIT OF VAVGOT appears thus between NOVAYA ZEMLIA and SAMOEDI. The engravers are Robert Scot and Samuel Allardice.

Size 6⅝" x 8⅜". *Scale* 1" = 500 Russian versts.

Published in Thomas Dobson, *Encyclopaedia, 16,* opp. 554.

787 [1796]

Description In scroll at lower left: SCOTLAND. In border at lower right corner: SCOT & ALLARDICE. Above top neat line at right corner: PLATE CCCCXLVI. Political divisions are noted. RGYLE SHIRE appears thus. The engravers are Robert Scot and Samuel Allardice.

Size 7" x 7½". *Scale* 1" = 50 miles.

Inset At upper right: SHETLAND ISLES. Size: 1½" x 1⁹⁄₁₆". Scale: None (1" = c. 65 miles).

Published in Thomas Dobson, *Encyclopaedia, 16,* opp. 722.

788 [1796]

Description In oval at upper left: ENGLAND / SCOTLAND / IRELAND / AND / WALES / FROM THE BEST AUTHORITIES / BY CYRUS HARRIS. Beneath oval: DOOLITTLE SCULP. Above top neat line: PUBLISHED BY THOMAS & ANDREWS. Many place names are given. The Shetland Islands break the inner neat line at the upper right. ISLE OF WIGT and LONDN appear thus.

Size 9⅞" x 7¾". *Scale* None (1" = c. 80 miles).

Published in Jedidiah Morse, *The American Universal Geography,* 3d ed., 2, opp. 98.

789 [1796]

Description [A Map of the River Rhine, from Nimeguen to Basle.] The following advertisement, bearing the date "March 26," appeared in the (Philadelphia) *Gazette of the United States*, April 1, 1796: "This day is published, at No. 201 Arch Street, and may also be had at Folwell's Printing Office, No. 33, in the same street, a map of the River Rhine, from Nimeguen to Basle, shewing the actual seat of war between the French and Austrians." The title is taken from the advertisement.

Size Unknown.   *Scale* Unknown.

Published Separately.

Location No copy located.

790 [1796]   *State* II (see also Map 766)

Description The letters in EUROPE are now solid instead of double lined. The worn plate has been recut considerably but no changes are noted. The engraver's signature in the lower right corner has not been recut and does not show on the copy examined. This is the fourth Morse map of Europe.

Published in Jedidiah Morse, *Geography Made Easy*, 5th ed., opp. p. 312.

791 [1796]

Description In oval at lower right: EUROPE / FROM THE BEST / AUTHORITIES. Beneath oval: ENGRAVED BY A. DOOLITTLE N.H. Above top neat line: PUBLISHED BY THOMAS & ANDREWS, BOSTON. ORLEAS appears for Orleans, ABERDEE for Aberdeen, and STR OF GIBRALTAR, but GIBRALTER town. The publishers are Isaiah Thomas and Ebenezer T. Andrews.

Size 7⅜" x 8¹⁵⁄₁₆".   *Scale* None (1" = c. 480 miles).

Published in Jedidiah Morse, *The American Universal Geography*, 3d ed., 2, front.

792 [1796]

Description In oval at lower left: FRANCE / DIVIDED INTO / CIRCLES / AND / DEPARTMENTS. In oval beneath title: DOOLITTLE SCULP: Above top neat line: PUBLISHED BY THOMAS & ANDREWS, BOSTON. Political divisions are noted. The NAMES OF THE / METROPOLITAN CIRCLES are given in a reference table at left center. Another table of EXPLANATION is given below it. The mileage figures on the scale of "British Statute miles" are inaccurate: "60," "80," and "100," should be substituted for 50, 60, and 70. ENCLAND appears thus and Carcassone as CAROASSONE. This map is very similar to Map 761.

Size 7½" x 8½".   *Scale* 1" = 80 British statute miles.

Published in Jedidiah Morse, *The American Universal Geography*, 3d ed., 2, opp. 348.

793 [1796]

Description In oval at lower left: NETHERLANDS / FROM THE BEST / AUTHORITIES. Below oval: DOOLITTLE SC:. Above top neat line: PUBLISHED BY THOMAS & ANDREWS, BOSTON. Political divisions are noted and many place names.

Size 7⅛" x 9".   *Scale* 1" = 24 British statute miles.

Published in Jedidiah Morse, *The American Universal Geography*, 3d ed., 2, opp. 342.

794 [1796]

Description In oval at lower left: POLAND / SHEWING THE CLAIMS OF / RUSSIA PRUSSIA & AUSTRIA / FROM THE BEST / AUTHORITIES. In lower left corner: DOOLITTLE SC:. Above top neat line: PUBLISHED BY THOMAS & ANDREWS, BOSTON. Above the title oval are three lines of REMARKS in which AUSTRA appears for Austria. Two large shaded areas appear and a note at the upper left explains that area "A" has been annexed by Russia, "B," by Prussia.

Size 7⅜" x 8⅜".   *Scale* 1" = 100 British miles (69½ to a degree).

Published in Jedidiah Morse, *The American Universal Geography*, 3d ed., 2, opp. 254.

795 [1796]

Description In oval at lower left: SWITZERLAND, / WITH ITS SUBJECTS & ALLIES / FROM THE BEST / AUTHORITIES. Beneath oval: DOOLITTLE SCULP. Above top neat line: PUBLISHED BY THOMAS & ANDREWS. This is a topographical map showing also the cantons and their boundaries. L ZURICH and ZURIEH are given thus.

Size 6⅞" x 8¾".   *Scale* 1" = 30 British statute miles (69½ to a degree).

Published in Jedidiah Morse, *The American Universal Geography*, 3d ed., 2, opp. 304.

796 [1797]

Description In scrolls at lower right: SPAIN / AND / PORTUGAL. Below title: VALLANCE SC. Above top neat line at right: PLATE CCCCLXXIII. The provinces are shown with their boundaries. Some topographical features appear.

Size 6½" x 8⅝".   *Scale* 1" = 120 British statute miles.

Published in Thomas Dobson, *Encyclopaedia*, *17*, opp. 619.

797 [1797]

Description In oval in upper right: A / CORRECT CHART / OF THE / BALTIC SEA, / ENGRAVED FOR / MALHAM'S NAVAL GAZETTEER. Below oval:

ROLLINSON SCULPT. N. YORK. Below bottom neat line at center: PUBLISH'D BY SPOTSWOOD AND NANCREDE BOSTON. This is a chart on Mercator's projection. DANTZICK is shown thus. No soundings are given. The chart was published by William Spotswood and Joseph Nancrede. The engraver is William Rollinson.

Size 9¼" x 7⅜". *Scale* 1" = 22 leagues.

Published in John Malham, *The Naval Gazetteer, 1,* opp. 71.

798 [¹797]

Description In oval at upper left: A / CORRECT CHART / OF THE / BAY OF BISCAY, / ENGRAVED FOR / MALHAMS NAVAL GAZETTEER. In oval below title: ROLLINSON SCT. N YORK. Below bottom neat line: PUBLISH'D BY SPOTSWOOD AND NANCREDE BOSTON. Many soundings and notes are given along the French coast.

Size 9⅜" x 7¼". *Scale* 1" = 16 leagues.

Published in John Malham, *The Naval Gazetteer, 1,* opp. 103.

799 [¹797]

Description In oval at lower right: A / CORRECT CHART / OF THE COAST OF / PORTUGAL, / ENGRAVED FOR / MALHAM'S NAVAL GAZETTEER. Above oval: HILL, SC. Above top neat line at center: PUBLISHED BY SPOTSWOOD & NANCREDE, BOSTON. A few soundings are given along the coast. The engraver is Samuel Hill.

Size 9⅜" x 7⁹⁄₁₆". *Scale* None (1" = c. 35 miles).

Published in John Malham, *The Naval Gazetteer, 2,* opp. 48.

800 [¹797]

Description In oval at lower right: A / CORRECT CHART / OF THE / ENGLISH CHANNEL / ENGRAVED FOR / MALHAMS NAVAL GAZETTEER. Under oval: ROLLINSON SCULPT. N. YORK. Beneath bottom neat line at center: PUBLISH'D SEPR. *1796* BY SPOTSWOOD AND NANCREDE BOSTON. Many soundings and notes are given throughout the Channel.

Size 7½" x 12⅛". *Scale* None (1" = 28 miles).

Published in John Malham, *The Naval Gazetteer, 1,* opp. 193.

801 [¹797]

Description In oval at lower right: A / CORRECT CHART / OF THE / GERMAN OCEAN, / ENGRAVED FOR / MALHAMS NAVAL GAZETTEER. In oval below title: ROLLINSON SCT. NEW YORK. Under

bottom neat line at center: PUBLISH'D BY SPOTSWOOD & NANCREDE BOSTON. This chart shows the North Sea from the STR. OF DOVER TO DOGGER BANK. No soundings are given.

Size 7½" x 9⅛". *Scale* 1" = 9 leagues.

Published in John Malham, *The Naval Gazetteer, 2,* opp. 488.

802 [¹797]

Description In oval at lower right: A / CORRECT CHART / OF THE / IRISH SEA, / WITH / ST. GEORGES CHANNEL / ENGD FOR MALHAMS NAVAL GAZETTEER. Beneath oval: ROLLINSON SCULPT. NEW YORK. Below bottom neat line: PUBLISH'D BY SPOTSWOOD AND NANCREDE BOSTON. No soundings are given.

Size 9⅜" x 7¼". *Scale* None (1" = 29 miles).

Published in John Malham, *The Naval Gazetteer, 1,* opp. 527.

803 [¹797]

Description In oval near upper center: A / CORRECT CHART / OF THE / MEDITERRANEAN SEA / ENGRAVED FOR / MALHAM'S NAVAL GAZETTEER. In oval below title: ROLLINSON SCULPT. N YORK. Below bottom neat line: PUBLISH'D BY SPOTSWOOD AND NANCREDE BOSTON. No soundings are given.

Size 7⅛" x 15¼". *Scale* 1" = c. 65 leagues.

Published in John Malham, *The Naval Gazetteer, 2,* opp. 132.

804 [¹797]

Description In oval at lower right: A / CORRECT CHART / OF THE / NORTH SEA, / ENGRAVED FOR / MALHAMS NAVAL GAZETTEER. Beneath oval: S. H. SC. Beneath bottom neat line at center: PUBLISHED BY SPOTSWOOD & NANCREDE, BOSTON. The engraver is Samuel Hill. No soundings are given.

Size 9¼" x 7⅜". *Scale* 1" = 75 leagues.

Published in John Malham, *The Naval Gazetteer, 2,* opp. 203.

805 [¹797]

Description Above top neat line: PLAN OF THE BLOCKADE OF CADIZ / BY THE / ENGLISH FLEET / UNDER THE COMMAND OF THE EARL OF ST. VINCENT, / AS TAKEN ON THE SPOT BY A BRITISH OFFICER, ON THE *18*TH OF MAY, *1797*. This rough plan of the British blockade of the Spanish fleet at Cadiz is accompanied by 21 lettered and numerical references printed beneath it. The drawing within the neat lines and without the title measures 4⅞″ x 5½″. While William Cobbett published this in a regular issue of his *Gazette,* he also issued a separate printing of the same map within a few days as evidenced by the following advertisement which appeared on September 27: "Just Published By Peter Porcupine An Accurate Plan of the Blockade of Cadiz . . . Elegantly printed on one sheet of superfine paper, suited for framing.—Price 12½ cents." The same advertisement appeared also in subsequent issues of the *Gazette.* No copy of this separate printing has thus far been discovered. Evans notes the same plan with the price being "9d." instead of "12½ cents." No copies are located. The plan as given on page 687 of the *Porcupine's Gazette* is at the upper center of a page with the headline: "Blockade of Cadiz" and with reports of the blockade being given in the accompanying columns.

Size 7½″ x 5½″.   *Scale* None (1″ = c. 2½ miles).

Published in (Philadelphia) *Porcupine's Gazette,* September 21, 1797; separately.

Reference Evans 31943.

Location No copy of separates located.

806 1797

Description In oval at lower right: AN / ACCURATE MAP / OF / EUROPE / COMPILED / FROM THE BEST / AUTHORITIES / *1797.* Much detail is shown. Modern Belgium is indicated as NETHE 11. Letters have been inserted to correct the spelling of ST. GEORGE'S CHAN. and STRAITS OF GIBRALTER [sic].

Size 8⅛″ x 9⅜″.   *Scale* None (1″ = 480 miles).

Published in Joseph Scott, *The New and Universal Gazetteer,* 2, opp. 400.

807 [1798]

Description Below lower neat line: PLAN OF THE FRENCH INVASION OF ENGLAND AND IRELAND, &c. This is an outline plan of Western Europe. Various ports are noted: TOULON, CARTHAGENA, BREST, etc., with dotted lines showing the contemplated routes of the invasion fleets. The plan is given at the top of a broadside, which measures 17½″ x 12½″, detailing the planned invasion. "Remarks on the Chart" are given at right bottom corner. Directly under this is: "Philadelphia: Printed by James Carey [1798]." James Carey published *Carey's United States Recorder* (Philadelphia) during most of this year (January 23 to August 30).

Size 7″ x 9″.   *Scale* None (1″ = c. 200 miles).

Published Separately.

Reference Evans 33753.

Location DLC.

808 1798 *State* II (see also Map 761; III post-1799, see below, Description)

Description The following imprint now appears below bottom neat line: PHILADA. PUBLISH'D BY J. STEWART & CO. FEBY. *17, 1798.* The third state appears in September 9, 1800, *Carey's General Atlas* with the figure "12" added at the upper left corner.

Published in John Gifford, [John Richards Green], *History of France, 4,* front.

809 [1798]

Description At top center above neat line of two part plate: WAR. At right: FIG. *1.* At extreme right: PLATE DXXV. At bottom right corner: LAWSON SC. This plate is divided in two equal sections: the upper, designated FIG. *1,* is a map-like representation of the manner of establishing an outpost; the lower portion carries no designation but is referred to in the text (*18* p. 751) as "Fig. 2" and is a map of the environs of Soest, in Westphalia, It is similar to Map 730. The engraver is Alexander Lawson.

Size 4 1/16″ x 6 3/16″ (on plate: 8¾″ x 6½″). *Scale* None (1″ = c. 1 league).

Published in Thomas Dobson, *Encyclopaedia, 18,* foll. 752.

810 [1798]

Description At top center above neat line of three part plate: WAR / ATTACK OF FORTIFIED PLACES. At extreme right: PLATE DXXXVI; in upper right corner of [Fig. 1]: PLAN / OF THE ATTACKS OF / LANDAU / IN *1713;* below bottom neat line at right corner: T. CLARKE SCULPT. The plate is divided into three sections. The upper comprising the map carrying the title given above, and showing part of Landau, in Bavaria, with the fortifications and nearby territory on that side (see *18,* p. 782). The lower section shows military details to a larger scale in two plans, designated FIG. 2, and FIG. 3. The engraver is Thomas Clarke.

Size 3⅞″ x 6¾″ (on plate: 9⅜″ x 7¼″). *Scale* 1″ = 200 fathoms.

Published in Thomas Dobson, *Encyclopaedia, 18,* foll. 784.

811 [1798]

Description At top center above neat line of two part plate: WAR. / ATTACK OF FORTIFIED

PLACES. At extreme right: PLATE DXXXVII; at right center: CROWN / WORK; at bottom right corner of plate: T. CLARKE SCULPT. This plate is divided into two sections. The upper part is a plan showing part of the details of the fortress of Philipsburg in 1734 (see 18, p. 784). The lower section is entitled: WATCH WORK and describes the mechanism of the watch. The engraver is Thomas Clarke.

Size 4⅜″ x 6⅜″ (on plate: 9½″ x 7⅜″). *Scale* 1″ = 140 feet.

Published in Thomas Dobson, *Encyclopaedia, 18*, opp. 808.

812 [1798]

Description At top center above neat line: WAR / PLAN OF THE CIRCUMVALLATION AND ATTACKS OF PHILIPSBURG IN 1734. Below neat line at bottom of plate: GRAVÉ PAR A. LAUSON 1798. At top right: PLATE DXXIX. This PLAN and the insets comprise two parts of a three part plate. For the third section see Map 813. This plan of Philipsburg is mentioned on page 768 of the *Encyclopaedia, 18*. The engraver is probably Alexander Lawson.

Size 6⅞″ x 6¾″ (on plate: 9⅜″ x 7⅜″). *Scale* 1″ = 550 fathoms.

Insets [a] Below map of Philipsburg: PLAN OF PART OF THE CIRCUMVALLATION OF PHILIPSBURG IN 1734. Size: 1⅜″ x 6¾″. Scale: 1″ = 58 F (feet).
[b] Below inset [a]: PROFILE OF DO. Size: 1½″ x 6¾″. Scale: 1″ = c. 2⅓ feet.

Published in Thomas Dobson, *Encyclopaedia, 18*, foll. 768.

813

Description At center of lower part of three part plate: PLAN OF PART OF A LINE OF CIRCUMVALLATION OF ARRAS IN 1654. At bottom of plate at lower right: GRAVÉ PAR A. LAUSON 1798. The plan is referred to on page 768 of the *Encyclopaedia, 18*. The engraver is probably Alexander Lawson. For the description of the upper portion of the plate see Map 812.

Size 2¼″ x 6¾″. *Scale* 1″ = 55 fathoms.

Inset At lower center: PROFILE OF DO. Size: ¾″ x 6¾″. Scale: 1″ = 3⅖ feet.

Published in Thomas Dobson, *Encyclopaedia, 18*, foll. 768.

814 [1798]

Description At upper left: BRITAIN / AND / IRELAND. Below title: J. T. SCOTT SCULP PHILADA.

Above top neat line at center: 7. The major divisions are indicated.

Size 3⅞″ x 2⁹⁄₁₆″. *Scale* 1″ = 300 miles (60 to a degree).

Published in John Gibson, *Atlas Minimus*, no. 7.

815 [1798]

Description In cartouche at upper left: DENMARK. Below bottom neat line at right: ENGRAV'D BY F. SHALLUS. Above top neat line at center: 25. The map shows political subdivisions and principal towns.

Size 3¹¹⁄₁₆″ x 2⁷⁄₁₆″. *Scale* 1″ = 54 miles (60 to a degree).

Published in John Gibson, *Atlas Minimus*, no. 25.

816 [1798]

Description At upper right: ENGLAND / AND / WALES. Beneath title: J. T. SCOTT SCULP. PHILADA. Above top neat line at center: 8. The county boundaries are shown and references to lists of names of the ENGLISH COUNTI. at the left and WELSH COUN. at the right.

Size 3¾″ x 2⅝″. *Scale* 1″ = 140 miles (60 to a degree).

Published in John Gibson, *Atlas Minimus*, no. 8.

817 [1798]

Description At upper left: EUROPE. Below title: J. T. SCOTT SCULP. PHILADA. Above top neat line at center: 2. The nations are indicated and their boundaries shown. Greenland appears north of Scandinavia.

Size 3¾″ x 2⅝″. *Scale* None (1″ = c. 19° latitude).

Published in John Gibson, *Atlas Minimus*, no. 2.

818 [1798]

Description At upper right: FRANCE / DIVIDED INTO / DEPARTMENTS. Beneath title: W. BARKER, SCULP. Above top neat line at center: 13. The department boundary lines are shown instead of the old provinces of the original map. The department names, however, are not given.

Size 3¹¹⁄₁₆″ x 2⁷⁄₁₆″. *Scale* 1″ = 280 miles (70 to a degree).

Published in John Gibson, *Atlas Minimus*, no. 13.

819 [1798]

Description At upper left: GERMANY / DIVIDED INTO / CIRCLES. Underneath title: J. T. SCOTT SCULP. Above top neat line at center: *17*. The map shows the larger political divisions.

Size 3⅞″ x 2⅝″. *Scale* None (1″ = c. 325 miles).

Published in John Gibson, *Atlas Minimus*, no. 17.

820 [1798]

Description At upper right: HUNGARY. Beneath title: J. T. SCOTT. Outside right neat line at center: *22*. Shown are Upper and Lower Hungary, Transylvania, and Esclavonia.

Size 2¹¹⁄₁₆″ x 3¹³⁄₁₆″. *Scale* 1″ = 150 miles.

Published in John Gibson, *Atlas Minimus*, no. 22.

821 [1798]

Description At upper left: IRELAND. Beneath title: J. T. SCOTT SCULP. PHILADA. Above top neat line at center: *10*. The county boundaries and names are shown.

Size 4¹³⁄₁₆″ x 2⁵⁄₁₆″. *Scale* 1″ = 80 miles (60 to a degree).

Published in John Gibson, *Atlas Minimus*, no. 10.

822 [1798]

Description At upper left: ITALY. Below title: J. T. SCOTT SCULP. PHILADA. Above top neat line at center: *15*. The map shows political divisions and adjacent islands. TURKY IN EUROPE appears thus beyond the GULF OF VENICE.

Size 3⅞″ x 2⁹⁄₁₆″. *Scale* 1″ = 330 miles (60 to a degree).

Published in John Gibson, *Atlas Minimus*, no. 15.

823 [1798]

Description In cartouche at upper left: NAPLES / AND / SICILY. Beneath title in cartouche: ROCHE ST. Above top neat line at center: *29*. Political subdivisions are shown and some towns.

Size 3¾″ x 2⁷⁄₁₆″. *Scale* 1″ = 140 miles (60 to a degree).

Published in John Gibson, *Atlas Minimus*, no. 29.

824 [1798]

Description At upper right: THE / NETHER- / LANDS. Beneath title: J. T. SCOTT SCULP. Outside right neat line at center: *12*. The boundaries of the Austrian, French, and Dutch provinces are shown.

Size 2⁹⁄₁₆″ x 3¾″. *Scale* 1″ = 70 miles (60 to a degree).

Published in John Gibson, *Atlas Minimus*, no. 12.

825 [1798]

Description At upper left: THE / NORTH EAST / PART OF / GERMANY. Beneath title: J. T. SCOTT SCULP. Above top neat line at center: *18*. The map shows political subdivisions and many towns.

Size 3¹⁵⁄₁₆″ x 2⁵⁄₁₆″. *Scale* 1″ = 180 miles (60 to a degree).

Published in John Gibson, *Atlas Minimus*, no. 18.

826 [1798]

Description At upper left: THE / NORTH WEST / PART OF / GERMANY. Beneath title: J. T. SCOTT SCULP. PHILADA. Above top neat line at center: *19*. The map shows political subdivisions and many towns.

Size 3⅞″ x 2⅝″. *Scale* 1″ = 120 miles.

Published in John Gibson, *Atlas Minimus*, no. 19.

827 [1798]

Description At upper left: POLAND. Beneath title: J. T. SCOTT SCULP. Outside right neat line at center: *23*. The map shows East Prussia and Poland with nine divisions.

Size 2⅝″ x 3¾″. *Scale* 1″ = 265 miles (60 to a degree).

Published in John Gibson, *Atlas Minimus*, no. 23.

828 [1798]

Description At upper left: PRUSSIA. Beneath title: J T SCOTT SCULP. Outside right neat line at center: *24*. Boundaries and some towns are indicated.

Size 2⅝″ x 3¹³⁄₁₆″. *Scale* 1″ = 75 miles.

Published in John Gibson, *Atlas Minimus*, no. 24.

829 [1798]

Description In cartouche at upper left: RUSSIA / IN / EUROPE. Below title in cartouche: ROCHE SCT. Above top neat line at center: *27*.

The map shows many political subdivisions and towns.

Size 3¹¹⁄₁₆″ x 2⁷⁄₁₆″.   *Scale* 1″ = 730 miles.

Published in John Gibson, *Atlas Minimus*, no. 27.

830 [1798]

Description   At upper left: SCOTLAND. Beneath title: J. T. SCOTT SCULP. PHILADA. Above top neat line at center: *9*. The county boundaries are shown. A list of REFERENCES is given at left center.

Size 3¹³⁄₁₆″ x 2⁹⁄₁₆″.   *Scale* 1″ = 107 miles (60 to a degree).

Published in John Gibson, *Atlas Minimus*, no. 9.

831 [1798]

Description   At upper left: SOUTH EAST / PART OF / GERMANY. Beneath title: J. T. SCOTT SCULP. PHILADA. Above top neat line at center: *20*. The map shows political subdivisions and many towns.

Size 3⅞″ x 2⅝″.   *Scale* 1″ = 144 miles (60 to a degree).

Published in John Gibson, *Atlas Minimus*, no. 20.

832 [1798]

Description   At upper left: SOUTH WEST / PART OF / GERMANY. Beneath title: J. T. SCOTT SCULP. Above top neat line at center: *21*. The map shows political subdivisions and some towns.

Size 3⅞″ x 2⁹⁄₁₆″.   *Scale* 1″ = 133 miles.

Published in John Gibson, *Atlas Minimus*, no. 21.

833 [1798]

Description   At upper right: SPAIN / AND / PORTUGAL. Beneath title: J. T. SCOTT SCULP. Outside right neat line at center: *14*. Political subdivisions are shown.

Size 2¹¹⁄₁₆″ x 3¹³⁄₁₆″.   *Scale* 1″ = 270 miles (60 to a degree).

Published in John Gibson, *Atlas Minimus*, no. 14.

834 [1798]

Description   In cartouche at upper left: SWEDEN / AND / NORWAY. Under title inside cartouche: ROCHE SCT. Outside right neat line at center: *26*. Some political subdivisions are included. Iceland in shown. References are given under and to the right of the cartouche.

Size 2⁷⁄₁₆″ x 3¹¹⁄₁₆″.   *Scale* 1″ = 480 miles.

Published in John Gibson, *Atlas Minimus*, no. 26.

835 [1798]

Description   At upper right: SWITZERLAND / WITH ITS / ALLIES. Beneath title: J. T. SCOTT SCULP. Outside right neat line at center: *16*. The map shows the political subdivisions, the larger towns, lakes, and rivers.

Size 2⁹⁄₁₆″ x 3¹³⁄₁₆″.   *Scale* 1″ = 60 miles.

Published in John Gibson, *Atlas Minimus*, no. 16.

836 [1798]

Description   In cartouche at upper right: TURKY [sic] / IN / EUROPE. Below title in cartouche: ROCHE SCT. Outside right neat line at center: *28*. The map shows political subdivisions and principal towns.

Size 2⅞″ x 3¾″.   *Scale* 1″ = 440 miles.

Published in John Gibson, *Atlas Minimus*, no. 28.

837 [1798]

Description   At lower right: THE / UNITED / PROVINCES. Beneath title: J. T. SCOTT SCULP. PHILADA. Outside right neat line at center: *11*. The province names and boundaries are given.

Size 2⅝″ x 3¹³⁄₁₆″.   *Scale* 1″ = 60 miles (60 to a degree).

Published in John Gibson, *Atlas Minimus*, no. 11.

838 [1798]

Description   At top above neat line: SKETCH OF THE HARBOUR AND ENVIRONS OF TOULON. Outside neat line at bottom right: T. CLARKE SCULPT. This is a map showing Toulon at the time of the English occupation of the city in 1793. The ENGLISH CAMP is shown on CAPE CEPET and two camps are shown of the besieging French forces, one east and one west of the city.

Size 5″ x 7⅝″.   *Scale* None (1″ = c. 2 miles).

Published in John Gifford, [John Richards Green], *History of France, 4*, opp. 422.

Reference   David M. Stauffer, *American Engravers, 2*, no. 415.

839 1799

Description At left center: A / NEW AND / ACCURATE MAP / OF / FRANCE / DIVIDED INTO DE-PARTMENTS, / WITH THE NETHERLANDS / &C. / *1799*. Below bottom neat line at center: EN-GRAVED FOR PAYNE'S GEOGRAPHY, PUBLISHED BY I. LOW NEW-YORK. At right corner: A. ANDERSON S. The METROPOLITAN / CIRCLES are listed at the left above the title.

Size 8⅝" x 8¾".   *Scale* 1" = 75 miles.

Inset At lower right corner: PLAN OF TOULON &C. Size: 1¾" x 1½". Scale: None (1" = c. 1½ miles).

Published in John Payne, *A New and Complete Universal Geography, 3,* opp. 607.

[c. 1799]   see Map 904.

AFRICA

840 [1790]

Description In oval at lower left: AFRICA / FROM THE BEST / AUTHORITIES. In lower right corner: R. SCOT SCULP. In border at upper right corner: PLATE IV. Some topographical features are noted and a number of place names.

Size 6¹⁵⁄₁₆″ x 8½″. *Scale* None (1″ = 850 miles).

Published in Thomas Dobson, *Encyclopaedia, 1,* opp. 228.

841 [1790]

Description In oval scroll at upper right: AFRICA. Outside left neat line at bottom: NO. VIII. Outside right neat line at top: DOOLITTLE SCULP N. HAVEN. The South Atlantic is labeled the ETHIOPIC / OCEAN; the Indian, the EASTERN / OCEAN.

Size 2¾″ x 4⅛″. *Scale* None (1″ = c. 2500 miles).

Published in Jedidiah Morse, *Geography Made Easy,* 2d ed., opp. p. 310.

842 [1790]

Description In vignette at upper right: AFRICA. Few place names are shown. SARA OR THE DESRT appears thus.

Size 2¾″ x 3⅞″. *Scale* None (1″ = c. 2500 miles).

Published in Benjamin Workman, *Elements of Geography,* 3d ed., opp. p. 115; ibid., eds. of 1793, 1795, 1796, and 1799.

843 [1791]

Description In oval at upper right: AFRICA. SARA OR THE DESERT is shown thus, and also the coast of ZANQUEBAR. This is the second Morse map of Africa.

Size 3⁵⁄₁₆″ x 6″. *Scale* None (1″ = c. 15° latitude).

Published in Jedidiah Morse, *Geography Made Easy,* 3d ed., opp. p. 310.

844 [1793]

Description In cartouche at lower left: AFRICA. Above top neat line: PUBLISHED BY THOMAS & ANDREWS BOSTON. Below bottom neat line center: ENGRAVED FOR MORSE'S AMERICAN GEOGRAPHY; at right: J. ALLEN SCT. The neat line is broken at the left center to show a corner of South America. Some topographical detail is noted. This is the third Morse map of Africa.

Size 6¾″ x 8⅛″. *Scale* None (1″ = c. 1000 miles).

Published in Jedidiah Morse, *The American Universal Geography,* 2, opp. 485.

845 [1794]

Description Above top neat line: A MAP OF BARBARY COMPREHENDING / MOROCCO, FEZ, ALGIERS, TUNIS AND TRIPOLI. Below title above neat line: SOLD BY MATHEW CAREY NO *118* MARKET-STREET PHILADA. / J. T. SCOTT SCULP. This is a political and topographic map of Northwest Africa. The interior desert area is noted as the: COUNTRY OF THE / HEMBRUM ARABS. SARDINIA breaks through the outer neat line at the upper right.

Size 5½″ x 10⅜″. *Scale* None (1″ = c. 105 miles).

Published in Mathew Carey, *Eine Kurtze Nachright Von Algier,* front.; idem, *A Short Account of Algiers,* front; ibid., 2d ed., front.

846 [1794]

Description In rectangle at upper right corner: AFRICA. Below neat line at lower right: DOOLITTLE SC. The title is shown in shaded letters. The parallels of latitude are not numbered. This is the fourth Morse map of Africa.

Size 3³⁄₁₆″ x 5¹¹⁄₁₆″. *Scale* None (1″ = c. 2000 miles).

Published in Jedidiah Morse, *Geography Made Easy,* 4th ed., opp. p. 393.

847 [1795] *State* I (II post-1799, see below, Description)

Description In oval at upper right: AFRICA / ACCORDING TO THE BEST / AUTHORITIES. Above top neat line: ENGRAVED FOR CAREY'S AMERICAN EDITION OF GUTHRIE'S GEOGRAPHY IMPROVED. Some topographical detail is shown and many place and area names. The CAPE VERD / ISLES break the neat lines at the upper left. The map appears in the September, 1800, edition of *Carey's General Atlas* with the figure "22" added at the upper left corner.

Size 13½" x 14". *Scale* 1" = c. 400 British statute miles.

Published in Mathew Carey, *Carey's General Atlas*, no. 22; idem, *The General Atlas for Carey's Edition of Guthrie's Geography Improved*, no. 22.

848 [1795]

Description At upper right: PLAN OF / SIERRA LEONE / AND THE / PARTS ADJACENT. / MDCCXCIV. At right under neat line: ENGRAV'D BY VALLANCE. This is a topographical map showing the land about the mouth of the Sierra Leone River belonging to the Company and also that granted to settlers.

Size 10¼" x 9½". *Scale* 1" = 1 mile 4½ furlongs.

Published in Sierra Leone Company, *Substance of the Report delivered by the Court of Directors*, front; ibid., 2d ed.

849 [1795]

Description In rectangle at upper right: AFRICA. C VEGRO is given on the southwest coast.

Size 2⅜" x 3¾". *Scale* None (1" = c. 2500 miles).

Published in Charles Smith, *Universal Geography Made Easy*, opp. p. 105.

850 [1796]

Description In rectangle at upper right: AFRICA. This is a re-engraving of Map 846. The parallels of latitude have been numbered and the title is now shown in solid instead of shaded letters.

Size 3⁹⁄₁₆" x 5¹¹⁄₁₆". *Scale* None (1" = c. 2000 miles).

Published in Jedidiah Morse, *Geography Made Easy*, 5th ed., opp. p. 393.

851 [1796]

Description At upper right: AFRICA / FROM THE BEST / AUTHORITIES. Beneath oval: DOOLITTLE SC:. At top center above neat line: PUBLISHED BY THOMAS & ANDREWS, BOSTON. Many place names are given and some topographical features. The GOAD / COAST appears for Gold Coast. This is the fifth Morse map of Africa.

Size 7⁹⁄₁₆" x 8⅜". *Scale* None (1" = c. 830 miles).

Published in Jedidiah Morse, *The American Universal Geography*, 3d ed., 2, opp. 597.

852 [1797]

Description In oval at left of center: A / CORRECT CHART / OF THE SOUTHERN COASTS OF / AFRICA, / FROM THE EQUATOR / TO THE CAPE OF GOOD HOPE. In oval under title: ENGRAVED FOR MALHAMS NAVAL GAZETR. Beneath oval: ROLLINSON SCULPT. NEW YORK. Below bottom neat line at center: PUBLISHD BY SPOTSWOOD AND NANCREDE BOSTON. The ocean south of Madagascar is named SOUTHERN PACIFIC OCEAN. Just below the Equator near the west coast appears ANZICO TO THE MICOKO. No soundings are given.

Size 7½" x 9⁹⁄₁₆". *Scale* 1" = 150 leagues.

Published in John Malham, *The Naval Gazetteer, 1*, opp. 15.

853 [1797]

Description In oval at right center: A / CORRECT CHART / OF THE WEST COAST OF / AFRICA. / ENGRAVED FOR / MALHAM'S NAVAL GAZETTEER. Below bottom neat line at center: PUBLISHD OCTOR *1796* BY SPOTSWOOD AND NANCREDE BOSTON. At right: B CALLENDER SCULP BOSTON. The coast is shown here from Tunis around Morocco to the Equator. ZAHRA OR DESERT OF BARBARY appears for the Sahara. The *14* FATHOM BANK is indicated off the GOLD / COAST.

Size 9¼" x 7⅜". *Scale* None (1" = c. 350 miles).

Published in John Malham, *The Naval Gazetteer, 1*, opp. 15.

854 [1798]

Description In oval at upper right: AFRICA. Below bottom neat line at right: SHALLUS SC. Outside right neat line at center: *4*. Some place names are noted.

Size 2⁷⁄₁₆" x 3⅝". *Scale* None (1" = c. 36° latitude).

Published in John Gibson, *Atlas Minimus*, no. 4.

855 [1798]

Description At upper left: BARBARY. Outside right neat line: *36*. The map is in two sections: the upper showing the western Barbary States; the lower section, Tripoli, Barca, and Egypt. The same neat line continues around both sections but the marginal degree line is broken.

Size 2⁷⁄₁₆" x 3¹¹⁄₁₆". *Scale* 1" = 550 miles.

Published in John Gibson, *Atlas Minimus*, no. 36.

856 [1798]

Description In rectangle at upper right: EGYPT, / NUBIA / AND ABISSINIA. Below title outside rectangle: W. BARKER, SCULP. Above top neat line: *38*. The boundaries are noted and some place names.

Size $3^{11}/_{16}''$ x $2^{1}/_{2}''$. *Scale* $1'' = 700$ miles.

Published in John Gibson, *Atlas Minimus*, no. 38.

857 [1798]

Description At lower left: NEGROLAND / AND / GUINEA. Outside right neat line: *37*. Boundaries are shown and some place names.

Size $2^{7}/_{16}''$ x $3^{11}/_{16}''$. *Scale* $1'' = 560$ miles.

Published in John Gibson, *Atlas Minimus*, no. 37.

858 [1798]

Description In oval at upper right: A NEW MAP / OF / AFRICA / FROM THE BEST / AUTHORITIES. Many place names appear and some topographical features. PAPT [sic] / OF / ASIA is given at the upper right.

Size $7^{1}/_{2}''$ x $9^{1}/_{8}''$. *Scale* None ($1'' = $ c. 830 miles).

Published in Joseph Scott, *A New and Universal Gazetteer*, first section pub. Philadelphia, July 3, 1798; idem, *The New and Universal Gazetteer, 1*, leaf B¹.

859 [1799]

Description In oval at lower left: AFRICA / FROM THE BEST / AUTHORITIES. Below title in oval: ROLLINSON. Below bottom neat line: ENGRAVED FOR PAYNE'S GEOGRAPHY PUBLISH'D BY J. LOW N. YORK. Many place names are given. The AUSGAR MORASS is shown in Northwest Africa.

Size $7^{3}/_{8}''$ x $8^{5}/_{8}''$. *Scale* None ($1'' = $ c. 830 miles).

Published in John Payne, *A New and Complete Universal Geography, 2*, front.

860 [1799]

Description In oval at left center: A / CORRECT MAP / OF THE / MEDITERRANEAN / SEA / WITH THE COUNTRIES / ADJACENT. Below lower neat line at center: ENGRAVED FOR PAYNE'S NEW & UNIVERSAL GEOGRAPHY, PUBLISHED BY I. LOW, N. YORK. Some topographical features are shown. Notes appear showing the landing place of Bonaparte and the site of Nelson's victory of the Nile. Many place names are given.

Size $7^{7}/_{16}''$ x $16^{1}/_{8}''$. *Scale* None ($1'' = $ c. $2^{1}/_{2}°$ latitude).

Published in John Payne, *A New and Complete Universal Geography, 2*, opp. 346.

861 [1799] *State* I (II post-1799, see below, Description)

Description In rectangle at left center: DISPOSITION / OF THE / ENGLISH & FRENCH / FLEETS, / AT THE COMMENCEMENT OF THE / ACTION, / AUGUST 1ST. *1798*. At right under cartouche: TANNER SC. Below neat line center: NEW YORK. PUBLISHED BY JOHN REID. MARCH 1ST *1799*. Soundings are shown in Abukir Road. A table is given on the page following identifying the ships. State II of this map was published in John Payne's *A New and Complete System of Universal Geography, 3*, opp. 699, with the imprint below the bottom neat line changed to read: ". . . John Low for Paynes Geography."

Size $8''$ x $12^{1}/_{4}''$. *Scale* None ($1'' = $ c. 1 mile).

Inset At right edge: A VIEW OF / BOKIER CASTLE. Size: $1^{7}/_{8}''$ x $6^{3}/_{8}''$. Scale: None.

Published in John Remmey, *An Account of the Present State of Egypt*, foll. p. 96.

862 [1799] *State* I (II post-1799, see below, Description)

Description In rectangle at upper right: EGYPT / FROM THE BEST / AUTHORITIES. At right under cartouche: TANNER SC. Below neat line center: NEW-YORK. PUBLISHED BY JOHN REID. MARCH 1ST. *1799*. Some topographical features are noted. The valley of the Nile is shown to Aswan. Many place names are given, both ancient and modern. State II of this map was published in John Payne's *A New and Complete System of Universal Geography, 3*, opp. 700, with the imprint below the bottom neat line changed to read: ". . . John Low for Paynes Geography."

Size $11^{3}/_{4}''$ x $7^{1}/_{8}''$. *Scale* $1'' = 20$ French leagues of 5000 toises.

Published in John Remmey, *An Account of the Present State of Egypt*, opp. p. 5.

ASIA

863 [1790]

Description In scroll at upper left: ASIA. Above top neat line at center: PLATE LIX. Some topographical features are noted and many place names. DE GAMA'S / LAND, COMPANYS LAND, and YEDSO are located north of Japan. MALACAN breaks the lower neat line.

Size 65⁄8″ x 81⁄2″. *Scale* None (1″ = c. 260 miles).

Published in Thomas Dobson, *Encyclopaedia*, 2, opp. 394.

864 [1790]

Description In oval scroll at upper left: ASIA. Outside left neat line near bottom: DOOLITTLE SC. N. HAVEN. Outside right neat line at top: NO. VII. The major countries are named. YESO Island is identified north of Japan.

Size 23⁄4″ x 41⁄8″. *Scale* None (1″ = c. 1000 miles).

Published in Jedidiah Morse, *Geography Made Easy*, 2d ed., opp. p. 300.

865 1790 *State* I (see also Map 891)

Description In decorative cartouche at upper left: AN ACCURATE / MAP OF THE / HOLY LAND / WITH THE AJACENT [sic] COUNTRIES / TAKEN FROM THE BEST / AUTHORITIES. / 1790. At left below title: ROLLINSON; at right: SCULPT.; in rectangle beneath title: ENGRAVED FOR THE AMERICAN EDITION OF / BROWN'S FAMILY BIBLE. This is a map showing the major cities and political divisions of the area. Major roads and trade routes are shown and some topographic features. According to Evans the printing of *The Self-Interpreting Bible* began in 1790.

Size 133⁄8″ x 91⁄8″. *Scale* 1″ = 40 miles (691⁄2 to a degree).

Published in *The Self-Interpreting Bible*, opp. "Joshua," Chap. xv.

Reference Evans 22348 and 24099.

866 [1790]

Description In vignette at upper left: ASIA. The major countries are named. SIREBIA appears thus.

Size 23⁄4″ x 4″. *Scale* None (1″ = c. 1000 miles).

Published in Benjamin Workman, *Elements of Geography*, 3d ed., opp. p. 111; ibid., eds. of 1793, 1795, 1796, and 1799.

867 [1791]

Description In decorated cartouche at upper right: THE / ANTIENT CITY / OF / JERUSALEM / AND PLACES ADJACENT. Directions identified on four sides of map outside neat lines: NORTH, EAST, SOUTH, and WEST. Below neat line at lower right: J NORMAN SC. Above neat line at top right: NO. XXVII. Above NORTH at top: ENGRAVED FOR THOMAS'S EDITION OF THE BIBLE. The various parts of the City, important buildings, and pools are identified in this pictorial plan.

Size 71⁄4″ x 101⁄4″. *Scale* None (1″ = c. 1⁄8 mile).

Inset At lower right: THE PLAN OF A GREAT HOUSE. Size: 17⁄8″ x 17⁄8″. Scale: (None).

Published in *The Holy Bible, containing the Old and New Testaments*, 2, opp. 485.

868 [1791]

Description In rectangle at top: ASIA. CORA appears for Korea, and KAMSZATKIA for Kamchatka. This is the second Morse map of Asia.

Size 59⁄16″ x 41⁄4″. *Scale* None (1″ = c. 32° latitude).

Published in Jedidiah Morse, *Geography Made Easy*, 3d ed., opp. p. 300.

869 [1792]

Description At lower right: AN ACCURATE MAP / OF THE / HOLY LAND / WITH THE / ADJACENT COUNTRIES / BY THOS. BOWEN. Below bottom neat line at right: A. ANDERSON SCULP. The map shows the primary cities and roads of the area and also some of the topographical features.

Size 113⁄16″ x 63⁄4″. *Scale* 1″ = 80 English miles.

Published in Flavius Josephus, *The Whole Genuine and Complete Works*, opp. p. 67; ibid., Philadelphia, 1795, opp. p. 67; ibid., Baltimore, 1795; *The Holy Bible*, Philadelphia, 1796.

870 [1792]

Description In vignette at upper center: A CORRECT MAP OF THE / COUNTRIES / SURROUNDING THE / GARDEN OF EDEN, / OR / PARADISE. / WITH / THE COURSE OF NOAH'S ARK DURING THE FLOOD, &C. Below bottom neat line at right: A. ANDERSON SCULP. This is a topographical map with contemporary political boundaries and surface features showing both ancient and more modern towns and cities.

Size 11⅜″ x 6⅝″. *Scale* 1″ = c. 85 miles.

Published in Flavius Josephus, *The Whole Genuine and Complete Works,* foll. p. 8; ibid., Philadelphia, 1795, foll. p. 8; ibid., Baltimore, 1795; *The Holy Bible,* Philadelphia, 1796; *The Holy Bible,* Philadelphia, 1799.

871 [1793]

Description In scroll at upper center: EAST / INDIES. Below title: S. ALLARDICE SC. Above top neat line at right: PLATE CCLIV. Many of the islands are named. JUVA appears for Java.

Size 6¹³⁄₁₆″ x 11″. *Scale* 1″ = 400 miles (60 to a degree).

Published in Thomas Dobson, *Encyclopaedia, 9,* opp. 218.

872 [1793]

Description On decorative ribbon at upper center: JERUSALEM. Below bottom neat line at left: A. ANDERSON SCULP. Above top neat line at center: ENGRAVED FOR THE AMERICAN EDITION OF MAYNARD'S JOSEPHUS. This is an ornate topographical map showing the principal buildings, monuments, and the several divisions of the city with its immediate surroundings.

Size 14″ x 16⁹⁄₁₆″. *Scale* 1″ = 320 sacred cubits.

Published in Flavius Josephus, *The Whole Genuine and Complete Works,* opp. p. 324; ibid., Philadelphia, 1795, opp. p. 324; ibid, Baltimore, 1795.

873 [1793]

Description In cartouche at upper left: ASIA. Above top neat line: PUBLISHED BY THOMAS & ANDREWS, BOSTON. Below bottom neat line: ENGRAVED FOR MORSES AMERICAN GEOGRAPHY BY A. DOOLITTLE N. H. Major place names are given and a few topographical features are indicated. NORTH / AMERICA is shown at the upper right corner. This is the third Morse map of Asia.

Size 6¾″ x 8³⁄₁₆″. *Scale* None (1″ = c. 910 miles).

Published in Jedidiah Morse, *The American Universal Geography, 2,* opp. 384.

874 [1794] *State* I (see also Map 884)

Description In rectangle at top: ASIA. At lower right outside right neat line: DOOLITTLE SC. PAR OF AFRICA is indicated thus; KAMSCHATKA appears thus. The engraver's name is very lightly cut. This is the fourth Morse map of Asia.

Size 5¾″ x 3³⁄₁₆″. *Scale* None (1″ = c. 35° latitude).

Published in Jedidiah Morse, *Geography Made Easy,* 4th ed., opp. p. 364.

875 [1794] *State* I (see also Map 887)

Description In rectangle at upper left corner: THE JOURNEYINGS OF / OUR SAVIOUR / JESUS CHRIST. Below neat line at bottom right: DOOLITTLE SC. This is a map of Palestine showing the tribes and districts of the country. The second "Bethlehem" is shown northeast instead of northwest of Nazareth.

Size 5¹¹⁄₁₆″ x 3¼″. *Scale* None (1″ = c. 41.5 miles).

Published in Jedidiah Morse, *Geography Made Easy,* 4th ed., opp. p. 366.

876 [1794] *State* I (see also Map 889)

Description In rectangle at lower right corner: A MAP / OF THE TRAVELS & VOYAGES / OF / ST. PAUL. Below neat line at lower right, lightly cut: DOOLITTLE SC. This is a historical map of the eastern Mediterranean lands as known in the time of St. Paul. The Mediterranean Sea north of Tripoli is marked ADRIA OR / THE ADRIATICK SEA.

Size 3⅜″ x 5¾″. *Scale* None (1″ = c. 220 miles).

Published in Jedidiah Morse, *Geography Made Easy,* 4th ed., opp. p. 367.

877 [1794] *State* I (see also Map 888)

Description In rectangle at top: PALESTINE OR THE HOLY LAND. Below neat line at lower right: DOOLITTLE SC. This is a historical map showing the route taken by Moses. Many place names are given. LANDND OF GOSHEN appears thus in northern Egypt.

Size 5¹¹⁄₁₆″ x 3¼″. *Scale* None (1″ = c. 80 miles).

Published in Jedidiah Morse, *Geography Made Easy,* 4th ed., opp. p. 396.

878 [1795] *State* I (II post-1799, see below, Description)

Description In oval near bottom center: AN / ACCURATE MAP OF / HINDOSTAN / OR / INDIA, / FROM THE BEST / AUTHORITIES. In oval below title: J. T. SCOTT SCULP. Above top neat line: ENGRAVED FOR CAREY'S AMERICAN EDITION OF GUTHRIE'S GEOGRAPHY IMPROVED. This is a political map showing some topographical features and many place names. This map appears in the September, 1800, edition of *Carey's General Atlas* with the figure "21" added at upper right corner.

Size 15⅝" x 16". *Scale* 1" = 150 miles (69½ to a degree).

Published in Mathew Carey, *Carey's General Atlas*, no. 21; idem, *The General Atlas for Carey's Edition of Guthrie's Geography Improved*, no. 21.

879 [1795] *State* I (see also Map 883; III post-1799, see Map 883, Description)

Description In oval at upper left: ASIA, / ACCORDING TO THE BEST / AUTHORITIES. Above top neat line: ENGRAVED FOR CAREY'S AMERICAN EDITION OF GUTHRIE'S GEOGRAPHY IMPROVED. This is a political map showing a few topographical features. The COMPANYS / LAND is shown north and west of Japan.

Size 13" x 13⅞". *Scale* None (1" = c. 560 miles).

Published in Mathew Carey, *Carey's General Atlas*, no. 19; idem, *The General Atlas for Carey's Edition of Guthrie's Geography Improved*, no. 19.

880 [1795] *State* I (II post-1799, see below, Description)

Description In oval at lower right: CHINA, / DIVIDED INTO ITS / GREAT PROVINCES / ACCORDING TO THE BEST / AUTHORITIES. In oval below title: B. TANNER SC. N. YORK. Above top neat line: ENGRAVED FOR CAREY'S AMERICAN EDITION OF GUTHRIE'S GEOGRAPHY IMPROVED. This is a political map with some topographical features shown. A short EXPLANATION is given at the bottom right. This map appears in the September, 1800, edition of *Carey's General Atlas* with the figure "20" added at the upper left.

Size 13¼" x 13⅞". *Scale* 1" = 190 British statute miles (69 to a degree).

Published in Mathew Carey, *Carey's General Atlas*, no. 20; idem, *The General Atlas for Carey's Edition of Guthrie's Geography Improved*, no. 20.

881 [1795]

Description In circle at upper right: A VIEW / OF THE DIVISION / OF THE LAND OF CANAAN / AMONG THE *12* TRIBES OF ISRAEL / THE SITUATION OF THE CITY AND / SANCTUARY &C. AS DESCRIBED / BY THE PROPHET EZEKIEL / CHAP XLV. XLVII. XLVIII / DELIN BY J. PURVES / *1788*. The names of the Tribes are given on their respective lands. The R. OF EGYPT is shown at the lower left.

Size 7⅛" x 9¾". *Scale* None (1" = c. 17 miles).

Inset At left: A SMALL / MAP OF EUROPE / ASIA AND AFRICA / TO SHOW THAT JERUSALEM / IS MOST CENTRICAL AND / CONVENIENT FOR A PLACE OF / GENERAL RESORT FROM / EVERY PART OF THE / WORLD. The only city noted is JERUSALEM. Size: sphere 5¹⁄₁₆" diam. Scale: None.

Published in Elhanan Winchester, *A Course of Lectures*, 2, opp. 110.

882 [1795]

Description In rectangle at upper left: ASIA. This is very similar to Map 866. More place names are given here: YESO I north of Japan, SAMARKAND, and a number of others. Siberia is spelled correctly.

Size 2⅜" x 3¾". *Scale* None (1" = c. 2600 miles).

Published in Charles Smith, *Universal Geography Made Easy*, opp. p. 84.

883 [1796] *State* II (see also Map 879; III post-1799, see below, Description)

Description Some of the lines have been strengthened, especially the coastal shadings. A clear passage of at least ½ mm., without shading, appears between the ends of the shading lines through URIEZ STR., located north of Japan, between COMPANYS / LAND and STATE I. This map appears in the September, 1800, edition of *Carey's General Atlas* with the figure "19" added at the upper left corner.

Published in Mathew Carey, *Carey's General Atlas*, no. 19.

884 [1796] *State* II (see also Map 874)

Description The lines have been recut in many places, including the coast line shading. The title now appears with solid instead of double lined letters.

Published in Jedidiah Morse, *Geography Made Easy*, 5th ed., opp. p. 364.

885 [1796]

Description In oval at upper left: ASIA / FROM THE BEST / AUTHORITIES. In oval below title: ENGRAVED BY DOOLITTLE. Above top neat line: PUBLISHED BY THOMAS & ANDREWS, BOSTON. This is a political map. NIPHAM is given for Nippon (Honshu Island); NEW GUINIA, for New Guinia. This is the fifth Morse map of Asia.

Size 7¾″ x 9″. *Scale* None (1″ = c. 13° 20′ latitude).

Published in Jedidiah Morse, *The American Universal Geography*, 3d ed., 2, opp. 456.

886 [1796]

Description In oval at lower center: HINDOSTAN / OR / INDIA / FROM THE BEST / AUTHORITIES. Below oval: DOOLITTLE SCULPT. Above top neat line: PUBLISHED BY THOMAS & ANDREWS, BOSTON. Some topographical features are noted. The MALDIVE ISLANDS are named but not shown. A short table of REMARKS is given at the upper right.

Size 7⅝″ x 8¼″. *Scale* 1″ = 300 British statute miles.

Published in Jedidiah Morse, *The American Universal Geography*, 3d ed., 2, opp. 532.

887 [1796] *State* II (see also Map 875)

Description The sea coast shading and some other lines have been recut. The shading lines along the coast measure about ⅛″ instead of the original 1⁄16″. The engraver's name has not been recut and is almost worn off.

Published in Jedidiah Morse, *Geography Made Easy*, 5th ed., opp. p. 372.

888 [1796] *State* II (see also Map 877)

Description Many of the lines have been recut. This state of the map may be identified by the coast line shading in the Red Sea. The portion along the east side of the Sinai Peninsula has not been recut, while the rest has been recut and makes a good impression.

Published in Jedidiah Morse, *Geography Made Easy*, 5th ed., opp. p. 371.

889 [1796] *State* II (see also Map 876)

Description Many lines have been recut. This state of the map may be identified by the comparative strength of the recut coast line shading and weakness of the mountain chain east of Palestine which was not recut. The engraver's name has almost disappeared.

Published in Jedidiah Morse, *Geography Made Easy*, 5th ed., opp. p. 367.

890 [1796]

Description In oval at upper left: PALESTINE / OR THE / HOLY LAND. Beneath oval: DOOLITTLE

SCULPT. Above oval: PUBLISHED BY THOMAS & ANDREWS. BOSTON. Many place names are shown. ADMA and LEBOIM join Sodom and Gomorrah at the bottom of the Dead Sea. The second "Bethlehem" is shown northeast instead of northwest of NAZAROTH [sic]. This is the second Morse map of Palestine.

Size 7½″ x 5 9⁄16″. *Scale* None (1″ = c. 33 miles).

Published in Jedidiah Morse, *The American Universal Geography*, 3d ed., 2, opp. 473.

891 1796 *State* II (see also Map 865)

Description The date following the title has been changed to *1796*. The statement now reads: . . . AMERICAN EDITION OF THE LIFE OF CHRIST.

Published in Paul Wright, *The New and Complete Life of Our Blessed Lord and Savior*.

892 [1797]

Description At upper left: CARTE / DE LA CHINE / DRESSÉE POUR SERVIR / AU VOYAGE DE L'AMBASSADE / DE LA COMPAGNIE DES INDES / HOLLANDAISES / VERS L'EMPEREUR DE LA CHINE, / DANS LES ANNÉES / *1794* & *1795*. Under title: GRAVÉE PAR VALLANCE. At center left: A MAP OF / CHINA / DESIGNED FOR THE VOYAGE / OF THE EMBASSY OF THE / DUTCH EAST INDIA COMPANY / TO / THE EMPEROR OF / CHINA / IN THE YEARS / *1794* & *1795*. This is a detailed topographical map of the coastal region of China from the Gulf of Chihli on the north to the delta of the Canton River in the south. The references on the map are explained in the "Itineraire Du Voyage fait par l'Ambassade Hollandaise vers l'Empereur de la Chine . . . ," *1*, LI–LX.

Size 42″ x 21¼″. *Scale* 1″ = 30 miles (60 to a degree).

Published in Andreas Everard van Braam Houckgeest, *Voyage de l'Ambassade, 1*, opp. XLIX.

893 [1797]

Description [Plan de la Ville de Pe-king.] A table of references: "Indications Pour le Plan de la Ville de Pe-king," is given in *1*, LXI–LXV, of this work. No such map has thus far been discovered.

Size Unknown. *Scale* Unknown.

Published in Andreas Everard van Braam Houckgeest, *Voyage de l'Ambassade*.

894 [1797]

Description In oval at upper center: A / CORRECT CHART / OF THE COASTS OF /HINDOSTAN, /

ENGRAVED FOR / MALHAM'S NAVAL GAZETTEER. Above oval: HILL, SC. Above top neat line: PUBLISHED BY SPOTSWOOD & NANCREDE, BOSTON. Several banks or shallow areas are noted but no soundings. The COUNTRY / OF / TIPPOO SULTAN is noted.

Size 7⅜" x 9⅛". *Scale* 1" = 60 leagues.

Published in John Malham, *The Naval Gazetteer*, 2, opp. 93.

895 [1797]

Description In oval near upper center: A / CORRECT CHART / OF THE / INDIAN OCEAN. / ENGRAVED FOR MALHAM'S NAVAL GAZETTEER. Below bottom neat line at center: PUBLISH'D SEPR. *1796* BY SPOTSWOOD AND NANCREDE BOSTON. At right: B. CALLENDER SCULPT BOSTON. CAPT CLOUGH'S PASSAGE *1764* is noted north of GREAT / ANDAMAN, and DUNCANS PASSAGE south of it. No banks or shallows are given.

Size 7⅜" x 9⅛". *Scale* 1" = 100 leagues.

Published in John Malham, *The Naval Gazetteer*, 2, opp. 208.

896 [1798]

Description At top right: PLAN / DE LA VILLE DE / MACAO / À LA CHINE / POSSÉDÉE PAR LES / PORTUGAIS / *1795*. At right center: PLAN / OF THE CITY OF / MACAO / IN CHINA / POSSESSED BY THE / PORTUGUESE / *1795*. At top left above neat line: VOL. II. PAGE *219*. At bottom right: VALLANCE SC. This is a detailed topographical map showing the City and the immediate opposite shore of the Canton River. Shallows are indicated but no soundings are given. The "Indications Pour le Plan de la Ville de Macao," explaining the references on the map, is given in 2, III–IV, of this work.

Size 18⅞" x 14⅝". *Scale* None (1" = c. 4500 feet).

Published in Andreas Everard van Braam Houckgeest, *Voyage de l'Ambassade*, 2, opp. 219.

897 [1798]

Description In scroll at upper left: ASIA. Below title: J. T. SCOTT SCULP. PHILADA. Outside left neat line at center: *3*. The major nations are noted.

Size 2⁹⁄₁₆" x 3¹³⁄₁₆". *Scale* None (1" = c. 36° latitude).

Published in John Gibson, *Atlas Minimus*, no. 3.

182

898 [1798]

Description At upper right: CHINA. Outside right neat line: *35*. The provinces are named.

Size 2⁷⁄₁₆" x 3⅝". *Scale* 1" = 800 miles.

Published in John Gibson, *Atlas Minimus*, no. 35.

899 [1798]

Description At lower left: INDIA / ON BOTH / SIDES THE / GANGES. Below title: J. T. SCOTT SCULP. Outside right neat line: *32*. Shown here are the Indian, Malay, and Indochinese peninsulas.

Size 2½" x 3¹³⁄₁₆". *Scale* 1" = 950 miles (60 to a degree).

Published in John Gibson, *Atlas Minimus*, no. 32.

900 [1798]

Description In rectangle at upper left: PERSIA. Beneath title in rectangle: J. T. SCOTT SCULP. Above top neat line: *31*. The map shows provinces and large towns.

Size 3¹³⁄₁₆" x 2½". *Scale* 1" = 640 miles (60 to a degree).

Published in John Gibson, *Atlas Minimus*, no. 31.

901 [1798]

Description At upper right: RUSSIA / IN / ASIA. Outside right neat line: *34*. The KINGDOM OF SIBERIA is noted.

Size 2⁷⁄₁₆" x 3⅝". *Scale* 1" = 1200 miles.

Published in John Gibson, *Atlas Minimus*, no. 34.

902 [1798]

Description At upper left: TURKY / IN / ASIA. Beneath title: J. T. SCOTT SCULP. Above top neat line: *30*. Shown here are Turkey proper, Persia, and the Arabian Peninsula.

Size 3¹³⁄₁₆" x 2½". *Scale* 1" = 1000 miles (60 to a degree).

Published in John Gibson, *Atlas Minimus*, no. 30.

903 [1798]

Description In oval at upper left: ASIA, / FROM THE LATEST / AUTHORITIES. In oval below title: ROLLINSON SCULPT. Below bottom neat line: ENGRAVED FOR PAYNES GEOGRAPHY PUBLISHED BY LOW & WILLIS N YORK. A few topographical features are noted and many place names.

Size 7⅜″ x 8¾″.   *Scale* None (1″ = c. 13° latitude).

Published in John Payne, *A New and Complete Universal Geography, 1,* opp. 3.

904 [c. 1799]

Description In oval at lower left corner: A MAP / OF THOSE / COUNTRIES / IN WHICH THE / APOSTLES /TRAVELLED: / IN PROPAGATING / CHRISTIANITY. / COMPILED AND ENGRAVED / BY / JOSEPH T. SCOTT. Above top neat line at center: SOLD BY THE PUBLISHER NO. 65 WALNUT-STREET PHILADA. Many towns and political and geographical districts are shown with a mixture of contemporary and ancient names. The lower neat line is broken for the Sinai Peninsula. The voyage of St. Paul from Jerusalem to Rome is shown by a dotted line. This map appears in some copies of *Carey's General Atlas,* Philadelphia, 1796, but it does not appear among those in the printed list until the 1802 edition of the *Atlas.*

Size 11⅛″ x 23½″.   *Scale* None (1″ = 100 miles).

Published Mathew Carey, *Carey's General Atlas,* at end (some copies only).

905 [1799]

Description In oval at upper left: A NEW MAP / OF / ASIA / DRAWN FROM THE BEST / AUTHORITIES.

Size 8″ x 9⁵⁄₁₆″.   *Scale* None (1″ = c. 800 miles).

Published in Joseph Scott, *The New and Universal Gazetteer, 1,* at leaf Z¹.

PACIFIC OCEAN

906 [1783]

Description In ornamental cartouche at upper right: CHART / SHEWING THE TRACKS / OF THE SHIPS EMPLOYED IN / CAPT. COOK'S / LAST VOYAGE TO THE / PACIFIC OCEAN; / IN THE YEARS / *1776, 1777, 1778, 1779*. This is a chart on Mercator's projection. PORT SR. FRANCIS DRAKE / OR DE LA BOGODA appears in 39° N. Latitude; NORTH WEST CONTINENT / OF AMERICA DISCOVER'D BY CAPT. COOK / *1778* appears at 70° N. Latitude.

Size 13⅛" x 12⅞".   *Scale* None (1" = c. 1200 miles).

Published in John Ledyard, *A Journal of Captain Cook's Last Voyage*, front.

907 [1796]

Description In lower left corner: SKETCH / OF / KARAKAKOOA BAY. / LAT. *19°. 28'* N. Lon. *204°. 0* E. / VARN. *8°. 0* E. *1779*. This is detailed chart of modern Kealakekua Bay on the Island of Hawaii showing the native settlements. A note indicates the spot where Capt. Cook was killed on February 14, 1779. This chart occupies the upper half of the same plate as Map 908, and was adapted from the inset of the same title appearing on a chart in the London, 1784, edition of this work (3, opp. 1). The name of the engraver, "Rollinson," appears at the bottom right of the plate.

Size 5¼" x 7⁵⁄₁₆".   *Scale* 1" = ⅓ "nautic" mile.

Published in James Cook and James King, *A Voyage to the Pacific Ocean*, opp. p. 148.

908 [1796]

Description In lower left corner: CHART / OF THE / SANDWICH ISLANDS. Below lower neat line at right corner: ROLLINSON. This is a chart showing the islands of Hawaii, Maui, Kahoolawe, and part of the island of Lanai. The engraver is William Rollinson. It occupies the lower part of the same plate as Map 907, and was adapted from the chart of the same title appearing in the London, 1784 edition of this work (3, opp. 1).

Size 7⅛" x 7⅜".   *Scale* None (1" = c. 24 miles).

Published in James Cook and James King, *A Voyage to the Pacific Ocean*, 3, opp. 148.

909 [1796]

Description In upper right corner: A SKETCH / OF THE ISLANDS / CALLED THE / MARQUESAS, / IN THE SOUTH PACIFIC OCEAN, / WITH SEVEN ADJACENT ISLANDS / LATELY DISCOVERED. Above top neat line at right: MASSA. MAG. The discovery dates and the latitudes are noted upon several of the islands.

Size 7³⁄₁₆" x 7¼".   *Scale* None (1" = c. 2° 20' latitude).

Inset At lower left: PORT MAIRE DE DIOS, OR RESOLUTION BAY. At the lower right corner of the inset map is inscribed the name: COOK. Size: 1⅞" x 1⅝". Scale: 1" = 1 mile.

Published in *Massachusetts Magazine*, 8 (1796), opp. 131.

910 [1796]

Description In upper left corner: A CHART / OF THE / SOUTHERN HEMISPHERE; / SHEWING THE TRACT OF / CAPT: COOK'S / LAST VOYAGE. Beneath title: ENGRAVED BY W. BARKER. This is a chart of the Pacific Ocean showing the track of Captain James Cook's last voyage with notations regarding the progress of the cruise. Hatch marks are given on the land surfaces. PHILIPINE / ISLES and I. FORMOSO are noted thus. See also Map 914.

Size 10⅜" x 8⅛".   *Scale* None (1" = 20° latitude).

Published in *The World Displayed, 8*, opp. 36.

911 1797

Description At lower center: CHART / OF THE NEW DISCOVERIES / EAST OF NEW HOLLAND / AND / NEW GUINEA / *1797*. Below bottom neat line at center: ENGRAVED FOR MORSE'S AMERICAN GAZETTEER. At right: CALLENDER SCP;. The explorations and discoveries of a number of Europeans are shown but not those of Captain James Cook. VAN DIEMEN'S LAND is attached to NEW HOLLAND.

Size 7¼" x 9⅞".   *Scale* None (1" = c. 1000 miles).

Published in Jedidiah Morse, *The American Gazetteer,* opp. "Tierra Austral."

912 [1798]

Description At upper left: EAST INDIA IS-LANDS. Beneath title: J. T. SCOTT SCULP. Above top neat line to left: *33.* Many islands are named.

Size 2⅝″ x 3¾″.   *Scale* 1″ = 1000 miles (60 to a degree).

Published in John Gibson, *Atlas Minimus,* no. 33.

913 [1798]

Description In oval at upper right corner: EAST / INDIES / FROM THE BEST / AUTHORITIES. Below oval: ROLLINSON SCULPT. Below bottom neat line: ENGRAV'D FOR PAYNE'S GEOGRAPHY PUB-LISH'D BY JOHN LOW NEW YORK. Some topograph-ical features are noted and many place names. India is also shown.

Size 7½″ x 10⁷⁄₁₆″.   *Scale* 1″ = 600 American statute miles.

Published in John Payne, *A New and Complete Universal Geography, 1,* opp. 312.

914 1799

Description In oval at upper center: A CHART / SHEWING THE TRACT OF / CAPT: COOK'S / LAST VOYAGE. / *1799.* Below bottom neat line: EN-GRAVED FOR PAYNE'S GEOGRAPHY, PUBLISHED BY I. LOW, NEW YORK. This chart is a re-engraving of Map 910. The PHILIPPINE / ISLES and I. FORMOSA are noted correctly, and hatch marks are now given on the ocean surface adjoining the land areas.

Size 10¼″ x 8″.   *Scale* None (1″ = c. 19° latitude).

Published in John Payne, *A New and Complete Universal Geography, 4,* opp. 521.

ARCTIC REGIONS

915 [1795] *State* I (II post-1799, see below, Description)

Description Across bottom of plate below map: A MAP OF THE COUNTRIES SITUATE ABOUT THE NORTH POLE / AS FAR AS THE 50TH. DEGREE OF NORTH LATITUDE. At lower right corner of plate: W. BARKER SCULP. At top of plate above map: ENGRAVED FOR CAREY'S EDITION OF GUTHRIE'S GEOGRAPHY IMPROVED. This is a polar projection map. Samuel Hearne's 1771 route to the Coppermine River is shown. The map also appears in the September, 1800, edition of *Carey's General Atlas* with "44" appearing in the upper right corner.

Size 10⅛" x 9¼".   *Scale* None (1" = c. 540 miles).

Published in Mathew Carey, *Carey's General Atlas,* no. 44; idem, *The General Atlas for Carey's Edition of Guthrie's Geography Improved,* no. 44.

References

Numbers refer to individual maps and charts and not to pages.

1. Adams, Randolph Greenfield, "The Cartography of the British Attack on Fort Moultrie in 1776," in *Essays Offered to Herbert Putnam* (New Haven, 1929), pp. 35–46. 592, 596.

2. ——, "William Hubbard's 'Narrative,' 1677: A Bibliographical Study," in Bibliographical Society of America, *Papers, 33* (1939), 25–39. 144.

3. American Antiquarian Society, *Proceedings . . . with the reports of the Council and Librarian* (Worcester, Mass., 1933–). 370

4. *American Chronicle* (New York). 324.

5. *American Magazine and Historical Chronicle* (Boston). 72–74, 81.

6. *American Magazine, containing a miscellaneous collection of original and other valuable Essays . . .*, ed. Noah Webster, Jr. (New York). 491, 667.

7. *American Museum* (Philadelphia). 6, 182, 477.

8. American Philosophical Society, *Early Proceedings of the American Philosophical Society for the Promotion of Useful Knowledge. Compiled by One of the Secretaries from the Manuscript Minutes of Its Meetings from 1744 to 1838* (Philadelphia, 1884). 300, 477.

9. ——, *Transactions of the American Philosophical Society . . .* (Philadelphia, 1771–). 300, 305.

10. *American Weekly Mercury* (Philadelphia). 726.

11. Anderson, Russell, "The Pease Map of the Connecticut Western Reserve," in *The Ohio State Archaeological and Historical Quarterly, 63* (1954), 270–78. 680.

12. Andrews, William Loring, *The Bradford map. The City of New York at the time of the granting of the Montgomerie Charter. A description thereof compiled by William Loring Andrews to accompany a facsimile of an actual survey made by James Lyne and printed by William Bradford in 1731* (New York, 1893). 378.

13. ——, "James Lyne's Survey; or, as it is better known, the Bradford Map," in *The Bookman, 11* (1900), 458–63. 378.

14. Archibald, Eugenie, *Catalogue of the William Inglis Morse Collection of Books, Pictures, Maps, Manuscripts, etc. at Dalhousie University Library, Halifax, Nova Scotia . . .* (London, 1938). 86

15. Armbruster, Anton, *Neu-Eingerichteter Americanischer Geschichts-Calendar, Auf das Jahr 1759* (Philadelphia [1758]). Evans 8198. PHi. 78.

16. ——, *Neu-Eingerichteter Americanischer Geschichts-und Haus Calendar, Auf das Jahr . . . 1760* (Philadelphia [1759]). Evans 8425. PHi. 50.

17. *Atlas des Colonies Angloises en Amerique* (Paris?, 17—?). Made-up atlas. MHi. 422.

18. Avery, Elroy McKendree, *A History of the United States and its People, from their earliest Records to the present time* (7 vols. Cleveland, 1904–10). 676.

19. Bailey, Francis, *Bailey's Pocket Almanac, being an American Annual Register, for the Year of our Lord 1785* (Philadelphia [1784]). Evans 18338. DLC. 113.

20. ——, *Bailey's Pocket Almanac, for the Year of our Lord, 1787* (Philadelphia [1786]). Evans 19488. 113.

21. Baltimore, Charles Calvert, 6th baron, *Articles of Agreement Made and Concluded Upon Between the Right Honourable the Lord Proprietary of Maryland, and the Honourable the Proprietarys of Pensilvania, &c. Touching the Limits and Boundaries of the Two Provinces . . .* (Philadelphia, B. Franklin, 1733). Evans 3710. DLC, MiU-C, PHi, RPJCB. 474.

22. Baltimore Museum of Art, *The World Encompassed. An Exhibition of the History of Maps held at the Baltimore Museum of Art October 7 to November 23, 1952 . . .* (Baltimore, Trustees of the Walters Art Gallery, 1952). 57, 298, 474–75, 497.

23. Bard, John, *A Letter to the Proprietors of the Great-Nine-Partners-Tract. On the Subject of Jacob Reigner & Company's Patented Land, to the Northward of the Fish Creek, in Dutchess County . . .* (New York, 1751). CSmH. 319.

24. Bartram, William, *Travels through North &*

REFERENCES

South Carolina, Georgia, East & West Florida, the Cherokee Country, the extensive territories of the Muscogulges, or Creek Confederacy, and the Country of the Chactaws . . . (Philadelphia, 1791). Evans 23159. BM, DLC, MBAt, MiU-C, MWA, NN, RPJCB. 628.

25. ———, *Travels . . .* (London [1792]). 628.
26. ———, *The Travels of William Bartram: Naturalist's Edition,* ed. Francis Harper (New Haven, 1958). 628.
27. Bates, Albert Carlos, "Check List of Connecticut Almanacs, 1709–1850," in American Antiquarian Society, *Proceedings,* N. S., 24 (1914), 93–215. 114, 542–44.
28. Baylies, Francis, *An Historical Memoir of the Colony of New Plymouth, Additions and corrections; with analytical index to the whole. By Samuel G. Drake* (Boston, 1866). 161.
29. Beers, Andrew, *The United-States Almanack, for the Year of our Lord Christ, 1783 . . .* (Hartford, Bavil Webster [1782]). 542, 544.
30. ———, *The United-States Almanack, for the Year of our Lord Christ, 1783 . . .* (2d ed.? Hartford, Bavil Webster [1782]). 543.
31. ———, *The United-States Almanack, for the Year of our Lord Christ, 1783 . . .* (3d ed.? Hartford, Nathaniel Patten [1782]). 544.
32. Belknap, Jeremy, *The History of New-Hampshire* (2 vols. Boston, 1791). Evans 23166. DLC, MBAt, MH, MHi, MiU-C, MWA, NHi, NN, RPJCB. 183.
33. ———, *The History . . .* (Dover, N.H., 1812). 183.
34. ———, *The History . . .* (Boston, 1813). 183.
35. Blodget, Samuel, *The Battle near Lake George in 1755 A Prospective Plan with an Explanation thereof by Samuel Blodget occasionally at the Camp when the Battle was fought. Reprinted in facsimile from the Edition published in London by Thomas Jefferys in 1756 with a Prefatory Note by Henry N. Stevens, F.R.G.S.* (London, 1911). 320.
36. ———, *A prospective-Plan of the Battle near Lake George, on the Eighth Day of September, 1755. With an Explanation thereof; containing a full, tho' short, History of that important Affair . . .* (Boston, 1755). Evans 7363. MB, MHi, MWiW, NHi, NN, RPJCB. 320–21.
37. Board of General Proprietors of Eastern Division of New Jersey, *A Bill in the Chancery of New-Jersey. At the Suit of John Earl of Stair, and Others. Proprietors of the Eastern-Division of New-Jersey; against Benjamin Bond, and some other Persons of Elizabeth-Town, distinguished by the Name of the Clinker Lot Right Men. With Three Large Maps, done from Copper-plates . . .* (New York, 1747). Evans 6021. DLC, MH, MiU-C, NN, RPJCB. 294, 397–98.
38. Boston, City of, Engineering Dept., *List of Maps of Boston published between 1600 and 1903 copies of which are to be found in the possession of the City of Boston or other collectors of the same. Reporting of Appendix I, Annual Report of the City Engineer. February 1, 1903* (Boston, 1903). 229, 243, 248.
39. ———, *List of Maps of Boston published subsequent to 1600 copies of which are to be found in the possession of the City of Boston or other collectors of the same. Reprint of Appendix J, Annual Report of the City Engineer. A Supplementary List to Appendix I, Annual Report of the City Engineer for the Year 1902. February 1, 1904* (Boston, 1904). 243.
40. *Boston Directory. Containing, a List of the Merchants, Mechanics, Traders, and Others, of the town of Boston . . .* (Boston, printed and sold by John Norman, 1789). Evans 22033. MB, MdHi, MiU-C. 243–44.
41. ——— (Boston, 1789). Reproduction published by Sampson and Murdock Company, Boston, 1930. 244.
42. *Boston Evening-Post.* 74, 79.
43. *Boston Gazette* (later *Boston Gazette and Country Journal*). 76, 119, 225, 325, 575.
44. *Boston Gazette and Country Journal.* 261.
45. *Boston Magazine.* 242.
46. *Boston News-Letter.* 46, 68, 160, 224, 325.
47. *Boston Weekly News-Letter.* 48, 75–76, 232, 727–28.
48. Bostonian Society, *Publications.* 234.
49. Braam Houckgeest, Andreas Everard van, *Voyage de l'Ambassade de la Compagnie des Indes Orientales Hollandaises, vers l'Empereur de la Chine . . .* (2 vols. Philadelphia, 1797–98). Evans 31860, 33448. CtY, DLC, NjP, NN, PPAmP. 892–93, 896.
50. Breck, Samuel, *Sketch of the internal improvements already made by Pennsylvania . . .* (2d ed. Philadelphia, 1818). 311.
51. Brigham, Clarence Saunders, *Journals and Journeymen: A Contribution to the History of Early American Newspapers* (Philadelphia, 1950). 69–70, 726.
52. ———, *Paul Revere's Engravings* (Worcester, Mass., American Antiquarian Society, 1954). 621.
53. Brinley, George, *Catalogue of the American Library of the late Mr. George Brinley of Hartford, Connecticut . . .* (5 vols. Hartford, 1878–93). 317.
54. British Museum, *Catalogue of Printed Maps, Plans, and Charts in the British Museum* (2 vols. London, 1885). 433.
55. Brown University, John Carter Brown Li-

brary, *The French and Indian War* (Providence, R.I., 1960). 44, 475.

56. ——, *In retrospect, 1923–1949. An exhibition commemorating twenty-six years of service to the John Carter Brown Library by Lawrence C. Wroth, Librarian* (Providence, R.I., 1949). 454, 474.

57. ——, "Notes" accompanying reproduction 1717 map (Providence, R.I., 1942). 44.

58. ——, *Report to the Corporation of Brown University, July 1, 1937* (Providence, R.I., 1937). 241.

59. ——, *Report . . . July 1, 1946* (Providence, R.I., 1946). 77.

60. ——, *Report . . . July 1, 1947* (Providence, R.I., 1947). 425, 454, 474, 680.

61. ——, *Report . . . July 1, 1949* (Providence, R. I., 1949). 475.

62. ——, *Report . . . July 1, 1956* (Providence, R. I., 1956). 128, 359, 400.

63. ——, *Report . . . July 1, 1958* (Providence, R.I., 1958). 692–94.

64. Brown, Lloyd Arnold, "The River in the Ocean," in *Essays Honoring Lawrence C. Wroth* (Portland, Me., 1951), pp. 69–84. 22, 721, 724.

65. Brunswick Township, Maine, Proprietors of, *An Answer to the Remarks of the Plymouth Company . . .* (Boston, 1753). Evans 6976. MWA, NN. 161, 163.

66. Burchard, Edward L., and Edward B. Matthews, "Manuscripts and publications relating to the Mason and Dixon Line . . ." in *Maryland Geological Survey*, 7 (1908), pt. 4. 456.

67. Burr, Nelson R., "The Federal City depicted, 1612–1801," in Library of Congress, *Quarterly Journal of Current Acquisitions*, 8 no. 1 (1950), 64–77. 531–32, 535.

68. Carey, Mathew, *Carey's American Atlas: containing twenty Maps and one Chart . . .* (Philadelphia, 1795). This is a reissue of the American maps in William Guthrie, *A New System . . .* (Philadelphia [1794–95]). Evans 28390, Phillips 1172, 1213, 1362, Sabin 10855. DGU, DLC, MH, MWA, PHi, PP, RPJCB. 24, 101, 103, 169, 185, 195, 213, 250, 284, 362, 414, 442, 483, 510, 568, 581, 601, 611, 642, 650, 687, 708.

69. ——, *Carey's American Pocket Atlas containing the following Maps . . . With a concise description of each State* (Philadelphia, 1796). Evans 30161, Phillips 1364, Sabin 10856. CSmH, DLC, MB, MWA, NHi, NN, PPL, RPJCB. 131, 174, 187, 197, 217, 253, 286, 367, 416, 445, 485, 513, 570, 584, 603, 613, 644, 652, 675.

70. ——, *Carey's American Pocket Atlas . . .* (2d ed. Philadelphia, 1801). Same entries as 1st ed.

71. ——, *Carey's General Atlas . . .* (Philadelphia, May 1, 1796). This is a reissue of the maps in Carey's *American* and *General* atlases. Evans 30162, Phillips 683, 1365, Sabin 10858. DLC, M, MB, MH, MiU-C, PPL, RPJCB. 23–25, 103, 132–33, 169, 185, 195, 213, 250, 284, 414, 442, 483, 510, 568, 581, 601, 611, 642, 653, 678, 687, 692, 708, 760–61, 763–64, 767–68, 770–74, 778–83, 847, 878–80, 883, 904, 915.

72. ——, *Carey's General Atlas* (Philadelphia, 1800). 23–25, 103, 133, 169, 185, 195, 213, 250, 284, 362, 414, 483, 510, 568, 581, 601, 611, 642, 653, 687, 692, 708, 760, 764, 767, 770–74, 778–83, 808, 847, 878, 880, 883, 915.

73. ——, *Carey's General Atlas* (Philadelphia, 1802). 678, 692, 904.

74. ——, *Carey's General Atlas* (Philadelphia, 1814). 23, 25, 414, 601, 678, 692, 772–74.

——, *Carey's War-Atlas . . . .* See Carey, *A General Atlas for the Present War . . . .*

75. ——, *Eine Kurtze Nachricht Von Algier . . . .* (Philadelphia, 1794). Evans 26734. MWA, RPJCB. 845.

76. ——, *The General Atlas for Carey's Edition of Guthrie's Geography Improved . . .* (Philadelphia, May 1, 1795). This accompanies William Guthrie, *A New System of Modern Geography: or, a geographical, historical, and commercial Grammar . . .* (1st Am. ed. 2 vols. Philadelphia [1794–95]). Phillips 6007. CtY, MiU-C, PPL. 23–25, 101, 132, 169, 185, 195, 213, 250, 284, 362, 414, 442, 483, 510, 568, 581, 601, 611, 642, 650, 687, 708, 759–64, 767–76, 847, 878–80, 915.

77. ——, *A General Atlas for the Present War. Containing six Maps and one Chart . . . Including Every Place in Europe and the West-Indies, in which the War has been carried on* (Philadelphia, Jan. 28, 1794). (Cover title: *Carey's War-Atlas: containing . . . .* This is the first known American printed atlas.) Evans 26741, Phillips 6003. DLC, MiU-C, MWA. 687, 759–64.

78. ——, *A Short Account of Algiers containing a Description of the Climate of that Country, of the manners and customs of the Inhabitants . . .* (Philadelphia, Jan. 8, 1794). Evans 26732. DLC, MB, MWA, MiU, NN, PP, RPJCB. 845.

79. ——, *A Short Account of Algiers and of its several wars against Spain, France, England, Holland, Venice, and other powers of Europe . . .* (2d ed. Philadelphia, Oct. 20, 1794). Evans 26733. RPJCB. 845.

80. *Carey's United States Recorder* (Philadelphia). 807.

81. *The Carlisle Gazette* (Pennsylvania). 479.

82. [Chapin, Howard M.], "Chronological Check List of Maps of Rhode Island in the Rhode

REFERENCES

Island Historical Society Library," in Rhode Island Historical Society, *Collections, 11* (1918). 251.

83. Charleston Library Society, *Catalogue of the Books belonging to the Charleston Library Society* ... (Charleston, S.C., 1826). 599.

84. Charlevoix, Pierre François Xavier de, *Histoire et description générale de la Nouvelle France, avec le Journal historique d'un Voyage fait par ordre du roi dans l'Amerique Septentrionnale* ... (Paris, 1744). 77.

85. Church, Elihu Dwight, *A Catalogue of Books relating to the Discovery and early History of North and South America forming a part of the Library of E. D. Church,* comp. and ed. George Watson Cole (5 vols. New York, 1907). 379.

86. Churchman, John, *An Explanation of the Magnetic Atlas, or Variation Chart, hereunto annexed; projected on a Plan entirely new, by which the Magnetic Variations on any part of the Globe may be precisely determined, for any time past, present, or future* ... (Philadelphia, 1790). Evans 22406. BM, DLC, MBAt, MHi, MiU-C, MWA, RPJCB. 6.

87. ——, *An Explanation of the Magnetic Atlas* ... (2d ed. London, 1794).

88. ——, *An Explanation of the Magnetic Atlas* ... (3d ed. New York, 1800). 6.

89. Clairac, Louis André de La Mamie de, *L'Ingenieur de Compagne: or, Field Engineer. Written in French by Chevalier De Clairac,* and translated by Major Lewis Nicola (Philadelphia, 1776). Evans 14678. CtY, DLC, MB, MiU-C, PPL. 731–42.

90. Clark, Matthew *[A complete Chart of the Coast of America, from Cape Breton into the Gulf of Mexico]* (Boston, published and sold by Matthew Clark, 1790). Issued without title page. Several of the charts are dated 1789 but the published volume was issued in 1790. Charts were also sold separately. Evans 21738, Phillips 300). CtY, DLC, MD, MDAt, MH, NN. 93–96, 165, 206–07, 306–07, 330, 567, 576–77, 598, 609, 625–27.

91. *Clarke's Charleston Directory with Large and Elegant Plan of the City Engraved by Ralph, One of the First American Artists* (Charleston, S.C., 1796) (Title taken from Dorothea N. Spear, *Bibliography,* p. 81.). 604.

Clements, William L., Library. *See* Michigan, University of.

92. Colden, Cadwallader, *The History of the Five Indian Nations depending on the Province of New-York in America* (New York, William Bradford, 1727). Evans 2849. BM, NN, RPJCB, ViU. 317.

93. ——, *The History of the Six Indian Nations in North America* . . . (Troy, N.Y.,

printed by Luther Pratt, 1797? Probably not published). Evans 31952. 375.

94. ——, *Papers relating to an Act of the Assembly of the Province of New-York for encouragement of the Indian trade, &c. and for prohibiting the selling of Indian Goods to the French, viz. of Canada ... With a Map. Published by authority* (New York, William Bradford, 1724). Evans 2512. NN, PHi, PP, PPAmP, RPJCB. 317.

95. Coleman, Kenneth, *The American Revolution in Georgia 1763–1789* (Athens, Ga., 1958). 611.

96. Colles, Christopher, *The Geographical Ledger and Systemized* [sic] *Atlas; Being an United Collection of Topograpaical* [sic] *Maps* (New York, 1794). This work was apparently never completed; only sheets noted are thus far known. Restrikes of several plates from Colles *Survey* also sometimes included. Evans 26781. 154–56, 309, 358.

97. ——, *A Survey of the Roads of the United States of America* (New York, 1789). Issued serially 1789–1792? Evans 21741. 265–71, 331–56, 401–12, 427–30, 480–81, 499–509, 546–66.

98. ——, *A Survey of the Roads of the United States of America 1789 by Christopher Colles,* ed. Walter W. Ristow (Cambridge, Mass., 1961), "Inventory of Extant Copies," pp. 115–16. 154–56, 265–71, 309, 331–56, 358, 401–12, 427–30, 480–81, 499–509, 546–66.

99. *Columbian Gazetteer* (New York). 685.

100. *Columbian Magazine* (Philadelphia). 208, 426, 431, 663, 668–69.

101. Condy, Jonathan W., *A Description of the River Susquehanna* . . . (Philadelphia, 1796). Evans 30338. DLC, MBAt, MH, MHi, MiU-C, MWA, NN, ScC. 311.

102. Connecticut (Colony), *The Public Records of the Colony of Connecticut* [1636–1776], *13* (Hartford, 1885). 264.

103. *Connecticut Courant* (Hartford). 304.

104. *Connecticut Gazette* (New London). 117, 304.

105. *Connecticut Gazette and the Universal Intelligencer* (New London). 261.

106. *Connecticut Journal* (New Haven). 109.

107. Cook, James, and James King, *A Voyage to the Pacific Ocean* . . . (3 vols. London, 1784). 907–08.

108. ——, *A Voyage to the Pacific Ocean* . . . (4 vols. New York, 1796). Evans 30274. MBAt, MWA, NN, RPJCB. 28, 907–08. *See also* Hawkesworth, John.

109. Council of Proprietors of the Western Division of New Jersey, *The Petitions and Memorials of the Proprietors of West and East Jersey, to the Legislature of New-Jersey, together with a Map of the State of New-*

190

Jersey, and the Country adjacent: and also an Appendix: containing extracts from several Original Papers, and Instruments, tending to elucidate the subject matter of the said petitions, &c. . . . (New York, 1784). Evans 18640. CSmH, N, NjHi, NjP, NjR, NN, RPJCB. 400.

110. ———, *The Petitions and Memorials of the Proprietors of West and East Jersey, to the Legislature of New-Jersey* . . . (New York [1785]). Evans 19126. MiU-C, N, NN. 400.

111. Cumming, William Patterson, *The Southeast in Early Maps with an annotated Check List of Printed and Manuscript Regional and Local Maps of Southeastern North America during the Colonial period* (Princeton, N.J., 1958). 294, 575, 578.

112. ———, *The Southeast in Early Maps with an annotated Check List of Printed and Manuscript Regional and Local Maps of Southeastern North America during the Colonial period* (2d ed. Chapel Hill, N.C. [1962]). 575.

113. Cutler, Manasseh, *An Explanation of the Map which delineates that part of the Federal Lands, comprehended between Pennsylvania west line, the Rivers of Ohio and Sioto, and Lake Erie* . . . (Salem, Mass., 1787). Evans 20312. DLC. 662.

114. ———, *An Explanation of the Map which delineates that part of the Federal Lands, comprehended between Pennsylvania west line, the Rivers of Ohio and Sioto, and Lake Erie* . . . (Newport, R.I., 1788). Evans 21037. CSmH, MiU-C, MWA, RHi. 662.

115. Daboll, Nathan, *Freebetter's New-England Almanack, for the Year of our Lord Christ, 1777* (Hartford, N. Patten [1776]). Evans 14725. CtHi, MWA. 385.

116. ———, *The New-England Almanack; and Gentleman's and Lady's Diary, for the Year of our Lord Christ, 1777* . . . (New London, Conn. [1776]). Evans 14724. MWA. 385.

117. *Daily Advertiser* (New York). 192, 377.

118. Davies, Benjamin, *Some account of the City of Philadelphia, the Capital of Pennsylvania and Seat of the Federal Congress* . . . (Philadelphia, 1794). Evans 26853. BM, DLC, MBAt, MWA, NHi, PPL, RPJCB. 461–62.

119. De Forest, Louis Effingham, ed., *Louisbourg Journals, 1745* . . . compiled for and published by the Society of Colonial Wars (New York, 1932). 70.

120. DesBarres, Joseph Frederick Wallet, *The Atlantic Neptune, published for the use of the Royal Navy of Great Britain* . . . (London, 1774–81). 482.

121. "A Description of the surprising Cataract, in the great River Connecticut," in *American Museum, 9* (1791), 254. 182.

122. Dobson, Thomas, *Encyclopaedia* (21 vols. Philadelphia, 1798–1803 [i.e. 1790–1803]). Evans states that the plates are copied from those drawn and engraved by Andrew Bell in *Encyclopaedia Britannica,* 3d ed. 13–17, 51, 432, 684, 701, 747–52, 755–57, 784–87, 796, 809–13, 840, 863, 871.

123. *Documents relative to the Colonial History of the State of New-York* . . . (15 vols. Albany, 1853–87). 317, 326.

124. *The Documentary History of the State of New-York; arranged under direction of the Hon. Christopher Morgan, Secretary of State,* ed. E. B. O'Callaghan (4 vols. Albany, 1849–51). 147.

125. Dow, George Francis, *The Arts & Crafts in New England, 1704–1775; gleanings from Boston newspapers relating to painting, engraving, silversmiths, pewterers, clockmakers, furniture, pottery, old houses, costume, trades and occupations, &c.* . . . (Topsfield, Mass., 1927). 75–76, 163, 224, 325, 575.

126. Drake, Samuel G., *The History and antiquities of Boston, the capital of Massachusetts and metropolis of New England, from its settlement in 1630, to the year 1770* . . . (Boston, 1856). 228.

127. ———, *See also* no. R28.

128. Drepperd, Carl W., *Early American Prints* (New York [1930]). 462, 537, 541.

129. Dunbar, Gary S., *Historical Geography of the North Carolina Outer Banks,* in Louisiana State University Studies, Coastal Series, no. 3 (Baton Rouge, [1958]). 575, 590.

130. Duncan, William, *The New-York Directory and Register, for the year 1791. Illustrated with a new and accurate Plan of the City, and part of Long-Island, exactly laid down, agreeably to the latest survey* . . . (New York, 1791). Evans 23337. MH, NHi, NN. 388.

131. ———, *The New-York Directory, and Register, for tre [sic] year 1792. Illustrated with a new and accurate plan of the City, and part of Long Island* . . . (New York, 1792). Evans 24281. CSmH, MH, NN. 389.

132. ———, *The New-York Directory, and Register, for the year 1792 [i.e. 1793] illustrated with a new and accurate Plan of the City and part of Long-Island* . . . (New York, 1793). Evans 25422. MH, NHi, NN. 389.

133. ———, *The New-York Directory, and Register, for the year 1794. Illustrated with a new and accurate plan of the City and part of Long-Island* . . . (New York, 1794). Evans 26919. CSmH, NHi, NN. 390.

134. ———, *The New-York Directory, and Register, for the year 1795. Illustrated with a new and accurate plan of the City and part of Long-Island* . . . (New York, 1795). Evans 28598. MWA, NHi, NN. 390.

REFERENCES

135. Dunlap, William, *A History of the Rise and Progress of the Arts of Design in the United States . . .*, A new illustrated edition. Edited with additions by Frank W. Bayley and Charles E. Goodspeed (3 vols. Boston, 1918). 68, 160, 163, 191.

136. *Dunlap's American Daily Advertiser* (Philadelphia). 460, 641.

137. Durrett, Reuben T., *John Filson, the First Historian of Kentucky . . .*, Filson Club, *Publications*, no. 1 (Louisville, 1884). 631, 639.

138. Ebeling, Christoph Daniel, *. . . Erdbeschreibung und Geschichte von Amerika . . .* (7 vols. Hamburg, 1793–1816). 479, 511.

139. *Encyclopaedia Britannica* (3d ed. Edinburgh, 1797 [i.e. 1788–97]). 784. *See also* Dobson, Thomas.

140. *The English Pilot. The Fourth Book. Describing the West-India navigation, from Hudson's-Bay to the River Amazones . . .* (London, 1721). 160.

141. Ethyl Corporation, *Lewis Evans and His Historic Map of 1755. First Known Document to Show Oil at the Industry's Birthplace* [New York, 1953?]. 299.

142. Evans, Charles, *American Bibliography by Charles Evans. A Chronological Dictionary of all Books, Pamphlets and Periodical Publications printed in the United States of America from the genesis of printing in 1639 down to and including the Year 1820 with Bibliographical and Biographical Notes* (14 vols. Chicago, 1903–59). Also, the Readex Microprint edition of Evans prepared by the American Antiquarian Society, Worcester, Mass. 1956–. 5, 9, 92, 111, 113–15, 119, 121, 127–28, 133, 137, 148, 170–71, 183, 192, 194, 200, 203, 211, 215, 220, 246, 251, 260–61, 272–73, 291, 295, 298, 311, 313–14, 320, 322, 328, 357, 361, 363, 375–76, 392, 422, 425, 431–33, 437, 456–57, 459, 464, 466, 468, 471, 473, 475, 479, 482, 486, 491, 493, 511, 515, 521, 523, 531, 534, 536, 544, 578, 582, 586, 590, 597, 621, 631, 641, 650, 653, 656, 660, 670, 676, 678, 680, 683, 753–54, 805, 807, 865.

143. Evans, Lewis, *Geographical, historical, political, philosophical and mechanical Essays. The first, containing an Analysis of a General Map of the Middle British Colonies in America; and of the Country of the Confederate Indians . . .* (Philadelphia, 1755). Evans 7411. CtY, MiU-C, MWA, NN. For other copies see Henry N. Stevens, *Lewis Evans*. 298.

144. ———, *Geographical, historical, political, philosophical and mechanical Essays. The first, containing an Analysis of a General Map of the Middle British Colonies in America; and of the Country of the Confederate Indians . . .* (2d ed. Philadelphia, 1755). Evans 7412. MWA; 2d ed., 2d issue, Evans 7413. NN. 298–99.

145. Federal Writers' Project, *Washington City and Capital* (Washington, D.C., 1937). 532.

146. Fielding, Mantle, *American Engravers upon copper and steel . . . A supplement to David McNeely Stauffer's American Engravers* (Philadelphia, 1917). 630.

147. Filson, John, *The Discovery, Settlement and Present State of Kentucke: and an Essay towards the Topography, and Natural History of that important Country . . . The Whole Illustrated by a New and Accurate Map of Kentucke and the Country adjoining, drawn from actual Surveys* (Wilmington, Del., 1784). 631–40.

148. ———, *The Discovery, Settlement and present State of Kentucke . . .* (New York [1962]). 635.

149. Fite, Emerson D., and Archibald Freeman, *A Book of Old Maps Delineating American History from the Earliest Days Down to the Close of the Revolutionary War* (Cambridge, Mass., 1926). 144, 425, 541.

150. Flavius Josephus [Joseph ben Matthias], *The whole genuine and complete works*, tr. George Henry Maynard, references by Edward Kimpton (New York, 1792 [pub. serially, 1792–94]). Evans 24437. CtY, MB, MH, MiU-C, MWA, NN. 18, 869–70, 872.

151. ———, *The whole genuine and complete works* (Philadelphia, 1795). Evans 28910. DLC. 869–70, 872.

152. ———, *The whole genuine and complete works* (Baltimore, 1795). 869–70, 872.

153. Fobes, Peres, *A History of the ancient Colony of Plymouth* [n.p., 1794?]. This volume was being prepared for publication in 1794 but no copy has been located. 212.

154. Ford, Worthington Chauncey, *Broadsides, Ballads, printed in Massachusetts 1639–1800*, in Massachusetts Historical Society, *Collections*, 75 (1922). 161.

155. Franklin, Benjamin, "A Letter from Dr. Benjamin Franklin, to Mr. Alphonsus Le Roy, Member of Several Academies, at Paris. Containing sundry Maritime Observations," in American Philosophical Society, *Transactions*, 2 (1786), 294–329. 721.

156. ———, *Maritime Observations in a Letter from Doctor Franklin, to Mr. Alphonsus Le Roy, Member of Several Academies, at Paris* (Philadelphia, 1786). MiU, MiU-C. 721.

157. ———, *The Papers of . . .*, ed. Leonard W. Labaree (New Haven, 1959), *1–*. 294, 474.

158. ———, "Remarks upon the Navigation from Newfoundland to New York, in order to avoid the Gulf Stream on one hand, and on the other the Shoals that lie to the southward of Nantucket and of St. George's Banks. By Dr. Franklin," in *American Museum*, 5 (1789), 213. 723.

159. Fraser, Donald, *The Young Gentleman and Lady's Assistant* . . . (2d ed. Danbury, Conn., 1794). Evans 27011. BM, MWA. 20.

160. ———, *The Young Gentleman and Lady's Assistant* . . . (3d ed. New York, 1796). Evans 30447. MWA. 20.

161. Futhey, John Smith, and Gilbert Cope, *History of Chester County, Pennsylvania, with genealogical and biographical sketches* . . . (Philadelphia, 1881). 477.

162. Gaine, Hugh, *Gaine's Universal Register, or, American and British Kalendar, for the year 1776* (New York, 1775). Evans 14057. CSmH, MBAt, MiU-C, MWA, NHi, NN, PHi, RPJCB. 382.

163. ———, *Gaine's Universal Register: or, American and British Kalendar, for the year 1778* (New York [1777]). Evans 15303. NHi, NN. 382.

164. Garrison, Hazel S., "Cartography of Pennsylvania before 1800," in *Pennsylvania Magazine of History and Biography, 59* (1935), 281–83. 298, 433.

165. *Gazette of the United States* (Philadelphia). 195, 274, 414, 483, 534, 611, 641, 789.

166. *General Advertiser* (Philadelphia). 753–54, 763.

167. *Gentleman's Magazine, The* (London). 77, 455, 476, 727–28.

168. *Geographical Gazetteer*, supplement to *Boston Magazine* (October 1784). 242.

169. Gibson, John, *Atlas Minimus: or, a new set of Pocket Maps, of various Empires, Kingdoms, and States, with Geographical Extracts relative to each. Drawn and engraved, by J. Gibson, from the best authorities. A new edition, revised, corrected, and improved* (Philadelphia, Apr. 14, 1798). Maps have been re-engraved from the 1792 (English) edition except for the map of France. The descriptive notes have been omitted on the American maps. Evans 33794, Phillips 691. DLC, MB, MiU-C, MWA. 36, 61, 715–18, 814–37, 854–57, 897–902, 912.

170. ———, *Atlas minimus: or, A new set of Pocket Maps of the several Empires, Kingdoms and States of the known World* . . . (London, 1792). Phillips, 676. 36, 61, 715–18, 814–37, 854–57, 897–902, 912.

171. Gifford, John [John Richards Green], *The History of France, from the earliest times, till the death of Louis Sixteenth* . . . (4 vols. Philadelphia, 1796–98). Evans 30489, 32189–90, 33796. DLC. 808, 838.

172. Gilman, Arthur, *The story of Boston, A study of independency* (Boston, 1889). 226.

173. Gilpin, John, "Observations on the Annual Passage of Herrings, by Mr. John Gilpin," in *Columbian Magazine, 1* (1786), 155–58. 722.

174. Gipson. Lawrence Henry, *Lewis Evans by Lawrence Henry Gipson to which is added Evans' A Brief Account of Pennsylvania. Together with Facsimiles of His Geographical, Historical, Political, Philosophical, and Mechanical Essays, Numbers I and II, wherein the author sets forth an analysis of a General Map of the Middle British Colonies* . . . *an Answer to the Objections* . . . *Also Facsimiles of Evans' Maps* (Philadelphia, 1939). 295, 297–99.

175. Goff, Frederick R., "The Federal City in 1793," in Library of Congress, *Quarterly Journal of Current Acquisitions, 9* (1951), 3–7. 527.

176. Goold, William, "Col. Arthur Noble, of Georgetown," in Maine Historical Society, *Collections, 8* (1881), 107–53. 163.

177. Gordon, William, *The History of the Rise, Progress, and Establishment, of the Independence of the United States of America* . . . (3 vols. New York, Hodge, Allen, and Campbell, 1789). Evans 21861. CtY, DLC, ICU, MiU, NjP, PPL, ViU. 150, 492.

178. ———, *The History of the Rise, Progress, and Establishment of the Independence of the United States of America* . . . (2d Am. ed. 3 vols. New York, Samuel Campbell, 1794). Evans 27061. MB, MHi, MWA, NN. 150, 495.

179. [Gottesman, Rita S.], *The Arts and Crafts in New York 1726–1776: Advertisements and News Items from New York City Newspapers* (New York, 1938). 47, 69, 324.

180. ———, *The Arts and Crafts in New York 1777–1799: Advertisements* . . . (New York, 1954). 377, 685.

181. Great Britain, Colonial Office, *Catalogue of the Maps, Plans, and Charts in the Library of the Colonial Office* (London, 1910). 497.

Green, John Richards. *See* Gifford, John.

182. Green, Samuel Abbott, *Ten Fac-simile Reproductions Relating to New England* (Boston, 1902). 145, 320–21.

183. ———, *Ten Fac-simile Reproductions Relating to Various Subjects* . . . (Boston, 1903). 203.

184. Griffen, Lloyd W., "Christopher Colles and His Two American Map Series," in Bibliographical Society of America, *Papers, 48* (New York, 1954), 170–82. 154–56, 309, 358.

185. Guthrie, William, *A New System of Modern Geography: or, A geographical, historical, and commercial Grammar* . . . (1st Am. ed. 2 vols. Philadelphia [1794–95]). These volumes were issued serially and the accompanying 45 maps were intended either to be inserted in the bound volumes or to be bound separately (*See* Carey, Mathew, *The General Atlas* . . .). Evans 25574, 27077, 28782, Phillips 6007, Sabin 29327. DLC, MBAt, MH, MiU-C, MWA, NN, OClW, Hi, RPJCB. R76.

REFERENCES

186. Hamilton, Sinclair, *Early American Book Illustrators and Wood Engravers 1670–1870 a Catalogue of a Collection of American Books* . . . (Princeton, N.J., 1958). 144, 729.

187. ——, "John Foster and the 'White Hills' Map," in Princeton University Library, *Chronicle, 14* (1953), 177–82. 144.

188. Hardie, James, *The Philadelphia Directory and Register: Containing the Names, Occupations, and Places of Abode of the Citizens; Arranged in Alphabetical Order* . . . (2d ed. Philadelphia, 1794). Evans 27089. NN, PP, PPL. 463.

189. ——, *A short Account of the City of Philadelphia, and of the different charitable and literary Institutions therein. Embellished with a correct Plan of the City* (Philadelphia, 1794). Evans 27090. MBA, NHi, RPJCB. 463.

190. Harlow, Thompson R., "The Moses Park Map, 1766," in Connecticut Historical Society, *Bulletin, 28* (1963), 33–37. 257–58.

191. Harris, Thaddeus M., *The Journal of a Tour into the Territory Northwest of the Alleghany Mountains; made in the Spring of the Year 1803. With a Geographical and Historical Account of the State of Ohio* . . . (Boston, 1805). 681.

192. Harvard University, Library, *A Catalogue of the Maps and Charts in the Library of Harvard University in Cambridge, Massachusetts* (Cambridge, 1831). 251, 274, 360, 590–91.

193. Hatch, John D., "Isaac Hutton, Silversmith," in *Antiques, 47* (1945), 32–35. 359.

194. Hawkesworth, John, comp., *A New Voyage, round the World in the Years 1768, 1769, 1770, and 1771* . . . *by Captain James Cook* (2 vols. New York, 1774). Evans 13324. CSmH, DLC, MiU-C, MWA, NN, RPJCB. 1. *See also* Cook, James.

195. Heart, Jonathan, "Account of some Remains of Ancient Works, on the Muskingum, with a Plan of these Works," in *Columbian Magazine, 1* (1787), 425–27. 663.

196. Heartman, Charles F., *Americana printed and in manuscript offered for cash* (Metuchen, N.J., 1930). 631.

197. [Henry E. Huntington Library & Art Gallery], *A Catalogue of Maps of America from the Sixteenth to the Nineteenth Centuries* (London, 1924). "Maps are now in Huntington collection"—slip attached to t.p. 71.

198. *Herald and General Advertiser* (Philadelphia). 479.

199. Holman, Richard B., "John Foster's Woodcut Map of New England," in *Printing & Graphic Arts, 8* (1960), no. 3. 144.

200. *The Holy Bible, containing the Old and New Testaments: with the Apocrypha* . . . (Worcester, Mass., Isaiah Thomas, 1791). Evans 23186. MB, MiU, MWiW-C, NN. 867.

201. *Holy Bible, The* (Philadelphia, Berriman & Co., 1796). 869–70.

202. *Holy Bible, The* (Philadelphia, 1799). 870.

203. Hubbard, William, *A Narrative of the Troubles with the Indians in New-England, from the first planting thereof in the Year 1607, to this present Year 1677* . . . (Boston, John Foster, 1677). Evans 231. *State* I of Map: NHi, NjP. 144; *State* II of Map: CSmH, ICN, MHi, MiU-C, MWA, MWiW-C, NhD, NN, PHi, RPJCB. 145.

204. Hugo, E. Harold, and Thompson R. Harlow, *Abel Buell a Jack of all trades* . . . *illustrated by a Chart* . . . (Meriden, Conn., 1955). 264.

205. Hulbert, Archer Butler, ed., . . . *Ohio in the Time of the Confederation* . . . Marietta College Historical Collections, *3* (Marietta, Ohio, 1918). 662.

206. Hunnewell, James Frothingham, *Bibliography of Charlestown, Massachusetts, and Bunker Hill* . . . (Boston, 1880). 247.

207. Hutchins, John Nathan, *Hutchins's Almanack or Ephemeris, for the Year of Christian account, 1759* . . . (New York, Hugh Gaine [1758]). Evans 8153. DLC, MiU-C, MWA, NHi. 81, 83.

208. ——, *Hutchin's improved: being an Almanack and Ephemeris of the motions of the Sun and Moon: the true places and aspects of the Planets; the rising and setting of the Sun; and the rising, setting and southing of the moon, for the Year of our Lord 1776* . . . (New York, Hugh Gaine [1775]). Evans 14125. DLC, MiU-C, NN. 235.

209. Hutchins, Thomas, *An Historical Narrative and Topographical Description of Louisiana, and West-Florida, comprehending the River Mississippi with its principal branches and settlements* . . . (Philadelphia, Robert Aitkin, 1784). Evans 18532. MWA. 490.

210. ——, *Proposals for publishing by subscription, a map* . . . *Philadelphia, October 15, 1781* (Philadelphia, 1781). 490.

211. ——, *A Topographical Description of Virginia, Pennsylvania, Maryland, and North-Carolina* . . . (London, 1778). 664–65.

212. ——, *A Topographical Description* . . . *reprinted from the original edition of 1778,* ed. Frederick Charles Hicks (Cleveland, 1904). 424, 676.

213. ——, *A Topographical Description* . . . (Boston, John Norman, 1787). Evans 20424. CSmH, DLC, MiU-C, NN, PHi, PPL, RPJCB. 658, 664–65.

214. Imlay, Gilbert, *A Topographical Description of the Western Territory of North America; containing a succinct account of its Climate, Natural History, Population, Agriculture, Manners and Customs* . . . (2 vols.

New York, Samuel Campbell, 1793). Evans 25648. BM, DLC, MH, MHi, MWA, NHi, NN, RPJCB. 495, 640, 672.

215. ——, *A Topographical Description . . .* (3d ed. London, 1797). 641, 672.

216. *An Impartial History of the War in America, Between Great Britain and the United States from its Commencement to the End of the War . . .* (3 vols. Boston, 1781–84). Evans 17241, 17610, 18617. CSmH, MH, MHi, MWA, RPJCB. 241.

217. *Independent Chronicle* (Boston). 148.

218. *Independent Gazetteer* (Philadelphia). 650.

219. Jefferson, Thomas, *Notes on the State of Virginia . . .* (2d Am. ed. Philadelphia, Nov. 12, 1794). Evans 27162. BM, MH, MHi, MWA, NN, RPJCB. 568.

220. ——, *The Papers of . . .* , ed. Julian P. Boyd (Princeton, N.J., 1950). 113.

221. Jeffreys, Thomas, *The American Atlas, or A Geographical Description of the whole Continent of America . . .* (London, 1776). 100.

222. ——, *A General Topography of North America and the West Indies. Being a Collection of all the Maps, Charts, Plans, and particular Surveys, that have been published of that part of the World, either in Europe or America . . .* (London, 1768). 181, 422.

223. ——, *North American Pilot* (London, 1777). 100.

224. Jillson, Willard Rouse, "Early Kentucky Maps (1673–1825)," in Kentucky State Historical Society, *Register, 47* (1949), [265]–93; *48* (1950), 32–52. 631, 640–45, 647, 650, 653.

225 ——, "Elihu Barker Map of Kentucky," in Kentucky State Historical Society, *Register, 21* (September 1923), no. 63, Supplement. 322–23. 641.

226. ——, *Filson's Kentucke,* Filson Club Publications, no. 35 (Louisville, 1930). 631.

227. ——, *The Kentuckie Country; an Historical Exposition of Land Interest in Kentucky prior to 1790, coupled with Facsimile Reproductions of the London 1786 Brochure of Alexander Fitzroy, and the "Whatman" Edition of John Filson's Map . . . with Critical Comment on Filson's Map, by Lawrence Martin . . .* (Washington, D.C., 1931). 639.

John Carter Brown Library. *See* Brown University.

228. Johnston, George, *History of Cecil County, Maryland, and the Early Settlements Around the Head of Chesapeake Bay and on the Delaware River, with Sketches of Some of the Old Families of Cecil County* (Elkton, Md., 1881). 477.

Josephus. *See* Flavius Josephus.

229. Karpinski, Louis C., *Bibliography of the Printed Maps of Michigan 1804–1880 with a series of over one hundred reproductions of maps constituting an Historical Atlas of the Great Lakes and Michigan . . . Including discussion of Michigan maps and map-makers, by William Lee Jenks* (Lansing, Mich., 1931). 111, 113, 128, 317, 660, 674.

230. Kihn, Phillis, "William Blodget, Map Maker 1754–1809," in Connecticut Historical Society, *Bulletin, 27* (1962), 33–50. 192, 272.

231. *Knoxville Register.* 656.

232. Landais, Pierre, *Memorial, to justify Peter Landai's conduct during the Late War* (Boston, 1784). Evans 18549. MBAt, MiU-C, MWA, NN. 743.

233. [Lear, Tobias], *Observations on the River Potomack, the Country adjacent, and the City of Washington* (New York, 1793). Evans 25711. DLC, MHi. 527.

234. ——, *Observations on the River Potomack . . .* (2d ed. New York, 1794). Evans 27209. DLC, MBAt, MH, MWA, NHi, NN. 527.

235. Ledyard, John, *A Journal of Captain Cook's last Voyage to the Pacific Ocean, and in quest of a North-West Passage between Asia & America; performed in the years 1776, 1777, 1778 and 1779. Illustrated with a Chart showing the tracts [sic] of the ships employed in this Expedition* (Hartford, 1783). Evans 17998. CSmH, DLC, MWA, NHi, RPJCB. 906.

236. LeGear, Clara Egli, "The New England Coasting Pilot of Cyprian Southack," in *Imago Mundi, 9* (1944), 137–44. 44, 67–68, 160.

——, *A List of Geographical Atlases . . . . See* Phillips, Philip L.

237. Lewis, Benjamin Morgan, *A Guide to engravings in American magazines 1741–1810* (New York, 1959). 491.

238. Library Company of Philadelphia, *Annual Report . . . 1960* (Philadelphia, 1961). 113.

239. [Lincoln, Benjamin?], *A description of the situation, climate, soil and productions of certain tracts of land in the District of Maine, and Commonwealth of Massachusetts* [n. p., 1793]. Evans 25720. ICN, MB, MBAt, NHi, NN, PPAmP, RPJCB. 167.

240. *London Magazine.* 421.

241. Longworth, David, *The American Almanack, New-York Register, and City Directory, for the twenty-first year of American independence. Containing most things useful in a work of the kind and embellished with an accurate map of the city, and a perspective of the Tontine city tavern . . .* (New York, 1796). Evans 30701. CSmH, MiU-C, MWA, NHi. 391.

242. ——, *Longworth's American Almanack, New-York Register, and City Directory, for the twenty-fourth year of American Inde-*

pendence (New York, 1799). Evans 35740. CSmH, MiU-C, MWA, NHi, NN. 395.

243. Love, William DeLoss, "The Navigation of the Connecticut River," in American Antiquarian Society, *Proceedings* N. S., *15*, (Worcester, Mass., 1902–03), 385–441. 259.

244. Low, John, *The New-York Directory, and Register, for the year 1796. Illustrated with a Plan of the City and part of Long-Island, laid down agreeably to the latest survey . . .* (New York, 1796). Evans 30706. NHi, NN. 393.

245. Low, Nathaniel, *An astronomical Diary; or, Almanack for the year of Christian aera, 1777* . . . (Boston [1776]). CSmH, MiU-C. 386.

246. Lowery, Woodbury, *The Lowery Collection, A Descriptive List of Maps of the Spanish Possessions within the present limits of the United States, 1502–1820*, ed. Philip Lee Phillips (Washington, D.C., 1912). 491.

247. Lunny, Robert M., *Early Maps of North America* (Newark, N.J., 1961). 110, 428.

248. McCorison, Marcus A., *Vermont Imprints 1778–1820: A check list of Books, Pamphlets, and Broadsides* (Worcester, Mass., 1963). 200.

249. McCormack, Helen G., "A Catalogue of Maps of Charleston based on the Collection of Engraved and Photostatic Copies owned by Alfred O. Halsey, Esq. of Charleston, South Carolina," in Charleston, S.C., *Year Book 1944* (Charleston, c. 1947), pp. 178–204. 599.

250. McDonald, Gerald D., "A Gift of *The New-York Gazette*," in New Public Library, *Bulletin, 40* (1936), 487–88. 47, 378.

251. McMurtrie, Douglas C., *Eighteenth Century North Carolina Imprints, 1749–1800* (Chapel Hill, 1938). 582, 586, 590.

252. M'Culloch, John, *A Concise History of the United States . . .* (Philadelphia, 1795). Evans 29002. DLC, P, PPL. 117.

253. ———, *A Concise History of the United States . . .* (2d ed. Philadelphia, 1797). Evans 32399. MWA. 140.

254. ———, *A Concise History of the United States . . .* (3d ed. Philadelphia, 1807). 140.

255. [———, comp.], *Introduction to the History of America . . .* (Philadelphia, 1787). Evans 20471. DLC. 115.

256. *Magazine of American History* (New York and Chicago). 541.

257. Maine Historical Society, *Collections* (Portland, Me. [1831–1906]). 214.

258. Malham, John, *The Naval Gazetteer; or, Seaman's complete guide. Containing a full and accurate account, alphabetically arranged, of the several coasts of all the countries and islands in the known world . . . illustrated with a correct set of charts from the latest and best surveys* (1st Am. ed. 2 vols. Boston, 1797). "Directions to the Binder for Placing the

Charts," 2, 574. The seventeen maps and charts engraved for the original English (London, 1795) edition by Samuel J. Neele are copied here. Evans 32415, Sabin 44119. CtY, DLC, MB, MH, MiU-C, MWA, NN, PHi, PPL, RPJCB. 35, 58–59, 698, 713, 797–804, 852–53, 894–95.

259. ———, *The Naval Gazetteer; or, Seaman's Complete Guide . . .* (London, 1795). 35, 58–59, 713.

Martin, Lawrence, "The Association of Filson's Map." *See* reference nos. 227, 631.

260. Mason, Charles, and Jeremiah Dixon, "Observations for determining the length of a degree of latitude in the provinces of Maryland and Pennsylvania, in North America," in Royal Society of London, *Philosophical Transactions, 57* (1768), 274–325. 497.

261. Massachusetts Historical Society, *Collections* (Boston, 1792–). 212, 490.

262. ———, *Prints, Maps and Drawings 1677–1822: A Massachusetts Historical Society Picture Book* (Boston, 1957). 75, 145, 163, 226, 541.

263. ———, *Proceedings of the Massachusetts Historical Society* (Boston, 1859–). 181, 227, 242–43, 245–46, 248, 320–21.

264. ———, *Special Publication* (Boston, 1912). 161, 163.

265. *Massachusetts Magazine, The* (Boston). 209, 245, 528, 909.

266. Mathews, Edward B., "Bibliography and Cartography of Maryland . . . ," in *Maryland Geological Survey, 1* (Baltimore, 1897), 229–401. 113.

267. ———, "The Maps and Map-makers of Maryland," in *Maryland Geological Survey, 2* (Baltimore, 1898). pt. 2. 511.

Matthias, Joseph ben. *See* Flavius Josephus.

268. Michigan, University of, William L. Clements Library, *Guide to the Manuscript Maps in the William L. Clements Library*, comp. Christian Brun (Ann Arbor, 1959). 658.

269. Miller, George Julius, "The printing of the Elizabethtown Bill," in Board of Proprietors of the Eastern Division of New Jersey, *Addresses before the Board of Proprietors of the Eastern Division of New Jersey. The printing of the Elizabethtown Bill in Chancery . . . George J. Miller Assistant to the Registrar of the Board of Proprietors of the Eastern Division of New Jersey* (Perth Amboy, N.J., Oct. 15, 1942). Pamphlet Series no. 1. 294, 397–98.

270. Milligan, Jacob, *The Charleston Directory and Revenue System* (Charleston, S.C. [1790]). Evans 22670. MH, ScC. 599.

271. Minick, Amanda Rachel, *A History of Printing in Maryland, 1791–1800, with a Bibliography of Works printed in the State during the Period* (Baltimore, 1949). 524.

272. *Month at Goodspeed's, The,* Goodspeed's Book Shop (Boston, 1929–). 233, 304, 387, 394, 638.

273. *Monthly Military Repository, The* (2 vols. New York, 1796–97). Evans 30807, 32492, Sabin 82379. 105, 139, 247, 373–74, 573, 606, 617.

274. Moore, John D., *A Journal during a Residence in France, from the beginning of August, to the middle of December, 1792* . . . (2 vols. London, reprinted New York, 1793–94). Evans 25838, 27341. NHi, NN. 765.

275. ——, *A Journal during a Residence* . . . (2 vols. Chambersburg, Penna., 1797). Evans 32493. CSmH, N, NN, OClWHi, PHi, PPA, PPL. 765.

276. More, Roger [pseud.], *Poor Roger, 1760. The American Country Almanack, for the Year of Christian Account 1760* (New York [1759]). Evans 8420. NN. 84, 421.

277. ——, *Poor Roger; or the American Country Almanack for the Year of Christian account 1761* (New York [1760]). Evans 8673. DLC. 323.

278. More, Thomas [pseud.], *Poor Thomas improved: being More's country almanack for the year of Christian account, 1761* (New York [1760]). Evans 8675. CSmH, MWA, NHi, NN. 146.

279. Moreau de St. Méry, Médéric Louis Élie, *Description Topographique et Politique de la Partie Espagnole de L'Isle Saint-Domingue* . . . (2 vols. Philadelphia, 1796). Evans 30817. DLC, MH, MWA. 693–94.

280. ——, *Description topographique, physique, civile, politique et historique de la partie Française de l'Isle Saint-Dominigue* . . . (2 vols. Philadelphia, 1797–98). Evans 32504, 34137. BM, DLC, MH, NN. 693–94.

281. ——, *Moreau de Méry's American Journey translated and edited by Kenneth Roberts [and] Anna M. Roberts* . . . (Garden City, N.Y., 1947). 693.

282. ——, *A Topographical and Political Description of the Spanish part of Saint-Domingo, containing, general observations . . . to which is prefixed, a new correct and elegant Map of the whole Island* . . . (2 vols. Philadelphia, 1796). BM, DLC, MBAt, MH, MWA, RPJCB. Evans 30818. 693.

283. ——, *A Topographical and Political Description* . . . (Philadelphia, 1798). Evans 34138. DLC, MWA, NHi, RPJCB. 693.

284. Morse, Jedidiah, *An abridgement of the American Gazetteer. Exhibiting in alphabetical order, a compendious account of the states, provinces, counties, cities* . . . (Boston, June 1798). Evans 34143, Sabin 50922. MH, MHi, MiU-C, MWA, NN, PHi, RPJCB. 63.

285. ——, *The American Gazetteer, exhibiting, in Alphabetical Order, a much more full and accurate account, than has been given, of the States, Provinces, Counties, Cities, Towns . . . on the American Continent* . . . (Boston, 1797). Evans 32509, Sabin 50923. CtY, DLC, IC, MH, MHi, MiU-C, MWA, NjP, NN, PPL, RPJCB. 60, 158, 357, 496, 618, 699, 714, 911.

286. ——, *The American Geography; or, A View of the Present Situation of the United States of America. Containing Astronomical Geography. Geographical definitions* . . . (Elizabeth Town, N.J., 1789). This is the 1st ed. of vol. 1 of *The American Universal Geography.* Evans 21978, Sabin, 50924. CtY, BMAt, MH, MiU-C, MWA, NjP, NN, RPJCB. 149, 491.

287. ——, *The American Universal Geography, or, A view of the present state of all the Empires, Kingdoms, States, and Republics in the known World, and of the United States of America in particular . . . Illustrated with maps* . . . (2 vols. Boston, 1793). Vol. 1 is the 2d ed. of *The American Geography* originally published in 1789. Imprint varies. Evans 25847, Sabin 50926. CtY, MB, MBAt, MHi, MiU-C, MWA, NjN, NN, PPL, PU. 19, 153, 168, 175, 214, 438, 494, 686, 706, 758, 844, 873.

288. ——, *The American Universal Geography . . . Illustrated with twenty-eight maps and charts . . . 3d ed., cor. and considerably enl. The introduction rev. and amended by Samuel Webber* . . . (Boston, 1796). Part I is the 3d ed., Part II is the 2d ed. of that volume. Evans 30824 vol. *1,* 30825 vol. 2, Sabin 50926 vol. *1.* CSmH, MB, MiU-C, RPJCB. 31, 33, 55, 188, 218, 287, 368, 417, 446, 514, 571, 585, 614, 645, 679, 695, 788, 791–95, 851, 885–86, 890.

289. ——, *Description of the Soil, Productions, commercial, agricultural and local advantages of the Georgia Western Territory* . . . (Boston, 1797). Evans 32510. MBAt, MHi, MiU-C, MWA, NN, RPJCB. 618.

290. ——, *Elements of geography: containing a concise and comprehensive view of that useful science . . . on a new Plan . . . illustrated with a neat Map of the United States, and a beautiful Chart of the whole World* . . . (Boston, December 1795). Evans 29112, Sabin 50935. CtY, MH, MWA. 26, 124.

291. ——, *Elements of geography: containing* . . . (2d ed. Boston, February 1796). Evans 30826, Sabin 50935. DLC, MH, MiU-C, MWA. 30, 124.

292. ——, *Elements of geography* . . . (3d ed. Boston, February 1798). Evans 34145, Sabin, 50935. MH, OClW. 37, 141.

293. ——, *Geography Made Easy. Being a short, but comprehensive System of that very useful and agreeable science* . . . (New Haven [1784]). Evans 18615, Sabin 50936. CtY, DLC,

MH, MiU-C, MWA, NHi, NN, RPJCB. 4, 112.

294. ——, *Geography Made Easy: being an abridgment of the American Geography. Containing, astronomical geography-discovery and general description of America . . .* (2d ed. Boston, 1790). Evans 22681, Sabin 50936. CtY, DLC, ICN, MiU-C, MWA, PPL, RPJCB. 7–8, 116, 702, 744, 841, 864.

295. ——, *Geography Made Easy: being an abridgement . . .* (3d ed. Boston, 1791). Evans 23579. DLC, NN. 11–12, 118, 705, 746, 843, 868.

296. ——, *Geography Made Easy: being an abridgement . . .* (4th ed. Boston, 1794). Evans 27351, Sabin 50936. DLC, MB, MH, MiU, MWA, PU, RPJCB. 21, 122, 766, 846, 874–77.

297. ——, *Geography Made Easy: being an abridgment . . .* (5th ed. Boston, 1796). Evans 30827, Sabin 50936. CtY, DLC, MHi, MWA. 32, 122, 790, 850, 884, 887–89.

298. ——, *Geography Made Easy: being an abridgment . . .* (6th ed. Boston, 1798). Evans 34146. DLC, MBAt, MH, MWA, RPJCB. 38, 62.

299. ——, *Geography Made Easy: being an abridgment . . .* (7th ed. Boston, 1800). Evans 38004. MH, MiU-C, MWA, NHi, NN, RPJCB. 38.

300. ——, *The History of America* (Philadelphia, 1790). Evans 22682. DLC, MWA. 51, 701.

301. ——, *The History of America* (2d ed. Philadelphia, 1795). Evans 29111. DLC, MWA, NN, RPJCB. 51, 701.

302. ——, *The History of America* (3d ed. Philadelphia, 1798). Evans 34147. DLC, MWA, PPL, RPJCB. 51, 701.

303. Morse, William Inglis, *The Land of New Adventure (the Georgian era in Nova Scotia)* (London, 1932). 86.

304. Mullin, John, *The Baltimore Directory for 1799, containing the Names, Occupations, and places of Abode of the Citizens . . .* ([Baltimore], 1799). MdBE, MdBP, MdHi, NHi, PPL. *See also* Dorothea N. Spear, *Bibliography*, p. 34. 525.

305. *The New American Magazine* [Woodbridge, N.J.]. 82.

306. New England Historical and Genealogical Society, *The New England Historical and Genealogical Register* [Boston, 1847–]. 177, 214, 248.

307. *New-Hampshire Gazette* (Portsmouth). 114.

308. [New Jersey (Colony)], *The Bill of Complaint in the Chancery of New-Jersey, brought by Thomas Clarke, and others, against James Alexander esqr., and others, commonly called the Proprietors of East-New-Jersey. Wherein the Title of the People of Elizabeth-Town to the controverted lands is fully exhibited, and the objections of the pretended Proprietors, stated, and refuted . . .* (New York, 1760). Evans 8550. NN. 399.

309. *New-Jersey Journal* (Chatham). 541.

310. *New London Gazette* (New London, Conn.) 304.

311. *The New-York and Country Almanack for the Year 1776* (New York [1775]). Evans 14344. MWA. 236.

312. New York (City), *Manual of the Corporation of the City of New York* (New York, 1851). 388.

313. ——, *Manual of the Corporation . . .* (New York, 1853). 394.

314. ——, *Manual of the Corporation . . .* (New York, 1857). 388.

315. New York (State), *Proceedings of the Commissioners of Indian Affairs, appointed by law for the extinguishment of Indian titles in the State of New York . . .* (Albany, 1861). 369.

316. *The New-York Directory, and Register, for the Year 1789. Illustrated with an accurate and elegant Plan of the City of New-York, and part of Long-Island, including the Suburbs, with all the Streets, Lanes, Public Buildings, Wharves, &c. exactly laid down, from the latest survey . . .* (New York, 1789). Evans 22021. DLC, MWA. 387.

317. *New-York Gazette*. 47, 84–85, 256, 317–18, 378–81.

318. New-York Historical Society, *Collections* [1868–]. 328.

319. ——, *The New-York Historical Society's Dictionary of Artists in America 1564–1860*, by George C. Groce and David H. Wallace (New Haven, 1957). 661.

320. *New-York Magazine; or, Literary Repository*. 97, 413, 529, 671, 673.

321. *New-York Mercury*. 324, 381.

322. *New-York Packet*. 6.

323. *The New-York Pocket Almanack, for the Year 1759 . . . by Poor Tom, Philomath* (New-York [1758]). Evans 8144. PHi. 80.

324. *New-York Weekly Journal*. 69.

325. *New-York Weekly Post Boy*. 70.

326. Norman, John, *The American Pilot, containing, the navigation of the sea coast of North America, from the Streights of Belle-Isle to Cayenne, including the Island and Banks of Newfoundland, the West-India Island, and all the islands on the coast . . .* (Boston, 1791). Evans 23637. CSmH, MH. 98–99, 151–52, 166, 308, 578, 600, 683, 704.

327. ——, *The American Pilot containing the navigation of the sea coast of North America . . .* (Boston, 1792). Phillips 4474a. DLC, MiU-C. 98–100, 151–52, 166, 210, 308, 578, 600, 683, 704.

328. ——, *The American Pilot containing the navigation of the sea coast of North America*

... (Boston, 1794). Phillips 4475. DLC, MB, RPJCB. 98–99, 102, 157, 166, 308, 580, 591, 683, 704.

329. Norman, William, *The American Pilot containing the navigation of the sea coast of North America, from the Streights of Belle-Isle to Cayenne, including the Island and Banks of Newfoundland, the West India islands, and all the islands on the coast* ... (Boston, 1794). CtY. 98–99, 102, 151, 157, 166, 210, 310, 580, 600, 688, 707.

330. ——, *The American Pilot containing the navigation of the sea coast of North America, from the Streights of Belle-Isle to Essequebo, including the island and banks of Newfoundland, the West-India islands, and all the islands on the coast. With particular directions for sailing to, and entering the principal harbours, rivers, &c.* .... (Boston, 1798). Phillips 1217. DLC, MB. 106–07, 159, 166, 221, 310, 589, 607, 688.

331. ——, *The American Pilot* ... (Boston, 1803). 157, 159, 166, 221, 310, 589, 607, 688.

332. ——, *The New East-India Pilot* ... (Boston, 1804). 688.

333. ——, *The New West-India Pilot* ... (Boston, 1803). 688.

334. [——, *A Pilot for the West-Indies; including the Coast of America and part of the Atlantic Ocean*] (Boston, 1795). RPJCB, Private coll. Mr. Thomas W. Streeter. 53, 629, 688–91, 709–10.

335. *The North American Pilot for Newfoundland, Labradore, the Gulf and River St. Laurence* ... (London, 1777). 100.

336. *North-Carolina Gazette* (Newbern, N.C.). 579, 586, 590.

337. *North Carolina Review* (Raleigh, N.C.). 582.

338. North Carolina (State), *The Acts of the General Assembly of the State of North-Carolina, passed during the Sessions held in the years 1791, 1792, 1793 and 1794* (Newbern, N.C., 1795). Evans 29221. DLC, NHi, NN. 579.

339. *Norwich (Conn.) Packet.* 5, 662.

340. Oberholtzer, Ellis Paxton, *Philadelphia; A History of the City and its People. A Record of 225 Years* (Philadelphia [1912]). 456.

341. O'Conor, Norres, J., *A servant of the Crown in England and in North America, 1756–1761* ... (New York, 1938). 378.

342. Ohio, Cooperative Topographical Survey, *Final Report ... Ohio Topographical Survey*, Christopher E. Sherman (4 vols. [Mansfield, Ohio, 1916–33]). 676, 681.

343. Palfrey, John Gorham, *History of New England* (5 vols. Boston, 1858–90). 231.

344. Paullin, Charles O., *Atlas of the Historical Geography of the United States*, ed. John K. Wright (New York, Carnegie Institution and American Geographical Society of New York, 1932) (Carnegie Publication 401). 171, 298.

345. Payne, John, *A new and complete system of Universal Geography; describing Asia, Africa, Europe and America; with their subdivisions of Republics, States, Empires, and Kingdoms ... Being a large and comprehensive abridgement of Universal Geography* ... (4 vols. New York, 1798–1800). Evans states that the work was first issued in 28 numbers—one each fortnight. Also: "There is an additional undated 8 vo. atlas with the imprint of Low and Willis." Evans vol. *1*, 34316, vol. *4*, 36047, Sabin 59284. DLC, MiU-C, NN, PHi, PP, RP. 39–40, 65, 142, 178, 190, 201, 222, 255, 292, 420, 518, 574, 608, 619, 657, 682, 700, 719, 839, 859–62, 903, 913–14.

346. [Pejepscot Company], *An Answer to the Remarks of the Plymouth Company* ... (Boston, 1753). DLC. 161–63.

347. *Pennsylvania Archives. Selected and arranged from Original Documents in the Office of the Secretary of the Commonwealth in conformity to the Acts of the General Assembly* (Philadelphia and Harrisburg [1852]). 260, 295, 298–99, 425, 432–33, 457.

348. Pennsylvania, Department of Internal Affairs, *Report of the Secretary of Internal Affairs ... Containing Reports of Surveys and Re-Surveys of the Boundary Lines of the Commonwealth, Accompanied with the same* ... (Harrisburg, 1887). 497.

349. *Pennsylvania Evening Post* (Philadelphia). 108.

350. *Pennsylvania Gazette* (Philadelphia). 203, 299, 327, 454, 474, 592, 630.

351. Pennsylvania, Historical Society of, *Pennsylvania Magazine of History and Biography*. 457, 476.

352. *Pennsylvania Journal* (Philadelphia). 86, 108, 302–3, 327, 592.

353. *The Pennsylvania Magazine* (Philadelphia). 89–91, 237–39, 489, 540.

354. *Pennsylvania Packet, and Daily Advertiser* (Philadelphia). 92, 111, 631, 660.

355. *The Philadelphia Almanack for the Year 1778* ... (Philadelphia [1777]). Evans 15553. DLC, PHi. 459.

356. Philadelphia (city), *The Committee appointed to examine into the Title of the Corporation to the north east Public Square, and the Boundaries of the same; and also to enquire, whether any, and what, encroachments have been made thereupon* ... (Philadelphia, Zachariah Poulson, Jr., 1797). Evans 32675. PHi. 469.

357. *Philadelphia Monthly Magazine or Universal Repository*. 472.

358. Phillips, Philip Lee, *The Beginnings of*

REFERENCES

Washington as described in Books Maps Views (Washington, D.C., 1917). 530–34, 536.

359. ———, *A Descriptive List of Maps and Views of Philadelphia in the Library of Congress 1683–1865. Issued by permission of the Library of Congress, as Special Publication Number Two of the Geographical Society of Philadelphia* (Philadelphia, 1926). 456–57, 467.

360. ———, *The First Map and Description of Ohio, 1787, by Manasseh Cutler. A bibliographical account, with reprint of the "Explanation"* . . . (Washington, D.C., 1918). 662.

361. ———, *The First Map of Kentucky by John Filson, a bibliographical account with facsimile Reproduction from the Copy in the Library of Congress* . . . (Washington, D.C., 1908). 631–32.

362. ———, Comp., *A List of Geographical Atlases in the Library of Congress with bibliographical notes* (6 vols. Washington, D.C., 1909–63). (vols. 5 and 6 comp. Clara Egli LeGear.) 567, 576–77, 692–93.

363. ———, *A List of Maps of America in the Library of Congress preceded by a List of Works relating to Cartography* . . . (Washington, D.C., 1901). 48, 113, 119, 139, 164, 220, 242, 298, 316, 357, 361, 380, 419, 422, 425, 456–57, 467, 477, 535, 539, 721.

364. ———, *List of Maps and Views of Washington and District of Columbia in the Library of Congress,* 56th Cong., 1st sess., Sen. Doc. 154 (Washington, D.C., 1900). 530, 534–35.

365. ———, . . . *Notes on the Life and Works of Bernard Romans.* Florida State Historical Society, *Publications,* no. 2 (Deland, Fla., 1924). 1, 109, 111, 147, 203, 261, 304, 621–22.

366. ———, *The Rare Map of the Northwest 1785 by John Fitch Inventor of the Steamboat. A Bibliographical Account . . . including some account of Thomas Hutchins and William McMurray* . . . (Washington, D.C., 1916). 111, 113, 660.

367. ———, . . . *Virginia Cartography: A Bibliographical Description* . . . Smithsonian Miscellaneous Collections 1039 (Washington, D.C., 1896). 6, 477.

368. *Photostat Americana Series; reproductions by the Massachusetts Historical Society,* 2d series, started January 1936, no. 55 issued on April 1, 1938. 317.

369. Pillsbury, John Elliot, "The Gulf Stream—A Description of the Methods employed in the Investigation, and the results of the Research," in U.S. Coast and Geodetic Survey, *Report of the Superintendent . . . June 1890* (Washington, D.C., 1891), Appendix 10, pp. 461–620. 721, 725.

370. *The Plea of the Colonies on the Charges brought against Them by Lord Mansfield, and Others, in a Letter to His Lordship. By a Native of Pennsylvania, London, Printed in the Year 1776* (Philadelphia, 1777). Evans 15713. PHi (*State* I of map) 2; MH, MiU-C, NN, PPAmP, PPL, RPJCB (*State* II of map) 3.

371. Plymouth Company, *Remarks on the Plan and extracts of Deeds lately published by the Proprietors of the Township of Brunswick* . . . [Boston, 1753]. MHi, MWA, NN, RPJCB. 161.

372. Ponce, Nicolas, engr., *Recueil de Vues des lieux Principaux de la Colonie Française de Saint-Dominique* . . . (Paris, 1795). Phillips 2717. DLC. 692–94.

373. *Porcupine's Gazette* (Philadelphia). 520, 805.

374. Pouchot, Pierre, *Memoir upon the late War in North America, between the French and English, 1755–60* (2 vols. Roxbury, Mass., 1866). 147.

375. Pownall, Thomas, *A Topographical Description of such parts of North America as are contained in the (annexed) Map of the Middle British Colonies, &c. North America* . . . (London, 1776). 295, 299.

376. [Price, Jonathan], *A Description of Occacock Inlet; and of its Coasts, Islands, Shoals, and Anchorages . . . Adorned with a Map taken by actual survey, by Jonathan Price* (Newbern, N.C., 1795). Evans 29351. Nc-Ar. 582.

377. Prince, Thomas, *Extraordinary Events the Doing of God, and marvellous in pious eyes. Illustrated in a Sermon at the South Church in Boston, N.E.* . . . (2d ed. Boston, 1747). Evans 6057. CSmH. 73.

378. *Proposals for publishing by subscription a correct map of the State of Vermont* (Ryegate, Vt., Oct. 27, 1795). 2 eds. 200. *See also* Marcus A. McCorison, *Vermont Imprints,* no. 368.

379. Proud, Robert, *The History of Pennsylvania, in North-America, from the original institution and settlement of that Province, under the first Proprietor, and Governor William Penn, in 1681, 'till after the Year 1742* . . . (2 vols. Philadelphia, 1797–98). Evans 32729, 34421. DLC, MBA, MiU-C, NN, PHi, RPJCB. 312.

380. Ramsay, David, *The History of the Revolution of South-Carolina, from a British Province to an Independent State* (Trenton, 1785). Evans 19211. CtY, DLC, MH, MiU-C, MWA, NN, PHi, PPL, RPJCB. 545, 593–97.

381. Reed, John, *An Explanation of the Map of the City and liberties of Philadelphia* (Philadelphia, 1774). Evans 13564. BM, DLC, MHi, PHi. 457.

382. Reid, John, *The American Atlas* . . . (New York, 1796). Evans 31078, Phillips 1216, 1366, Sabin 104830. DLC, ICN, MB, MdAN, MdBP, MiU-C, NN. 57, 136, 176, 189, 198, 201, 219, 254, 289, 371, 418, 450, 516–17, 537–38, 572, 587, 605, 616, 646–47, 655, 697, 712.

383. ——, *The American Atlas* . . . (New York [1796?]). Has cover title: The Atlas for Winterbotham's History of America. 1796. Sabin 69016. NN. 57, 136, 176, 189, 198, 201, 219, 254, 288, 371, 418, 450, 517, 537, 572, 587, 605, 616, 647, 655, 697, 712. *See also* R534.

384. Remmey, John, *An Account of the Present State of Egypt* . . . (New York, 1799). Evans 36202. CtY, DLC, MH, MWA, N, NHi, NN, PPL. 861–62.

385. *Report of the resurvey of the Maryland-Pennsylvania boundary part of the Mason Dixon Line*, in *Maryland Geological Survey*, 7 (Baltimore, 1908). 497.

386. Romans, Bernard, *A concise natural History of East and West Florida; containing an Account of the natural produce of all the southern part of British America* . . . , *1* (New York, 1775). No copy known of 2d vol.—L.C. card. Evans 14440. DLC, MBAt, MiU-C, NN, PHi, RPJCB. 487–88, 621–24.

387. ——, *A concise natural History of East and West Florida . . . A facsimile reproduction of the 1775 edition with introduction by Rembert W. Patrick. Floridiana Facsimile & Reprint Series.* (Gainsville, Fla., 1962). 488, 623–24.

388. ——, *Philadelphia, August 5, 1773. Proposals for printing by subscription. Three Very Elegant and Large Maps of the Navigation, to, and in, the new ceded Countries* [Philadelphia, 1773]. RPJCB. 621.

389. *The Royal American Magazine*, (Boston). 659.

390. Royal Society of London, *Philosophical Transactions* [1665/66–]. 497, 784.

391. Sabin, Joseph, *Bibliotheca Americana. A Dictionary of Books relating to America, from its discovery to the present time. Begun by Joseph Sabin, and continued by Wilberforce Eames for the Bibliographical Society of America* . . . (20 vols. New York, 1868–1936). 104–05, 311, 525.

392. Sackett, Nathaniel, *A Memorial &c.* (New York, 1785). Evans 19232. DLC, MiU-C, NN, OClWHi. 661.

393. St. Clair, Arthur, *Proceedings of a General Court Martial, held at White Plains, in the State of New-York . . . for the Trial of Maj. Gen. St. Clair, August 25, 1778* . . . (Philadelphia, 1778). Evans 16141. CSmH, MWA, NN. 328.

394. Saint Pierre, Jacques de Henri Bernardin, *Studies of Nature* (3 vols. Worcester, Mass. 1797). Evans 32796. BM, DLC, MH, MWA, NN. 34.

395. ——, *A Vindication of Divine Providence; derived from a philosophic and moral Survey of Nature and of Men* . . . (2 vols. Worcester, Mass., 1797). Evans 32797. MWA, NN, RPJCB. 34.

396. *Salem* (Mass.) *Mercury.* 662.

397. Salomon, Nathan Ben [pseud.], *An Astronomical Diary or Almanack for 1786* (New Haven [1785]). Evans 19108. CtHi, DLC. 114.

398. Samoual, Jean Baptiste, and Louis Samoual, *Description of a Plantation, situated at Petit St. Louis, near Port-de-Paix in the northern part of Hispaniola* . . . [Boston, 1796]. Evans 31158. MBAt, MHi, MWA. 696.

399. Saur, Christoph, *Der Hoch-Deutsch Americanische Calender auf das Jahr* . . . *1761* (Germantown, Pa. [1760]). Evans 8619. MWA. 87.

400. ——, *Der Hoch-Deutsch-Americanische Calender, auf das Jahr* . . . *1773* . . . (Germantown, Pa. [1772]). Evans 12417. PHi. 729.

401. Scharf, John Thomas, *Chronicles of Baltimore; being a complete History of "Baltimore Town" and Baltimore City from the earliest period to the present time* (Baltimore, 1874). 524, 526.

402. ——, *History of Maryland, from the earliest period to the present day* (Baltimore, 1879). 474.

403. Scharf, John Thomas, and Thompson Westcott, *History of Philadelphia 1609–1884* . . . (3 vols. Philadelphia, 1884). 454–55.

404. Schmidt, Martin F., "Existing Copies of the 1784 Filson Map," in *Filson Club Historical Quarterly,* 28 (1954), 55–57. 631.

405. Schöpf, Johann David, . . . *Reise durch einige der mittlern und südlichen Vereinigten Nordamerikanischen Staaten* . . . (2 vols. Erlangen, 1788). 113.

406. Schuylkill and Susquehanna Navigation, *An Historical Account of the Rise, Progress and Present State of the Canal Navigation in Pennsylvania. With an Appendix, containing, Abstracts of the Acts of the Legislature . . . to which is Annexed, "An Explanatory Map"* (Philadelphia, 1795). Evans 29474. Sabin 84620-1. DLC, MH, MHi, MiU-C, MWA, RPJCB. 443.

407. Scott, Joseph, *An Atlas of the United States* . . . (cover title) (Philadelphia, 1796). A reissue of the maps in the 1795 Scott *Gazetteer.* Phillips 4521a. DLC. 125, 173, 186, 196, 216, 252, 285, 366, 415, 444, 484, 512, 569, 583, 602, 612, 643, 651, 674.

408. ——, *Atlas of the United States 1795–1800 Featuring maps produced by Joseph Scott*

(Cleveland [1960]). 173, 186, 196, 216, 252, 285, 366, 415, 444, 484, 512, 569, 583, 602, 612, 643, 651, 674.

409. ——, *A New and Universal Gazetteer* (1st Section Philadelphia, July 3, 1798). 858.

410. ——, *The new and universal Gazetteer; or, Modern geographical Dictionary . . . To which is added, a new and easy introduction to geography and astronomy . . . Illustrated with twenty-five maps, an armillary sphere, and several diagrams . . .* (4 vols. Philadelphia, 1799–1800). Evans 34519, 36282, Sabin 78330. DLC, MB, MWA, NWM, PPL. 42, 66, 173, 186, 196, 216, 252, 293, 366, 415, 444, 484, 512, 569, 583, 602, 612, 643, 651, 674, 720, 806, 858, 905.

411. ——, *The United States Gazetteer: containing an authentic description of the several states. Their situation, extent, boundaries, soil, produce, climate, population, trade and manufactures . . . Illustrated with nineteen maps* (Philadelphia, 1795). First known gazetteer of the United States. The maps were drawn and engraved by Joseph Scott (p. vi of Preface). The pages are not numbered, the maps being placed opposite the descriptions which are alphabetically arranged. Evans 29476, Sabin 78331. DLC, DI-GS, ICN, MB, MiU-C, MWA, PPL, RPJCB, ViU. 125, 173, 186, 196, 216, 252, 285, 366, 415, 444, 484, 512, 569, 583, 602, 612, 643, 651, 674.

412. *The Self-Interpreting Bible: containing the Sacred Text of the Old and New Testaments . . .* (New York, Hodge and Campbell, 1792). Evans states the printing of this edition began in 1790. Evans 24099. CSmH, CtY, DLC, MiU-C, NjP, RPJCB. 865.

413. Shurtleff, Nathaniel B., *List of Printed Maps of Boston* (Boston, 1863). 227, 246.

414. ——, *A Topographical and Historical Description of Boston* (Boston, A. Williams and Co., Old Corner Bookstore, 1871), and (Boston, Printed by request of City Council, 1871). 224, 227, 229, 231, 242–43, 246.

415. Sierra Leone Company, *Substance of the Report delivered by the Court of Directors of the Sierra Leone Company to the General Court of Proprietors Thursday, March 27th, 1794* (Philadelphia, 1795). Evans 29513. BM, DLC, MHi, MWA, NN. 848.

416. ——, *Substance of the Report delivered by the Court of Directors of the Sierra Leone Company . . . To which is prefixed Memoirs of Naimbanna, an African Prince* (Philadelphia, 1799). Evans 36310. MWA, NN, PPL, ViU. 848.

417. Smith, Charles, *The American Gazetteer, or Geographical companion. Containing a general and concise account, alphabetically arranged of the states, principal cities, post-towns, ports of entry, harbours, rivers, bays, capes, lakes &c. of the American union* (New York, 1797). Evans 32841. MWA, NN. 139.

418. ——, *The American War, from 1775 to 1783, with plans* (New York, 1797). Evans 32842. MBAt, NN, RPJCB. 105, 247, 373–74, 573, 606, 617.

419. ——, *Universal Geography made easy; or, A new geographical Pocket Companion: comprehending, a description of the habitable World . . .* (New York, 1795). Evans 29521. MWA, NN, RPJCB. 27, 54, 126, 711, 777, 849, 882.

420. Smith, Daniel, *A Short Description of the State of the Tennassee* [sic] *Government, or the Territory of the United States south of the River Ohio, to accompany and explain a Map of that Country* (Philadelphia, 1793). Evans 26168. BM, DLC, MBAt, MH, MWA, RPJCB. 650.

421. ——, *A short Description of the State of the Tennassee* [sic] *lately called the Territory . . .* (2d ed. Philadelphia, Mar. 9, 1796). Evans 31199. MWA. 653.

422. Smith, Justin H., *Arnold's March from Cambridge to Quebec, A Critical Study . . .* (New York, 1903). 163.

423. Smith, William, *An examination of the Connecticut claim to lands in Pennsylvania, with an appendix, containing extracts and copies of original papers* (Philadelphia, 1774). Evans 13629. CSmH, DLC, ICN, MBAt, MHi, MiU-C, MWA, NN, RPJCB. 257, 260.

424. [——], *An Historical Account of the Expedition Against the Ohio Indians, in the Year 1764. Under the Command of Henry Bouquet, esq., Colonel of Foot, and now Brigadier General in America . . .* (Philadelphia, 1765). Evans 10167, Sabin 84616. CSmH, DLC, MiU-C, NN, PHi, PPL, RPJCB. 424, 658.

425. Society of Colonial Wars, *Annual Register of Officers and Members of the Society of Colonial Wars . . .* (New York, January 1896). 70.

426. South Carolina (Province), *The Report of the Committee, of Both Houses of Assembly of the Province of South-Carolina, appointed to inquire into the causes of the disappointment of success, in the late Expedition against St. Augustine . . .* (Charleston, S.C., 1742). Evans 5063. NN. 620.

427. Spear, Dorothea N., *Bibliography of American Directories through 1860* (Worcester, Mass., 1961). 246, 525, 604.

428. Spieseke, Alice Winifred, *The First Textbooks in American History and their compiler John M'Culloch,* Teachers College, Columbia University Contributions to Education, no. 744 (New York, 1938). 113, 115, 117, 140.

429. Stafford, Cornelius William, *The Philadel-

phia Directory, for 1797: containing the Names, Occupations, and Places of Abode of the Citizens . . . (Philadelphia, 1797). Evans 32868. MH, MWA, NHi, PPL. 470.

430. Stauffer, David McNeely, *American Engravers Upon Copper and Steel* . . . (2 vols. [New York], 1907). 75–76, 108, 144, 170, 208, 214, 272, 300, 320, 324–25, 327, 381, 387, 394, 413, 448, 456, 462, 477, 531, 541, 838.

431. Stearns, Samuel, *The North American's Almanack for the Year of our Lord, 1777* (Worcester, Mass. [1776]). Evans 15096. CtY, DLC, MiU-C, MWA, NN. 383.

432. Stedman, Charles A., *The History of the Origin, Progress, and Termination of the American War* (2 vols. London, 1794). 247, 373, 606, 617.

433. Steiner, Abraham G., "Account of some Old Indian Works, on Huron River, with a Plan of them, taken the 28th of May, 1789," in *Columbian Magazine, 3* (1789), 543–44. 669.

434. Stephens, Thomas, *Stephen's Philadelphia Directory, for 1796; or, Alphabetical Arrangement: containing the Names, Occupations, and Places of Abode of the Citizens* . . . (Philadelphia [1796]). Evans 31235. DLC, MB, MH, MiU-C. 467.

435. Stevens, Henry N., *Lewis Evans His Map of 1752 recently brought to light (with a facsimile of the same) Additional notes to the second edition of an essay published in 1920 entitled Lewis Evans His Map of the Middle British Colonies in America* (London, 1924). 295, 297.

436. ——, *Lewis Evans His map of the Middle British Colonies in America a comparative account of eighteen different editions published between 1755 and 1814 Second Edition with numerous corrections and additions including some account of his earlier map of 1749 the whole illustrated by twenty-four facsimiles of titles and maps* (London, 1920). 295, 298–99.

437. Stevenson, Roger, *Military Instructions for Officers detached in the Field* . . . (London, 1770). 730.

438. ——, *Military Instructions for Officers detached in the Field* . . . (Philadelphia, 1775). Evans 14475. DLC, MB, MiU-C, MWA, MWiW-C, NN, PPL, RPJCB. 730.

439. Stiles, Ezra, *A History of Three of the Judges of King Charles I* . . . (Hartford, 1794). Evans 27743. CSmH, MB, MH, MiU-C, MWA, NN, RPJCB. 249, 275–83.

440. Stinehour, Roderick, "But there are More Questions," in *Printing & Graphic Arts, 8* (1960), 125. 144–45.

441. Stokes, Isaac N. Phelps, *The Iconography of Manhattan Island 1498–1909. Compiled from Original Sources and illustrated by photo-intaglio reproductions of important Maps Plans Views and Documents in Public and Private Collections* (6 vols. New York, 1915–28). 128, 224, 317–18, 331, 378–80, 394.

442. Stokes, Isaac N. Phelps, and Daniel C. Haskell, *American Historical Prints Early Views of American Cities, etc. from the Phelps Stokes and other collections* (New York, 1932). 109, 128, 202–03, 224, 248, 318, 320, 378, 394, 456, 462, 465, 521, 531, 541.

443. Streeter, Thomas W., *Americana-Beginnings: A Selection from the Library of Thomas W. Streeter shown in honor of a visit of the Hroswitha Club on May 3, 1951* (Morristown, N.J., 1952). 144, 497, 531.

444. ——, "Princeton's Mason and Dixon map," in *Princeton University Library, Chronicle, 16* (1954–55), 97–99. 497.

445. "Subscription List for a map of the 'Four New England States' 1785 From an Original List of Subscribers in the Society's Collections," in The Bostonian Society, *Publications, 9* (1912), 129–34. 148.

446. Sullivan, James, *The History of the District of Maine. Illustrated by a new correct Map of the District* (Boston, 1795). Evans 29589. BM, DLC, ICN, MH, MiU-C, MWA, NN, RPJCB. 171.

447. Swem, Earl Gregg, "Maps relating to Virginia in the Virginia State Library and other Departments of the Commonwealth . . . ," in the Virginia State Library, *Bulletin, 7* (1914), 37–263, 568, 572.

448. Talman, C. Fitzhugh, "Climatology of Haiti in the Eighteenth Century," in *Monthly Weather Review and Annual Summary, 34* (1906), 64–73. 694.

449. Tatham, William, *Proposals for publishing a large and comprehensive Map of the southern division of the United States of America* (Richmond, 1790). 493.

450. *Telegraphe and Daily Advertiser* (Baltimore). 524.

451. Thompson, Edmund B., *Maps of Connecticut before the year 1800. A descriptive list* . . . (Windham, Conn., 1940). 256–57, 259, 261–63, 272, 291.

452. Thruston, Rogers C. B., "Filson's History and Map of Kentucky," in *Filson Club History Quarterly, 8* (1934), 1–38. 631, 636.

453. *Times and District of Columbia Daily Advertiser* (Alexandria, Va.). 539.

454. Tobler, John, *The Pennsylvania Town and Country-Man's Almanack for the Year of our Lord 1761* . . . (Germantown, Pa. printed and sold by C. Sower [sic] [1760]). Evans 8748. MWA. 87.

455. Trumbull, Benjamin, *A Complete History of Connecticut, Civil and Ecclesiastical, from the emigration of its first planters from England in MDCXXX, to MDCCXIII* (1 vol.

Hartford, 1797). Evans states it was reprinted with a second volume, New Haven, 1818; and New London, 1898. Evans 32942. CtHi, ICN, MH, MiU-C, MWA, NN. 291.

456. Trumbull, James Hammond, *List of Books printed in Connecticut 1709–1800* ([Hartford], 1904). 259, 304.

457. Truxton, Thomas, *Remarks, Instructions, and Examples relating to the Latitude and Longtitude* . . . (Philadelphia, 1794). Evans 27823. BM, CSmH, DLC, MB, MBAt, MWA. 22.

458. Turner, Charles Henry Black, comp., *Some records of Sussex County, Delaware* (Philadelphia, 1909). 475.

459. U.S. Bureau of the Census, *A Century of Population Growth from the First Census of the United States to the Twelfth, 1790–1900* (Washington, D.C., 1909). 60, 158, 462, 496.

460. ———, *Heads of Families at the First Census . . . Connecticut* (Washington, D.C., 1908). 290.

461. ———, *Heads of Families at the First Census . . . Maine* (Washington, D.C., 1908). 176.

462. ———, *Heads of Families at the First Census . . . Maryland* (Washington, D.C., 1907). 516.

463. ———, *Heads of Families at the First Census . . . Massachusetts* (Washington, D.C., 1908). 219.

464. ———, *Heads of Families at the First Census . . . New Hampshire* (Washington, D.C., 1907). 189.

465. ———, *Heads of Families at the First Census . . . New York* (Washington, D.C., 1908). 372.

466. ———, *Heads of Families at the First Census . . . North Carolina* (Washington, D.C., 1908). 588.

467. ———, *Heads of Families at the First Census . . . Pennsylvania* (Washington, D.C., 1908). 451.

468. ———, *Heads of Families at the First Census . . . Rhode Island* (Washington, D.C., 1908). 254.

469. ———, *Heads of Families at the First Census . . . South Carolina* (Washington, D.C., 1908). 605.

470. ———, *Heads of Families at the First Census . . . Vermont* (Washington, D.C., 1907). 199.

471. ———, *Heads of Families at the First Census . . . Virginia* (Washington, D.C., 1908). 572.

472. U.S. Congress, *American State Papers. Documents, Legislative and Executive, of the Congress of the United States, from the First Session of the First to the Second Session of the Tenth Congress, Inclusive* . . . (Washington, D.C., 1834). 443.

473. U.S. Library of Congress. Div. of Maps, *An account of the activities . . . year ending June 30, 1939* (Washington, D.C., 1940). 127–28.

474. ———, *District of Columbia Sesquicentennial of the Establishment of the Permanent Seat of the Government. An Exhibition in the Library of Congress, Washington, D.C., April 24, 1950 to April 24, 1951* (Washington, D.C., 1950). 532–33, 535.

475. ———, *Ohio the Sesquicentennial of Statehood 1803–1953* (Washington, D.C., 1953). 662.

476. ———, *Report of the Librarian of Congress for the fiscal year ending June 30, 1904* (Washington, D.C., 1904). (later, *Annual Report*.) 76, 170.

477. ———, *Report . . . 1906*. 214.

478. ———, *Report . . . 1907*. 359, 479.

479. ———, *Report . . . 1915*. 181, 520.

480. ———, *Report . . . 1916*. 291, 520.

481. ———, *Report . . . 1929*. 296.

482. ———, *Report . . . 1930*. 297–98.

483. ———, *Report . . . 1940*. 193.

484. ———, *Report . . . 1941*. 258.

485. U.S. Senate, *Maps of the District of Columbia . . .* (Washington, D.C., 1852). 530, 535.

486. *Universal Asylum and Columbian Magazine, The* (Philadelphia). 527.

487. Vail, Robert William Glenroie, *The Voice of the Old Frontier* (Philadelphia, 1949). 161, 167, 313–17, 319–20, 322, 361, 375–76, 490, 631, 650, 662, 676.

488. Vermont (State), *Records of the Governor and Council . . . 1822–1831*, vol. 7 in Vermont, *Records of the Governor and Council of the State of Vermont* . . . (8 vols. Montpelier, 1873–1880). 147.

489. Vermont, Secretary of State, *State Papers of Vermont, Volume One, Index to the Papers of the Surveyors-General* (Rutland, 1918). 198.

490. Verner, Coolie, "The Aitken Map of Virginia," in *Imago Mvndi, 16* (1962), 152–56. 540.

491. ———, "The Maps and Plates appearing with the several Editions of Mr. Jefferson's 'Notes on the State of Virginia,'" in *The Virginia Magazine of History and Biography, 59* (1951), 21–33. 568.

492. ———, "Some observations on the Philadelphia 1794 editions of Jefferson's *Notes*," in *Papers of the Bibliographical Society of the University of Virginia, Studies in Bibliography, 2* (1949–50), 201–04. 568.

493. Vietor, Alexander O., "The Bauman map of the siege of Yorktown," in the Yale University Library, *Gazette, 21* (1946), 15–17. 541.

494. ———, "Printed maps," in Helen Comstock, ed., *The Concise Encyclopedia of American Antiques, 2* (New York, 1957), 437–43. 161, 163, 184, 261, 474.

495. *Virginia Gazette* (Williamsburg). 727.

496. Volney, Constantin François Chasseboeuf,

Comte de, *The Ruins: or A Survey of the Revolutions of Empires* (New York, 1796). Evans 31517. MBAt, MWA, NN, RPJCB. 29.

497. ———, *The Ruins . . .* (Philadelphia, 1799). Evans 36661. CSmH, CStbS, CtY, MiU-C, MB, MWA, NjP, RPJCB. 29, 43.

498. Wainwright, Nicholas B., "Scull and Heap's map of Philadelphia," in *The Pennsylvania Magazine of History and Biography, 81* (1957), 69–75. 454.

499. ———, "Tale of a Runaway Cape The Penn-Baltimore Agreement of 1732," in *The Pennsylvania Magazine of History and Biography, 87* (1963), 251–93. 474, 497.

500. Walton, John, *John Filson of Kentucke* (Lexington, Ky. [1956]). 631.

501. Warren, Isaac, *The North American's Almanack, for the Year of our Lord Christ, 1777* (Worcester, Mass. [1777]). Evans 15212. MH. 384.

502. Waters, Willard O., comp., "American Imprints, 1648–1797 in the Huntington Library, Supplementing Evans' *American Bibliography*," in the Huntington Library, *Bulletin*, no. 3 (February 1933), pp. 1–95. 147, 170, 379.

503. Watson, John Fanning, *Annals of Philadelphia and Pennsylvania, in the olden time; being a collection of memoirs, anecdote, and incidents of the City and its Inhabitants . . .* (2 vols. Philadelphia, 1856–57). 475.

504. Weatherwise, Abraham [pseud.], *Father Abraham's Almanac. For the year of our Lord 1761* (Philadelphia, William Dunlap [1760]). Evans 8766. MWA. 84, 421.

505. ———, *Father Abraham's Almanack (on an entirely new plan) for the year . . . 1759* (Philadelphia, William Dunlap [1758]). Evans 8280. MHi, MWA, PHi. 83.

506. ———, *Father Abraham's Almanack (on an entirely new plan). For the Year of our Lord 1759 . . .*, printed at Philadelphia by William Dunlap for G. Noel, bookseller (New York [1758]). Readex Microprint edition of Evans states no copy found. Evans 8281. 83.

507. ———, *Father Abraham's Almanack . . . for . . . 1759* (New York, Hugh Gaine [1758]). Evans 8282. MWA. 83.

508. ———, *Father Abraham's Almanack . . . for . . . 1759,* printed at Philadelphia for Daniel Henchman (Boston [1758]). MHi, NHi, PHi. 83.

509. ———, *Weatherwise's Federal Almanack, for the Year of our Lord, 1788 . . .* (Boston, [1787]). Evans 20860. CSmH, DLC, MWA. 662, 666.

510. Weiss, Harry B., "John Norman, engraver, publisher, bookseller . . . ," in New York Public Library, *Bulletin*, 38 (1934), 3–14. 108, 302–03, 327.

511. West, Benjamin, *Bickerstaff's New-England Almanac for . . . 1776* (Norwich, Conn. [1775]). CSmH, CtHi, MHi, MWA. 240.

512. West, John, *The Boston directory, containing the names of the inhabitants, their occupations, places of business, and dwelling-houses . . .* (Boston, June 1796). Evans 31619. BM, DLC, MB, MBAt, MHi, MiU-C. 246.

513. ———, *The Boston Directory . . .* (Boston, 1798). 246.

514. ———, *The Boston Directory . . .* (Boston, 1800). 246.

515. Wheat, Carl Irving, *1540–1861 Mapping the Transmississippi West . . . The Spanish Entrada to the Louisiana Purchase 1540–1804* (5 vols. in 6, San Francisco, 1957). 5, 57, 60.

516. Whitehill, Walter Muir, *Boston A Topographical History* (Cambridge, 1959). 224, 227, 234.

517. Whitney, Peter, *The History of the County of Worcester, in the Commonwealth of Massachusetts . . .* (Worcester, 1793). Evans 26481. BM, ICN, MB, MHi, MiU-C, MWA, NN, RPJCB. 211.

518. Williams, George H., "Maps of the territory included within the State of Maryland, especially the vicinity of Baltimore," in Johns Hopkins University, *Circulars* (Baltimore, 1893), *12,* no. 103. 526.

519. Williams, Jonathan, Jr., "Memoir of Jonathan Williams, on the use of the Thermometer in discovering Banks, Soundings &c.," in American Philosophical Society, *Transactions, 3* (1793), 82–100. 724.

520. ———, *Memoir on the use of the Thermometer in Navigation. Presented to the American Philosophical Society, held at Philadelphia, for promoting useful knowledge, by Jonathan Williams, Jun. one of the Secretaries. Extracted from the Third Volume of their Transactions now in the Press* (Philadelphia, 1792). Evans 25040, Sabin 104297. BM, NHi. 724.

521. ———, *Memoria sobre el uso del Termómetro en la navegacion presentada a la Sociedad Filosófica de Filadelfia para promover los conocimientos utiles por Jonathan Williams uno de sus secretarios. Sacada del volumen tercero de sus Transacciones Filosóficas. Traducida del idioma ingles de orden de s. m.* (Madrid, 1794). RPJCB. 724.

522. [———], *Thermometrical Navigation being a Series of Experiments and Observations, tending to prove, that by ascertaining the relative heat of the sea-water from time to time, the passage of a ship through the Gulph Stream, and from deep water into soundings, may be discovered in time to avoid danger, although (owing to tempestuous weather,) it may be impossible to heave the lead or observe the Heavenly Bodies. Extracted from*

REFERENCES

the American Philosophical Transactions. Vol. 2 & 3, with additions and improvements (Philadelphia, 1799). Evans 36722. CtY, DLC, MH, MHi, MiU, MWA, NN, PHi, PPL, RPJCB, ViU. 725.

523. Williams, Samuel, *The Natural and Civil History of Vermont* (Walpole, 1794). Evans 26478, 28094. BM, DLC, MH, MWA, NN, RPJCB. 194.

524. [Williams, W.], *First Principles of Geography* (Charleston, S.C., 1798). Evans 35032. DLC. 41.

525. [Williamson, Charles], *Description of the Genesee Country, its rapidly progressive population and improvements: in a series of letters from a Gentlemen to his Friend* (Albany, 1798). Evans 35033. DLC, MH, MiU-C, MWA, NHi, PPL. 313, 376.

526. [——], *Description of the settlement of the Genesee Country, in the State of New-York. In a series of Letters from a Gentleman to his Friend* (New York, 1799). Evans 36727. Copies containing *State* I of map: NHi, NN, Private coll. of Mr. Robert W. G. Vail; *State* II: NHi; *State* III: DLC, MiU-C, MWA, NHi. 314–16.

527. ——, *Observations on the proposed state road from Hudson's River, near the City of Hudson, to Lake Erie, by the Oleout, Catherine's, Bath, and Gray's Settlement, on the western bounds of Steuben County* (New York, 1800). 316.

528. Williamson, Joseph, *A Bibliography of the State of Maine from the earliest period to 1891* . . . (2 vols. Portland, 1896). 161, 170–71.

529. Winchester, Elhanan, *A Course of Lectures, on the Prophecies that remain to be fulfilled* . . . (2 vols. Norwich, Conn., 1795). Evans 29907. NN. 881.

530. Winsor, Justin, *The Memorial History of Boston, including Suffolk County, Massachusetts. 1630–1880.* (4 vols. Boston, 1881). 225–29, 234, 243, 246, 248.

531. Winsor, Justin, ed., *Narrative and Critical History of America* (8 vols. Boston and New York, 1889). 84, 113, 298, 322, 386, 660, 674.

532. ——, [Remarks on John Fitch Map], in Massachusetts Historical Society, *Proceedings,* 2d Ser., 7 (Boston, 1891–92), 364–66. 660.

533. Winterbotham, William, *An Historical, Geographical, Commercial, and Philosophical View of the United States of America* . . . (4 vols. New York, 1796). DLC, DN, MB, MiU-C, NjP, NN, PPL. 537, 648–49.

534. ——, [The Atlas for Winterbotham's History of America 1796] (Cover title). This accompanies his *An Historical Geographical . . . View of the United States* . . . (1st Am. ed. New York, 1796). Evans 31647. 28, 56, 135, 176, 189, 198, 219, 254, 288, 371–72, 418, 450, 516, 537, 572, 587, 605, 615, 646, 654, 697, 712.

535. Workman, Benjamin, *Elements of geography . . . The second edition . . .* (Philadelphia, 1790). First issue of second edition. Evans 23091, Sabin 105474. NNA. 9, 115, 703.

536. ——, *Elements of geography . . . The second edition . . .* (Philadelphia, 1790). Second issue of second edition. No copy located. 9, 115, 703.

537. ——, *Elements of geography . . . The 3d edition . . .* (Philadelphia, 1790). First issue. Evans 23092, Sabin 105474. CtY, DLC, MWA, PPAmSwM, PU, RPJCB. 10, 52, 117, 745, 842, 866.

538. ——, *Elements of geography . . . The fourth edition . . .* (Philadelphia, 1793). Evans 26509, Sabin 105474. NNC, PHi, PU. 10, 52, 120, 703, 745, 842, 866.

539. ——, *Elements of geography . . . The fifth edition . . .* (Philadelphia, 1795). Evans 29924, Sabin 105474. MH, NN, PHi. 10, 52, 120, 703, 745, 842, 866.

540. ——, *Elements of geography . . . The sixth edition . . .* (Philadelphia, 1796). Evans 31661, Sabin 105474. CtY, MWA, PHi, PU, RPJCB. 10, 52, 703, 745, 842, 866.

541. ——, *Elements of geography . . . The seventh edition . . .* (Philadelphia, 1799). Evans 36740, Sabin 105474. CtY, MWA, PHi. 10, 52, 120, 140, 703, 745, 842, 866.

542. *The World displayed; or, a curious Collection of Voyages and Travels* . . . (8 vols. Philadelphia, 1795–96). Evans 29926, 31664. CSmH, MiU-C, MWA, NN. 910.

543. Wright, Paul, *The new and complete Life of Our Blessed Lord and Savior, Jesus Christ: that Great Example, as well as Savior of Mankind* . . . (New York, 1795). Evans 29928. MWA, NN. 891.

544. Wroth, Lawrence Counselman, *Abel Buell of Connecticut Silversmith Type Founder & Engraver* (New Haven, 1926). 109–10, 259, 264, 621.

545. ——, *Abel Buell* (rev. ed. Middletown, Conn., 1958). 109–10, 259, 264, 621.

546. ——, *An American Bookshelf 1755* (Philadelphia, 1934). 295–96, 298.

547. Wroth, Lawrence C., and Marion W. Adams, *American Woodcuts and Engravings, 1670–1800,* . . . with an introduction by Clarence S. Brigham (Providence, R.I., 1946). 77, 144, 658.

548. Wroth, Lawrence C., "Joshua Fisher's 'Chart of Delaware Bay and River,'" in *The Pennsylvania Magazine of History and Biography,* 74 (1950), 90–109. 475–76.

549. ——, *Some American contributions to the art of navigation, 1519–1802* (Providence, R.I., 1947). 475–76, 721, 724.

550. ———, "Some American contributions . . . ," in Massachusetts Historical Society, *Proceedings, 68* (October 1944—May 1947), 72–112. 475–76.

551. ———, "Source Materials of Florida History in the John Carter Brown Library of Brown University," *Florida Historical Quarterly, 20* (1941–42), 3–46. 621.

552. ———, "The Thomas Johnston Maps of the Kennebec Purchase," in *In Tribute to Fred Anthoensen, Master Printer* (Portland, Me., 1952), pp. 77–107. 161, 163.

Index of Names

Numbers refer to individual maps and charts; numbers preceded by the letter "R" signify entries in the *Reference* section.

A., R. *See* Aitken, Robert.
Abernethie, Thomas, 593–94, 596, 599
Adams, Marion W., R547
Adams, Randolph G., 144
Adlum, John, 432
Aitken, Robert, 89–92, 203, 237–38, 489, 540, 730–31, 734, 736–37, 740, 742, R209, R490
Alexander, James, 295, R308
Allardice, Samuel, 462, 520, 684, 755–56, 786–87, 871
Allen, Joel Knott, 272
Allen, John, 758, 844
Allen, William, 454–55
American Antiquarian Society, *Proceedings*, R27, R52, R142, R243
American Geographical Society, R344
American Museum, R121, R158
American Philosophical Society, *Transactions*, R155, R519–22
Amherst, Jeffrey, baron, 325
Amory, Thomas C., 246
Anderson, Alexander, 134, 190, 201, 222, 292, 518, 574, 646, 673, 839, 869–70, 872
Anderson, J., 413
Andrews. *See* Thomas & Andrews.
Andrews, Ebenezer T., 571, 791–95
Anthoesen, Fred, R552
Antiques, R193
Anville, Jean Baptiste B., Duke d', 49
Arbuthnot, Mariot, 593
Armstrong, John, 422
Arnold, Benedict, 92

Bailey, Francis, 113, 115
Baker, Charles, 211
Baltimore, Charles Calvert, 6th baron, 474, R499
Bancker, Evert, Jr., 400
Baptiste, Jean, 696
Barker, Elihu, 641–43, R225
Barker, Oliver, 641
Barker, William, 16–17, 23, 128, 131, 169, 217, 253, 255, 286, 311, 367, 414, 420, 445, 452, 483, 510, 513, 570, 584, 591, 601, 611, 613, 642, 644, 652, 675–78, 687, 752, 761, 770–72, 776, 818, 856, 910, 915
Barnard, Thomas, 330
Bauman, Sebastian, 541, R492

Bayley, Frank W., R135
Belcher, Jonathan, 228
Belknap, Jeremy, 183
Bell, Andrew, 784, R122
Bellin, Jacques Nicolas, 77, 118–19, 123, 126, 131, 149, 660, 674, 679, 692
Bennett. *See* Sayer & Bennett.
Bennett, John, 108, 476, 592
Berriman & Co., R201
Berry, Edward, 765
Bibliographical Society of America, *Papers*, R2, R184
Biddle, Mary, 456
Birch (or B. Birch), 661
Birch, William, 419
Blanchard, Joseph, 181
Blodget, Samuel, 320
Blodgett, William, 192, 272, R230
Blunt, Edmund M., 220
Board of Proprietors of the Eastern Division of New Jersey, R269
Boggs, Benjamin R., 455
Bolitho, John, 476
Bonaparte, Napoleon, 860
Bond, Benjamin, R37
Bonner, John, 224–26, 228
Bonnor, George, 41
Bonsall, Joseph H., 456
Bookman, The, R13
Boone, Daniel, 631
Boston, City Council of, R414
Boston Magazine, R168
Bostonian Society, R445
Bouquet, Henry, 424, 630, 658, R424
Bowen & Co., 694
Bowen, Emanual, 160
Bowen, Thomas, 869
Bowes, Joseph, 470, 472
Boyd, Julian P., R220
Boydell, John, 471
Boydell, Josiah, 471
Bradford, William, 317–18, 378–80, R12–13, R92, R94
Bradley, Abraham, Jr., 127–28, 158, 496
Bradt, John, 359

INDEX

INDEX

J. W. *See* W., J.

Jefferson, Peter, 298, 422, 540, 660

Jefferson, Thomas, 113, R491–92

Jeffreys, Thomas, 77, 181, 298, 320, 422, 629, 689, 691, R35

Jenks, William Lee, R229

Jervis, John, Earl of St. Vincent, 805

Jessup, Ebenezer, 329

Jessup, Edward, 329

John, Earl of Stair, R37

Johns Hopkins University, *Circulars*, R518

Johnson, Guy, 658

Johnson, Sir William, 320, 324

Johnston (or Johnson), Thomas, 71, 76, 161, 163, 191, 227–29, 320, 322, R552

Johnston, William, 582, 590

Jones, (Benjamin?), 43

Jones, Ephraim, 163

Jones, Phineas, 161, 163

Keatinge, George, 524

Kemble, Robert, 413

Kennedy, Robert, 497–98

Kennedy, William, 631

Kentucky State Historical Society, *Register*, R224–25

Kimpton, Edward, R150

King, James, R107–08

Kitchen, Thomas, 163

Klockhoff, H., 147, 262

Labaree, Leonard W., R157

Lafayette, Marie Joseph P. Y. R. G. du Motier, Marquis de, 541

Langdon, Samuel, 181

Larkin, Ebenezer, 618

Laurie & Whittle, 629, 689, 691, 710

Lauson, A. *See* Lawson, Alexander.

Lawrence, John, Sr., 295

Lawson, Alexander, 809, 812–13

Leach, John, 148

LeGear, Clara Egli, R362

L'Enfant, Pierre Charles, 527, 530–31, 534

LeRoy, Alphonsus, R155–56

Lewis, Samuel, 101, 123, 137, 169, 173, 185, 187, 213, 362, 371, 414, 418, 442, 448, 510, 568, 581, 601, 678

Library of Congress, R359, R361–64

Library of Congress, *Quarterly Journal*, R67, R175

Lightfoot, Benjamin, 422

L'Isle, Guillaume de, 317

Livingston, H(enry?), 671

Lobach, David, 455

Loring, B. & J., 179

Lotter, Tobias C., 455

Louisiana State University Studies, R129

Low, Esther, 190

Low, John, 65, 142, 201, 222, 255, 292, 420, 518–19, 574, 608, 619, 700, 719, 839, 859–62, 913–14

Low & Willis, 39–40, 903, R345

Lownes, Caleb, 239

Ludlow, Israel, 681

Lukens, John, 425

Lurting, Robert, 378

Lydius, John, 295

Lyne, James, 378, 380, R12–13

M'Comb, James, Jr., 387

McCorison, Marcus A., R378

M'Culloch, John, R428

Macklennan, John, 47

McMurray, William, 111, 660, R366

Maerschalck, F., 380

Maine Historical Society, *Collections*, R176

Malham, John, 35, 58–59, 698, 713, 797–804, 852–53, 894–95

Man, Thomas, 457–58

Mansfield, Lord, R370

Marietta College, R205

Martin, David, 247, 371, 373–74, 418, 450, 516, 697

Martin, François-X., 586

Martin, Lawrence C., 232, R227

Maryland Geological Survey, R66, R266–67, R385

Mason, Charles, 425, 497–98

Mason and Dixon Line, 425, R66

Massachusetts Historical Society, R368

Massachusetts Historical Society, *Collections*, R154

Massachusetts Historical Society, *Proceedings*, R532, R550

Matthews, Edward B., R66

Maverick, Peter Rushton, 316, 370

Maxwell, William, 413

Maynard, George Henry, 872, R150

Meers, 610

Melish, John, 511

Merrill, Phinehas, 184

Mifflin, Thomas, 432–33, 462

Miller, Andrew, 163

Miller, Francis, 325

Miller & Moss, 456

Mitchell, John, 101, 109

Molineux, Frederic, 449

Montgomerie, John, 378

Monthly Weather Review, R448

Moore, Sir Henry, 326

Moore, Philip, 511

Moreau de St Méry, Médéric Louis Élie, 693

Morgan, Christopher, R124

Morris, Robert Hunter, 475

Morse, Jedidiah, 4, 12, 19, 21, 26, 31, 33, 38, 55, 60, 62, 112, 118, 122, 124, 141, 149, 158, 175, 188, 357, 491, 496, 585, 614, 618, 686, 695, 699, 702, 705–06, 714, 744, 746, 758, 766, 790, 843–44, 846, 851, 868, 873–74, 885, 890, 911

Morse, William Inglis, *Collection*, R14

Mortier. *See* Cóven and Mortier.

Moses, 877

Mott, Samuel, 257

Mount and Page, 476

Mulgrave, Lord. *See* Phipps, Constantine J., 2d Baron Mulgrave.

Murray, John, 4th Earl of Dunmore, 540

212

INDEX